D0303431

THE MASOCHISTIC PLEASURES OF
SENTIMENTAL LITERATURE

Copyright © 2000 by Princeton University Press
Published by Princeton University Press, 41 William Street
Princeton, New Jersey 08540
In the United Kingdom: Princeton University Press
Chichester, West Sussex

Library of Congress Cataloging-in-Publication Data

Noble, Marianne
The masochistic pleasures of sentimental literature / Marianne Noble
p.   cm.
Includes bibliographical references and index.
ISBN 0-691-00936-8 (cloth : alk. paper)
ISBN 0-691-00937-6 (pbk. : alk. paper)
1. American literature—Women authors—History and criticism.
2. Psychoanalysis and literature—United States—History—
19th century. 3. Women and literature—United States—History—
19th century. 4. American literature—19th century—History and
criticism. 5. Erotic literature, American—History and criticism.
6. Warner, Susan, 1819–1885. Wide, wide world. 7. Stowe, Harriet
Beecher, 1811–1896. Uncle Tom's cabin. 8. Dickinson, Emily,
1830–1886—Criticism and interpretation. 9. Sentimentalism in
literature. 10. Masochism in literature. 11. Pleasure in literature.
12. Sex in literature. I. Title.
PS147.N63   2000
810.9′353—dc21   99-048831   CIP

This book has been composed in Galliard

The paper used in this publication meets the minimum
requirements of ANSI/NISO Z39.48-1992 (R1997)
(*Permanence of Paper*)

www.pup.princeton.edu

Printed in the United States of America

10 9 8 7 6 5 4 3 2 1

10 9 8 7 6 5 4 3 2 1
(Pbk.)

THE MASOCHISTIC PLEASURES
OF SENTIMENTAL LITERATURE

Marianne Noble

PRINCETON UNIVERSITY PRESS   PRINCETON, NEW JERSEY

Contents

Acknowledgments

IN THE course of writing this book, I have turned for assistance to the minds and hearts of many colleagues and most of the people close to me, and it is a deep pleasure to express my gratitude and admiration to them. Jonathan Loesberg, Paula Bennett, Suzanne Juhasz, and Jim Berg read multiple drafts of the book, engaging extensively in different ways, offering suggestions, asking probing questions, and participating in ongoing dialogues that helped me know my thoughts more fully. Their contributions were crucial for the success of the project. Priscilla Wald and Robert Ferguson were not only extremely insightful, encouraging, and professional dissertation directors, but they stayed in for the long haul, supporting the project—and me—through every step on its way to final publication. They are model scholars, emotionally supportive and intellectually rigorous, and I feel privileged to have worked with them. Though Alan Levine entered the project later on, he also involved himself deeply with the manuscript, posing acute questions and making exceptionally good suggestions. For the graceful expression of complex, nuanced arguments, I am grateful to Victoria Wilson-Schwartz, who not only knows more about the Elsie Dinsmore books than anyone should but whose meticulous editing of the final draft was at times little short of miraculous.

My deep thanks also go to the many colleagues who offered suggestions on shorter sections of the book: Elizabeth Ammons, Elizabeth Barnes, Ann Douglas, Andrea Kerr, Mary Loeffelholz, Michael Manson, Robert K. Martin, Jeannie Pfaelzer, Jo Radner, Roberta Rubenstein, Eric Savoy, Vanessa Schwartz, Richard Sha, Susan Belasco Smith, Robert McClure Smith, and Laura Wexler. Lacey Wooton-Don, Jeff Edwards, and Eve Rosenbaum were devoted and encouraging research assistants, for which I thank them exuberantly. I am also glad to thank Deborah Malmud for her professional and effective work as my editor. And finally, I want to express my gratitude and admiration for the members of the Nineteenth-Century American Women Writers Study Group and other scholars working in this field. Their pathbreaking research underlies every page of this book, and their nurturing collegiality is a vivid testimony to the kinds of transformations female scholars can and should make in academia.

I am glad to thank my colleagues at American University for their friendship and intellectual stimulation, and the graduate students in my Whitman/Dickinson classes and my summer seminars on sentimentalism for their encouragement and provocation. I am happy to thank the American University senate, the American University College of Arts and Sciences, the American Council of Learned Societies, and Columbia University for financial support to complete various stages of this project. And I am grateful to the U.S. taxpayers for my steady access to the unparalleled resources of the Library of Congress and the assistance of the reference librarians there.

I am grateful to Johns Hopkins University Press for permission to reprint here those portions of chapters 4 and 5 that appeared under the titles "Ecstasies of Sentimental Wounding in *Uncle Tom's Cabin*" (*Yale Journal of Criticism* 10.2 [1997]: 295–320); "Dickinson's Sentimental Explorations of 'The Ecstasy of Parting'" (*Emily Dickinson Journal* 5.2 [1996]: 280–84); and "The Revenge of Cato's Daughter: Dickinson's Masochism" (*Emily Dickinson Journal* 7.2 [1998]: 22–47). I am grateful for the permission from the University of Iowa Press to reprint those sections of chapter 3 that appeared as "'An Ecstasy of Apprehension': The Gothic Pleasures of Sentimental Fiction" in *American Gothic: New Interventions in a National Narrative*, edited by Robert K. Martin and Eric Savoy. All Dickinson poems are reprinted by permission of the publishers and the Trustees of Amherst College from THE POEMS OF EMILY DICKINSON, Variorum Edition, Ralph W. Franklin, ed., Cambridge, Mass.: The Belknap Press of Harvard University Press, Copyright © 1998 by the President and Fellows of Harvard College. Copyright © 1951, 1955, 1979 by the President and Fellows of Harvard College.

Finally, it is an enormous pleasure to thank my family and friends for their unflagging love and support: Heather Drew, Mary B Fort, Helene Edmonds, Thew Elliott, Sue Hatch, Kathy Hepler, Leah and Stuart Johnson, Mary Kraus, Florence Lusk, Kaye Noble, Alec Noble, and Jennifer Rich. I promise now to return all of your phone calls. I thank my cousin Bob Edmonds for being everything a loving friend could possibly be. Above all, I thank my parents, my mother, Dr. Mary Noble, and my father, Herbert Noble, Jr., who both always inspired and encouraged my hunger for knowledge and beauty. The book is dedicated with love and deep gratitude to them.

THE MASOCHISTIC PLEASURES OF
SENTIMENTAL LITERATURE

Introduction

"Weird Curves": Masochism and Feminism

In 1881, Lucy Larcom, an American poet well known in her day, published "Fern Life," a poem that intermingles meditations upon nature with religious and cultural observations. One of the themes "Fern Life" addresses is the resilience of women in the face of cultural oppression. Women, Larcom suggests, are like ferns, which have constraints upon their lives that make it difficult for them to grow in a normal way into recognizably healthy and beautiful plants. The first line of the poem suggests that sometimes it is hard even to recognize them as alive at all: "Yes, life! Though it seems half a death" (231). The remark appears to be addressed to someone who is surprised by the vitality asserted in the title, "Fern Life." It suggests that women, like ferns, in fact *are* alive, despite expectations to the contrary. The poem goes on to imply that women will assert their right to develop themselves, to create their own art despite conventions dictating that they merely "pencil rare patterns of grace / Men's footsteps about" (231). In the fifth and seventh stanzas, Larcom indicates that social limitations will not prevent women's self-fulfillment, but they *will* force them to seek unexpected means for self-realization:

> Yet why must this possible more
> Forever be less?
> The unattained flower in the spore
> Hints a human distres.
>
> To fashion our life as a flower,
> In weird curves we reach,—
> O man, with your beautiful power
> Of presence and speech!
>   (qtd. in Walker, *Nineteenth* 232)

Lacking the beautiful powers of "presence and speech" that men have—discouraged from asserting themselves physically and verbally—women have to reach in weird curves. But the poem does not lament victimization; it is about "Fern *Life*," the fact that women will make accommodations in order to find pleasure and power within the cultural circumstances in which they find themselves. I want to suggest in this book that the pronounced strain of masochism that is evident in a good deal of nineteenth-century American women's sentimental writing is one such "weird curve."[1]

By calling the masochism in sentimental literature a "weird curve," I emphasize that it is in some sense unnatural, a reaction to the constraints upon women's lives. But it is also a form of self-expression, beautiful—or at least fascinating—once one can see beyond its weirdness. Consider, for example, Maria Brooks's "The Obedient Love of Woman Her Highest Bliss" (1827):

> To every blast she bends in beauty meek;—
> Let the storm beat,—his arms her shelter kind,—
> And feels no need to blanch her rosy cheek
> With thoughts befitting his superior mind.
>
> Who only sorrows when she sees him pained,
> Then knows to pluck away pain's keenest dart;
> Or bid love catch it ere its goal be gained,
> And steal its venom ere it reach his heart.[2]

In what way might we see in this masochistic poem a weird curve? Is it anything more than a conventional, conservative nineteenth-century view of female nature—that a woman's true desire is to submit, obey, and suffer for her man? Well, yes and no. The poem uses a conventional discourse of eroticized martyrdom and female submission in order to create a dark fantasy of erotic love. By focusing upon pain, the poem draws attention to the female body, so that "the highest bliss" is envisioned in physical terms. In the second line, for example, imagining submission to a beating storm is a way of fantasizing about the loving sensations of a man's embrace. Similarly, in the second stanza, the images of being punctured by a keen dart and feeling its venom are ways of imagining being penetrated and flooded in a loving but painful way. The physicality of pain in this poem—the blasting, bending, beating, blanching, and plucking—is also the physicality of romantic love, and the intensity of pain is also somehow the intensity of desire for pleasure. Expressing desire for physical pleasure by fantasizing about submission is neither reactive nor subversive: it is a weird curve, a way of circumventing prohibitions on both female embodiment and female artistry.

Some feminist readers might look upon this poem purely as a tragic sign of the repressive manipulation of Brooks's desire by a misogynist patriarchy. Others might argue that it is more powerful, a roundabout way of criticizing the very patriarchal oppression it seems to celebrate. But I seek to offer a more complex and subtle analysis of sentimental masochism than such a victim/subversion dichotomy invites. In this book, I argue that the masochism in nineteenth-century American women's sentimentality can be seen as an opportunity for agency that presented itself to authors *within* the ideological constraints of the culture. Brooks's poem is as obedient as it possibly could be, and yet, as the erotics of its violent imagery suggests, it is submissive with a vengeance. This is not to suggest that the poem is ironic or subversive; Brooks does not "get one over on the patriarchy." To the contrary, the poem is immersed in patriarchal ideology and represents an effort to maximize the pleasure of a fantasy whose character has been patriarchally determined. Power is not antithetical to the "woman's highest bliss" but constitutive of it. The masochism in sentimentality—neither subversive nor purely reactive—makes available the "bliss" of reveling in fantasized submission to power.

In claiming that such a poem is masochistic, this book challenges many recent feminist approaches to sentimentalism, which have argued that the pleasures the genre offered female readers lay not in its celebration of the pleasures of submission but in its assertion of female desires for autonomy and agency. Certainly one would not have to look far to see a critique of the patriarchy in "Obedient Love of Woman Her Highest Bliss": it so starkly represents the violence of romantic ideologies that it could be read as an exposé of them. Such a reading might appeal to feminist critics because it would seem to consolidate a legacy of writing by morally superior women who are indignant at the brutality inflicted upon them yet capable only of subversive resistance.

But to find in such works only a powerless critique of patriarchal brutality is to create a false picture of the trajectory of American literary history. Female sentimental authors were not simply victims who were silenced or forced to function as mouthpieces for patriarchal ideology, nor simply virtuous crusaders for truth and justice. They were authors eager to empower themselves and ambitious to explore and put into words their thoughts on a range of subjects not confined to tender love, regional portraiture, and womanly desires for kindness and compassion. They had selfish desires, violent fantasies, contradictory ambitions, and competing identifications—as did men. This is not to say that Brooks longed for her own physical abuse, not even subconsciously. Rather, she was exploiting a culturally overdetermined form of self-expression for the pleasures and powers she derived from it. To ignore the complex pleasures of a poem like "Obedient Love" is to strip it of the lurid, violent erotics that is its most interesting—albeit disturbing—feature. It is to flatten out its anguished, complex, and perverse transcription of physical and emotional desire, reducing its emotional landscape to merely black and white outlines of sanctionable female feelings.

Masochism in sentimental fiction cannot be univocally celebrated as an empowering rhetorical device, though, for it is also both symptom

and agent of the ideological manipulation of female desire. Brooks probably did not intentionally eroticize patriarchal violence in "Obedient
Love of Woman Her Highest Bliss"; rather, that eroticization derives at
least partially from prevalent discourses associating violence and eroticism. And that discursive pattern had significant negative ramifications
for female readers, who derived from such literature the terms of their
own erotic desire. As Michelle Masse says of the Gothic, which resembles the sentimental in this respect, "what characters in these novels represent, whether through repudiation, doubt, or celebration, is the
cultural, psychoanalytic, and fictional expectation that they *should* be
masochistic if they are 'normal' women" (2).[3] A poem like "Obedient
Love of Woman" has a similar effect upon readers, consolidating undesirable patterns of desire and reinforcing one of the most oppressive and
abiding fictions of feminine identity—that of an essential female
masochism.[4]

The eroticism of sentimental suffering was a double-edged sword,
functioning both as a discursive agent for the proliferation of oppressive
ideologies and as a rhetorical tool for the exploration of female desire. In
other words, to the extent that such literature influenced women's un-
derstandings of their own sexuality, training them to experience their
desire vicariously through that of a man, or prompting them to be attracted to violent men, it was an agent of the construction of oppressive
gender roles. Yet, to the extent that eroticized representations of suffering made available a language of passion, desire, and anger, they were an
important form of literary agency.

My reader might object: "I see how the masochism in sentimentalism
is oppressive, but what about the other side of the sword? How empowering was it for a woman to engage in self-exploration in a language that
oppressively determined the very results she was supposedly discovering?
Did that language actually assist self-discovery, or did it rather determine what the author "found" inside herself? How empowering could
it be for women to use the master's language in the quest for a female
erotics?" Not empowering at all, many theorists of female sexuality have
concluded, and much feminist theorizing of the past twenty years has
sought a genuine language of female desire or has looked into literary
history for ways female authors subverted the dominant language.[5]
Some theorists have proposed that all female sexual desire expressed in
patriarchal language is false desire, and therefore that no exploration of
patriarchally determined desires is genuine self-exploration. A collective
paper produced by the women of A Southern Women's Writing Collective, who call themselves Women Against Sex (WAS), exemplifies the
extreme limit to which this position might be taken: "Though we realize

that many women, including WAS members, have had self-described affirmative sexual experiences, we believe that this was in spite of and not
because the experiences were sexual. We also recognize that as women
in this patriarchal culture, we have not escaped the socially constructed
dynamic of eroticized dominance and submission; that is, dominance
and submission is *felt* in our bodies as sex and therefore 'affirmative'"
(513). They have themselves physically felt the pleasures of eroticized
dominance, but because these pleasures diverge from their conception
of "true" female pleasure, they reject them. Going so far as to claim that
"if it doesn't subordinate women, it's not sex," they advocate "radical
celibacy" as the only imaginable form of resistance to the inevitable patriarchal deformation of female desire (515). This manifesto is not only
oppressively self-distrusting, it is also antithetical to women's self-empowerment, leaving women only with the dubious powers and pleasures
of self-loathing and self-denial. Their boldly stated belief that women
can empower and pleasure themselves only by denying the legitimacy of
their feelings and by trying to feel what they wish to feel locates all epistemological certainty outside themselves, in a body of theory written by
others.

As scholarship of the past thirty years has shown, desire is not something added onto a preexisting subject but rather is itself constitutive of
subjectivity. The women of WAS might argue that ideologically generated desires are not *true* desires, but surely that is precisely what they
are. They are not essential, innate, natural, or prior to language and culture, nor are they immutable, but they are *real* components of a
woman's subjectivity, fundamental to who she is. If the self is a social
construction, then the repudiation of all politically incorrect desire is, in
a real sense, the repudiation of the self. In her landmark essay "Feminine
Masochism and the Politics of Personal Transformation," Sandra Lee
Bartky explores precisely this problem with what she calls the "sexual
voluntarist" position, the belief that "[a]rmed with an adequate feminist
critique of sexuality and sufficient will power, any woman should be able
to alter the pattern of her desires." Sexual voluntarism, she argues, represents a "shallow view of the nature of patriarchal oppression," which
does not merely preach the desires it wishes its subjects to experience
but creates subjectivities deeply invested in power (57).[6] Because desire
is constitutive of self, altering one's desire is frequently a more compli-
cated and systemic procedure than simply willing a change in oneself.[7]
On the other hand, one cannot simply endorse the "liberal" belief that
a woman can therefore feel free to embrace whatever desire she feels,
since desire itself has been "colonized" (51), and therefore the "free"
indulgence of desire is impossible.[8] Certainly both self and desire can be

changed, but it it is not therefore true that all self-exploration must begin from the premise that dominant fictions can be repudiated and rendered irrelevant at will.[9]

If feminists seek to transform oppressive patterns of female desire within patriarchal culture into more self-affirming desires, they would do well to recognize the double-edgedness of masochism, since transformation is only likely to occur through a clear recognition not only of the ways that masochistic desire undermines women's lives but also through acknowledgment of the needs that women have met, or have tried to meet, through masochism. I build upon, without reproducing, the scholarship of the past thirty years that has extensively analyzed the oppressive aspects of eroticized domination: the undesirability of a patriarchally determined female masochism that might cause women to embrace their own harm is one of the basic premises motivating this entire project. But transformation requires a deep understanding, not simply willpower. The particular contribution of this book is the observation that failing to recognize the powers and pleasures women have sought in exploiting dominant discourses of desire will impede the transformation of desire. More specifically, this book observes that the effort to come to terms with masochistic desire in nineteenth-century American women's sentimentality must acknowledge not only that patriarchal culture oppressively eroticizes violence but that patriarchally determined desires are real desires. Recent feminist literary critics have extensively analyzed language experiments in which nineteenth-century authors strain against ideologically determined desires in a quest for their true desire.[10] These are crucial, enlightening studies, and my book serves not as a challenge but as a complement to them. But subversive resistance and linguistic subterfuge are not the only weapons in the arsenal of nineteenth-century authors. The dominant language that eroticizes women's suffering and their submission to male dominance has itself frequently been an important means of exploring and expressing desire. The desires and fantasies that the dominant language enables a woman to articulate are indeed ideologically overdetermined, but they are also real. And they can generate gripping representations *not* of feminist longings opposed to dominant fictions but of the pleasures of the dominant fictions themselves.[11] And these fictions, far from irrelevant, are the narratives by which many people live; in effect, these fictions constitute their reality.

Recently a number of theorists have analyzed the erotic pleasures of masochism, focusing mostly upon either male subjectivity or foundational ontology. Leo Bersani, for example, proposes that sexuality is a pleasurable sensation of shattering, of experiencing "that which is intolerable to the structured self." It depends, he argues, on "the gap in human life between the quantities of stimuli to which we are exposed and the development of ego structures capable of resisting . . . those stimuli. The *mystery* of sexuality is that we seek not only to get rid of this shattering tension but also to repeat, even to increase it. In sexuality, satisfaction is inherent in the painful need to find satisfaction." And therefore, he deduces, sexuality "could be thought of as a tautology for masochism. . . . [It] is ontologically grounded in masochism" (*Freudian* 38–39). An ontological theory of masochism such as this stands apart from the cultural gendering of sadism and masochism: the pleasures of masochism are available to both men and women. Is it not possible that, even given the oppressive gendering of masochism in Western culture, women might have found within that culturally imposed form of eroticism similar avenues for pleasure and excitement?[12]

Recent scholarship has also emphasized how masochistic fantasies can represent forms of agency as well as pleasure, again largely focusing either upon men or upon human beings in general. Deleuze, as well as Nick Mansfield, Carol Siegel, and Laura Frost, represent the masochistic position as one of self-empowerment through apparent repudiation of power. Yet, few critics have considered the possibility that female masochism might serve similar purposes.[13] Surely, it will be insisted, this is because masochism was *transgressive* for the male (resistant to dominant gender norms), while it was *programmatic* for the female. But a dichotomy between transgression and capitulation is too simple, stuck in the rut of resisting Freud's postulate of an essential female masochism. On the most basic level, masochistic fantasy offers women the same possibilities for empowerment through repudiation of power that it offers men: the position of being *done to* can be a powerful stance for seizing political and social agency, coercing the doer to obey not through force of arms but through force of self-esteem. As Deleuze puts it, "The masochist's apparent obedience conceals a criticism and a provocation. He simply attacks the law on another flank" (88). Histrionic victimization is a particularly effective strategy for self-empowerment in a liberal society in which most citizens want to be seen as nonviolent and compassionate.[14]

The refusal to acknowledge the ways that masochism may have served women as a mode of power derives from a limited and limiting understanding of women's relationship to power, which is not simply a force wielded by men against women but instead is available for people in all social positions to wield for their own ends. As Elizabeth Grosz writes, power is not something done to people but rather is the medium in which all people operate:

> until very recently, . . . power has been seen as the enemy of feminism, something to be abhorred, challenged, dismantled, or at best something to be shared more equally, a thing which can be divided in different ways. Power is

not the enemy of feminism but its ally. The goal of feminism cannot simply involve the dismantling of power, or its equal distribution, for power must be understood as that which administers, regulates, enables, as well as disqualifies and subordinates. If feminists believe that their goal is to abandon power, to "not play power games" they have already lost in a game from which they cannot withdraw. Feminism must aim at the reordering of power, not its elimination, that is, at the expedient use of power and its infinite capacities for transformation and rewriting. . . . Power is not something that feminism should disdain or rise above for it is its condition of existence and its medium of effectivity. ("American" 7–8)

Women have not been simply victims of power; like men, they have been formed by it and have operated within its constraints and regulations.[15]

The erotics of masochism can serve as a case in point; masochism is indeed an oppressive pattern of female desire, but women have also found both power and pleasure within the eroticization of domination. Consider the following contribution in the *Kinsey Report*: "I'm a woman who considers myself to be quite secure, confident, and assertive in my dealings with others. My husband and I still have a mutually exciting and satisfying sex life after nearly 20 years together. I am not hesitant about hinting when I'd like to have sex or about making the first move, but during intercourse itself I usually fantasize that I am being forced to have sex with a gangster, pirate, or other intimidating sort of man—which I end up enjoying" (Reinisch 93). To assert that the patriarchal manipulation of desire, and only that, is acting upon this woman would be simply wrong. She has been taking advantage of the eroticization of male violence for twenty years, thereby enjoying security, self-confidence, self-assertiveness, and physical pleasure with her husband. She even uses the words "mutually exciting," suggesting that she thinks of her sex life in terms of equality and reciprocity, notwithstanding the fantasy of submission that she finds erotically stimulating. This woman is not simply a victim of patriarchal power games. She is playing them.

Yet I do not simply want to side with those who might celebrate that fact. How did this scenario become erotically charged for this woman? Does her erotic desire have negative effects on her self-esteem, agency, or authority, effects of which she is unaware? Certainly, nineteenth- and twentieth-century women have in fact all too frequently been the victims of power games, actual victims of the "intimidating sort of man."[16] Many women learn to experience their desire vicariously through that of the male, to submit to coercive sex rather than privilege their own desire, to keep quiet about sexual harrassment or assault. In order to enable women to come to terms with their own erotic desire, it is important to acknowledge that there might be detrimental aspects to their masochistic fantasies, even as we celebrate the inventiveness and ingenuity of their coping strategies. B. Ruby Rich thoroughly considers both sides of the debate over masochism, but few discussions of the masochism in nineteenth-century women's literature have engaged in such a simultaneous inquiry.[17]

If my project challenges approaches to nineteenth-century sentimental literature that univocally celebrate its subversive resistance to the patriarchy or lament its powerless manipulation by the patriarchy, my project is in line with scholarship that foregrounds the way this literature enabled women to wield power through complicitous alignment with hegemonic ideologies.[18] The masochism in nineteenth-century sentimental literature is not simply a symptom of or polemic against women's oppression by men (though it is both); it is also a rhetorical device, wielded with mixed benefits. White middle-class women—the implied readers of sentimental literature—were hardly powerless in the nineteenth century, and the failure to recognize their complicitous use of power sanitizes or whitewashes their actions.[19] The masochism in sentimentality is part of that complicitous use of power, a fact that has been largely ignored by critics of sentimentalism. While feminist critics in the 1970s read it as proof of the disempowerment of nineteenth-century women,[20] critics in the 1980s, eager to rescue these works and their authors from aesthetic purgatory and moral culpability by emphasizing their unique forms of feminism, insisted that the books were not masochistic at all.[21] Nina Baym, for example, explicitly states that one representative character (Fleda in Warner's *Queechy*) who willingly suffers "is not a masochist" (*Woman* 151); rather, her behavior constitutes a conscious accommodation to reality that enables her to acquire personal autonomy. But Baym's position misrepresents masochism. The fact that masochism serves important needs does not make it less masochistic, just more comprehensible. It is important to retain the label "masochism" in our discussion of nineteenth-century sentimentalism, even as we recognize the needs that masochism has met, for renaming all apparent feminine masochism as "something else" forecloses avenues for transformation that a critical look at the situations inspiring masochism might open.

Imposing our own template of wishes on nineteenth-century women's literature prevents genuine exploration of what we actually do find there. Janice Radway's study of Harlequin romances, *Reading the Romance*, exemplifies such an imposition. Even though she writes about twentieth-century mass fiction rather than nineteenth-century women's sentimentalism, the theoretical assumptions underlying her study also underlie the 1980s feminist studies of nineteenth-century literature, and *Reading the Romance* therefore serves as a useful representative contrast for my own study. Radway insists that contemporary Harlequins are not masochistic, even though the typical plot features a heroine who is raped by a man who subsequently repents of his rape and persuades her to marry him, and even though readers admit that they find "a little forceful persuasion" attractive in their romances (75). Since the heroines dislike rape, since rape fantasies serve important psychological needs for Harlequin readers, and since she assumes masochism cannot be helpful, Radway concludes that she has refuted "what several analysts have said of romantic heroines and of the women who identify with them, which is that they masochistically enjoy being brutalized, terrorized, and hurt by men."[22] While it is probably true that these women do not enjoy brutality, surely the regularity with which heroines desire rapists, despite their dislike of rape, and are attracted to emotionally abusive men, despite their dislike of abuse, indicates that the books are masochistic, if masochism is also understood as a form of fantasy or erotic daydream and not only as a label for the real-life choices a person makes in concrete situations. Cruelty is the single most characteristic feature of the sexy Harlequin hero; and though he ultimately repents, the fact that the paradigm almost invariably features a reformed-rapist-as-hero cannot be coincidental. Rather, his sexual violence and the uncontrollability of his desire for the heroine are erotic. Radway concedes that the heroes uniformly display hard, angular, severe, and dark features, as well as contemptuous, disdainful personalities, but since "what all of the heroines want is tenderness and nurturance," not pain, she insists the books are not masochistic (144–45).

What she fails to recognize is that virtually *all* masochists long for tenderness and nurturance. As Bernhard Berliner writes, "The masochist has a particularly great need for being loved in the passive infantile way. . . . The masochist appears as if he loves his suffering, as if suffering were the aim of an instinct. This is not true. Suffering is very much unwanted by him and makes him really unhappy. However, he cannot but accept suffering because it is the price he has to pay for his particular gratification. Seeking pain is a way of avoiding a greater pain, or of acquiring love, for the masochist" (323–25). Berliner overstates his case when he claims that suffering never makes masochists happy, but he is certainly right that masochists see suffering as an undesirable fee they must pay for the love they crave. The Harlequin heroine and the Harlequin reader desire tenderness in their romances, but since they see cruelty and domination as the keys to procuring that tenderness and are therefore erotically attracted to such behaviors, their desires are nonetheless masochistic. I read Radway's discussion of Harlequin novels as a sensitive and timely study of the way that masochistic fantasy meets crucial psychological and material needs for female readers. However, her refusal to apply the label "masochistic" unfortunately legitimizes and fails to challenge the oppressive pattern of desire that she identifies. Change will only occur through a recognition of the double-edgedness of masochistic fantasies: their costs *and* their usefulness.

Such dismissive approaches to the masochistic patterns that are all too evident in both Harlequins and nineteenth-century sentimental literature derive, I suspect, from an understandable resistance to Freud's association of femininity with masochism, which has justifiably angered feminists for almost a century by implicitly authorizing a view of woman as essentially attracted to abuse.[23] Freud's essentializing of female masochism has put women in the position of needing to prove they do not want to be abused, to insist that they do not secretly enjoy coercion and domination. But focusing solely upon rebutting Freud's theory of an essential female masochism fails to engage the deeper issue of masochism's social construction, as well as its ontological and religious aspects. The fact is, some women, even some feminists, experience an erotic attraction to domination, despite their commitment to gender equity. A wide variety of ideas and images provoke human erotic desire, and for women, as for men, this can include fantasies of coercion and domination. For example, Nancy Friday's compendium of women's erotic fantasies, *My Secret Garden*, features scenarios of rape and sadomasochism. To say that women do not experience masochistic desire is effectively to deny to women the same complex interiority as men. Female sexuality does not always have to be something women would be proud to discuss in public. Women are as capable of experiencing unspeakable desires that run counter to their conscious senses of who they are and their political, social, and religious values as men are. As B. Ruby Rich writes, fantasy is "a sphere apart, shaped by social and psychological factors but lacking any inherently linear relationship to action itself, positioned finally in a . . . complex dialectic with the active life" (533). It is neither irrelevant nor directly correlative. Recognizing the distinction between fantasy and real-life desires—and allowing room for sexual fantasies—is a crucial next step for feminists exploring female sexuality.

This book is not intended as a study of the self-defeating behaviors that people perform in their lives, nor of actual sadomasochistic activities. Rather, it is a genealogy of the discourses that produce masochistic *fantasies*. It studies nineteenth-century literature by women in which violent images and tropes serve as the language of erotic desire.[24] I do not use the word "masochism" to refer to concrete behaviors but rather to identify an attraction to domination that is frequently, though not exclusively, an erotic attraction. I do not necessarily mean the enjoyment of pain (what Freud calls "algolagnia"). I tend to agree, rather, with Simone de Beauvoir, who writes: "Pain, in fact, is of masochistic significance only when it is accepted and wanted as proof of servitude" (though, like Berliner, she overstates her case in order to reiterate that in masochism pain is not the aim of an instinct). Beauvoir is emphatic that masochistic fantasies are not an index to actually desired behavior. "It is a mistake to seek in fantasies the key to concrete behavior; for fantasies are created and cherished as fantasies. The little girl who dreams of violation with mingled horror and acquiescence does not really *wish* to be violated, and if such a thing should happen it would be a hateful calamity" (398–99). Beauvoir's theory of masochism parallels my own understanding of women's masochistic fantasies: woman's status as man's "other" in Western culture strips her of subjectivity and propels her to seek both vicarious existence and transcendence as the cherished possession of an idealized man. But the case is more complex than that, for, as numerous feminist commentators upon masochism insist, "Western women" are not necessarily any more masochistic than men are, and so to attribute the problem to sweeping generalizations about Western women is to foster potentially damaging stereotypes and misconceptions.

Indeed, where theories of masochism tend to run into trouble is when they posit simple, universal explanations for what is a complex phenomenon. Indeed, no simple, comprehensive theory of the origins of any form of sexual desire is forthcoming. Sexual researchers Robert Stoller and Ethel Specter Person both acknowledge this truth and coin metaphors that illuminate the complexity of any endeavor to understand the origin of a sexual desire. Person coins the term "sex print" to refer to the "individualized script" that elicits erotic desire for each person, his or her "erotic signature," constructed along with his or her social identity.[25] Stoller coins the term "microdot," which refers to an encoding device used by the Nazis, whereby a page of information was condensed into a tiny photograph the size of a dot. Sexual desire, he argues, is a microdot: a densely compacted pile of personal and cultural information compressed into a particular image that is personally exciting for that particular individual. It is a sexual microchip coded with cultural, historical, genetic, biological, experiential input. Any attempt to understand a form of desire such as masochism must take into account not only this multiplicity of forces converging to create it but also their interplay with each other.

This book makes no attempt to formulate a comprehensive theory of the origins of masochistic desire. Its goal is more specific: to analyze the role of culturally and historically specific discourses in shaping the masochistic fantasies in mid-nineteenth-century American sentimentalism. This kind of targeted discourse analysis, while it lacks universal explanatory power, provides a crucial complement to other kinds of approaches that have recently been adopted. Stoller, for example, takes a basically psychoanalytic approach, vividly displaying the complexity of a masochistic microdot by writing an entire book, *Sexual Excitement*, about one erotic fantasy of one patient, "Belle," whose masochism he attributes largely to her interactions with her two relatively dysfunctional parents. His approach is simultaneously illuminating and frustrating. The correlation between certain traumatic incidents in childhood and Belle's erotic fantasy is convincing, but one suspects that there is more to erotic desire than the family romance. What about cultural representations of eroticized violence? What about the young woman's religious upbringing, her region, her ethnicity and its relationship to the dominant culture, her socioeconomic standing and the position of women within that bracket? Answers to such questions might be found through a focused analysis of the language of her fantasies, a consideration, for example, of where her words and images are used elsewhere in her culture and what associations those uses carry.

Studying discourses of desire not only enhances a psychoanalytic methodology, like Stoller's, but also sociological ones, like those of John Noyes and Jessica Benjamin. In *The Mastery of Submission*, Noyes adopts a cultural-studies perspective, explaining the rise of masochism in terms of Michel Foucault's observation in *The History of Sexuality* that in modern culture, the operations of power become eroticized. For Noyes, the nineteenth- and twentieth-century phenomenon of masochistic desire is best understood as a corollary to certain transformations of the workings of power in modern society. A "liberal" idealization of "civilized" nonviolent behavior coexists with the need for "real men" to wield effectively the tools and mechanisms of social control. While to be civilized, men must submit to restraint and discipline, to be manly, they must use their cultural power to subjugate others. Rather than suffer nervous breakdowns, some of those who find the clash untenable parody social violence through fantasies of violence turned against themselves— thereby identifying simultaneously as liberal and as manly subjects. In locating a crisis of masculinity at the core of masochistic desire, Noyes repudiates Freud's postulate of an essential female masochism. In fact, Noyes proposes that women experience masochistic desire only vicariously through unconscious identification with male masochists.[26] Given my own focus, I see this as an obvious shortcoming of Noyes's basically magnificent book, a shortcoming that has its roots in his commitment to his own broad assertions about the nature of liberalism in modern Western culture. But not all masochism is about the male crisis over liberalism; for example, the masochistic imagery in Emily Dickinson's "Master" letters—in which a Daisy kneels at the knee of her Master—is more directly comprehensible through consideration of the Calvinist and sentimental discourses used in the books Dickinson read than through broad consideration of the contradictions in male subjectivity inherent in liberal culture.

Like Noyes, Jessica Benjamin makes broad and useful characterizations about culture in general, but unlike him, she virtually fuses masochistic desire with the female subject position in modern Western society. Blending a feminist interpretation of Western culture with an object-relations psychoanalytic emphasis upon the importance of mutual recognition between a mother and child, she attributes masochistic desire to a breakdown in that drama of recognition: ontologically insecure children will secure the affirmation "I exist" either by hurting another (sadism, male) or by submitting to another's blows (masochism, female). The masochistic tendency, she argues, derives from the fundamental positioning of woman as man's other in Western culture, a positioning that renders women vulnerable to a fear of male abandonment and therefore likely to privilege connectedness of any kind—including the connectedness of erotic domination—rather than acquiesce to an aloneness that means nonrecognition and therefore nonexistence.

But Benjamin's link between masochism and femininity cannot account for the fact that masochism is as prominent among men as it is among women, nor can it account for the fact that it is far from the norm even among women. Her theory usefully demonstrates how masochism is related to cultural norms of female identity construction, but it is not as broadly characteristic of women in Western culture as she suggests. Rather, it applies to culturally specific patterns of female desire transmitted by equally specific discourses. She claims that gender-related patterns in parenting determine a child's identity, and that for many girls, this early construction of identity will subsequently manifest itself in the language of masochistic desire. But such a theory presumes a preexisting masochistic desire that invents masochistic language to describe itself, rather than vice versa, and frequently, the *language* of desire arises *prior* to the form of desire itself, influencing rather than merely expressing that desire.[27]

Attention to this linguistic dimension resolves some of the open issues in Benjamin's book. For example, Benjamin convincingly shows how Western social organization prompts a girl to seek vicarious access to identity rather than autonomy, to believe that as a woman, she is "nothing" alone. And she proposes that the fear of abandonment intrinsic to such a precarious form of subjectivity might induce a woman to idealize a powerful man, since he would have to prove himself capable of sustaining the burden of personhood for both of them. Benjamin proposes that because of conventions of male identity in Western culture, the woman learns to idealize a " 'heroic' sadist," someone who assures her of his strength specifically in acts of abusing her (119). She theorizes that while men identify themselves through contemptuously separating from their mothers and only reconnect with that lost first love object via the symbolic vehicle of sexual intercourse, women never fully individuate from their mothers, continuing their maternal identification and experiencing desire only vicariously through the desire for the man's desire (Benjamin 74–83). Because the man expresses his individuality through acts that dominate the female, she develops the desire to be dominated. Even though she does not want to be a subordinated person, she has no choice, because that is the only social position she can imagine. But this argument that a girl miserably acquiesces to a desire she despises does not make intuitive sense. If a girl came to understand that motherhood is a despised position in the culture, would that understanding really foster in her a desire to be despised? She might submit, but would her desire also fall in line? This problem in Benjamin's theory can be resolved, however, by considering the frequently religious language in which the "'heroic' sadist" is invoked. As I demonstrate, tracing this figure backward to representations of God offers a more plausible explanation of how a woman might come to find such a figure attractive. Thus, it is not enough to have a broad theory of the origins of sexual desire in general or masochism in particular; for a more complete understanding of the development of sexual desire, we must consider the particular discourses within which desire blooms.

Language does not entirely determine desire, but it plays a more active role than theorists of masochism have granted to it. In order to suggest the nature of the study I am engaged in, I would like to cite two examples of how language plays a determining role in shaping people's erotic experiences. The first is an interview that Robert Stoller and Gilbert Herdt conducted with a tribal Indonesian woman. She uses precisely the same word to label both what we call "orgasm" and the pleasurable physical feelings she experiences while breast-feeding her child (163–64). As it turns out, recent American studies indicate ample scientific basis for equating these two activities, since the same hormone is secreted in a woman's body during both nursing and vaginal or clitoral orgasm.[28] It is our culture, phobic about maternal sexual desire, that linguistically separates these experiences, and it is our language of love that therefore makes it difficult for those of us who think in it to recognize and actually feel the sameness of these two forms of loving experience. Of course, these two feelings of love are not completely identical, and certainly Western women can and have experienced this similarity— language does not have complete autonomy over experience—but our language problematizes that association. This example suggests that in analyzing any particular expression of desire, we cannot necessarily seek the essential desire that language supposedly articulates without paying close attention to how that language is itself integral to the desire. The prevailing theories of masochism need to attend not only to the signifier and to the signified but to the mediation between them.

The second example not only demonstrates how attention to the language of desire sheds light on the etiology of masochism but also raises some of the knotty theoretical issues that emerge from a psycholinguistic analysis like mine. In his moving and persuasive polemic against corporal punishment, *Spare the Child*, Philip Greven demonstrates that children raised within a context of evangelical Protestant discourses associating corporal punishment with love sometimes develop sadomasochistic tendencies. Greven writes, "Love and fear, pain and suffering, power and authority, and unquestioning obedience—the leitmotifs of evangelical and fundamentalist Protestantism for many centuries—are often the roots from which sadomasochism in all its beneficial and destructive manifestations arises. The association of love and pain is inescapable when corporal punishments are used" (176). He documents numerous instances in which Protestant disciplinary ideologies lead to sadomasochistic desire. One of these focuses upon the effects of "discipline" on children schooled in a small apocalyptic Protestant sect (founded in 1972), the Northeast Kingdom Community Church at Island Pond, Vermont. The promotional literature of the sect states: "we discipline our children according to the Word of God. We love our children; we do not abuse them; we discipline them . . . the infliction of pain upon a child's rear end . . . is not child abuse, but rather their salvation." But Greven, and one father whose daughters spent time there, disagree; they believe that the sect's equation of "love" with "the infliction of pain upon a child's rear end" generates masochism. The father wrote: "I have an eight-year-old girl who is a masochist. She equates love with beatings." Greven quotes a tape recording this father made of himself speaking with his daughters shortly after he withdrew them from Island Pond. In it, the two girls urge their father to spank them:

> "We want to feel decent," say the voices on the tape. "If you don't discipline us then our hearts will never change. . . . Yeah, do something like that. Do something like spanking us, or hit us. . . . Spank us or put us in the corner. . . . Do you rather put us in the corner, Papa? . . .
> "I want to love you children," says [their father]. "I want to do what the Lord would have me do for you."
> "I know, the Lord wants you to spank us if we're disobedient. If you love us . . . then you'll spank us. If you spank us, then you love us. If you don't spank us, then you don't love us." (Greven 175)

Close consideration of this dialogue suggests that the desires of these two children to be spanked are directly attributable to the language that was spoken to them at Island Pond. Their word choices—"We want to feel decent"; "our hearts will never change"; "If you spank us, then you love us"—suggest the presence of external influences, and the agent of transmitting those influences appears to be a violent strain within the language used at their school. The girls do not simply speak; rather, they seem to be spoken by their culture. But we cannot, therefore, simply say that they are the brainwashed victims of a cult and therefore don't *really* want to be spanked. Who are we—who is anybody—to say what another person's *true* desire is? How can we distinguish between brainwashing and good breeding, between healthy desires and unhealthy ones, between a cult and a legitimate spiritual community? We can imagine that these girls—restored to loving parenting and a more conventional life—might stop expressing a desire to be spanked. But if this were to happen, then surely we would do better to say that their desire has not been *restored* but *changed*. While under the influence of the Island Pond community, they *do* desire to be spanked. If, as detached observers, we want to separate these girls' expressions of desire from some hypothetical true desire—to specify, perhaps, that the language of spanking and discipline is simply these girls' best means of expressing desires for parental love and personal self-esteem—we must nonetheless recognize that they have, at least partially, a *real* desire to be spanked.

How much autonomy do we want to grant to the language of desire? How sincere are these girls' expressions of desire? These questions are unanswerable, yet the quest for answers lies at the heart of this book. As the example of the Indonesian language of breastfeeding suggests, language has a fair amount of influence over our experiences of the world. The metaphors in which we understand our experience do not completely determine our experience and our desire, but they do influence them. The authors I analyze in this book associate images of submission and violence with erotic desire. To what extent is this intentional, and to what extent nonvoluntary? To what extent does it represent their desire, and to what extent is it a distorted expression of desire for something really quite different? Examining the relationship between these authors' expressions of desire and the Calvinist discourses associating punishment with love helps us explore these questions, but it does not resolve these ambiguities once and for all. There is certainly no way to know whether the authors actually desired domination in any direct or simple way. Fantasies are not direct expressions of desire. As with the young girls at the Island Pond school, there is no direct relationship between Susan Warner's, Harriet Beecher Stowe's, and Emily Dickinson's verbal expressions of masochistic desire and their fundamental psychology. But there is *some* relationship between them.

This necessarily ambivalent position on the autonomy of language with relation to desire spills over into an equally ambivalent position on the status of the literary works that I am studying: are they simply language acts, aesthetic objects divorced from their authors? Are they, by contrast, accurate signs of their authors' desires? Once again, I imagine them in a space somewhere in between. I read the works I analyze as fantasies, neither diary entries nor pure language acts.[29] Robert McClure Smith has pointed out the instability and relative autonomy of erotic fantasies, observing that "Fantasy scenarios are specifically constructed in order to permit multiple and shifting identifications" ("Masochistic Aesthetic" 1). They are both intentional and unintentional. In fantasies, authors exert their control over material whose nature is influenced by the culture, and which comes to them predominantly from their own unconscious. Fantasies are aesthetic products informed by desire, not transcripts of desire, and the degree of authorial intention in them varies and cannot easily be ascertained. The works I analyze mediate between unconscious levels of desire and conscious levels of authorial intention; they cannot be said to describe real-life desires. As fantasies, these works occupy a position somewhere between a voice that is masochistic and an actual desire for suffering. Because fantasy exists in a realm apart from actual experience, it is important to resist the kind of taxonomizing impulse the father in Greven's anecdote indulges when he calls his daughters "masochists." I would say rather that the literature I analyze is masochistic in ways that its authors partially, but not entirely, control.

The nineteenth-century sentimental authors discussed in this book are influenced by the discourses of the culture out of which they emerge, which prompt them to represent sexuality in terms of domination and promote desires for such experiences by associating them with ecstatic pleasures. Contradictorily, these authors are also women who are committed to the autonomy of the self, partially because of their roots in Calvinism, partially because of ideologies of American individualism, and partially because they are ambitious artists. They are therefore in a double bind, conflicted between their understanding of selfhood and their language of sexuality. Masochistic fantasies of the loss of self-control are a way of resolving that conflict, a way of responding to culturally determined forms of desire *and* of maintaining aesthetic and personal control. Their artworks are simultaneously products of the imagination and products of craft: syntheses of desire and intentionality, the unconscious and the conscious.

Recent scholarship on the linguistic determination of experience varies according to discipline. Following the lead of Michel Foucault, poststructuralist philosophers such as Judith Butler contend that there is no meaningful physical experience prior to the language governing its experience.[30] Scholars of many persuasions in the highly contested field of psychoanalytic theory take a similar, though less radical, position by arguing that language creates an "official version" of experience (Juhasz, "Object" 143). Physical and life scientists, by contrast, typically see experience as a direct function of sensual perception, and they regard language as a mere encoding of prior experience for the purposes of relaying that experience to others (Gumperz and Levinson 39). (The hormonal continuity between breast-feeding and orgasm suggests the relevance of such a perspective.) Linguists John Gumperz and Stephen Levinson argue for a middle ground between linguistic and biological determinism, calling for a theory that blends the autonomy of sensory experience with the autonomy of the organizing function of language.[31] I advance such a theory in this book, describing the interplay between the physical sensations produced by sentimentalism and the discourses in which they are experienced. The operations of sympathy produce a sensation of sheer physical affect: "the sight of other people's anguish causes very real anguish to me," writes Montaigne.[32] But in nineteenth-century sentimental literature, that anguish is experienced within the context of predominant discourses of the era associating affliction with romantic and religious love. That shared version of reality, as transmitted by language, informs the reader's experience of sympathetic pain.

My analysis of the language of desire is partially informed by Jacques Lacan's theory of language *as* desire. It is not that I accept Lacan's claim that his theories are true but rather that, like Margaret Homans, I find that his theories encapsulate a *myth* about the relationship between women and language that has considerable resonance for my subject. Like Lacan's psychoanalytic paradigm, nineteenth-century sentimentalism frequently centers upon a nostalgic longing for a lost maternal symbiosis that was necessarily renounced in the process of acquiring an adult identity. And like Lacan, the authors I analyze frequently suppose that maternal plenitude must be rejected in order for an individual to acquire a meaningful identity in the social system through speaking the dominant language. Only men can perform such a rejection, so that women therefore are culturally silenced, represented as the background from which male authoritative subjects distinguish themselves in the act of speaking.[33] The authors I analyze frequently acquiesce to or at least respond to this formulation, often presuming a conflict between femininity and speech or femininity and presence. Masochistic writing can be seen as their response to this conflict, in that it accommodates an impulse toward female erasure *and* an impulse for female aesthetic activity. It is a self-denying form of presence. The fact that the authors I analyze present this Lacanian perspective on language and gender does not prove that Lacan is right, but rather that he has put his finger on a powerful formulation about the relationship between language, gender, and identity.

Like many intrepid critics tempted by the seductive vortex of Lacanian theory, I discovered while writing this book a contradiction in his work: while his theoretical work, taken as a whole, urges us to look to the cultural origins of subjectivity by locating those origins in language, it also simultaneously universalizes male and female identities in ahistorical and transcultural ways that limit its explanatory power. Although my book is at times inspired by his and a number of other psychoanalytic models, it is specifically indebted to none and does not seek to engage in debate over their relative merits. Rather, I seek the origins of women's literary masochism more in history than in theory, though theory helpfully guides my interpretation of historical data. Masochism is more culturally and historically specific than theorists suggest, frequently arising in conjunctions with ideals of ethereal femininity, innocence, self-sacrifice, and a disciplined work ethic—such as characterized northeast American, nineteenth-century, middle-class Protestant culture (though obviously it occurs elsewhere). From its religious roots, one can trace the spread of masochism at least partly through nineteenth-century sentimentalism, the mass medium that disseminated such ideas on a wide scale and thereby defined a coherent value system for many female readers. This literature is therefore particularly useful for twentieth-century readers interested in female masochism, enabling them to understand the historical and cultural foundation of the contemporary phenomenon. By addressing the links between literary expressions of desire in the sentimental community and the discourses of love prevalent in the culture from which they spring, this study provides the historical and cultural contexts sorely needed by many of the broad cultural psychoanalytic theories of female masochism, if they are to be believable and useful. It begins with two chapters addressing the role of discourse in the production of female masochistic desire, and it then considers the varying uses made of those discourses by important authors of the era. The tenor of the book also gradually changes from an opening emphasis upon the patriarchal determination of women's desire to an increasing emphasis upon women's self-determination through appropriation and exploitation of masochistic discourses of desire.

Chapter 1 identifies two major antebellum discourses in the northeastern United States that encouraged women both to interpret domination as a sign of the love of a man endowed with subjectivity and to express their desire for his love in tropes of wounding and violence. Nineteenth-century sentimentalism is frequently informed by the notorious ideology of "true womanhood," which implicitly idealizes a noncorporeal woman. One of the important attractions of masochism is that it makes available to a woman who endorses "true womanhood" a way of imagining her own embodiment and her own desire for physical pleasure, thereby restoring to presence a female body that that ideology effectively erases. An equally influential discourse affecting the use of masochism in the sentimental works I study is the the evangelical language of the Second Great Awakening, the Protestant revival movement that swept across the Northeast in the decades preceding the Civil War. Evangelical discourse is important in the etiology of sadomasochism because its language consistently links corporal punishment with love. In particular, the providential theory of affliction, according to which pain is a sign of God's love, can be seen as an important progenitor of masochistic desires in antebellum women's sentimentalism.

Admittedly, the notion that pain is sent by God as a sign of his love is not born with John Calvin but is as old as Christianity itself; it is particularly characteristic of Pauline theology. But since the authors I analyze all come from Puritan backgrounds, I concentrate on the Calvinist tradition. While the psychological traits associated with masochism as a form of sexual fantasy—a desire for perfection, a fear of intimacy as a kind of assault upon the self, a particularly emphatic sense of individuated selfhood—are by no means limited to Protestantism, they are indeed characteristic of it. Study of Calvinist discourse is therefore especially illuminating with regard to the development of masochism. Certainly, the fact that Jean Jacques Rousseau (whose *Confessions* features a number of masochistic fantasies) was raised in Geneva, on a diet of sentimental romances, is highly suggestive of correlations among sentimentalism, Calvinism, and masochism. Without a doubt, though, a broader consideration of the religious influences on masochistic desire is called for, and I hope that this book will spark diverse studies of these influences.

However, while evangelical Protestantism plants an important seed associating love with punishment, domination, and/or cruelty, it does not in and of itself link that love with eroticism. But as I show in chapter 2, the mechanisms of sentimentalism foster such an association, yoking the Calvinist idealization of affliction to the painful affect that is a central component of all sentimental literature. As the bestselling didactic children's tale *Elsie Dinsmore* and the pro-slavery apologia *The Planter's Northern Bride* demonstrate, sentimental representations of domination frequently function not simply as tropes for love but as building blocks for patriarchally determined erotic desire.

The next three chapters consider the uses of the language of sentimental masochism in three of the most important women's literary works of the day: Susan Warner's sentimental bestseller, *The Wide, Wide World* (1851); Harriet Beecher Stowe's blockbuster epic, *Uncle Tom's Cabin* (1852); and the poetic corpus of one of America's greatest poets, Emily Dickinson. For a number of reasons, these three literary products

are ideal for analyzing the development of female expressions of masochistic desire. First, they are useful because they feature a variety of ap-
plications of the discourses of sentimental masochism: Warner uses it
unself-consciously for an exploration of feminine romantic desire within
a religious context; Stowe uses it with a certain amount of self-consciousness for the political purpose of energizing the abolitionist movement; Dickinson uses it for highly self-aware explorations into the nature of power, eroticism, and identity. Secondly, Warner and Stowe
wrote two of the most popular books of the entire nineteenth century,
so we can take it for granted that they appealed to a great many readers
and influenced them. Juxtaposing two writers who enjoyed widespread
mass popularity with a more private, exclusively "literary" author illustrates that the language of sentimental masochism was not only oppressive and widespread but also available for appropriation, manipulation,
and exploitation.

The three writers initially seem disparate: Warner is a social conservative whose explicit endorsement of traditional female roles includes an
unconscious but pronounced attraction to masochism. Stowe is an out-
spoken activist who consciously takes a stand against patriarchal and racial injustice, but the grounds of her rebellion unintentionally reinforce
oppressive cultural norms, including feminine masochism. Dickinson is
a poet who rejects masochism and the social institution of marriage that
she believes fosters it, but she deliberately appropriates the popular discourse of sentimental masochism as a literary device. The very disparities
among these three writers are useful, however, precisely because they
expose in stark relief the predominant features these women have in
common, thereby underscoring the cultural patterns underlying their
usage of sentimental masochism. Two of these patterns are particularly
significant. Warner, Stowe, and Dickinson all came from strongly patriarchal families that valued intellectual development for daughters as well
as sons, even though they endorsed an ideology of separate spheres for
men and women that denied women professional ambition. These authors were also emotionally and intellectually absorbed with the evangelical culture of the Second Great Awakening and tended to associate
self-renunciation with pleasure, in keeping with their religious background. These two commonalities, it will be shown, played a key role in
the process leading them to sentimental masochism in their quest for a
language that was amenable to their aesthetic and intellectual aspirations
but also responsive to intense pressures impeding their writing.

The chapter on Susan Warner most clearly straddles the line that informs the entire book—the line between masochism as a form of feminine agency and masochism as a symptom of the cultural oppression of
women. Demonstrating that *The Wide, Wide World* is heavily influenced

by masochistic tropes proliferating in the culture at large, I analyze masochism as a limited and limiting—but effective—means of imagining physical pleasure without damaging culturally sanctioned ideals of female identity. The text both fosters *and* explores the erotics of domination. Masochism is clearly not an innate desire in *The Wide, Wide World*, since the text vividly displays the manipulation of its heroine's desire— but it is nonetheless a real form of expressing desire.

Like *The Wide, Wide World*, *Uncle Tom's Cabin* is a sentimental text in which dominant ideologies associating suffering with pleasure render masochism a powerful expressive device. And the mixture of manipulation and agency that Stowe discovers in using that expressive device leads her to a particularly ambivalent position. Stowe advocated a politics of feelings, and her representations of tortured slaves and her efforts to make readers feel their pain derived from an effort to force readers to identify with the victims of American injustice. The juxtaposition of those images with evangelical imagery of the ecstasies of wounding, however, invited readers to experience the feeling of another's pain as ecstatic. The further association of those ecstasies with sexually charged images of black men had the effect of eroticizing that sympathy. As in the case of Warner, the erotics of sympathy in *Uncle Tom's Cabin* results from the juxtaposition of sentimental and evangelical discourses. But in *Uncle Tom's Cabin*, the eroticization complicates the book's politics. Sentimentalism, this chapter demonstrates, is shot through with sadomasochistic pleasures that complicate its overtly humanitarian motives.

The final chapter addresses the most sophisticated and intentional use of such pleasures. It demonstrates that Emily Dickinson was hardly imprisoned by patriarchal constructions of desire but rather exploited them for her own purposes. Dickinson's usage of sentimental masochism most dramatically challenges the "sexual voluntarist" critique of masochism, according to which the only pleasure possible for a woman lies in resistance to dominant forms of desire. This chapter demonstrates that Dickinson exploited dominant discourses of desire not ironically nor subversively but with relish, indulging the pleasures that the culture associated with female submission. Her writing epitomizes the possibilities for female self-expression to be found in the weird curves of sentimental masochism.

One

Masochistic Discourses of Womanhood

IN 1850, the issue of women's rights was all the rage in America. The first official women's rights convention, held at Seneca Falls, New York in July 1848, had declared that "all men and women are created equal," and at its close the members had agreed to reconvene at a much larger, highly publicized National Woman's Rights Convention in Worcester, Massachusetts in October 1850. But though these women's rights activists sought to speak out on behalf of all women, they were far from enjoying unanimous support among women—to say nothing of men. A striking example of the kind of opposition they faced from women appeared in the April 1850 edition of *Godey's Lady's Book*, one of the most popular and influential ladies' magazines of the nineteenth century. It was a short story, "Woman's Rights," in which the author, Haddie Lane, politely but pointedly attacks the women's rights advocates as selfish, lazy, and irreligious. Over the course of this story, the narrator, also named Haddie, learns that the true meaning of women's rights differs considerably from the rather lighthearted meanings being bandied about at the boarding school from which she has just returned.

In the opening scene, Haddie is engaging in high-spirited banter with her male cousin, and when she teasingly threatens to kill him if he refuses to concede her "rights," Haddie's Aunt Debbie decides things have gone far enough. She takes her niece on a journey through their village to teach her that woman's rights are sacred duties which should not be treated lightly. In each of the encounters in this story, the increasingly chastened Haddie learns that woman's rights always entail either suffering or self-sacrifice. She and her aunt have the "right" to carry a heavy basket of food to a poverty-stricken but upright single mother and her grimy "urchins." They encounter a dying young woman who insists, "I am in dreadful agony sometimes—yet, believe me, I would not be as I once was for all the wealth of worlds. I am far happier now," having "gladly changed" from "a proud girl to a humble sufferer" (270). When they encounter Ellen Stuart, a woman whose long-suffering patience and thankless darning had drawn her husband back from alcoholism and who now enjoys "rural felicity," Aunt Debbie asks, "Which would you rather be, the proud, wealthy woman, sneering at household duties, and endeavoring wildly to revolutionize the world; or Ellen Stuart, humble and hard-working though she be, rejoicing in the thought that her patient forbearance and the blessed old stocking have wrought this change?" Her niece answers, "Not the *virago*, for the wealth of worlds" (272).

Contemptuous of self-indulgence in the women's rights movement, the story not only romanticizes pain and suffering but encourages women to seek out physical abuse. Haddie learns, for example, that domestic violence is another of woman's rights when she encounters her friend Fanny Carlton, who is out walking with her father. They "had approached nearly to where we stood, when the old man's foot struck against some obstacle in the path. He with difficulty suppressed a loud cry of pain; but, lifting his arm quickly, gave his daughter a blow so heavy that she reeled forward, and would have fallen but for a friendly cedar which stood near. . . . [A]t this shameful blow her color faded; an expression of pain crossed her face. . . . Mr. Carlton walked as fast as his foot would allow, muttering curses and imprecations; while Fanny seemed to have forgotten the blow, so tenderly did she support the old man" (271–72). Far from being angry at her father, Fanny "blame[s] her own carelessness" and insists, "I am doing penance, Haddie; I used to be such a rover. But my father likes me near him; and he has so few enjoyments that I am glad I can help him to forget his sufferings" (272). Aunt Debbie insists that submission to paternal violence is another one of "woman's rights." "Fanny is learning a lesson of self-denial, of patience; and though it may seem an unenviable right to you to be able to 'bless them that curse you,' we must think of 'the great reward' which Fanny will obtain in heaven" (272). The story shifts from justifying suffering to advocating it. There is a crucial distinction between enjoying the sense of agency that may involve some suffering (for example, in carrying a heavy basket of food to the poor) and characterizing violence as a not "unenviable" right. It may be true that in learning to bless one's persecutors, a person can experience a moral triumph, but that is a "right" shared by all people. By including subjection to paternal violence in a catalogue of "woman's rights," the story fails to distinguish between suffering as a means to an end and suffering as an end in itself. Deriving pleasure from submission to unwarranted violence is not a right: it is masochism.

This story is not anomalous; indeed, its appearance in *Godey's*— widely recognized at the time as the standard of genteel taste—indicates that its values and the language in which they are articulated represent the mainstream of midcentury genteel culture. But how could such a tale be read by a significant portion of the women in antebellum America without arousing their ire? What could lead the editor, Sarah Josepha Hale—an advocate for women's education, property rights, and professional opportunities—to publish it? How could she presume that her readers would both like and benefit from a story in which suffering is not a lamentable human inevitability but a significant right for women? The goal of this chapter is to explore these questions, to understand how a masochistic discourse of a female attraction to violence became a recognizable and acceptable feature of the mid-nineteenth-century literary landscape.

In part, the answer to these questions is latent in the discursive and cultural context of the story, which is the product of antebellum Protestantism in the northeastern United States. In order to understand the pleasure Fanny takes in paternal violence, for example, it is crucial to address the religious context of the story. Aunt Debbie posits suffering as a "right" because it enables (or, rather, forces) Fanny to turn to God and so gain "the great reward" of an eternity in heaven. Receptivity to masochism is linked to spiritual transcendence. The Protestant doctrine underlying this belief system is the notion of providence, according to which affliction is a manifestation of God's love, sent to force individuals to turn away from earthly comforts and toward heavenly support. As Mary Rowlandson reminds herself in her 1682 captivity narrative, "'For whom the Lord loveth he chasteneth, and scourgeth every Son whom he receiveth.' (Hebrews 12.6) . . . 'It is good for me that I have been afflicted.' The Lord hath showed me . . . That we must rely on God Himself, and our whole dependance must be upon Him" (172–73).

More immediate influences on a text like "Woman's Rights" might have been popular hymns, sermons, and tracts of the antebellum period. Consider the following stanzas from three hymns from Henry Ward Beecher's popular *Plymouth Collection*.

> On my heart each stripe be written,
> Wherewith Thou for me wert smitten;
> Each deep wound that I may be
> Wholly crucified with Thee.

> And can my heart aspire so high,
> To say—"My Father God!"
> Lord, at Thy feet I long to lie,
> And learn to kiss the rod.

> Wait, then, my soul, submissive wait,
> Prostrate before His awful seat;
> And, 'mid the terrors of His rod,
> Trust in a wise and gracious God.[1]

Hymns such as these undergird the masochistic affirmations in a story like Haddie Lane's "Woman's Rights." Fanny Carlton's interpretation of her father's blows as a "right" is rooted in providential theories of affliction, which encourage Christians to recognize love and compassion in the chastening paternal rod. The enormous popularity and familiarity of such hymns provided a frame of reference enabling *Godey's* readers to respond positively to "Woman's Rights." This kind of Puritan discourse forms one thread in a complex tapestry of cultural forces encouraging nineteenth-century female readers to associate male violence with love and pleasure.

Of course, hymn writers did not gender the pleasures of the scourging rod. But the discourses of womanhood in ascendancy during the first half of the nineteenth century had the effect of making metaphors like those used in the hymns particularly applicable to women. As this chapter shows, it is the intersection of two of these discourses—true womanhood and Calvinism—that made antebellum middle-class culture so receptive to masochistic stories like Haddie Lane's "Woman's Rights." True womanhood implicitly idealizes an impossible notion of "female nature" according to which a woman has neither a body nor an independent existence. This ideal therefore makes the destruction of female autonomy seem natural and desirable. As we shall see, this perspective is reinforced by prevailing religious ideals, according to which the destruction of individual autonomy paves the way for a transcendent union with God. As diaries by women caught up in the Second Great Awakening—a massive revival movement in the first half of the nineteenth century—reveal, religious perspectives idealizing violence provide a pattern for thinking about marriage. Both conversion and marriage promise a blissful expansion of being for the one who relinquishes individual existence. The juxtaposition of these two discourses, then, has the effect of making the whole notion of submission to the destruction of the female self seem natural and even ecstatic for women, more of a "right" than a misfortune.

———————

One of the most important ideologies linking Calvinist affirmations of suffering to women in particular was the notion that independent female existence, though possible, was unnatural.[2] This attitude is vividly reflected in the legal status of a wife, as defined by the eighteenth-century English legal theorist Sir William Blackstone: "In marriage, the husband and wife are one person in law; that is, the very being or legal existence of the woman is suspended during the marriage, or at least is incorporated and consolidated into that of the husband: under whose *cover* she performs everything; and is therefore called in our law-french a *feme-covert*. . . . [A] man cannot grant anything to his wife, or enter into covenant with her: for the grant would be to suppose her separate existence;

and to covenant with her, would be only to covenant with himself"
(430). In effect, a woman's legal personhood died in marriage; her "very
being" was "suspended." According to the law, it would be ludicrous to
permit covenants between husband and wife, because a wife *was* her
husband.

The influence of Blackstone, an English jurist who was the first to
study and elucidate the entirety of English law, can hardly be overstated.
His four-volume *Commentaries on the Laws of England* (1765–69) was
revered both in England and America. It served as the basis of university
legal education in both countries, was read by most of the Founding
Fathers, and was extensively used during the formation of the American
legal system following the American Revolution. Certainly, laws do not
necessarily determine how people regard themselves, but Blackstone appears to have captured in this principle of coverture—if not actually determined—an attitude that in fact was widespread in the culture: a
woman relinquishes all independent existence in marriage and is completely dependent upon her husband. Only he has subjectivity; she has
none. The writings of nineteenth-century women's rights activists react
against the pervasiveness of this attitude. The well-known British feminist Frances Cobbe objected to the treatment of women as "relative
creatures," demanding that approaches to "woman as adjective" be re-
placed by "woman as noun."[3] And American women's rights advocates,
including Elizabeth Oakes-Smith (author of the popular 1842 poem
"The Sinless Child") and Thomas Wentworth Higginson (a renowned
advocate for abolitionism and feminism) explicitly refer to Blackstone's
principle of coverture as both cause and symptom of the unjust treatment of women (Higginson, *Alphabet* 147–48). Oakes-Smith, for example, protests that Blackstone represents woman as "incompetent,
being held as an infant, a chattel, an idiot in law" (*Woman* 71). But she
also recognizes an enormous appeal in the ideals underlying the law of
coverture. After quoting Blackstone, she writes that the "extract, remarkable alike for the force and beauty of its expression, would seem to
imply that the philosophy of law is not greatly at variance with the truth,
recognizing that unity of life and feeling which our Saviour himself defines to be the true marriage" (70). Though she goes on to insist that
the ideal was rarely achieved in real marriages, she acknowledges in principle the beauty of the ideal of the unity of person in marriage, an ideal
she relates to spiritual union. Feminist legal historian Marylynn Salmon
concurs that such a union, though widely recognized to be impossible,
was cherished as an ideal of marriage to be pursued and upheld: "Unity
of person, the principle advertised so well by William Blackstone in his
commentaries on English law (1765–69), represented little more than
an ideal in Anglo-American law . . . [But as] an ideal, lawyers, judges,

and lawmakers all upheld the principle. For early Americans, as for the English, spousal unity represented a goal of the law, hoped for but never realized, worshiped and ridiculed at the same time" (14). She adds, "As an ideal, unity of person found greater favor in the North, where courts gave men more control over family property" (40). Hence, we find in the North poets like Emily Dickinson reiterating the mystical ideal of spousal unity in such verses as "Brain of His Brain— / Blood of His Blood— / Two lives— One Being—now—" (246).

Women's rights activists and detractors contested this early American ideal throughout the nineteenth century, playing out its material battles over women's property in courts of law and its philosophical battles over woman's nature in literature, medicine, parlors, and pulpits. Many moderate women sought to walk a line between the radicals and the conservatives by asserting their need for material and social powers but locating those powers in the social forms produced by coverture. An editorial denouncing the Seneca Falls Convention on behalf of women's rights appeared in 1848 in the Philadelphia *Public Ledger and Daily Transcript*: "A woman is nobody. A wife is everything. A pretty girl is equal to ten thousand men, and a mother is, next to God, all powerful. . . . The ladies of Philadelphia, therefore . . . are resolved to maintain their rights as Wives, Belles, Virgins, and Mothers, and not as Women" (Gurko 93). The author is saying that woman in the abstract may be without rights, but in her role as belle, wife, maiden, or mother, she has far more power than men through her influence over men. Through roles defined in relation to men, women not only control men but gain property and power, and so the autonomy and independence sought by the feminist agitators in Seneca Falls, this editorial suggests, are more likely to strip women of the considerable power they enjoy as sexual beings than it is to empower them. This editorial is a witty slap at the radicals, but though perhaps lighthearted in tone, it is nonetheless a sincere affirmation of the powers and pleasures of the pedestal. As such, in retrospect we can see that it serves to disempower women by consolidating the declining but still vigorous principle of the *feme covert*. In locating women's power in the abdication of independent rights, it exemplifies the functioning of power through the production of subjectivity: the editorialist affirms the subject positions of middle-class wife and belle, along with the ideology that locates pleasure in the erasure of female autonomy, because the woman finds both power and pleasure in the subjectivity accessed vicariously through men.

In retrospect, this editorial also offers an important indication of how the ideal underlying the doctrine of coverture related to the production of masochistic fantasies in nineteenth-century women. Its central assumption—"a woman is nobody"—undergirds the process by which male dominance is eroticized. According to the spirit, if not the letter, of the law of coverture, in order to exist as a meaningful social being, a woman must relinquish her independent self; in order to empower herself, she must eschew all personal agency and seek true power as an adjunct to a man endowed with both identity and agency. But using a man as her only bridge to social existence positions the adjectival woman in a precarious situation, vulnerable to psychic and social collapse if separated from the man whose presence makes her meaningful. In a culture in which a single woman is "incomplete," as the British liberal manufacturer and influential essayist William Rathbone Greg claimed in his 1862 essay "Why Are Women Redundant?" pain and domination might well seem preferable to solitude, because they would dramatically foreground the presence of a subject through whom the woman could find "complete" existence.[4] As Michelle Masse writes, "The greatest incentive for masochism is stated with wry brevity by a patient: 'I guess if you're a victim, you're never alone.' Someone is always there for the masochist, even if only as mental representation" (45).[5]

As Masse, following both Jessica Benjamin and Simone de Beauvoir, demonstrates, the precarious contingency of female identity in patriarchal culture has tended to foster female masochistic fantasies. Dependent upon the signs of the other's presence and that other's power for the most fundamental sense of her identity, many a woman is led to idealize a man who manifests his power in his willingness to discipline and punish her. Her preference for violent signs of his presence—rather than, say, nurturing or jocular signs—is at least partially attributable to the language in which the destruction of independent female subjectivity was couched in the nineteenth century. Frequently the specific discourses associated with coverture associated femininity with ethereal noncorporeality, and as we shall see, this association unfortunately played directly into a masochistic affirmation of severity, discipline, and punishment.

Implicit in the mystical ideal underlying the law of coverture is a notion that by nature, a woman is bodiless, since every vestige of her independent self, including her body, was to become subsumed to that of her husband. This impossibility, though rarely articulated explicitly, was widely implied. As Nancy Armstrong observes, British conduct books of the late eighteenth and early nineteenth centuries idealize not "a woman who attracts the gaze as she did in an earlier culture, but one who fulfills her role by disappearing into the woodwork" (80). Rejecting outmoded aristocratic notions of the female body as an object for the display of male power, she demonstrates, bourgeois domestic fiction insisted that a woman's essential being lay not in her body but in her interiority: "By implying that the essence of the woman lay inside or underneath her surface, the invention of depths in the self entailed making the material body of the woman appear superficial" (76). Feminist American historians tend to represent this contrast between two perspectives on the female body in religious rather than class-oriented terms. Rather than contrasting "aristocratic" and "bourgeois" perspectives, they contrast an outmoded religious view of woman as the carnal inheritor of Eve's depravity with the burgeoning ideal of angelic womanhood, an ideal emphasizing woman's innate passionless purity.[6] But the English economic and American religious perspectives are not all that different: the ideal of the female body as an object for the display of man's power essentializes—as does the outdated religious view—a woman whose identity is defined by her carnality. Middle-class Protestant culture, by contrast, essentializes a woman whose identity is not only defined by her interiority but is actually undermined by her body.

In their rejection of the outmoded views of women as ornamental objects with no meaningful interiority, many middle-class nineteenth-century women enthusiastically endorsed the new representations of women.[7] Indeed, the ideal of disembodied passionlessness was, in a sense, liberating, freeing them from the tyranny of being viewed as mindless, an assumption that made female education pointless and female professionalism consequently impossible. The noncorporeality of "true womanhood" effectively made women seem to be moral, not carnal, beings, with important purposes other than the gratification of male desire. In *Woman in America* (1850), Maria McIntosh writes, "But while all the outward machinery of government, the body, the thews and sinews of society, are man's, woman, if true to her own not less important or less sacred mission, controls its vital principle. Unseen herself, working, like nature, in secret, she regulates its pulsations, and sends forth from its heart, in pure and temperate flow, the life-giving current" (25). The body is man's; woman, by contrast, is "unseen" and works "in secret." And bodiless purity bestows upon her a "sacred" social role of considerable importance and power: she is the spirit animating the government and other social organizations.

Ideals of bodilessness may also have seemed enticing since they implicitly circumvented oppression stemming from the notion that a woman's body was the property of her husband. According to Salmon, the law of coverture arose from a commitment among lawmakers to protect husbands' access to their wives' bodies. If a wife were independently subject to the law, she could be put in jail, depriving her husband of his legally protected right to her sexual and household services. Consider the argument of Tapping Reeve, Connecticut supreme court justice and author of the first treatise on domestic relations published in the United States, who wrote in 1816 that the right of a husband to the person of his wife "is a right guarded by the law with the utmost solicitude; if she could bind herself by her contracts, she would be liable to be arrested, taken in execution, and confined in a prison; and then the husband would be deprived of the company of his wife" (Salmon 42). And this eventuality, Reeve concluded, "the law will not suffer."[8] Given such attitudes toward the female body, it is not surprising that many women found refreshment in the new views of women as bodiless, passionless, and innately spiritual.

The law of coverture, then, contradictorily underwrote both the notion that a woman's body was designated for her husband's use and (via the ideal of ethereality implicit in legal invisibility) the notion that a woman in fact had no body at all. In "Women's Suffrage: The Reform against Nature," when the famous spokesman for Victorian Protestantism Horace Bushnell cites the law of coverture in a discussion of female nature, he uses metaphors that suggest both attitudes toward the female body: "The man, as in fatherhood, carries the name and flag; the woman, as in motherhood, takes the name on herself and puts it on her children, passing out of sight legally, to be a covert nature included henceforth in her husband" (*Selected* 168). And the justification he offers for this disappearance implicitly idealizes a woman who either has no body, or one that exists purely for male consumption:

> [A man's] look says, Force, Authority, Decision, Self-asserting Counsel, Victory. And the woman as evidently says, "I will trust, and be cherished and give sympathy and take ownership in the victor, and double his honors by the honors I contribute myself." . . . One is the force principle, the other is the beauty principle. . . . Enterprise and high counsel belong to one, also to batter the severities of fortune, conquer the raw material of supply; ornamentation, order, comfortable use, all flavors, and garnishes, and charms to the other. . . . They are positivity and receptivity, they are providence and use, they are strength and beauty, they are mass and color, they are store-house and table, they are substance and relish, and nothing goes to its mark or becomes a real value till it passes both. (168)

Bushnell begins with the suggestion that a true woman's body will suggest its own nonexistence, since a man's "look" is described in capitalized nouns that emphasize a powerful presence, while a woman's is captured in lowercase passive constructions that deny corporeal presence and deflect subjectivity onto him. The passive voice indicates the adjectival nature Bushnell idealizes in woman; while the man has "mass" and "substance," the woman is a disembodied aura of "receptivity" and "ornamentation." Bushnell also includes substantive metaphors for women, but these tend to create a picture of a being available for consumption:

"flavor," "garnish," "table," "relish." Either disembodied—lacking "mass" and "substance"—or embodied in order to appease someone else's appetites, a woman was positioned in an uneasy relationship to her own body in assertions like this one.

It is important to keep in mind that true womanhood was a vigorously challenged norm of social behavior, asserted frequently by conservatives only to be pooh-poohed by advocates of what Frances Cogan calls "real womanhood." Nonetheless, many of its prescribed behaviors remained the dominant signs of gentility and good manners and were therefore both cultivated and prized for the class distinction they imparted. Signs of noncorporeality were particularly sought out by middle-class women in middle class communities of the Northeast, where "true womanhood" and Calvinist perfectionism exerted their most significant influence, where ideologies of coverture were taken most seriously, and where the promises of power through self-erasure were most likely to be believable. But even in working-class communities, in which self-denial was a more dubious mode of empowerment, such markers of class distinction were sought.[9] Negation of the signs of embodiment through manners, attitudes, and beliefs was one of the fundamental processes involved in constructing a bourgeois identity; a woman pursuing candidacy for "true womanhood" was trained to behave in such a way as to suggest her own physical absence. In *The Wide, Wide World*, for example, Susan Warner idealizes Alice Humphreys, "a person who supplied what was wanting everywhere; like the transparent glazing which painters use to spread over the dead color of their pictures; unknown it was she gave life and harmony to the whole" (205). A body, in this quotation, is what a "true woman" is *not*; its negation is central to the production of an ideal of gentility. A process of ongoing negation of the female body can be seen as a central component of the creation of an "angel in the house." Obviously, literal disembodiment is impossible, but through decorous behavior, a woman could minimize the impression created by her body. She could suggest that she was more ethereal than carnal. When John Humphreys tells Ellen Montgomery, "I see you and hear you; but without any disturbance," he implicitly affirms her true womanhood by praising her ability to minimize the effects of her body (461). Having learned to be present but convey an impression of absence, Ellen is able to enjoy the status and privilege associated with genteel womanhood.

Such examples fall into the category of what Judith Butler (borrowing from Julia Kristeva) calls "abjection," the process by which one constructs one's social identity by identifying and repudiating that which one is not.[10] A quotation from Hannah More's 1808 novel *Coelebs in*

Search of a Wife articulates quite clearly the central role played by abjection of the body in the construction of "true womanhood."[11] The protagonist describes the perfect wife: "She is not a professed beauty, she is *not* a professed genius, she is *not* a professed philosopher, she is *not* a professed wit, she is *not* a professed anything" (133–34, emphasis in original). The question of what the ideal woman *is* elicits the following response: "'She is,' replied I, 'from nature—a woman, gentle, feeling, animated, modest. She is by education, elegant, informed, enlightened. She is, from religion, pious, humble, candid, charitable'" (134). All of the things the ideal woman is *not* are nouns; all of the things she *is* are adjectives, except the first: a woman. As represented by More, "true womanhood" is a conceptual framework, a cluster of poses constituted through erasure. No substantive can be associated with woman because nineteenth-century culture idealizes a woman who is by nature insubstantial.

The ideal of female noncorporeality promises the true woman a social position of the first importance ("it was she gave life and harmony to the whole"), but leaves that position ever vulnerable to the incessant assault of her own body. Conduct books regularly promised women that gentleness, modesty, and affectionate service would win them true and important power through influence.[12] But the multitude of friendly promises of power through modesty frequently imply unfriendly threats if a woman does not display "retiring," "unobtrusive" behaviors. The president of the New York State Teachers' Association put it quite forcefully. Following Susan B. Anthony's successful delivery of a speech in 1856, he said, "Madam, that was a splendid production and well delivered . . . but I would rather have followed my wife or daughter to Greenwood cemetery than to have had her stand here before this promiscuous audience and deliver that address" (Gurko 197).[13] Likewise, one popular 1822 conduct book, William B. Sprague's *Letters on Practical Subjects to a Daughter*, warns, "Beware also of an ostentatious manner. By this I mean that kind of manner which savors too much of display; which indicates a disposition to make yourself too conspicuous." The overly visible female provokes "a feeling of disgust" (83).[14]

Such warnings were not simply ideals preached to deaf female ears. In Britain, Mary Poovey notes, "by the last decades of the eighteenth century, even to refer to the body was considered 'unladylike'" (*Proper* 14). Poovey quotes Hester Thrale (most known to posterity as the intimate friend of Samuel Johnson), who reported that when she read aloud from the *Spectator*, "even the Maid who was dressing my Hair, burst out o' laughing at the Idea of *a Lady* saying her Stomach ach'd, or that something stuck between her Teeth" (14). Similar attitudes toward the female body governed nineteenth-century American society, as the midcentury diary of Anna LaRoche, daughter of an eminent Philadelphia doctor, exemplifies. The following two entries afford an instructive contrast: the first describes men's liberty to be physically present, and the second describes a girl's attempt to assume a similar liberty:

> Feb 26th 1863—On the 23rd I went to the Democratic Club. . . . We went in the reserved seats while Papa sat on the platform. . . . the crowd arose & cheered & screamed . . . after a second of silence the cheers arose once more—men waved their hats & hdkfs all those upon the platform arose & helped to increase the noise—as for Papa I declare that he not only waved his hat but his cane & hdkfs both & I am not certain that he did not wave his legs & arms—such was his excitement.

> May 17th 1863 . . . I had an amusing letter from Penn [a female friend] who says she stood on the door step as the Democrats were passing & cried "Bravo democrats"—it was immediately responded to by cheers which caused her enraged family to seize her by the back & draw her in.

Anna is "amused" not by the fact that Penn appeared in public but by Penn's transgression of the implied taboo against drawing attention to her presence. A woman was to negotiate the contradiction between her own embodiment and the ideal of bodilessness through a self-effacing form of presence, acting *as though* she lacked a body. Fanny Fern similarly describes the social proscriptions against signs of female presence: "I'm glad we are all free; but as a woman—I shouldn't know it, didn't some orator tell me. Can I . . . clap my hands at some public speaker when I am nearly bursting with delight? Can I signify the contrary when my hair stands on end with vexation? . . . Bah!—you know I can't. '*Free*!' Humph!"[15] Of course she *could* do these things; the fact is that in a deep sense she does not want to, since she does not want to jeopardize her status as a genteel woman. Though free in the abstract ("we are all free"), she is unfree because of who she is socially. This extract from Fern, like the extract from Anna LaRoche's diary, exemplifies Michel Foucault's claim that power works not through repression (saying "no") but positively, through the production of subjectivity. Because they value the benefits associated with their subject positions, Fern and La-Roche are regulated by their own desires.

It must be observed, however, that the ideal of noncorporeality was also under attack from feminists. Thomas Wentworth Higginson satirizes it: "The Invisible Lady, as advertised in all our cities a good many years ago, was a mysterious individual who remained unseen, and had apparently no human organs except a brain and a tongue. You asked questions of her, and she made intelligent answers; but where she was, you could no more discover than you could find the man inside the

Automaton Chess-Player. Was she intended as a satire on womankind, or a sincere representation of what womankind should be?"[16] As Joanne Dobson comments after quoting this excerpt, though Higginson recognizes that social attitudes toward women are progressing, he also "recognizes how entrenched in mainstream thinking the ideal of female reticence is, lamenting that 'the opinion dies hard that she [woman] is best off when least visible'" (67). In 1890, a female doctor indicated that society had not progressed as rapidly as reformers had hoped it would; she felt the need to insist that "Woman has certain inalienable rights, and first and foremost among them is the right to occupy as much room in space as nature intended she would."[17]

Higginson also connected ideologies of female bodilessness with an attraction to domination, violence, and pain. Observing with disgust an ideology that makes "self-effacement" appear "delightful," "*Bene vixit qui bene latuit*" ("She has lived well who has kept well concealed") (*Women and Men* 14–15), he argues that women are "systematically taught from childhood up that it is their highest duty to efface themselves, or at least keep out of sight" (*Women and Men* 12). This disastrous instruction brings them to a masochistic state in which they advise each other to "Lie down on the floor and let your husband trample on you, if he will"(*Alphabet* 121–22). Higginson concedes, "There is a certain charm in it, no doubt—in feeling that self is absolutely annulled, that we live only for others or for some one other. But this is, after all, to quit the helm of our own life" (*Women and Men* 84).

Though Higginson indicates a causal link between the ideal of female noncorporeality and female masochism, he does not explain how the one produces the other. He sees masochistic behaviors as implicit in the invisibility and annihilation he associates with coverture. But the link can be more clearly established: some of the literature of the era that is committed to true womanhood suggests that the ideal of a bodiless woman produces emotions of personal inadequacy and guilt, emotions that in turn lead to a masochistic desire for domination. Julia Ward Howe's aptly titled poem "Woman" idealizes a "vestal priestess proudly pure / But of a meek and quiet spirit . . . And mood so calm that naught can stir it." But though it opens with a paean to static, self-effacing femininity, the poem ends with a confession of personal inadequacy: "I would that I were she!"[18] The poem affirms and illustrates the abiding force of true-womanhood ideology, which was debated, not antiquated, during this time period and it indicates that the ideology generated feelings of personal inadequacy. Spiritual counselors promoting the ideal of ethereal femininity promulgated feelings of personal failure and self-distrust, of the kind that Howe expresses. Rev. Sprague, for example, urges female readers to guard vigilantly against the senses, which are always ready to undermine their purity. He warns them to avoid occasions that might "throw you into the power of these invisible tyrants [evil thoughts], or to lead you even in the smallest degree, to relax your circumspection. You should especially guard the senses" (163). Sprague's book went through eleven editions over a thirty-four-year span from 1822 to 1855, indicating an abiding, widespread interest in his ideas and a corresponding steady dissemination of the belief that the true woman is threatened by her body and its senses.

The anxiety toward the body that accompanies the bodiless ideal makes guilt fundamental to the existence of the woman aspiring to the status of "true woman." Rather than criticize the ideology of noncorporeality—which, because it is implicit, is difficult to recognize—some women, seeking the status of gentility associated with true womanhood, affirm its principles, lament their own weak characters, and rededicate themselves to the tasks it requires. They describe efforts to achieve self-restraint and self-denial, celebrate successes, worry about lapses, and idealize men who respect their efforts and even assume some of the painful burden of their discipline. Ellen Montgomery, for example, adores her "brother" John because he never flatters her nor lets her off the hook but instead consistently demonstrates his love in severity and acts of prohibition: "of one thing, she was perfectly sure . . . that if any thing were not right she should sooner or later hear of it. But this was a censorship Ellen rather loved than feared" (461).

Jo March in Louisa May Alcott's *Little Women* is another young woman who suffers from guilt over her own intransigent corporeality and marries a man who helps her discipline herself in order to be a true woman. Jo is constantly berating herself for her failure to live up to the ideal of tranquillity and placidity that is expected of women in her social circle. Filled with physical energy and volatile passions, she "found her greatest affliction in the fact that she couldn't read, run, and ride as much as she liked" (36). Her lack of physical and emotional self-control causes her great guilt. In one scene, in which she agonizes that her passion has nearly caused the death of her sister, she asks her mother, Marmee, how she manages to control her temper and "keep still." Marmee says that her mother used to help her, but when she died, "I had a hard time, Jo, and shed a good many bitter tears over my failures, for in spite of my efforts I never seemed to get on. Then your father came. . . . He helped and comforted me, and showed me that I must try to practice all the virtues I would have my little girls possess, for I was their example" (76). But sometimes his advice and excellent example are insufficient. Jo observes, "I used to see Father sometimes put his finger on his lips, and look at you with a very kind but sober face, and you always folded your lips tight or went away: was he reminding you then?"

(76–77). And Marmee responds, "Yes. I asked him to help me so, and he never forgot it, but saved me from many a sharp word by that little gesture and kind look" (77). This recollection of her husband's discipline stimulates Marmee's love. She begins to cry, saying, "speaking of Father reminded me how much I miss him, how much I owe him" (77). Following in her mother's footsteps, Jo ultimately chooses not to marry her dear friend Laurie, because, as Marmee puts it, "You are too much alike and too fond of freedom" (304). Jo chooses instead a more disciplined, sober man, Professor Bhaer, who lets her know that he disapproves of the low sensation fiction she writes, awakening Jo's love for him in the very act of finding fault with her.[19]

Men like John Humphreys, Mr. March, and Professor Bhaer, who were willing to assist women in the difficult task of self-control, may not have been too difficult to find in middle-class, Protestant communities of the Northeast, where ideologies of coverture were taken most seriously. Writings of influential men from these communities suggest that the restraint of the female body was an important mechanism for the production of masculinity, as well as femininity. *Letters on Practical Subjects* (already quoted) offers a useful representative example of how erasure of female corporeality played a role in the construction of manhood as well as womanhood. Its author, Rev. William Buell Sprague, deliberately seeks this representative role, claiming in *The Annals of the American Pulpit* to speak for the American clerical mind as a whole. Sprague exerted a considerable influence on the women who are the subject of this book: Emily Dickinson received *Letters on Practical Subjects* as a gift from her father; and according to the biographer of Susan and Anna Warner, the sisters appreciated a fan letter received from the renowned Rev. Sprague more than any other tribute they received.[20] In *Letters*, Sprague includes the following anecdotal lesson:

> When a woman takes up the weapons of theological warfare . . . the native loveliness of female character is instantly eclipsed. The modest and retiring virtues, which are the peculiar ornament of your sex, can never find a place amidst the din and clashing of religious combatants. It was my lot, not long since, to encounter a sturdy female polemic in a stage coach; and I must confess that, after a little while, she succeeded in driving me effectually from the field; not because I was apprehensive of being crushed by the weight of her arguments, but because, when I came to reflect, it cost me less mortification to yield to her the honor of an apparent triumph than to keep the attitude which I had incautiously taken of discussing the most momentous of all subjects, in such circumstances, with a talking female, whose element was controversy. (141)

Sprague is purportedly describing the verbosity of this "talking female," but the terms he uses emphasize her corporeality: "sturdy," "driving me," "crushed by the weight." Simply by using the word "female" (an insult in the nineteenth century)[21]) he is drawing attention to the woman's body. Webster's 1848 *American Dictionary of the English Language* defines "female" as "one of the sex which conceives and brings forth young," while the *Oxford English Dictionary* defines "female" as "belonging to the sex which bears offspring." In other words, "female" rudely draws attention to the body itself. Sprague's repeated use of this epithet 'female" in conjunction with the terms focusing upon the polemic's corporeality suggests that female presence, offensively asserted in her verbal and nonverbal manners, is contemptible, and a woman should conceal her body ("eclipse" it) or seek to minimize it through an impression of frailty, nonsturdiness.

The need to "eclipse" signs of the female body is as essential to Sprague's sense of his own heroic manhood as it is to his notion of femininity. His representation of theology as chivalric combat ("weapons of theological warfare," "din and clashing of religious combatants," "driving me from the field," "the honor of an apparent triumph") is probably not representative of the attitude the majority of Americans in 1822 would have taken toward religious discussion. At that time, religion was declining in prestige as a career for men relative to business and politics. Prior to the American Revolution, nine of the colonies had "established" churches; citizens were required by their governments to attend and maintain them, and public life centered around church life. But in the decades following the Revolution, churches were disestablished, state by state, a process culminating in the disestablishment of the Congregational Church in Massachusetts in 1833. As Ann Douglas argues, disestablishment is symptomatic of the fact that after the Revolution, Americans were increasingly locating the "din and clashing" of life's struggles in political and business spheres, leading many clergymen to feel, anxiously, rather like women. One minister, Orville Dewey, wistfully insisted, "I am *not a clergyman*," since he believed that clergymen are "not fairly thrown into the field of life . . . [but rather] hedged around with artificial barriers, . . . a sort of moral eunuchs" (230–31). If Sprague were to admit the sturdy woman's equal authority in the sphere of theology, he would further the marginalization and feminization that were locating clergymen out of "the field of life." Sprague elevates himself in his own eyes by contrasting his own spiritualized abstraction with the female polemic's corporeality. In doing so, he displays the schizophrenic approach to the female body that Lacan describes: woman is represented as the brute matter from which man differentiates himself, but with which he futilely seeks to reconnect in an etherialized form through symbolic practices. Sprague's chivalric quest is such a symbolic practice; he, as knightly cleric, fights on behalf of the lady, not with her.

While the effect of such discourses of male chivalry and contempt for female corporeality is, for the male, the consolidation of manhood, for the female reader, it is more destabilizing. The young reader whom Sprague was addressing might well come to feel discomfort with her own body, and perhaps guilt or shame at her own inability to minimize the signs of her own presence. For example, Emily Dickinson, who owned *Letters on Practical Subjects,* expresses the kind of antagonism toward the body promulgated by clerical attitudes like Sprague's when she writes, "I do not care for the body, I love the timid soul, the blushing, shrinking soul; it hides, for it is afraid, and the bold obtrusive body—Pray, marm, did you call *me?*" (L#39).²² This attitude of hostility toward her own body is not entirely characteristic of Dickinson's sensibility, though; in fact, a longing to *affirm* the body and embodied forms of love also runs throughout her poetry. But in response to the evangelical fervor of the Second Great Awakening that was sweeping through Amherst, and also in response to the middle-class ideal of noncorporeal true womanhood, at the age of twenty she espouses the conventional view of the body as intrinsically unspiritual.

In associating the boldness and obtrusiveness of the body with a servant, presumably vulgar and immodest, Dickinson also reiterates the widespread attitude that female corporeality is lower-class. That classist attitude toward the female body, conventional in middle-class Protestant circles, conflicted with the equally conventional Protestant work ethic. The notion that female embodiment was lower-class, unspiritual, and unfeminine limited the sphere of appropriate activity for genteel women. Conduct books, sermons, magazines, novels—even physiology textbooks and popular health manuals—represented stasis and tranquillity as ideal female attitudes, with the result that the number of activities available to the nineteenth-century middle-class woman was limited. While seventeenth- and eighteenth-century American ideologies emphasized women's membership in an economic household, "true womanhood" idealized what Nancy Armstrong calls "labor that is not labor," work that produced no sweat and required no muscles (75). It was not ornamental in the aristocratic way, but neither was it productive in a vulgar, lower-class way. In accordance with the work ethic, the "true woman" was to work, but many forms of real work ran counter to the new ideals of tranquil femininity. In *The Wide, Wide World,* when Alice Humphreys commands Ellen Montgomery, "Arise. Shine!" it is not surprising that Ellen requests specific details ("how can I shine?"). And Alice provides a virtual nonanswer: "in the faithful, patient, self-denying performance of every duty" (239). Ellen cannot imagine, and Alice cannot specify, what Ellen should do, because the duties are less important than the fact of self-denial. Any concrete activity would assert one's body and presence, while self-gratifying acts, equally problematically, assert the legitimacy of the self. To be an angel was, according to nineteenth-century ideals, to be powerful, but to be angelic was precisely not to do anything, but simply to incarnate goodness. The female now shouldered single-handedly the oft-noted contradiction within Puritanism between the ideal of selflessness and the individuality implicit in Puritan introspection. Her job was to focus upon herself in a guilt-ridden effort to deny her self.[23]

Certainly, there were many activities for middle-class women that were deemed both useful and decorous: teaching, visiting the sick, nurturing children, performing domestic labor. But frequently, even these activities were described in terms of nonlabor. In *The House of the Seven Gables*, for example, in a scene in which the cheerful middle-class heroine Phoebe Pyncheon cleans her bedroom, Hawthorne describes her as "one of those persons who possess, as their exclusive patrimony, the gift of practical arrangement. It is a kind of natural magic. . . . What was precisely Phoebe's process, we find it impossible to say. She appeared to have no preliminary design, but gave a touch here, and another there" (71–72). In making a room formerly inhabited by spiders, mice, and rats comfortable for herself, Phoebe uses, not a broom and bucket, but "natural magic." She acts, and yet the impression produced by the description of her action is one of nonactivity, of artless influence rather than embodied action.

The conflict between ideals of bodilessness and the Protestant work ethic was crucial to the flourishing of female masochism. According to Cheryl Walker, in response to "the restrictions placed upon their sex," the "limitation and confinement" that put recognizable forms of heroism off-limits for women, some Puritan women turned their energies upon themselves, fantasizing about martyrdom and rigorous discipline. Walker writes, "American women poets [raised in Puritan households] manifested an early and intense fascination with heroic sacrifice and martyrdom. Both Elizabeth Oakes-Smith and Lucy Larcom pored over Foxe's *Book of Martyrs*, (as did Anne Bradstreet) and longed to model themselves on these saintly figures" (73–74). (Emily Dickinson also read Foxe.) Oakes-Smith even indulged in what she called "self-inflicted torture" in order to prove to herself that she could take pain if she had to:

I renewed my study of Fox's "Book of Martyrs.". . . I knew from the first that I was of a flimsy make, and might not be able to bear any great pain even for a great cause, for I fainted at even a slight hurt of any kind. Accordingly I tested myself in various ways such as holding my fingers in the blaze of a candle; but as I always fainted from the pain, I saw that I was not at all like the martyrs of whom I read. . . . My mother fell ill from pleurisy, for which a blister had been supplied. I made critical inquiries about this blister which seemed to cause so much suffering, and when I learned that it caused a pain like a burning flame, I hailed it as just the thing I required to test my ability to endure. I watched my opportunity and secured enough of the black mixture to spread a plaster of considerable size, which I bound on just below the knee, and went to my pillow with an exultant sense of heroism. In the night the pain wakened me, but I bore it without a murmur lest I should waken my sister. I was very happy despite of pain, for I had learned that I could bear it.

At length came the hour of rising. I was conscious of lassitude, but did not anticipate anything serious. I jumped out of bed and began to draw on my stockings. I knew no more. I had fainted and was carried into my mother's room. (*Autobiography* 35–36)

Both Walker and Oakes-Smith see this behavior as a direct response to a Puritan upbringing. Intentionally causing herself pain can be seen to respond in particular to the twin ideals of usefulness and mortification of the flesh. Oakes-Smith longs for physical activity to perform on behalf of "a great cause" and doubts her own fortitude, but the only method she identifies to challenge her own physical limits is self-inflicted suffering. The problem of female activity—what was a woman to *do* to express her allegiance to norms of selflessness and bodilessness—fostered numerous such fantasies of self-torture and martyrdom among women raised in the Puritan tradition.[24]

Conduct books and religious biographies went so far as to promote such fantasies of martyrdom. In *Letters on Practical Subjects*, for example, Sprague's devotion to female noncorporeality leads him to idealize Harriet Newell, a martyred young woman known for doing just about nothing: "Perhaps there has been no individual in modern times to whom the church is more indebted for elevating the standard of benevolent enterprise in the female sex," he speculates (190). Newell was one of the first female American missionaries; she traveled to India in 1812, when she was nineteen, but before she could begin her work, she found "that the hand of death was upon her and she was sinking suddenly, though calmly, to her rest" (190). Sprague discusses Newell in the context of a chapter addressing appropriate avenues for female *enterprise*; his selection of a woman who died before her life work even began as a role model for female activism is absurd in the extreme; he *does not* select Ann Judson, Newell's companion on the trip, who at that moment was vigorously pursuing missionary activities, the romantic exoticism of which renders her memoirs fascinating even today. Newell was a better model of female usefulness for him, because her death enabled her to be the abstract female force he found so lovely, unburdened of the body he found so threatening. Newell's death did nothing to detract from her activist capabilities, he insists; to the contrary, she became more fully herself once she had shed her corporeal constraints: "she did not cross the ocean and make her grave in that foreign land to no purpose. . . . [Her death marks] one of the brightest eras in the history of her missionary operations" (191). The activism implied in "eras" and "histories" almost conceals the fact that Newell's death is the *only* event in the history of her missionary operations.

Harriet Newell became something of a minor saint, represented by the American Baptist Publication Society, for example, as "an example of Christian heroism unheard of before" (Langstroth 19). The society said, "It is this splendid heroism upon which the stream of light through breaking clouds of neglect sheds such a halo of splendor around her name [and] . . . her short but eventful life" (19). The society made this claim and published her biography "with the prayer that it will influence many young women who feel their lives are too obscure or too weak to be of much use for God" (Langstroth 2): "Her work was short, her toil soon ended, but see what it does for humanity! Her high example should cheer the missionaries of all coming time. Heathen lands are now dotted over with the graves of martyrs; missionary women sleep on almost every shore, some are lying beneath the ocean depths" (28). While presumably it is the missionary work itself that is idealized, the phrasing privileges not the action but the dying.

Harriet Newell's memoirs and their dissemination and reception afford a useful, representative study of how Puritan representations of women's lives encouraged masochism as an appropriate female desire in accordance with prevailing ideologies of womanhood. A number of tributes written during the century following Newell's death emphasize the important theme that a woman does not need a body to be alive in her truest sense. Langstroth's tribute to Newell asserts, "The life of a really Christlike woman must recede physically to appear in its true proportion" (2). And Pastor Nathaniel Ragland devotes half of his 1900 tribute to Newell to descriptions of her decline, death, and posthumous influence, including two chapters describing her grave—the view from it, the inscription on it, its setting, and the various feelings many people have had upon visiting it—only to insist that she is not really dead. "The voice of Harriet Newell, for three quarters of a century, has been heard from that lonely grave under the evergreen tree in the burial-ground at Port Louis," Ragland writes, fascinated by the paradox of her undiminished vitality. "Though dead, she has been speaking through all these years in many tongues and in many lands. Countless multitudes have heard the voice of her supplication" (54). Lovingly imagining the scene of her death as "a place where angels would like to stay their waving wings," and he imagines no change in her state from living to dead:

"Like a river, with green and shaded banks, she flowed without a murmur into the waveless sea, where life is rest" (46).

The hagiography of Harriet Newell is to a certain extent determined by a sermon preached upon the occasion of Newell's death by the Reverend Mr. Sprague's colleague Leonard Woods. Approximately twenty-five editions of her letters and diary were published over the thirty-four-year period following her death, and Woods's sermon was appended to most of them, reinforcing the message that martyrdom is an important form of female agency. Ostensibly addressing Newell's mother, Woods says, "It must afford you particular satisfaction to contemplate *the usefulness of her life.* . . . so lovely in her character, so useful in her life, so resigned in her sufferings, so tranquil and happy in her death. . . . Nor is she less precious, or the less *yours*, because she is absent from the body and present with the Lord" (27, emphasis in original). Though "absent from the body," Newell remains an abiding presence, of sorts.[25]

Woods's sermon implies that suffering is a prime mode of female pleasure as well as usefulness. Observing that pain was good for Newell, Woods writes, "Times of persecution and distress have a favorable influence upon Christian character. In such seasons . . . [Christians] are reduced to the necessity of feeling that they have no other interest, and no hope of enjoyment from any other quarter. Accordingly, they make a more unreserved surrender of everything for Christ . . . Yea, *they rejoice in their sufferings, and gladly fill up what is wanting of the afflictions of Christ in their flesh for his body's sake, which is the Church*" (Woods 8–9, emphasis in original). Certainly Christian hostility to the body is not confined to Calvinism, but it is indeed typical of it. In interpeting the life of Harriet Newell, Woods draws upon some of the most masochistic and anticarnal passages in Pauline theology. The quotation from Paul's Letter to the Colossians (1:24), for example, exemplifies a strain in Christianity that socialist theologian Dorothy Soelle calls "Christian masochism," (9) a strain she finds particularly virulent in the writings and legacy of John Calvin. There is a crucial difference between accepting the pain that may accompany enlightenment and seeking out pain for itself, and like many fundamentalist Calvinists, Woods advocates the latter. He admonishes Christians to welcome their sufferings, which God sends to remind them that pleasure is transitory and to force them to seek relief from the hand that dealt it. (Soelle calls such an approach to God "theological sadism.") The quotation from Paul turns this inverted meaning of suffering into a paradoxical representation of physical health as a state of spiritual illness. The physically healthy person is "wanting" affliction, wounded from insufficient suffering; good Christians, therefore, desire ("want") distress in order to fill that wound. Paul implicitly posits Christ's pierced body as the touchstone of spiritual health, and physical health as a metaphor not only for the sickness of the individual's soul but for the sickness of the church. In welcoming affliction into his or her own physical body, the Christian can paradoxically help to heal the wounds in Christ's spiritual body.

The receiving, passive body performing this heroic work is implicitly female, since the Church, the body of Christ, was traditionally female, his "bride," a gendering that was consolidated by the popularization of the angelic ideal in the late eighteenth and early nineteenth centuries.[26] As ideologies of female nature shifted from an emphasis on her depraved carnality to an emphasis on her disembodied spirituality, ideologies of women's work shifted toward women's passive suffering on behalf of both genders: she was to do nothing apart from trying to be pure and receiving healing affliction for the sake of Christ's body on earth. While God theoretically demands of all Christians absolute submission and bodily renunciation, in nineteenth-century practice, such submission is particularly demanded of females—hence Woods's sermon preached upon an occasion of female martyrdom. Horace Bushnell observes that because "[w]e Americans take up some very crude notions of subordination, as if it implied inferior quality, character, power," we rarely expect men to imitate Christ. However, he says, we should respect the suffering and submission that women endure: "The highest virtues . . . belong to the subject conditions. . . . Was Mary inferior because she was a lowly, subject woman? Was her holy thing, her son, inferior because he was subject, in his beautiful childhood, and subject all his life long, down to the last hour's breath and the last nail driven?" (*Selected* 169–70) Obviously not. Like Christ, women find their agency and heroism in passive martyrdom, right down to "the last nail driven." But as Diane Price Herndl writes, "When women are taught that illness and death offer them the best route to power, we all suffer the loss of possibilities" (3).

One of the "loss[es] of possibility" that Newell suffered was her coming to believe that her body was a spiritual enemy without which she would be better off. In her diary, Newell focuses relentlessly on the need to subdue her body. Indeed, she correlates good physical health with bad spiritual health, just as Woods does in her eulogy. "March 3rd, 1811 Oh this cold, stupid heart! I long for wings to fly away from earth, and participate [in] the holiness and pleasures of the saints within the veil. I have had this day a greater sense of my depravity, and of my inability to create exercises pleasing to God, than I recollect having ever had before. I think I feel my need of a physician, if I have no heart to apply to one" (86). The warm physical body is "cold" in spiritual terms, and Newell therefore longs to be free of it. Her "spiritual" physician will help her detach from the carnal world, help her find "wings to fly away from earth." And because the earthly body is in some sense the source and symbol of her "depravity," it serves as the foundation for a number of metaphors she uses elsewhere to express her spiritual difficulties: "My past transgressions rose like great mountains before me. The most poignant anguish seized my mind; my carnal security fled; and I felt myself a guilty transgressor, naked before a holy God."[27] "Carnal security," a self-confidence born of good health, is also a source of damning indifference to God. When she endures ongoing painful migraines, Newell believes that God is stripping her of her dangerous good health, leaving her like Eve, "naked before God," with all of her sinful, carnal depravity on full display so that she may be truly healed.

This familiar Calvinist attitude toward "the natural body" provides the terms for Newell to express spiritual desire as well as guilt. "1810 Feb 18 He has again laid his chastising rod upon me, by afflicting me with sickness and pain. But 'I will bear the indignation of the Lord, because I have sinned against him.' . . . afflictions are good for me. . . . Let my dear heavenly Father inflict the *keenest* anguish, I will submit; for he is infinitely excellent, and *can* do nothing wrong" (61–62). Because bodily health ironically leaves her in no need of spiritual healing, she tries to "rejoice in [her] sufferings," as Woods says all true Christians do, because they direct her toward spiritual health. Just as the discourse of bodily depravity provides the terms of her guilt, so too the masochistic aspects of Calvinism provide a language in which she couches her religious longings.

To judge from her diary, Newell's life was governed by the ongoing effort to suppress all worldly desires, and she was continually plagued with guilty feelings over her failure to detach fully from what she repeatedly calls "the glittering toys of the earth." On her deathbed, she insisted that the guilt associated with human carnality was an excessive burden to carry, and she longed to be free of it, in order finally to achieve the purity that her corporeality precluded. She said that thoughts of her imminent demise were "cheering and joyful beyond what words could express." And when she was told that she would not live through another day, she rhapsodized, "*Oh joyful news! I long to depart*," adding that death appeared "*truly welcome and glorious*."[28] When her husband asked her if she would be willing to live longer, she replied, "yes, if I could live better than I have ever yet done. But I have had so much experience of the wickedness of my heart, that if I should recover, I should expect the remainder of my life to be much like the past; and I long to get rid of this wicked heart and go where I shall sin no more" (244–45). Perpetually on the brink of self-corruption, Newell longs for release from a physical existence that appears hell-bent on leading her into temptation. Perhaps such talk on a deathbed might be expected from men as well as women.

What is startling is that absolutely nothing *else* is expected or obtained from the history of her supposedly activist life.

While Calvinism itself can be seen as masochistic, with its emphasis on the depravity of the body and the providential notion that divine love is manifested in affliction, its practitioners are not necessarily masochists— people who associate domination and suffering with pleasure. But a number of the discursive features of Calvinism encourage nineteenth-century female followers to seize upon the masochistic aspects of their religion as the discourse in which they express their private guilts and desires. The ideology of coverture plays an important part in this process, because it implicitly idealizes female bodilessness. Female fantasies of martyrdom are further promoted by Calvinist hagiographies that promote suffering and death as ideal forms of female usefulness. Of course, this pattern is almost as old as Christianity itself. In *Alone of All Her Sex*, Marina Warner discusses numerous cases of female martyrdom throughout history that have been celebrated as models of female virtue. But Calvinist doctrine in particular fosters female masochistic desire because of the particularities of its understanding of religious desire—a form of desire that paves the way for the eroticization of patriarchal violence.

It has long been noted that Calvinism produces a particularly individuated notion of selfhood. While a Christian denomination like Catholicism features a host of saints, a Virgin Mother, and a hierarchy of ecclesiasticals mediating between each soul and God, Calvinism refuses all mediation. As Harold Frederic would write in *The Damnation of Theron Ware* at the end of the nineteenth century, Catholics "are held up by the power of the true Church . . . they have help, and you [Protestants] are walking alone" (273–74). The Puritan self is more defined by impermeable boundaries between the Me and the Not-Me than are selves in more communal cultures, which are defined by relatively fluid borders, so that intimacy with others can enhance rather than undermine a notion of identity. But because the Calvinist self is defined through an isolating individualism, intimacy tends to threaten the integrity of that self. Jonathan Edwards's intellectual descendant Ralph Waldo Emerson reveals the threat that social intercourse poses to selves in the Puritan tradition when he writes, "Society everywhere is in conspiracy against the manhood of every one of its members." Gloria Anzaldua offers useful metaphors for conceptualizing the distinction; she distinguishes between the sharp "boundaries" of an individualist culture and the porous "borders" of a more communal culture, arguing that the former are a distinct characteristic of the dominant American conception of identity. Sacvan Bercovitch concurs. In *The Puritan Origins of the American Self*, he cites as evidence of the greater individuation of

Anglo colonists the fact that the (Catholic) Spanish conquerors "regarded the country as the Indians' and native recruitment as essential to their design of colonization"; by contrast, "[t]he Puritans, despite their missionary pretenses, regarded the country as *theirs* and its natives as an obstacle to *their* destiny as Americans" (141). Others are represented as an obstacle to the American Puritan's sense of destiny, and merging is not part of the vision for social future.[29]

For people whose identities are defined by stark individuation, the blurring of personal boundaries may feel more like a threatening assault upon the self than a comfortable intimacy. It is no surprise, therefore, that the American Puritan frequently conceived of intimacy with others in tropes of violence against the self, as is exemplified in the phraseology Edwards uses to describe his desire "to be united to Christ": "I felt withal an ardency of soul to be, what I know not otherwise how to express, than to be emptied and annihilated; to lie in the dust, and to be full of Christ alone" (450) Such expressions linking violence and rapture are, admittedly, fundamental to Christianity, a religion rooted in suffering, submission, and martyrdom. But the tendency to associate intimacy with a total loss of self and a collapse of the boundaries of identity—and a consequent tendency to express the desire for intimacy and transcendence in terms of violence—is particularly characteristic of those influenced by John Calvin.

These tendencies characterize American transcendentalism as thoroughly as they do American Calvinism, for, as Perry Miller and Sacvan Bercovitch have variously demonstrated, transcendentalism is an outgrowth of Puritanism. The transcendental self is in many respects a Puritan self, and it therefore comes as no surprise that transcendentalism also uses tropes of violence to represent the desire to transcend the self. Although Emerson does not express a desire specifically to be annihilated, his conception of transcendent ecstasy does require the negation of selfhood: "all mean egotism vanishes. . . . I am nothing; I see all" (24). For Emerson, as for Newell, the boundaries of the self become permeable and incoherent in the moment of ecstasy: not an "I" at all but simply a perceiving, noncontrolling "transparent eyeball," "the currents of the Universal Being circulate through" him. But this sensation of escape from the rigid confines of identity is inseparable from violence: the dangling modifier in the following sentence in *Nature* reinforces this incoherence. "Standing on the bare ground . . . all mean egotism vanishes." The loss of a coherent identity is reflected in the loss of a grammatical subject. In addition, the middle part of this same sentence also uses a violent image to capture the notion of ecstasy: "my head bathed by the blithe air and uplifted into infinite space." According to grammatical logic, the only thing that could be "uplifted into infinite space" is Emerson's head! In fact, in *Seeing and Being,* Carolyn Porter has aptly described this as a decapitation (106). While Emerson presumably did not consciously envisage physical violence as necessary to achieve a rapturous union with the infinite, his Puritan legacy renders violence to identity as characteristic of his language of transcendence as it is of the language of his evangelical kinswoman Harriet Newell.

In a sense, then, there is something masochistic about transcendentalism. As we will see in chapter 5, this correspondence stems not only from the Puritan legacy but from the romantic sublime, an aesthetic tradition at play in Emerson's transparent-eyeball passage. But there is a significant difference between transcendentalist and Calvinist perspectives on the violence of ecstasy, a difference relating to their perspectives on human nature. Transcendentalism is optimistic: "A man is a god in ruins," Emerson says in *Nature* (53), and transcendent rapture represents the apotheosis of human potential. Calvinism, by contrast, is pessimistic about human nature, and its discourses of rapture frequently emphasize an assault upon the humanity that stands between the soul and its expansion into the infinite. Harriet Newell, for example, writes, "I have ardently longed to depart and be with Jesus," and "Willingly will I let go my eager grasp of the things of time and sense and flee to Jesus" (17).[30] To join with Jesus—or anyone else—the Puritan self must die. And so a language of death can be a language of desire. Of course, a loss of ego is the foundation of any mystical experience, but Puritans tend to dwell upon the self-hating and self-destructive aspects of Christian mysticism. As Ann Taves points out, the typical Puritan conversion narrative begins with an expression of self-loathing, turns then to renunciation of self, and ends with a description of being flooded with power or ecstasy. Twelve-year-old Newell writes, "I was lost in raptures. . . . This is too much for me, a sinful worm of the dust, deserving only eternal punishment"(14).[31] This passage demonstrates the intermingling of self-loathing, renunciation, and ecstasy, each of which can call to mind each of the others. The intensity of her self-loathing seems to serve as an expressive technique for conveying the intensity of her rapture, and the magnitude of the term "eternal punishment" captures the intensity of her desire for transcendence. Here and throughout the discourses of the Second Great Awakening, self-abasement functions as a metonym for the ecstasy of religious fusion.

Puritan notions of selfhood also enable examination and discipline to function as tropes of intimacy. On March 13, 1810, Newell writes: "How engaged am I in the concerns of this world! . . . Why this awful distance from God? 'Search me, O God, and know my heart, try me, and know my thoughts'" (65). "The world"—and the body that is part of it—is a barrier to intimacy with God. Thus, Newell uses the trope of divine examination (searched, tried, and known) to express her religious desire. Just as worldly concerns separate her from God, so the opaque body protects her guilty heart and thoughts. Surveillance and examination will enable—indeed force—her to unburden the guilty secrets that distance her from him, enabling him to "know" her.

And the longing for intimacy more particularly produces a longing for a divine "'heroic' sadist," a figure who demonstrates his love in a heroic willingness to hurt her. "1809, March 10 How awfully depraved is the natural heart! Every day I can see more and more of my own apostacy from God. . . . Break, compassionate Immanuel, Oh *break* this stony heart of mine, and *compel* me to live an obedient child" (64–65). Frustrated by her inevitable failure to live up to her religious ideals, Newell longs, not for the strength to do it, but for someone to *make* her do it. In her despair, she requests, not a greater degree of agency, but to be stripped of all vestiges of it. Annihilation is so thoroughly the term in which she conceives her desire to merge with God that the one who will "break" her is "compassionate." This diary entry features the same doctrine that underlies Susan Warner's idealization of John Humphreys, whose "censorship Ellen rather loved than feared" (461). In both cases, the masochistic desire for domination actually represents a longing for intimacy, expressed in the terms of a culture that conceives of intimacy as a violation of the self, as well as a longing for agency and personhood in a culture that denies those capacities to women.

All of these metonyms for intimacy—discipline, surveillance, death, abjection, compulsion—can also function as expressions of eros. After Newell decides to go to India, where she expects to die, she writes, "Aug 14: In the Paradise of God, every rising wish, that swells the heart of the celestial inhabitant, is immediately gratified. O for a dismission from this earthly tabernacle—O for an entrance into those lovely mansions! My soul pants for the full enjoyment of God. I cannot bear this little spirituality—this absurd indifference; I long to be swallowed up in endless fruition! When shall I die—when shall I live forever?" (125). Her longing for a mystical fusion posits death as a harbinger of the delights of plenitude, in contrast to the sense of incompleteness she experiences in the "little spirituality" of worldly life. To be alive is to feel gaps between desire and completion, while merging with God—being "swallowed up in endless fruition"—is a state of "full enjoyment." Newell's desire for "endless fruition" implicitly compares death to a generative, womblike state in which need and satisfaction are instantaneous, in which self and other are one. The terms she uses to describe this state suggest the presence of eros: an internal undefined desire that is "rising," that "swells" and "pants" for "full enjoyment." It may be that eighteen-year-old Newell's betrothal to her husband had stimulated sexual desires—in one letter, she mentions a troublingly carnal attraction to him—but without turning to theories of sublimation, we might more simply observe that in Newell's culture, an expression of religious desire *is* an expression of eros, a loving desire for another. It is no surprise that in her diary, Newell often expresses her love for God in terms that sound quasi-erotic: "Oh the real bliss that I have enjoyed . . . The hour of sweet release will shortly come"; "a heart burning with love"; "Descend thou holy Spirit: Breathe into my soul a flame of ardent love."[32]

Tropes of the destruction of individuality can express the desires of both religious and sexual love, a connection that has been noted by a number of recent theorists. In "Master and Slave," for example, Jessica Benjamin argues that masochism represents a desire for transcendence. In religious cultures, such desires traditionally focus upon God, but "[t]he experience of losing the self . . . is increasingly difficult to obtain except in the erotic relationship. Consequently, sexual eroticism has become the heir to religious eroticism" (296). Michel Foucault similarly observes that in a religious culture, explorations of a longing to escape the limitations of the self are frequently articulated in the trope of a longing to merge with God, while in a secular world, transgressive fantasies (such as the sadomasochism of Bataille or Sade) play the role formerly played by religious longing. "Transgression carries the limit right to the limit of its being"; in a "movement of pure violence," it reveals "that which imprisons it" ("Preface" 34–35). "Perhaps," he muses, "the emergence of sexuality in our culture is an 'event' of multiple values: it is tied to the death of God and to the ontological void which his death fixed at the limit of our thought; it is also tied to the still silent and groping apparition of a form of thought in which the interrogation of the limit replaces the search for totality" (50).

Both of these theories positing a relationship between violence and transcendence explicitly cite Georges Bataille's ontological explanations of the relationship between death and eroticism. And while Bataille universalizes what I have been arguing is a culturally specific phenomenon, he is nonetheless exceptionally helpful for understanding masochism, because he presents vivid metaphors that crystallize a relationship between violence, eroticism, and religious transcendence that is frequently present in modern, Western culture. In *Erotism*, Bataille argues that all erotic and religious desire is a longing to eradicate the separation of oneself from everything else. "Between one being and another, there is a gulf. . . . We are discontinuous beings, individuals who perish in isolation in the midst of an incomprehensible adventure, but we yearn for our lost continuity. We find the state of affairs that binds us to our random and ephemeral individuality hard to bear. Along with our tormenting desire that this evanescent thing should last, there stands our obsession with a primal continuity linking us with everything that is" (15). Because continuity of being necessarily entails the destruction of "this evanescent individuality," eroticism (like religious transcendence) is intrinsically violent, he proposes. "In essence, the domain of eroticism is the domain of violence, of violation. . . . The whole business of eroticism is to destroy the self-contained character of the participators as they are in their normal lives" (17). Religious ecstasy entails much the same destruction of the self—hence the preponderance of violent religious rituals designed to produce a mystical transcendence for their practitioners.

Bataille is probably wrong to universalize the relationship between violence and eros; they are not necessarily associated in all cultures and eras.[33] Baumeister notes that such associations are far more prevalent during the post-Enlightenment era, when the self has become a considerably more complex, symbolic, and potentially constraining entity. But Calvinist tropes of desire do lend themselves to Bataille's theory, because they similarly derive from an idea of a self created through difference and isolation. Likewise, though Bataille inappropriately universalizes the gendering of domination and submission, his theories do aptly describe the gendering of dissolution and absorption in Northeast-American middle-class culture of the early nineteenth century. Bataille writes, "The transition from the normal state to that of erotic desire presupposes a partial dissolution of the person as he exists in the realm of discontinuity. . . . In the process of dissolution . . . [t]he passive, female side is essentially the one that is dissolved as a separate entity. But for the male partner the dissolution of the passive partner means one thing only: it is paving the way for a fusion where both are mingled, attaining at length the same degree of dissolution" (17). As analysis of discourses of "true womanhood" suggests, what Bataille represents as a universal law of gender division grounded in anatomy is to a great extent the product of social construction, accomplished by specific discourses and broad social factors. Women had to be trained to long for dissolution, and men had to learn a desire for absorption. However, Bataille's theory offers useful metaphors and images to understand how desire works within a culture in which dissolution and absorption are associated with ecstasy.

We can see in Puritan diaries and sermons the linguistic means by which women were trained to think of eros masochistically, in terms of their own dissolution. We can also see in such texts how Puritanism not only offered tropes of violence and domination as metonyms for transcendent eros but also facilitated the slippage from human-divine relations to wife-husband relations. In part this association was fostered by the Puritan notion of "covenant," a contract between two parties establishing a hierarchy and placing rights and obligations upon both. Of course, covenant is not, in origin, a Puritan idea, but a biblical one. The rainbow in the story of Noah's Ark, for example, is a potent sign of God's covenant with humanity. Covenant is fundamental to Judaism and to all branches of Christianity. But it received a renewed emphasis in Protestantism. Covenant ideas governed areas as diverse as marriage, government, and religion, and though marriage was one covenant and religion another, in practice their terms were frequently used interchangeably, so that the terms of one covenant would explain and legitimize the terms of the other. In his *Journal*, for example, John Winthrop points to one covenant (marital) in order to justify another kind of covenant (civil) and then grounds both in human beings' (religious) covenant with God.[34] Under the covenant paradigm, he suggests that husbands and kings are like God, a simile that implicitly authorizes interchangeability among these three types of authority.

This interchangeability was part of the common vocabulary, as is evident in an 1852 poem written by Emily Judson, who married Harriet Newell's fellow missionary Adoniram Judson after the death of his first wife, Ann (who had been Newell's closest friend). Featuring the same delight in providential affliction as is found in Newell's diary, the poem displays how providential and covenant theology associated male-authored violence with love, ecstasy, and even erotic delight:

Submission

Stricken, smitten, and afflicted,
Saviour, to Thy cross I cling;
Thou hast every blow directed,
Thou alone canst healing bring.

Try me till no dross remaineth,
And whate'er the trial be,
While thy gentle arm sustaineth,
Closer will I cling to Thee.

Cheerfully the stern rod kissing,
I will hush each murmuring cry;
Every doubt and fear dismissing,
Passive in Thine arms will lie.

And when through deep seas of sorrow,
I have gained the heavenly shore,
Bliss from every wave I'll borrow,
And for each will love Thee more.

Judson compares the agonies of God's afflictions to "deep seas," adding that she will obtain "bliss," not *despite* those "deep seas of sorrow," but

directly from them. Suffering intensifies her love and serves as a powerful trope for it: to kiss the stern rod is to express her love; to be stricken,
smitten, and afflicted is to feel God's love. Indeed, for each wave of sorrow that she encounters, she "love[s God] more." Though the Savior
wields a "stern rod," his arm is "gentle," because he only raises it against
her to draw her nearer to union with him. It is a metonym for intimacy.
But what is particularly striking is that the metaphor Judson uses to express her longing for religious intimacy could also be used to express
marital intimacy: "Passive in Thine arms will lie." Sexual and religious
eros are associated through the mediating figure of the chastening rod.

The interchangeability of God and husband fostered by the Puritan
notion of covenant is exemplified in another diary from the Second
Great Awakening, *The Memoirs of Mrs. Abigail Bailey*, which recounts
the life of an eighteenth-century Congregationalist wife and mother
whose husband was guilty first of violence, then of adultery, and ultimately of incest. Bailey composed her *Memoirs* in 1792, covering in it
the years from her marriage in 1767 up to her divorce settlement in
1792. She describes the events of her married life, attempting to understand her suffering through the lens of Congregationalist theology. Like
any autobiography, her memoirs are not a disinterested, pure transcript
of the "truth"; as Bailey was writing, she was also attempting to pressure
her husband into granting a financially beneficial property settlement by
threatening him with public exposure. The memoirs are centrally concerned with Abigail's own piety and the religious fulfillment she finds in
submission, a narrative choice that may have unconsciously been influenced by a desire to secure the approval of a community whose support
was likely to prove crucial to her future existence. But the memoirs were
not published till twenty-three years later, upon her death in 1815,
when her minister, Ethan Smith, arranged for the publishing house of
Samuel T. Armstrong (who published both his own *Dissertation on the
Prophecies* and the *Memoir* of Harriet Newell around the same time) to
print and market twenty-five hundred copies of Bailey's memoirs for de-
votional use. Their appearance so many years after the fact would have
rendered invisible the self-promoting aspects of her focus upon her own
virtue, and the memoirs would have been received purely as an illustration of the ecstasies rewarding the dutifully submissive wife. In other
words, though Abigail was a strong and determined woman with complex motives for writing, the circumstances under which her memoirs
were published would have made them seem a relatively straightforward
illustration of the popular hypothesis that female pleasure and power
come through submission and suffering.

Abigail Abbott was born in 1746 in New Hampshire. Four years after
she joined the church, at the age of eighteen, she married Asa Bailey,

who began physically abusing her within a month, had an affair with a hired woman, attempted to rape another, and after the birth of their fourteen children, began sexually and physically abusing their sixteen-year-old daughter Phebe. His character was hard and unyielding, as Abigail's description of a whipping he inflicted upon Phebe indicates: "He seized his horse whip, and . . . fell to whipping her without mercy. She cried, and begged . . . [but he acted] as though he were dealing with an ungovernable brute; striking over her head, hands, and back; nor did he spare her face and eyes; while the poor girl appeared as though she must die" (75–76).[35] As a devout churchgoer, Bailey represents all such events within a religious framework. For example, describing her own first encounter with her husband's violence, she writes, "I now began to learn, with trembling, that it was the sovereign pleasure of the allwise God to try me with afflictions in that relation, from which I had hoped to receive the greatest of my earthly comforts" (57).

Abigail is not a masochist, but her narrative contains some masochistic tendencies. Astonishingly, the grief Bailey feels when her husband abuses their daughter stems from feelings of abandonment and jealousy. She laments, "All his tender affections were withdrawn from the wife of his youth, the mother of his children. My room was deserted, and left lonely . . . while this one daughter engrossed all his attention" (71). Evidently, even after well over a decade of brutal treatment, Abigail continues to desire Asa's presence in her bedroom. Brutality is not as bad as abandonment. But faced with the patent fact of his desertion in the episode with their daughter, Bailey turns to God, deriving keen religious pleasures from the feeling of submitting to her husband's tyranny; she comes to understand Asa's abuse as a manifestation of God's loving chastisement. "For some time I could not obtain a comforting view that those unusual afflictions [Asa's incestuous activities] were in mercy, and not in judgment; for the rod seemed so severe" (73). But once she accepts a providential interpreation of Asa's abuse, she finds deep pleasures in her predicament:

> I now thought God dealt mercifully with me, in sustaining and comforting me under my affliction. As the flood of iniquity increased, so my faith and trust in God increased. In piercing trials, I felt myself, and all that was dear to me, in the hands of Him, who is my covenant God in Christ; and hence could say, "It is the Lord, let him do what seemeth him good." I now felt that I had more reason to be astonished at the tenderness in which God dealt with me, than to complain of this, or of any trial, which I ever endured. (74)

Abigail associates the "piercing trials" of marital infidelity with "tenderness," mercy, and comfort because religious doctrines encourage such associations. And so the increase in her suffering increases her sense of intimacy with Christ: "I was enabled to realize, with solemn awe and delight, that my words, actions, and secret thoughts, were all naked and open to the eyes of Him" (83). And this feeling of physical exposure is a prelude to a sensation of rhapsodic union that she can best convey in an array of highly sensualized metaphors foregrounding the physical intermingling of her body with Christ's body:

> My soul seemed to be emptied of the creature; and filled with the Creator. I sweetly felt the truth of those words of Christ; "In that day ye shall know that I am in the Father, and you in me, and I in you." "Abide in me, and I in you." "If a man love me, he will keep my words; and my Father will love him; and we will come unto him, and will make our abode with him." "The Comforter, whom the Father will send in my name, shall abide in you." For sometime, I was so swallowed up in God, that I seemed to lose a view of all creatures. I do not know that I had a thought of myself. I seemed hid from a sight of the world in an ocean of bliss. (85)

The quotations Bailey calls to mind to describe the religious ecstasy that she experiences during her period of abuse reiterate again and again a physical intermingling. She feels God's indwelling Spirit, and she also feels "swallowed up in God"; they are inside each other. Eros denied in one arena is experienced in another. The overall impression conveyed by this part of Abigail's memoir is that submission to domestic violence is rewarded by a sublime and sensual merging of self with God.

The "piercing trials" of Asa's violence and his marital abandonment metaphorically perform the annihilation of the self that paves the way for a form of love experienced as God inside the self, or the self inside of God. Thus, as the following quotation indicates, piercing, love, and union are linked in Abigail's mind: "While I pleaded God's gracious promises, and felt the most piercing sense of my own unworthiness, I felt a solid peace and heavenly calmness, and intense love to God the Father, Son and Holy Ghost. I was struck with wonder at the union between Christ and believers. This union, I felt a humble confidence that I did enjoy" (86). God's love pierces, because it comes only with acknowledgment of unworthiness and the renunciation of oneself, but suffering is worth the cost because it paves the way for an intimate, ecstatic union with Christ. Harriet Newell expresses pleasure at the thought of being broken; Abigail Bailey thinks in terms of piercing. But in both cases, affliction is linked with a transcendent form of eros, and the language of that eros is the language of the passive, submissive, or pierced body, flooded with God's love or even penetrated by God's body. Like Bataille, Abigail Bailey and Harriet Newell suggest that continuity with others is inseparable from violence to oneself.

The air of sexual scandal and sexual desire that characterizes the memoirs constitutes them as one strand in the complex discursive web associating affliction with pleasure throughout Protestant communities of the Northeast during the first half of the nineteenth century. Though Abigail never expresses a desire for suffering, she does continue to experience sexual desire for the husband who abuses her. Her memoirs associate male violence with female pleasure because of the slippage facilitated by the notion of covenant: submitting to Asa's afflicting rod produces in Abigail ecstasies of religious intimacy conceived in physical terms, and because husband and God were used interchangeably in Puritan discourse, the text can be said to associate the pleasures of loving intimacy with a husband's chastening rod.

Read in the context of this scandalous story, the following Watts hymn, which Bailey quotes in her *Memoirs*, consolidates the masochistic association of love with affliction:

The darkness of Providence

Lord, we adore thy vast designs,
Th'obscure abyss of providence!
Too deep to sound with mortal lines,
Too dark to view with feeble sense.

Now thou array'st thine awful face
In angry frowns, without a smile:
We, through the cloud, believe thy grace,
Secure of thy compassion still.

. . . .

Dear Father, if thy lifted rod
Resolve to scourge us here below;
Still let us lean upon our God,
Thine arm shall bear us safely through.

Abigail copied this hymn into her journal (154) because she believed God had sent it to her to sustain her during her difficulties. Lines such as "Dear Father, if thy lifted rod / Resolve to scourge us here below; / Still let us lean upon our God, / Thine arm shall bear us safely through" may have performed this sustaining function in private, but they also had the effect of linking Asa's actual scourging rod with God's loving, sustaining arm in the arena in which her memoir was received.

The pleasures inherent in the Puritan association of affliction with eros might well have been an important factor in women's enthusiastic responses to the Second Great Awakening. In addition to the satisfactions of agency they enjoyed in joining religious associations and the sense of independence, purpose, and enthusiasm that the revival movement provided, many women, in their private religious accounts, recorded the pleasures of a transcendent intimacy.[36] While prevailing ideologies abjected the female body, fantasies of piercing, breaking, discipline, surveillance, and martyrdom paradoxically provided a roundabout way of imagining physical intimacy and physical manifestations of religious ecstasy. To image the female body submissive before divine affliction was to imagine the body receptive to the flooding of ecstasy.

Two

Sentimental Masochism

WE HAVE SEEN that ideologies representing women's identity as by nature relative or contingent can inspire in the would-be "true woman" an oppressive longing to merge her female self with that of a far more important, powerful man. The implicit ideal of a noncorporeal woman, which inspires guilt in the woman for her invariable failure to accomplish perfect self-restraint, can direct that longing toward a man who manifests his power in acts of severity. And Puritan doctrines locating power and transcendent pleasures in total self-abnegation, interpreting affliction as a sign of love and authorizing associations between husbands and God, foster an attraction to a man who manifests his love in acts of discipline and punishment. However, while Puritanism associates discipline, surveillance, and affliction with love, and while it frequently describes religious ecstasy in terms that could also describe erotic pleasure, it is not in and of itself masochistic, if by that term we mean something resembling its original definition in Richard von Krafft-Ebing's *Psychopathia Sexualis*:

> By masochism I understand a peculiar perversion of the psychical sexual life in which the individual affected, in sexual feeling and thought, is controlled by the idea of being completely and unconditionally subject to the will of a person of the opposite sex; of being treated by this person as by a master, humiliated and abused. This idea is colored by lustful feeling; the masochist lives in fantasies, in which he creates situations of this kind and often attempts to realize them. . . . I feel justified in calling this sexual anomaly "Masochism," because the author *Sacher-Masoch* frequently made this perversion, which up to his time was quite unknown to the scientific world as such, the substratum of his writings. (86–87)

Neither Abigail Bailey nor Harriet Newell fantasizes about being humiliated or abused by a man, so neither is what Krafft-Ebing would call a masochist. But both do associate "the idea of being completely and unconditionally subject to the will of" *God* with pleasure; they often think of that subjection in terms that resemble those of ecstatic sexual submission; and they link God and human males in their writings. But we have yet to see how the Calvinist association of violence with love in turn becomes associated with sexuality. That is the goal of this chapter.

In nineteenth-century America, the discourses of Calvinism and coverture serve as the foundation of a recognizably masochistic desire through the agency of sentimentalism. Sentimentalism plays this key role because, while not masochistic in itself, it is closely linked to masochism, historically and structurally. Like masochism, sentimentalism can be read, broadly, as a quest for a state of union, or plenitude. And like masochism, sentimentalism describes a world in which pain is an avenue toward achieving that desired state of oneness. When providential theories of pain are read in the context of sentimental affirmations of sympathetic suffering, the result is an implicit link between pain and a mystical pleasure of transcendent union. And when the juxtaposition is used to characterize heterosexual romance—as it frequently is in nineteenth-century women's sentimentalism—the effect is pronouncedly sexualized and therefore recognizably masochistic.

The Parallel Structures of Sentimentalism and Masochism

American sentimentalism is an aesthetic and philosophical tradition with roots both in the Scottish Enlightenment and in the sentimental movement in eighteenth-century Europe. The cult of sensibility, starring the benevolent "man of feeling," arose in the late seventeenth and eighteenth centuries as a direct challenge to Hobbesian pessimism and Calvinist determinism, the latter of which tended to see human nature as inherently sinful, the body and the feelings as sites of corruption and confusion, and passion as "the devil in the inside of man" (Herget 3). (Strictly speaking, therefore, sentimental Calvinism is an oxymoron.) Sprague's admonition, "You should especially guard the senses; for these are the principal avenues through which vain thoughts find their way into the soul," exemplifies the Calvinist distrust of the body and the feelings. In the late seventeenth century, a growing reaction among the latitudinarian clergy in England rejected such pessimistic attitudes toward human nature, maintaining instead that human beings are naturally inclined to virtuous actions because of the pleasurable feelings such actions generate and because of the unpleasurable feelings of not doing them. As one of those clergymen put it, "when we see a miserable Object, Nature it self moves our Bowels to Compassion, and our Hands to give."[1] In 1711, the third earl of Shaftesbury, a student of John Locke, published his *Charakteristicks of Men, Manners, Opinions, Times*, which enjoyed widespread influence in Europe over the course of the eighteenth century. It blended Locke's faith in the senses as our most fundamental and reliable source of knowledge with the latitudinarian emphasis upon a benevolent (rather than depraved) human nature. Out of this blend emerged Shaftesbury's theory of a "moral sense" in addition to the familiar five physical senses, an innate human faculty that determines right and wrong by allowing one person to experience another's pains and pleasures through sympathetic identification, to know intuitively and experientially rather than through reason. The moral sense was an embodied, feeling-based form of cognition that seemed to many people to redeem both human nature and the human body.[2]

Shaftesbury's protégé Francis Hutcheson brought this concept of an innate and sympathetic moral sense to Scotland, where it influenced the developing epistemological, moral, and aesthetic philosophies of the Scottish Common Sense school of philosophy. Like Shaftesbury and the latitudinarians, Hutcheson emphasized the moral value of sympathy. Spectacles of suffering, he wrote in 1755, naturally provoke sympathy and benevolent actions: "The misery of one beloved, while it continues and is attended to, is incessant pain to the observer. . . . [T]here is a natural impulse, implanted for the kindest reasons, forcing us to such spectacles of misery, which generally brings relief to the sufferers" (145). Four years later, in 1759, Hutcheson's student Adam Smith, more famous today as the author of *The Wealth of Nations*, wrote one of the era's most influential theories of the relationship between sympathy, morality, and community, *The Theory of Moral Sentiments*, which represents sympathy as the foundation of any moral society. Sympathy, Smith speculates, arises from an impartial internal spectator inside all of us who allows us to change places with a sufferer and put that other's interests before our own. "His agonies, when they are thus brought home to ourselves, when we have adopted and made them our own, begin at last to affect us, and we tremble and shudder at the thought of what he feels" (2). When we make another's agonies "our own," in a sense we *become* that other. "By the imagination we place ourselves in his situation, we conceive ourselves enduring all the same torments, we enter as it were into his body, and become in some measure the same person with him, and thence form some idea of his sensations, and even feel something which, though weaker in degree, is not altogether unlike them." And that experience, a "great restraint upon the injustice of mankind," produces benevolent behavior spontaneously (8). Under the influence of sympathy, we do unto our neighbors what we would have our neighbors do unto us, because our neighbors *are*, in a sense, ourselves.

The principles of Common Sense philosophy were a central component of the early American education system; according to Perry Miller, they were America's "official metaphysic" for over half of the nineteenth century, read by the Founding Fathers and by most of the major authors of antebellum American literature, both male and female.[3] For example,

Susan Warner repeatedly mentions in her journal that she has been read-ing Dugald Stewart of the Common Sense tradition and his intellectual precursor, David Hume. Harriet Beecher Stowe noted that Common Sense philosophers were some of her most formative influences. And since the father of Mary Virginia Terhune and her sister insisted that they be educated "as if they were boys and preparing for college," their training doubtless exposed them to the Scottish philosophy that has been described as "probably the most potent single tradition in the American Enlightenment" and "the most important intellectual devel-opment in late-eighteenth-century America."[4] The sentimental literary tradition has its roots in this broad philosophical trend, and to this ex-tent it is an outgrowth of—rather than a reaction against—the Enlight-enment.[5] In keeping with its moral principles, sentimental authors ideal-ized characters who sympathized with and assisted those who suffered; they encouraged readers similarly to feel the experiences of fictional characters, to seek the truth of a book through emotional and physical identification; they urged them to adopt appropriately humanitarian be-haviors accordingly. They endorse an epistemology that is neither purely rational nor purely sensual but blends both in a form of apprehension that is best—though imperfectly—understood as "intuition," consulta-tion with the "heart," or simply "feeling."[6] As Lydia Sigourney wrote in a public letter printed alongside a poem sympathetic to the plight of the Cherokee, "It will be alleged that we have viewed this subject solely through the medium of *feeling*. This was our intention."[7]

In that it brings people together through sympathetic extensions into each others' experiences, the sentimental project is one of unification. It idealizes the recognition in others' experiences of counterparts to one's own, thereby eradicating the gaps between individuals and fostering a oneness among them that Puritanism tended to preclude. As Elizabeth Barnes writes, in her analysis of Smith and his legacy in early American novels, "Something is 'sentimental' if it manifests a belief in or yearning for consonance—or even unity—of principle and purpose" (23).[8] Senti-mentalism is not confined to the Anglo-American tradition, of course; it was especially influential on the continent. And while the continental traditions had their own literary and philosophical genealogies, all shared with Anglo-American sentimentalism an emphasis upon a union forged through sympathy. David Denby, in his study of sentimental nar-rative in French literature from 1760 to 1820, likewise observes that sentimentalism aims at a state of union: "the text, read and wept over, is to be the site of a community of like minds drawn together by their common reaction to a common scene" (80). And not only does the text unite readers; the typical plot centers on union. According to his analysis of the prototypical structure of the genre, an initial state of union is disrupted by a misfortune or a villain, resulting in a piteous state "which must then be overcome as a condition of the re-establishment of an ulterior happiness, which will represent the closure of the text" (Denby 72). On these twin conditions—loss of union and drive toward its restoration—"are built the dynamic of the narrative, the sense of meaningfulness and purposiveness which are the basis of the listener's potential interest in and identification with the tale" (74). In terms of both reader response and theme, sentimental plots are built around a quest for unity, and sentimental tears are shed over sundered unions.

In keeping with the rise of a secular culture, the sentimental plot frequently conceives of the unity that has been ruptured in psychological rather than religious terms: intimate relationships between mother and child, or husband and wife, or friend and friend.[9] The paradigmatic plot of what Nina Baym calls "woman's fiction" involves a young heroine who is sundered from a unity enjoyed with her mother and family, set adrift upon the world, and driven to recreate that lost state of plenitude, usually in marriage. But sentimental texts that fall outside Baym's classification, such as *Uncle Tom's Cabin*, also have the same core of sundered domestic relationships. Stowe writes that Uncle Tom sheds "just such tears, sir, as you dropped into the coffin where lay your first-born son" (34). Figuring the pain of loss as a universal experience that transcends differences of gender and culture, Stowe presumes she can enable readers to enter into Tom's experience by displaying his grief while at the same time appealing to their memories of their own painful separations.[10] In sentimentalism, readers "enter, as it were, into another person," not simply by imaginatively observing others' suffering, but by witnessing and simultaneously recalling their own suffering, in particular the painful interpersonal separations that to some degree or other are part of their own past experiences. Sentimentalism does not simply idealize the compassionate observation of another; it offers an intuitive and visceral understanding of the other's fear and anguish. A state of union, then, is achieved through suffering, which is the mechanism enabling one to "enter into" another person, as it were.

One of the most frequently represented forms of separation in sentimentality is that of mother and child. *Charlotte Temple, Hope Leslie, The Wide, Wide World, Uncle Tom's Cabin, Ruth Hall, Our Nig, Incidents in the Life of a Slave Girl, The Hidden Hand, Retribution, The Planter's Northern Bride, Malaeska Indian Wife of the White Hunter, Elsie Dinsmore,* and *Iola Leroy* all feature mother-child separation as a core trauma, if not *the* core. (*The Lamplighter* and *St. Elmo* emphasize separation from a grandfatherly type of man who is compared to a mother.) Stowe explicitly states that the separation of mothers from children constitutes the emotional core of *Uncle Tom's Cabin*. Referring to the death of her son Charley in 1849, Stowe wrote, "It was at his dying bed and at his grave that I learned what a poor slave mother may feel when her child is torn away from her," adding that "much that is in that book had its root in the awful scenes and bitter sorrows of that summer" (C. E. Stowe 203–4). Such scenes, which resemble what Mary Ann Doane labels "maternal melodramas,"[11] are particularly effective methods for provoking emotional affect, because they awaken a trauma with which all people can identify: the separation of mother and child. If they have not experienced such a separation from the parent's perspective, they have from that of the child. People may experience this trauma to different degrees, depending upon culture, gender, and individual circumstances, but a certain degree of individuation from one's primary caretaker is necessary to go about one's business in the world. Sentimentality exploits the pain of that ontological wound; ironically, allusions to loss in the genre function as a unifying mechanism.

Because the lost state of unity that is central to the sentimental imagination is so frequently a mother-child bond, "mother" often functions in sentimental literature as a figure of plenitude. "The Quaker Settlement" in *Uncle Tom's Cabin*, extensively discussed in recent criticism, exemplifies the sentimental alignment of motherhood with plenitude and presence. Rachel Halliday, who is described as having both an "ample, motherly form" and an "ample wing," is above all a figure representing abundance and generosity. Stowe writes that she "never looked so truly and benignly happy as at the head of her table. There was so much motherliness and fullheartedness even in the way she passed a plate of cakes or poured a cup of coffee, that it seemed to put a spirit into the food and drink she offered" (223). This famous chapter equates maternal plenitude with home and heaven; under Rachel's influence, for example, George Harris feels, "This, indeed, was a home,—*home*,—a word that George had never yet known a meaning for; and a belief in God, and trust in his providence, began to encircle his heart, as, with a golden cloud of protection and confidence, dark, misanthropic, pining atheistic doubts, and fierce despair, melted away before the light of a living Gospel, breathed in living faces" (224). The matriarchal home, in sentimentalism, is heaven on earth, and, as Jane Tompkins puts it, the ideal mother, such as Rachel Halliday, is "God in human form" (*Designs* 142).

This well-known image of a sacred sphere of plenitude is a vivid example of the transformation of American religion from the rigidly patriarchal Trinitarian Calvinism of Cotton Mather and Jonathan Edwards to a new theology that Leslie Fiedler calls "sentimental love religion" and Laurence Buell calls "Calvinism romanticized."[12] Rejecting the image of

God as an enraged Jehovah dangling the sinner over a burning pit, the new theology tended to conceive of him as a loving, compassionate mother. Horace Bushnell, for example, wrote, "We sleep in his bosom, even as a child in the bosom of its mother" (*Moral* 27), and Henry Ward Beecher said that a mother's love is "a revelation of the love of God"(qtd. in McLoughlin 88). Such comparisons are particularly prominent in nineteenth-century sentimental fiction; indeed, sentimental fiction plays an important role in developing and disseminating them.[13] In *The Lamplighter*, Maria Cummins celebrates a "mother's love, a love which is the highest, the holiest, the purest type of God on earth" (108). In *The Minister's Wooing*, Mrs. Marvyn nearly goes insane trying to love the wrathful, masculine God who appears to have damned her son for all time, but she is able to love God when her black servant, Candace, compares him to her own maternal self: "'Come, ye poor little lamb,' she said, walking straight up to Mrs. Marvyn, 'come to old Candace!'—and with that she gathered the pale form to her bosom, and sat down and began rocking her, as if she had been a babe. . . . 'Why de Lord a'nt like what ye tink,—He *loves* ye, honey! Why, jes' feel how *I* loves ye" (736). And in *The Wide, Wide World*, shortly after Ellen is tearfully wrenched from her mother, she meets Mr. Marshman, a clergyman who urges her to turn toward God, who he implies is a better mother. Depicting Ellen's mother in glowing terms, he insists that God is just like that, only more so. "Is he not even to-day taking away your dear mother for the very purpose that he may draw you gently to himself and fold you in his arms?" In *Uncle Tom's Cabin*, in a chapter significantly entitled "Reunion," Stowe describes the death of St. Clare. When the doctor observes "his mind is wandering," St. Clare objects, "No! it is coming *Home*, at last!" And his passing collapses the distinction between home, mother, and heaven: "Just before the spirit parted, he opened his eyes, with a sudden light, as of joy and recognition, and said "*Mother!*" (456) In sentimentality, home and mother are the secular counterpart to heaven and God.

The effect of the turn in sentimental literature toward a theology of a maternal God and a concordantly sacred domestic sphere is to collapse the distinction between sacred quests for religious transcendence and secular quests for domestic union. The search for a spouse with whom to create a domestic union is conceived in sacred terms, while the search for God is conceived in maternal terms. As Leslie Fiedler puts it, in the sentimental Protestant novel, "marriage becomes the equivalent of bliss eternal" (45). A passage from Caroline Lee Hentz's *The Planter's Northern Bride* exemplifies the way that sentimentalism blurs the distinction between domestic quests and religious ones by comparing both religious and marital unions to the union of a mother and child. The scene occurs shortly after the heroine, Eulalia, has married Mr. Moreland, undergoing a painful separation from her parents. She and her new husband are on a boat, heading to their new home:

> They were on the sea—the deep, deep sea, and though gliding comparatively near the coast, it was invisible to the eye, and the view had all the boundlessness and grandeur of the ocean's midst. Eulalia sat on deck, by her husband's side, with glory above her and glory below, and both the downward and the upward glory were reflected on her soul, making an intense inward glory, which was again reflected resplendently from her face. Gently rocked on the undulating waters, cradled on the arm of Moreland—that arm which seemed to her as the wing of an angel, protecting and sheltering her,—bathed in that calm, celestial light, that deep, tranquil, silver ocean, whose horizon was another silver ocean, distinguishable only by a kind of quivering splendour, fanned by a pure and inspiriting breeze, Eulalia approached nearer a state of beatitude than she had ever dreamed of attaining. Oh! to be borne on for ever over those rippling diamonds, thus companioned, soul linked to soul, heart bound to heart—looking up to heaven, seeing nothing but heaven, earth only a memory, something far off and separate—could there be a Paradise more holy and blissful? . . . "There is but one thing wanting to complete the magic of the scene," said Moreland, . . . "and that is music. Sing one song or hymn, my Eulalia." . . . Eulalia looked up and smiled, while the moisture gathered in her eyes. She was carried back to her native home; she was in the folding of a mother's arms . . . (199)

In this fantasy, marriage is both a return to infancy and a religious transcendence. Hentz compares the boundlessness of the sea not only to the union of husband and wife but also to a cradle, a mother's arms, an angel's arms, and an ecstatic fusion with the divine spirit in Paradise. She portrays romantic love as a merging with something infinitely "deep": a woman loses her identity in a diffused meld with a man whose divinity is most comprehensible and imaginable through comparison to a mother. Eulalia cries over the pain of her lost maternal union, but her desire for that lost plenitude has been fulfilled with a maternal substitute, a husband who rocks her and protects her beneath his sheltering angelic wing and, like God, fills her soul with "an intense inward glory." This union, which typifies the ideal sentimental union, is a pure plenitude that is simultaneously maternal, sexual, and sacred.

In this passage, Eulalia is basking in a "quivering splendour" that resembles what Julia Kristeva calls the "chora"; Eulalia is no longer her individuated self, but rather is merged with everything that is, in a sensual, nonsymbolic experience of cool breezes, undulating waters, and gentle rocking. The chora, Kristeva proposes, is a state characterizing the early life of an infant, a state of bodily drives, pulsations, and integration with the mother and the world, which she represents for the infant.[14] Communication occurs through touch and vocalizations: murmuring, humming, and other nonsymbolic, musical uses of the voice. Identity, Kristeva proposes, is born out of a painful separation from and negation of this chora. In order to produce the fiction of a coherent, individual "self," every person must first undergo a process called abjection, repudiating that which represents the "not-me." The abject includes not only disgusting, antilife things like pus, corpses, and vomit but also the mother, who represents a threat to the child's individual identity. Abjection is followed by the process of constructing an identity in language, where symbolization and signification replace the "semiotic" meaning of presymbolic communication in the chora. What Kristeva calls the semiotic remains present in adult language, however, in the rhythm, musicality, and other nonsymbolic forms of poetic expression that disrupt coherent, singular meanings in conventional symbolic communication. It is thus altogether fitting that music, which evokes the maternal presence, should complete the marital/maternal bliss Eulalia enjoys with her husband.

In this psychological construct (and others), "mother" is the privileged signifier for totality. And while the underlying drive in sentimentalism is toward a blissful state of nonindividuation, understood as maternal fusion, the road to that ideal frequently leads through paternal domination and violence.[15] Sentimentalism does not reject, but exploits, symbolic discourses. For example, though Hentz idealizes a regressive union with a maternal, angelic man who represents plenitude and benevolence, whenever that union is threatened—as it is in the novel both by a slave rebellion and by a false claimant to his hand—he restores the union through acts of violence that force submission, on his own terms, to the order that he represents. And broken unions are the basic staple of all sentimentalism, leading to a situation in which authority, and a willingness to use violence to enforce it, are essential aspects of a male hero's desirability—as they are of the Calvinist God's.

Consider a scene from the end of *The Planter's Northern Bride*, in which Moreland puts down a slave rebellion:

> Vulcan, the blacksmith [a rebellious slave], stood firm and unmoved as the anvil in his forge. All his dark and angry passions had been whetted on the edge of the murderous weapons hidden beneath his shop, and made red hot by the flames of the midnight furnace. His stubborn knees refused to bend, and a sullen cloud added luridness to his raven-black face.
>
> Moreland and he stood side by side;—all the rest were kneeling. The beams of the departing sun played in golden glory round the brow of Moreland; the

negro seemed to absorb the rays,—he looked of more intense, inky blackness.

"Vulcan!" said his master, "if you expect my forgiveness, ask it. Dare to resist me, and you shall feel the full weight of my indignation."

"I'm my own master," cried the blacksmith, in a morose, defying tone. "I a'int a gwine to let no man set his feet on my neck." . . .

The face of Moreland turned pale as marble, and lightnings kindled in his eyes. To brute force and passion he had nothing to oppose but moral courage and undaunted will; but he paused not to measure his strength with the muscles swelling out, like twisting serpents, in the negro's brandished arm. Laying his right hand commandingly on his shoulder, he exclaimed:—

"There is but one master here. Submit to his authority, or tremble for the consequences!" (505–6)

The aptly named Vulcan is associated with every satanic, infernal image Hentz can compress into a few paragraphs, while Moreland, with sunbeams playing "in golden glory round [his] brow" and the rest of the slaves kneeling round about him, is God. As God, Moreland *is* the realm of plenitude sought in both erotic and religious quests. But one of the key signs of his desirability is his readiness to do battle with Vulcan. Like the heavenly Master, Moreland shows his authority—and his love—in his capability, and willingness, to subjugate.

Eulalia, however, shows her worthiness of his love in her absolute tractability. In sentimentalism, the happy union—of husband and wife, of planter and slave—is a divine plenitude comparable to a mother-child union, but it is predicated upon the power and authority of a masterful man. It is therefore significant that the signs of Moreland's authority regularly function as signs of his romantic desirability in Hentz's imagination: "'How good, how noble you are!' cried Eulalia, for the first time throwing her timid arms round his neck; then, blushing at her boldness, would have withdrawn them, but he imprisoned them in his own, and retained her in willing bondage" (343). Though Eulalia seeks a quasi-maternal plenitude, not subjugation, in marriage, the phrase "willing bondage" indicates that they are linked. Hentz probably uses such phrases to justify her pro-slavery stance, as if to say "Domination and possession are attractive in other social relations, such as marriage, so why not concede that they are beautiful in the relationship between master and servant?" But what that means is that she is exploiting, on behalf of her political agenda, what she assumes will be the reader's already positive feelings toward eroticized domination in romantic fantasies. Consider another example: "'But come, my Eulalia,'—there was inexpressible grace and tenderness in the manner in which he thus expressed his ownership—never had her name sounded so sweet, never had the possessive pronoun seemed so significant or appropriate" (305–

6). Moreland is indeed maternal—"tender" and "sweet"—but his "possessive" assertion of "his ownership" is crucial in identifying him as a safe and irresistible avatar of domestic plenitude. When Moreland asks Eulalia, "what will you call me?" she does not even consider using a possessive pronoun and even refuses to call him by his first name, because "That would sound too familiar for me. I feel too much reverence to admit of it" (345). She settles upon his last name, without the "Mister." And the privilege of this bold degree of familiarity, Hentz writes, constitutes for her "one more link in the golden chain of love and confidence, wreathed round her heart" (345–46). Moreland is a holy person who inspires "reverence," and given the Puritan tendency to express love for God in terms of a desire for violence, and given Hentz's own conservative political agenda, it is no surprise that Hentz describes love for him in terms of being chained, imprisoned, and enslaved.

To the extent that sentimental romances appropriate violent Calvinist discourses in their evocation of an ideal union, as Hentz does here, they resemble the transgressive fantasies that Julia Kristeva describes in *Powers of Horror*. Representations of horror can produce what Kristeva calls a *jouissance*, an orgasmic bliss, because they invoke the possibilities of reintegration with lost parts of one's original wholeness, understood as a mother. This reintegration repels, because it means one's own death, but entices, because it represents the ecstasy of boundless union with everything. Her theory of the ecstasies of abjection resembles Bataille's theory that both sacred and secular fantasies of merging with totality are essentially violent. But Kristeva adds to Bataille's basic construct the psychological insight that individuals often conceive of the fusion with the "all" as a state of symbiosis with the mother. Hentz's fantasy of a marriage that is comparable to maternal fusion and accomplished through the man's authority is a good example of how violent discourses can invoke an erotic and religious notion of a blissful totality-conceived-as-mother.

Kristeva's theory of the pleasures of horror literature has frequently been applied to Gothic fiction, but not to sentimentalism. But the link between horror and an ecstatic expansion of the self is as fundamental to sentimentalism as it is to the Gothic. Sentimentalism does not exploit horror only to the extent that it uses mystical Calvinist notions; rather, its central rhetorical device—sympathy—is itself violent, in that it is predicated on another's suffering. In identifying with another's pain, readers experience an expanded sense of self and a union with alterity that resembles the jouissance Kristeva ascribes to abjection. The mechanisms of sympathetic union, like the mechanisms of Gothic horror fiction, mirror and duplicate the message of the providential theory of affliction, according to which experiences of pain (sent by God) are precursors to an ecstatic state of sacred union. Horror is therefore central to the sentimental, as Philip Fisher demonstrates in his anatomy of the genre.

In *Hard Facts*, Fisher explores an image drawn from Rousseau, which, he claims, contains in miniature "the primary psychology of sentimental narration itself" (105). It features "an imprisoned man who sees, through his window, a wild beast tearing a child from its mother's arms, breaking its frail limbs with murderous teeth, and clawing its quivering entrails. What horrible agitation seizes him as he watches the scene which does not concern him personally! What anguish he suffers from being powerless to help the fainting mother and the dying child" (105). Fisher observes that readers of sentimental fiction are in the position of the imprisoned man, seized by "horrible agitation" over a "scene which does not concern [them] personally." Like him, they witness a scene of horror which they are helpless to prevent; their feelings cannot lead to action.[16] Like Fisher, Cathy Davidson also locates violence at the core of the sentimental, distinguishing the genre from the Gothic according to the detachment of the reader.[17] In both genres, she claims, the reader experiences terror along with the victim. While the reader of the Gothic is an active participant, so that the identification produces anxiety and fear, the reader of sentimental fiction is sidelined, unable to help but forced to watch. These differing perspectives on a common core of violence account for the differing reader responses: heart-pounding terror for the Gothic reader, heart-wrenching tears for the sentimental reader. But in both genres, pleasure arises from a fantasized experience of suffering, which stimulates a sensation of expansion beyond the limitations of coherent identity, a breakdown of identity possibly leading to a sensation of limitless totality of being. Sentimentalism tends to *celebrate* the maternal character of that fusion with the all, while the Gothic emphasizes the terrifying nature of a maternal merge that is associated with death, but in both genres, "mother" functions as a figure for totality.

To the extent that the core of sentimental narration is a union conceived of as a maternal symbiosis and achieved through the experience of identifying with another's pain, it bears a striking resemblance to the overarching structure of masochism. A number of recent psychological theories of masochism have argued that it is fundamentally a quest for a sense of oneness with everything. Georges Bataille describes a desire, ontological in origin, to achieve a state of "continuity" between self and other, a symbiosis that signifies the death of oneself but allures with the promise of wholeness. Roy Baumeister basically concurs, relating the rise of such desires in modern culture to the rise of increasingly individuated and imprisoning notions of selfhood in contemporary life. Masochism, he proposes, is an effort to escape this imprisoning self of modernity and experience an expansion of being. Leo Bersani similarly emphasizes the shattering of the self in masochism, an opening up of the self to otherness, to "that which is intolerable to the structured self" (*Representation* 148). Nick Mansfield, emphasizing the masochist's control over the theatrical staging of his or her own shattering, argues that masochism is a state of "total subjectivity," in which the masochist is both an individual self *and* is merged with totality. Of course, all of these theorists concur that the masochist focuses upon suffering as the avenue to achieving this state of expansion. As Kristeva proposes, fantasies of violence express a longing to shatter the boundaries of the self in order to remerge with totality in a state of ecstatic nonidentity.

John Noyes's theory of the rise of masochism as a form of pleasure is basically in line with these other theories, though he addresses in particular how specific technological and cultural features of modernity promote violent fantasy as a way to imagine transcending the self:

> Masochism takes control of the technologies that produce subjectivity as cultural stereotypes. It develops elaborate strategies for framing the collapse of socially sanctioned identities, and it performs this collapse as a pleasurable abandonment of identity. . . . It relies upon the pleasurable disappearance— and controlled reappearance—of the subject. . . . Societies that develop political technologies to control and discipline the bodies of their subjects must reckon with the possibility that individuals will put these technologies to alternative uses. This is what happens in the case of masochism. It draws on stereotypes of violence and technologies of control in order to convert them into technologies of pleasure. In the process it perpetuates these stereotypes, but it does this—so its proponents would argue—in a way that renders them harmless, parodies them. (4–5)

Modern technological society requires that males both be model liberal subjects—civilized and nonviolent—and at the same time participate in large cultural schemes that are characterized by subterranean violence. As examples of the latter, he includes the forceful control of lower classes and wars fought for ideological or commercial reasons. Some men, alert to these contradictions in the definition of their being, find the competing identifications untenable and respond by turning the very technologies of discipline—whips, handcuffs, leather—against themselves as harmless technologies of pleasure.

But Noyes's focus upon the construction of male subjectivity allows for the possibilities of female masochism only by imagining that female masochists identify with male masochists. This theory may well be correct as far as women's actual practice of masochistic sex games—which is of central interest for Noyes—is concerned. However, in the realm of literary fantasy, there is a whole range of expressions of female masochistic desire that are not easily explained in Noyes's terms and that predate the period he discusses. In nineteenth-century sentimental works, women do not identify with male masochists; indeed, such figures are rejected in them. Rather, the requirements for attractive male characters are steep: they must be, like Horace Moreland, both very virile and very gentle, both aggressively paternal and quietly maternal. By excluding female literary masochistic fantasies from his study, Noyes fails to recognize that nineteenth-century sentimental fiction established and popularized the gender norms against which his own *fin-de-siècle* masochists revolt. He also fails to recognize that sentimental fiction models for subsequent masochists the ways that submission can be linked to transcendence of the self. The spankings and stern lectures in sentimental fiction may sound like camp today, but they are in fact the originals, the prototypes that camp representations are mimicking. When twentieth-century male masochists engage in theatrical rituals of violence against the self as a form of transcending the self, they are imitating in parodic ways patterns established in sentimental works.

Masochism as a sexual practice and as a form of erotic fantasy would not have taken the forms it has today were it not for the sentimental literature that provided many of its most characteristic images. One of the most important contributions of nineteenth-century sentimental fiction to the rise of sexual masochism in the culture at large is the apotheosis of the godly mother. As we have seen, "mother" is a figure representing plenitude in sentimental fiction, and the impetus to transcend the limited self is frequently expressed as a regressive longing to remerge with one's mother. Husbands are therefore frequently endowed with maternal characteristics of loving plenitude as well as paternal ones of powerful discipline. The sanctification of motherhoood is not, of course, solely attributable to sentimental fiction, but it *is* a sentimental phenomenon, widely disseminated to the population through sentimental literature. It is also a crucial psychological foundation for the masochistic sensibility. As we have seen, Bernhard Berliner observed in 1940 that "The masochist has a particularly great need for being loved in the passive infantile way. . . . He is fixated on the love objects of his early childhood . . . [and sees suffering as] the price which he has to pay for his particular gratification" (323–25). Like the sentimentalist, the masochist nostalgically longs for the safety and bliss associated with a preoedipal, maternal bond, and like the sentimentalist sees suffering as the road to that ecstatic ideal of union, and therefore conceives of his or her desire in terms of violence or domination. Even though the regressive aspects of masochism have been recognized at least since Berliner published his article, the extent to which masochism at its core is a longing for maternal symbiosis has been insufficiently considered in many studies of masochism.

Gilles Deleuze's *Coldness and Cruelty* is the first major theory to address masochism as a regressive desire in which "mother" is the privileged signifier for that ideal of totality: "In the case of masochism the totality of the law is invested upon the mother" (90). Masochistic fantasy, he argues, expresses a desire for maternal symbiosis by means of an elaborate, theatrical regression fantasy in which "Eros is desexualized and humiliated for the sake of a resexualized Thanatos" (120).[18] Gaylin Studlar, who attempts to restate Deleuze's theory of masochism in everyday language, writes, "Masochism forces us to reconsider the power of a desire . . . born out of infantile helplessness and the dangerous bliss of symbiosis" (49). The masochist, she claims, following Deleuze, wishes "to restore identification and oneness with her [the mother, a figure of idealized wholeness] and be reborn into a 'new man devoid of sexual love' who represents the denial of sexual difference and rejection of the father's sexuality" (43). The Deleuzian masochist is a man whose attraction to cold, punitive women represents a rejection of conventional representations of male sexuality. Since Deleuze does not explore how female masochism relates to his construct, he does not point out that a female also seeking maternal fusion does not need to repudiate conventional symbolic representations of female sexuality but rather can exploit them. Female fantasies of being disciplined by a punishing father are not socially transgressive. Nor are they incompatible with a quest for maternal fusion. For as we have seen, if the goal of female masochistic fantasy—like that of male masochistic fantasy—is the dissolution of self and expansion into a totality conceived as "mother," the road to that goal is, in the female masochistic fantasy, paternal discipline and punishment. And, as the pattern established by religious systems such as Calvinism suggests, focusing upon the violence of transcendence can call to mind the ecstatic aspects of transcendence. More specifically, in texts blending sentimentalism and Calvinism, suffering is a metonym for an ecstasy typically conceived as maternal fusion. Both male and female forms of masochism are regressive, as Deleuze indicates, but female masochism can exploit conventional sexual norms, while male masochism repudiates them.

Both sentimentalism and masochism emerge from Western cultures of the late eighteenth and early nineteenth centuries, an era during which the meaning of "mother" and the self's relation to "mother" was changing. Only at this time did motherhood become the primary signifier of plenitude, wholeness, and nurture. As many feminist historians have argued, in America this understanding of "mother" is a historically contingent product of changes in family organization that swept across the nation between 1785 and 1815.[19] Conventional representations of family life during the earlier, colonial era feature an extended household that intermingles public and private spheres, a little commonwealth ruled by the father with the mother playing the role of "helpmeet" rather than official nurturer or symbol of domestic plenitude. The rise of industrial labor dramatically transformed the family structure. As increasingly men began to work outside the home in industry and the professions, child care became more and more the special province of women, and care on a paternal model or care shared by both parents yielded to a more exclusively female "mothering" (Bloch 105). Representations of family in the antebellum decades increasingly emphasize intense one-on-one emotional bonds, a shift that corresponds to an increasing divergence between public and private spheres. As Bloch demonstrates, the debates over wet-nursing illustrate this shift. Wet-nursing was customary on both sides of the Atlantic during the colonial era, and the clergy had traditionally deplored it on religious grounds. Between 1785 and 1815, however, they began to emphasize the detrimental *psychological* effects of wet-nursing other than its sinfulness. The language of religion yields to that of psychology.

The mother-child bond idealized in psychological discussions of identity may not be a universal truth but a socially constructed one, a new narrative about how people are, rooted in transformations of family life in the late eighteenth and early nineteenth centuries, when the psychological effects of motherhood became increasingly ideologically significant. As theorists like Julia Kristeva, Janine Chasseguet-Smirgel, Jane Gallop, and Ann Cvetkovich have pointed out, mother and child harbor aggressive feelings toward each other as well as symbiotic ones. Freud's postulate of a universal, idealized memory of a blissful bond between mother and child might well, then, be a construct created after the child had grown up, and not during childhood itself. An adult suffering from the agonizing constraints of excessive individuation that characterize the modern era might well articulate his sense of alienation in terms of a nostalgic longing for a mythological period of perfect maternal love supposedly experienced before a gap between the "me" and the "not-me" gave birth to the oppressive illusion of a coherent and individuated self. Of course, nostalgia is not new; what is new in the nineteenth and twentieth centuries, is the maternal character of a longing that formerly might have been pictured forth as a "Golden Age," or as "Eden," or as "Paradise." What is also new in this era is the rise of masochism and sentimentalism, both of which express a desire that had formerly been understood as a religious quest for spiritual transcendence in the modern terms of a nostalgic, erotic longing for reunion with "mother."

Let us digress for a moment to see just how central to post-Freudian psychological thinking is this link between masochistic desire and a longing for maternal fusion. We will then return to the nineteenth century to see how sentimental literature played an important role in consolidating the pattern of association that has become familiar today. In *Camera Lucida* (1981), a study of photography by eminent critic and theorist Roland Barthes, we find a vivid example of the links I have been trying to establish. Though he is writing neither about masochism nor sentimentalism, certain of his offhand remarks and claims exemplify how thoroughly masochism and sentimentalism converge in a common pursuit of transcendence or totality—conceived in the signifier "mother" and accessed through suffering. In this study of photography, Barthes says he is taking a "sentimental," rather than scholarly, approach to photography: "I was interested in photography only for 'sentimental' reasons; I wanted to explore it not as a question (a theme) but as a wound: I see, I feel, hence I notice, I observe, and I think" (21). The essence of sentimentalism, he indicates, is an experience of suffering. Like nineteenth-century sentimental authors and eighteenth-century Common Sense philosophers, he suggests that sentimental knowledge derives from feelings grounded in physical experience: "I make myself the measure of photographic 'knowledge,' he writes, asking "what does my body know of photography?" (9). To know sentimentally is to know with the body, to privilege a primary gut response to cognition over a secondary intellectual one. Barthes implies, though never asserts, that the pleasure of such a sentimental approach is masochistic; to consider photographs sentimentally is to wait for an experience he calls a *punctum*. Certain photographs will contain this *punctum*: a detail that stimulates inside him a physical response of "tiny jubilations, as if they referred to a stilled center, an erotic or lacerating value buried in myself" (16). This sentimental laceration is erotic, he claims, because it is not only internally felt but provokes desire for something external, propelling his imagination outside of himself. "The *punctum*, then, is a kind of subtle *beyond*—as if the image launched desire beyond what it permits us to see . . . toward the absolute excellence of a being, body and soul together" (59). For Barthes, the experience of this sentimental wound operates as a gate between himself and alterity, seeming to puncture his skin, opening him up to an experience of continuity between himself and "absolute excellence" in the "subtle *beyond*."

This simultaneity of desire and gratification in the *punctum* calls to mind the afflictions sent by the Calvinist God, which both awaken in the Christian a desire for fusion with God and are metonymically linked to the gratification of that desire. As Jane Gallop observes, "When Barthes talks about the sting and the wound and the arrow that pierces me, he is pointing to a tradition of mysticism. In European thought, mysticism is the great tradition of openness to alterity, of receptivity to being overwhelmed by otherness" (155). But there is a similar tradition in American thought as well. As we saw in the writings of Harriet Newell and Abigail Bailey, affliction is frequently a way to imagine God's pure presence, since it simultaneously suggests the dismantling of the self and seems in itself to be a powerful indication of God's presence. For Calvinists, affliction evokes notions of an ecstatic transcendence and reunion with God; in a secular context, the sentimental wound evokes a different form of transcendence, by creating a bridge that crosses the divide between oneself and a suffering other, enabling a reader to extend beyond the conventional boundaries of the self and to "enter into" another person.[20]

Barthes understands that merge with alterity as, at its core, a maternal merge. Like Stowe and other sentimentalists, Barthes identifies the underlying drama in the sentimental wound as one of maternal separation. In his effort to locate the "essence" of photographic pleasure, Barthes proceeds, as he says, phenomenologically, looking at stacks of photographs, sentimentally permitting his body to receive whatever wounds they may inflict. The photograph that he singles out from all the others as the essential photograph with the sharpest *punctum* portrays his mother as a young girl. She had recently died when he wrote *Camera Lucida*, and the photograph inspires in him a bittersweet fantasy of reunion with her. For Barthes, an appeal to the anguish of separation from his mother turns out to be the essence of the erotic pleasure he associates with the sentimental wound. In linking an experience of pain to an erotic sensation that, at root, is a longing for his mother, Barthes not only encapsulates the essential dynamic of masochism but indicates its inextricable link to sentimentalism.

Barthes is predisposed to associate maternal separation with sexuality, perhaps because of his grounding in the works of his contemporary Jacques Lacan, who sees the traumatic separation of mothers and children as the core of both human identity and sexual desire. In his famous essay "The Mirror Stage," Lacan proposes that a very early separation from the mother represents the source of all desire. An infant, he imagines, acquires an illusory sense of coherence by imagining itself in the eyes of its mother (or through identifying with its mirror image) and perceiving itself as a separate individual. In other words, an infant acquires an identity by thinking something like "She sees me." The "me," then, arises through "her" gaze, and therefore is inextricably other than "she," contingent upon her difference. Absence of the mother (or "other," more purely) and yearning for the state of non-

individuation that fusion with her represents is, therefore, the agonizing core of identity. Desire is born at the first moment of individuation,
Lacan speculates; desire is the longing to fill the gap at the core of
being, to reunite with the totality of existence that the maternal body
had once represented. And since unfulfillable desire is the foundation
of identity, full gratification would destroy the self. Hence, people turn
to sexuality as a symbolic compensation for that ontological *désir*, for
substitutes for the impossible goal of the pure plenitude of maternal
presence.[21]

Although Lacan and Barthes assert that sexuality is a symbolic expression of an ontological drive for maternal fusion, sexuality has not always
been understood in such maternal terms. Nineteenth-century sentimentalism played an important role in the process by which this nostalgia for
maternal plenitude became associated with sexuality. In order to discuss
how it did this, it will be useful first to borrow a word, "propping," from
Barthes's fellow poststructuralist theorist Jean Laplanche. Beginning
with the broad claim that our experiences of physical sensations are always shaped by the language and cultural attitudes contextualizing
those experiences, Laplanche attempts to explain how language could
operate as the agent by which the animalistic instinct for copulation becomes associated with a particular form of desire. No sexual desire is
inborn, he proposes; rather, it is a cultural construct. He speculates that
this construction occurs during infancy, positing that at a certain moment, the drive is stimulated at the same time that a child is acquiring a
more abstract system of ideas. The effect of the simultaneity is that an
idea, conceived in language, "leans" on, or is "propped" on, the drive.
A particular form of desire, then, is a product of metonymy, which is
essentially to say, a product of linguistic association.

"Propping" is a good metaphor for expressing the association of
"ecstasies of pain" and affect in sentimental literature. And it is that
propping of idea on affect that makes sentimentalism such an important
component of the rise of masochism as a form of desire in modern culture. As we have seen, sentimental authors strive to make their readers
feel the pain of the characters they write about, specifically by focusing
upon ruptured mother-child unions. Though it is an emotional pain, it
is nonetheless felt in the body: virtually all respondents to sentimental
literature acknowledge their physical responses, as we will see in chapter
4. Many describe a reaction in the bowels, or a sensation of twisting or
wrenching of the heart, or the jangling of nerves, and always, there is a
copious stream of tears. At the same time that readers experience the
painful rupture of maternal bonds, there circulate in sentimental texts
multiple variations on the theme that pain is a sign of love, that suffering

is a metonym for a transcendent ecstasy best conceived as the restoration of that mother-child bond. The propping of the idea on the affect can be for the reader a felt experience of an ecstasy of pain. And if the ecstatic impetus is couched in sexual terms, as it frequently is, the result is a consolidation of the idea that that felt experience of sympathetic pain is also a felt experience of sexual pleasure. This blend of sympathetic pain and sexual desire is fundamental to the development of masochism as it comes to be known in the twentieth century.

I would like now to turn to two examples of the propping of ideas of erotic desire on the painful experience of sentimental affect, in order to see how sentimentalism consolidates and disseminates many of the fundamental notions of modern masochism, such as are seen in Barthes's *Camera Lucida*. First, we will examine Lydia Sigourney's "The Suttee" as a representative example of how sentimental literature associates suffering with sexual pleasure through the propping of sexual discourses on the sentimental wound of maternal separation. We will then turn to another excerpt from *The Planter's Northern Bride* that encapsulates the entire process outlined in this chapter.

Lydia Sigourney's "The Suttee" (1827) uses sexual images to characterize the mother-child bond and a language of sexual longing to characterize mother-child separation. It is therefore a good example of how sentimentality eroticizes the pain of maternal separation. In the poem, Sigourney emphasizes the pathos of such a separation as a way to popularize opposition to the Hindu practice called "suttee," the burning of a wife on the funeral pyre of her dead husband, and covertly, perhaps, to criticize Western marriage laws that tie women to a "loathsome partner." But its use of the sentimental wound is represented in sexual language that produces a distinctly masochistic effect:

The Suttee

She sat upon the pile by her dead lord,
And in her full, dark eye, and shining hair
Youth revell'd. —The glad murmur of the crowd
Applauding her consent to the dread doom,
And the hoarse chanting of infuriate priests
She heeded not, for her quick ear had caught
An infant's wail. —Feeble and low that moan,
Yet it was answer'd in her heaving heart,
For the Mimosa in its shrinking fold
From the rude pressure, is not half so true,
So tremulous, as is a mother's soul
Unto her wailing babe. —There was such wo
In her imploring aspect, —in her tones

Such thrilling agony, that even the hearts
Of the flame-kindlers soften'd, and they laid
The famish'd infant on her yearning breast.
There with his tear-wet cheek he lay and drew
Plentiful nourishment from that full fount
Of infant happiness, —and long he prest
With eager lip the chalice of his joy. —
And then his little hands he stretch'd to grasp
His mother's flower-wove tresses, and with smile
And gay caress embraced his bloated sire, —
As if kind Nature taught that innocent one
With fond delay to cheat the hour which seal'd
His hopeless orphanage. —But those were near
Who mock'd such dalliance, as that Spirit malign
Who twined his serpent length mid Eden's bowers
Frown'd on our parents' bliss. —The victim mark'd
Their harsh intent, and clasp'd the unconscious babe
With such convulsive force, that when they tore
His writhing form away, the very nerves
Whose deep-sown fibres rack the inmost soul
Uprooted seem'd. —
            With voice of high command
Tossing her arms, she bade them bring her son,—
And then in maniac rashness sought to leap
Among the astonish'd throng.—But the rough cord
Compress'd her slender limbs, and bound her fast
Down to her loathsome partner.—Quick the fire
In showers was hurl'd upon the reeking pile;—
But yet amid the wild, demoniac shout
Of priest and people, mid the thundering yell
Of the infernal gong,—was heard to rise
Thrice a dire death-shriek.—And the men who stood
Near the red pile and heard that fearful cry,
Call'd on their idol-gods, and stopp'd their ears,
And oft amid their nightly dream would start
As frighted Fancy echoed in her cell
That burning mother's scream.[22]

The poem urges its reader to identify and sympathize with the tortured woman. The language in which it describes her body facilitates an Anglo-American reader's identification: her breast is like a "chalice of joy," a Christian, Western symbol that—like the "fount of happiness" and the clichéd "flower-wove tresses"—invites readerly identification.

Likewise, the primary focus in this poem, the violent separation of mother and child, facilitates identification, since virtually all readers can identify with the trauma of maternal separation to some degree or another—certainly more than they can identify with being burned alive. As in much nineteenth-century sentimentality, Sigourney exploits that commonality of experience in order to enable readers to feel a degree of pain through identification. They can approximate the feeling of the burned mother's pain, and they will presumably oppose the barbaric practice of wifeburning out of a newly *felt* conviction that it is wrong. (Identification with the barbaric men is prevented by their representation as Satanic, "wild, demoniac," "infernal" people who call on "idol-gods." They are merely sadistic "others," serving the central, sympathetic action of the poem.)

Sigourney's contemporary reader might well have experienced what Halttunen calls a disturbingly pleasurable, "aggressive kind of voyeurism" in connection with the gut reaction of sympathetic pain provoked by this sentimental poem; Halttunen demonstrates that such pleasures were widely associated with the sentimental reading experience.[23] "The Suttee" invites such an experience by characterizing "agony" as "thrilling," and by focusing upon a beautiful young woman tied up, physically exposed, and tortured before a crowd of enthusiastic men, whose "hoarse chanting," applause, and "glad murmur" indicate their pleasure in the horrible action. The image of "the rough cord / [that] Compress'd her slender limbs" also indicates a masochistic aesthetic, fetishizing the beauty of the woman's body through contrast to its rough bondage.

The mother and child desire each other; the mother's breasts are "yearning" for the child, who in turn sees them as storehouses of "joy" and "happiness." And Sigourney subtly suggests that their desire for each other is a sexual desire, since she compares it to the desire of man and woman: that of Adam and Eve. When she compares the priests in "The Suttee" to Satan in the form of a snake watching the bliss of Adam and Eve, she writes in an offhand way that suggests that she believes her reader will be intimately familiar with the scene to which she is referring. Where would readers in 1827, in Protestant New England, be most likely to derive their knowledge of this particular scene? Almost without a doubt, from Milton's *Paradise Lost*. While for us today, a deep familiarity with this text cannot be assumed, Sigourney probably did assume such a familiarity in most of her readers. Thus, when she writes that the priests "mock'd" the mother and child stealing a last moment together, and then compares them to "that Spirit malign / Who twined his serpent length mid Eden's bowers / [and] Frown'd on our parents' bliss," she is almost certainly alluding to the most sexual passage in *Paradise*

Lost, in which Milton focuses on the envy of Satan as he lustfully watches Adam and Eve engaging in sexual intercourse:

> aside the Devil turn'd
> For envy, yet with jealous leer malign
> Ey'd them askance, and to himself thus plain'd.
>   Sight hateful, sight tormenting! Thus these two
> Imparadis't in one another's arms
> The happier *Eden*, shall enjoy their fill
> Of bliss on bliss, while I to Hell am thrust
>   (book 4, 503–8)

Sigourney strongly suggests the influence of Milton simply in her use of blank verse, like his. She also repeats a number of key words from the famous passage, including "malign" and "bliss." And the effect of comparing the mocking crowd to an envious Satan watching Adam and Eve making love is the creation of a sexual air not only in the mother-child relationship but in the entire situation of a jealous satanic crowd watching and interrupting an act of loving union. As is characteristic of the genre, the mother is a figure of plenitude, and a child's union with her is the prototype of the pleasure of adult sexuality. The reader is encouraged to feel the mother's suffering, and the air of erotic, "thrilling agony" in the poem is propped on that spectatorial suffering, making possible an experience of masochistic pleasure.[24]

A more fully developed example of the same kind of propping is found in *The Planter's Northern Bride*, in a passage which offers a mise-en-scène for how sentimentalism works and also illustrates how notions of both sexual and religious pleasure might have propped themselves upon internal experiences of sentimental affect, prompting a reader to associate sympathetic suffering with sexual desire or religious pleasure. As this scene opens, Eulalia has sought out her minister for spiritual comfort: she fears that she cannot marry her beloved Moreland, because of her father's opposition to her union with a southerner. By way of consolation, the minister tells her a story from his own early life. When his fiancée, Emma, died shortly before their marriage by falling over a cliff while horseback riding, he plunged into despairing anguish, until:

> One of those blessed servants of God, who are appointed for a peculiar mission, found me, and dragged me up out of the depths of the abyss of blackness in which my soul was plunged; he poured oil and balm into my wounds, bound them in the swaddling bands which wrapped the babe of the manger, and left me not till he had laid me a weeping penitent at the foot of the cross. Then a divine warmth penetrated my heart. I looked upon this world only as the dim vestibule of a great and glorious temple . . . and I said, "Let me guide

my fellow-pilgrims over the tottering planks to the beautiful shores of the promised land,—that land whose celestial beauties my eyes have been opened to behold." I said, "O, my God! I dedicate myself to thee, body and soul, in life and death, for time and eternity." Eulalia, I have been true, as far as poor frail humanity can be, to the solemn vows of my great consecration. I can see now why I was led through such a thorny path. My soul was so wedded to earth, nothing but a mighty wrench could have torn it from my grasp. (134–35)

This story typifies the conversion paradigm: extreme pain is providential, since only a "mighty wrench" could break the minister's excessive attachment to the earth. Once he submitted to God's will, he was born again, nurtured by a distinctly maternal minister, flooded with "divine warmth," and absorbed into a lasting, ecstatic relationship with a God who showed his love in his willingness to inflict great pain.

But what is particularly fascinating is that Eulalia goes through a similar "conversion" experience as she listens to the minister, suggesting that *identificatory* pain can produce a similar sensation of misery and an opening up to receive grace. First, the pain: Eulalia "was gazing, in imagination, on the mangled body of Emma, at the foot of that awful precipice,—on the horse and the rider, both quivering and bleeding in the agonies of death,—on the anguish of surviving friends; she was dwelling on the appalling uncertainty of every earthly blessing,—the terrible penalty love is doomed to pay for its short dream of joy,—on the sad, sad doom of mortality; she wept as if her heart would break,—wept for herself, wept for her minister, and for all the sons and daughter of humanity" (133–34). Like a reader of sentimental fiction, Eulalia "gaz[es] in imagination" upon a gory spectacle, feels the pain along with the characters, and weeps.[25] She undergoes in fantasy the anguish of separation that must inevitably rupture any loving union ("the terrible penalty love is doomed to pay for its short dream of joy"), and this pain provokes in her a consciousness of the tragedy of mortality, unleashing a flood of tears.

Thus far, her sympathetic experience mirrors the minister's. However, when he reached that state of consciousness, he was propelled toward a religious union; when Eulalia reaches it, she is propelled toward a marital union. Although she is ashamed of her worldly selfishness and the narrow scope of her concerns, which have persisted despite this story (recounted to make her think in larger, less personal terms), Eulalia is forced to confess that she remains most concerned about her relationship with Moreland. The minister comforts her by indicating that he believes she and Moreland will soon marry, a private union of northerner and southerner that will help to unify North and South: "I believe

Providence has a mission for you to perform, the way of which will be made smooth beneath your feet. You will be a golden link of union between the divided interest of humanity" (136). Providence afflicts both the minister and Eulalia with the agony of separation as a precursor to an ecstatic union. That suffering stimulates desire for reunion, but whereas the minister experiences such a union in the form of religious rapture, Eulalia becomes "a golden link of union" in marriage. But as we have seen, religious ecstasy and marital ecstasy are not really all that different in sentimental novels. Both religious transcendence and marriage represent an ecstatic loss of self and expansion into something infinitely large that, in sentimental literature, is best conceived through comparison to a mother's tender love and protection. And in both cases, that ecstatic expansion is contingent upon a prior experience of pain. The masochistic pleasures of sentimental suffering are to a large extent contingent upon an erotic character in the discourses propped upon suffering. As we shall see in the next section, such discourses were all too frequently present in nineteenth-century women's sentimentalism.

"The Lineaments of the Divine Master"

In *Woman in America* (1850), Maria McIntosh describes a "political inequality, ordained in Paradise, when God said to the woman, 'He shall rule over thee,' and which has ever existed, in every tribe, and nation" (22). Her 1863 novel *Two Pictures* tells the story of a woman who seems to challenge this law by seeking to live independently but, after almost dying from exhaustion, gratefully relinquishes her independence in order to marry a virile, masculine protector, "the type to her of a guardian Providence" (437). The novel closes with an image of her

> Resting . . . as she had never rested before. . . . Where was her pride, her independence now? All exchanged for the sweetness of entire trust in the large heart, the clear judgment, the firm will of him whom she had chosen for her earthly guide. She had exercised wisely her woman's right of choice, and the result was this ineffable peace. What could the poor, vain ranters about woman's independence have given her in exchange for it? Ah! They know not how sweet it is to "obey," when obedience has been preceded by "love and honour." Only see that he whose rule you accept bears the lineaments of the Divine Master, and be assured your highest happiness and truest happiness in this, as in every relation, will be found in obedience to God's arrangements. (449)

Implying that marital self-renunciation is as "sweet" as religious self-renunciation, this passage illustrates that the paradigm of "covenant" tended to render God and the human male interchangeable. A woman in search of rest, peace, and entire trust should assert herself sufficiently to demand a man who resembles God, and then yield herself up to him. It may well be that her failure to locate a man up to her lofty standards— a combination of maternal nurture and paternal mastery—led to McIntosh's decision never to marry, or it may be that all too frequently in her culture, the implicit sign that a man bore "the lineaments of the Divine Master" was his willingness to be a human master: to dominate, discipline, and afflict his beloved.

Most married women probably got over the idea that husbands are like God—Fanny Fern grew rich mocking such notions—but nonetheless countless sentimental novels and poems associate the man whom a woman loves with God, and the means by which they do so is through displaying his authority in a streak of violence or severity. Maria Evans Wilson's novels exemplify this eroticization of domination. In *St. Elmo* (1866), for example, a character claims that the heroine, Edna, would only marry if "she learned to love, almost against her will, some strong, vigorous thinker, some man whose will and intellect master hers, who compels her heart's homage" (193). Edna, not surprisingly, is so mastered, and the man who subjugates her is a cruel, despotic rake who is converted to Christianity through her efforts and becomes a godly preacher. He remains violent in character, but because he wields violence on behalf of the good, he is eminently attractive. It is not that Evans and McIntosh are indifferent to women's intellectual and artistic aspirations. To the contrary, their novels focus upon women's hunger for such attainments. But they also present individual cultivation not as an end in itself but as a step on the road to the highest form of female existence, which is the transcendence achieved in Christian marriage.

Martha Finley's *Elsie Dinsmore* (1867) affords a useful case study of how the convergence of sentimentalism and Calvinism establishes this pattern of eroticizing male violence and promoting masochistic desire on the part of female readers. Although the erotic relationship in it is between father and daughter rather than husband and wife, it is nonetheless particularly useful for this study, because its masochistic eroticism is so overt and because of its overwhelming popularity and significance in American literary history. One of countless nineteenth-century tales in which a human abuser partakes of the powerful, ecstatic attractions of the divine disciplinarian, *Elsie Dinsmore* was also one of the biggest best-sellers of the century, for three generations outselling every other novel for juveniles, with the exception of *Little Women*. The best-seller for its publisher in 1868, *Elsie Dinsmore* remained in print for fifty years and was read by an estimated twenty-five million, predominantly young, female readers. It exerted a considerable influence upon the underlying romantic assumptions of a considerable portion of the American population.

This sentimental, masochistic blockbuster tells the didactic story of a pious nine-year-old whose mother died at her birth and whose father subsequently abandoned her. She is consumed with desire, not for an erotic union, but for the total plenitude of a parent-child union, symbolized by her missing mother. Elsie is thrilled when her handsome father returns, but devastated when he withholds his affection, offering attention only in the form of imperious prohibitions and stern punishments. She submits to his autocratic ways dutifully though not eagerly, continually castigating herself for the imperfection of her submission to him: although she does everything he demands, sometimes she feels resentful, and although she never complains, once (to her great shame) she fails to silence a friend who criticizes her father. Elsie believes that only perfect submission will win his love, and, as portrayed by Finley, she is right, for once the last vestiges of her will have been eradicated and she is completely subjugated, Elsie's father pledges wholehearted, abiding love, and the story ends with Elsie denied nothing, basking in a bliss of plenitude, enjoying not only her father's love and desire but the luxury of material possessions and rich foods.

But the bulk of the book addresses how female submission to male violence is the avenue to such plenitude. An exemplary passage, midway through the book, links love with criticism, punishment, and severe prohibition. In it, Elsie has been subjected to the humiliating punishment of having her hand tied up as a sign of a malfeasance. When company arrives and she begs permission to leave the public space, Horace says, "I shall not let you go, if it were only to punish you for getting off the seat where I bid you stay, without permission. You will have to learn that I am to be obeyed at all times, and under all circumstances. Sit down, and don't dare to move again until I give you leave" (173–74). Forbidden to leave, Elsie gazes "with affectionate admiration into his face," thinking, "How handsome my papa is!" Finley adds, "She admired her father, and loved him, oh! *so* dearly" (172). After an hour on the stool, Elsie is given permission to go to bed, for which she thanks her father "in a humble little voice," promising, "I will try to be a good girl always." But when Horace refuses to kiss her goodnight, she grieves violently: "papa wouldn't kiss me! he said I was too naughty. O mammy! will he ever love me now?" (175). This story is about a girl's quest for love, and the only path to love imaginable in this sentimental story is perfect obedience. Because Elsie's lovelessness is attributed to the few remaining vestiges of her own will, fantasies of punishment are fantasies of desire, since they image the destruction of her self that will win her the permanent love she craves. Therefore, Horace's humiliating severity elicits from his daughter love, admiration, and an erotic admiration of his handsomeness and longing for his kisses.

This association of punishment with love is rooted in Finley's Puritanism. When Horace autocratically forbids Elsie to enter the meadow where the rest of the children play, his God-like refusal to explain what appears to be a whim frustrates both Elsie and the reader; but one morning Elsie descends to discover that he has killed a large, poisonous snake in that very meadow. Finley didactically articulates the moral: Horace always "has some good reason for his commands, even although he may not choose to explain it all" to her (104). His violence and cruelty are signs of his loving protection, and though submission to them is painful, it is less so when they are understood as manifestations of love. The other children in the book are represented as being deprived of the discipline that will make them "better" and therefore more lovable. Permissive love is not true love; severity is. The snake in the meadow is an obvious allusion to Satan in the Garden of Eden, making it clear that Horace is to be understood as God-like. Indeed, the entire tale is a Christian allegory, built on the traditional Christian promise: people anger God through their heretical resistance to his will, but if they relinquish all claims to self-will, they will be flooded with grace, "claimed" by God's abiding love, and transported to his heavenly home.

To be sure, on the surface Horace's severity toward Elsie is censured, and eventually he bitterly repents of it and begs God to forgive him. But who is more charismatic and attractive in the Elsie novels? Her stern, abusive father or her future gentle, kind husband, Edward Travilla? Horace's abusive streak is part of an undercurrent making him appear attractive, not because we love arrogance and cruelty, but because we love power. Like the prototypical male hero in the contemporary Harlequin-type novels Janice Radway discusses, the hero of the Elsie novels must be transformed from a tyrant into a strong and virile crusader for justice. But the initial streak of despotism is the key to his desirability, because it establishes his strength and vitality, which remain part of his permanent psychological profile. Goodness without power is boring. Even before Horace's change of heart, Finley paves the way for seeing his abusiveness as a sign of attractiveness by linking his severity to God's severity. It enables us to see in him "the lineaments of the divine Master." After all, his brother is equally cruel to Elsie, but lacking the allegorical connection to God, Arthur simply comes off as a bully, whereas Horace never does.

Horace Dinsmore illustrates the extent to which godly violence can lend an ecstatic air to a sentimental text. One day, furious that Elsie's copybook is blotted, Horace threatens what Elsie correctly suspects will be a whipping if she ever presents a blotted copybook again. She imagines this whipping with a mixture of dread and desire: "Oh, he couldn't, *couldn't* mean that! how could I ever bear it! and yet if it would make me really good, I think I wouldn't mind the pain" (184). It is not that Elsie wants to be hurt, but rather that she longs to be "really good," and she acquiesces to and even welcomes punishment if it will help her be what ideologies of true womanhood idealize. When Elsie's enemy Arthur frames her by blotting the copybook, Horace is overwhelmed with rage and "drag[s] her from the room, for he was terribly angry, his face fairly pale with passion," up to his bedroom, where he intends to inflict a "severe punishment." Crying that "Horace will half kill Elsie" (202), his sister Lora runs up to tell him the truth and, pushing open the door, sees a terrifying image: "he had a small riding whip in his hand, and Elsie stood beside him pale as death, too much frightened even to cry, and trembling so that she could scarcely stand" (203). In this tableau, Horace seems to demonstrate what Jonathan Edwards calls "the wrath of the infinite God" whom Elsie has offended "infinitely more than ever a stubborn rebel did his prince" ("Sinners in the Hands of an Angry God"). Like Edwards, Elsie dreads the punishment of the Father, but it nonetheless inflames her love for him, because it demonstrates his commitment to save her by taking whatever steps are necessary to make her "really good." Although she dreads punishment, she dreads lovelessness more, and she is convinced that her persistent will is the cause of her unlovability. So, the more Horace threatens her, the more she loves him.

The reader, I think, would feel a mixture of anger at Horace and horrified pity for Elsie. But those emotions are associated in the text with love and intimacy. After all, the scene just quoted gives rise to the following encounter:

> Elsie's papa took her in his arms, saying in loving, tender tones, "My poor little daughter! my own darling child! I have been cruelly unjust to you, have I not?"
>
> "Dear papa, you thought I deserved it," she said, with a burst of tears and sobs, throwing her arms around his neck, and laying her head on his breast.
>
> "Do you love me, Elsie, dearest?" he asked, folding her closer to his heart.
>
> "Ah! so very, *very* much! better than all the world beside. O papa! if you would only love me."
>
> "I do, my darling, my own precious child," he said, caressing her again and again. "I do love my little girl, although I may at times seem cold and stern; and I am more thankful than words can express that I have been saved from

punishing her unjustly. . . . ah! I fear it would have turned all her love for me into hatred; and justly too!"

"No, papa, oh! no, *no*! *nothing* could ever do that . . . . [S]he timidly pressed her quivering lips to his cheek. (204–5)

Elsie does not love her father's violence, but she loves him for the power he demonstrates in his willingness to inflict it. Love is overlaid on a framework of violence and pain.

Because of the associations of ecstasy with pain in the religious background to the book, Horace Dinsmore's violence—really his only distinguishing character trait—imparts a Gothic thrill to *Elsie Dinsmore*. His threats to whip his daughter or mutilate her (it is elsewhere jokingly suggested, for example, that he might cut her hand off) indicate a God-like intention to break down her resistance to grace, to force her to submit in order to receive what Abigail Bailey called the "oceans of bliss" associated with full submission to the chastening rod. The near-whipping of Elsie is a turning point in the tale, for it symbolically enacts Elsie's total annihilation and Horace's total willingness to effect that annihilation. Sentimental allusions to a God-like man willing to crush the female self appeal to the fearful but exciting desire to achieve the state of nonidentity that Bataille calls "continuity" and that is figured as "God the Father" here. As we have seen, sentimental fiction exploits terror, drawing upon a core scene of violence perpetrated upon an innocent and helpless victim, but fostering tears of pity over the inevitability and unmerited nature of the pain or annihilation.

Much of the godly violence in *Elsie Dinsmore* is tinged with eroticism because of a plethora of subtle and not-so-subtle cues that eroticize the relations between Elsie and her father. In an early scene, Horace Dinsmore gazes upon his daughter while she is horseback riding, "thinking of a time, some eight or nine years before, when he had assisted another Elsie [Elsie's mother] to mount her horse, and had ridden for hours at her side" (74). His daughter and wife bear the same name, and as he recalls his wife, "an emotion of tenderness began to spring up in [Horace's] heart," seemingly conflating paternal and marital love. On another occasion, after Elsie's will has been completely vanquished, Horace watches her read the Bible. "The darling!" he thinks, "she is lovely as an angel, and she is *mine*, mine only, mine own precious one; and loves me with her whole soul. Ah! how can I ever find it in my heart to be stern to her?" (228). Shortly thereafter, under the influence of this possessive desire, he hustles Elsie upstairs upon his return from a long trip, and they indulge the ecstasies of their reunion in his bedroom, in private. Subsequent books focus upon the conflicts between Horace and Elsie's suitors, culminating in overt eroticism in the fourth book of the

Elsie Dinsmore series. In one scene, Elsie "glide[s]" across the floor, "drop[s] gracefully at his feet" and, laying her hands on his knees, looks lovingly up at her father. He, "passing one hand caressingly over her shining hair," effuses, "My darling, how very, very lovely you are," adding, "there is no flaw in your beauty!" (*Elsie's Womanhood* 17). Moments before her wedding to his own closest friend, Horace bursts into Elsie's bedroom, banishing all others with "a slight motion of his hand." "'My darling!'" murmured the father in low, half tremulous accents; putting his arm around the slender waist. 'My beautiful darling! How can I give you to another?' and again and again his lips were pressed to hers in long passionate kisses" (123–24). His burning kisses are more the mark of erotic than paternal love.

In consolidating this pattern of eroticized paternal violence, *Elsie Dinsmore* is a masochistic influence upon its young readers, urging them to associate female submission with erotic pleasure. But its masochism may not be completely oppressive. It may indeed foster in female readers an attraction to a man who demonstrates his love and affection in acts of violence and discipline and in male readers a belief that they need to be authoritative in order to be attractive to women. But just because *Elsie Dinsmore* preaches the ecstasies of informed submission is no reason to think that its readers *accepted* that message. Indeed, the interplay between the text and a potentially resisting reader authorizes anger as well as passivity.[26] Berliner observes that the desire to express unacceptable anger is one of the principle causes of masochistic behavior: "Suffering is the weapon of the weak and unloved where undisguised aggression is dangerous. The masochistically exhibited suffering excuses the [masochist's] aggression, partially conceals it, serves its new repression, and disarms retaliation. Masochism is a way of hating without great risk" (331). Many recent studies of masochism have similarly addressed the way that fantasies of suffering constitute an indirect form of hostility for the person who cannot express anger directly.[27] In the eyes of a just God, the superego, or an implied reader, the victim of unmerited suffering looks blameless and pure, while his or her abuser looks detestable. Projection into that onlooker's mind affords indirect access to anger, since the onlooker speaks on behalf of the fantasizer, who can remain mute in accordance with social proscriptions against the expression of anger. Relating a case history in support of Berliner's thesis, psychologist Robert Stoller describes a masochistic female patient who routinely implied that his own behaviors were sadistic, and he realizes that being positioned as sadist made him feel manipulated by her and uncomfortable with what an implied onlooker might make of him. Masochism, he observes, was his patient's effort to express hostility indirectly.[28]

Elsie Dinsmore exemplifies the way that masochistic fantasies function as expressions of anger, aggression, and hatred. Horace Dinsmore—unlike God, whom he emulates—is so unjust in his punishments that his abuse affords Elsie the narcissistic pleasures of looking virtuous and innocent in the eyes of an implied third party. In one scene, for example, Horace naively believes a wicked schoolteacher's false accusations against Elsie: "'Is it *possible!*' said he frowning angrily, adding, 'I shall certainly punish you, for I will never allow anything of the kind.' As he spoke he picked up a small ruler that lay before him, at the same time taking Elsie's hand" (189). He decides instead to make Elsie drink a glass of water and eat a slice of chokingly dry bread. "'Now, Elsie,' said her father, in a tone of great severity, 'never *dare* to show me such a temper as this again; you will not escape so easily next time; remember I am to be obeyed *always*; and when I send you anything to eat, *you are to eat it.*'" Didactically, Finley states the obvious: "It had not been temper at all, and his unjust severity almost broke her heart; but she could not say one word in her defense." But the word "unjust" says it for Elsie; it authorizes frustration and anger toward the gullible father in the minds of both nineteenth- and twentieth-century readers, who know that innocent Elsie does not deserve what she gets. Words in Elsie's defense spontaneously arise in the mind of the reader, who completes the expression of anger on behalf of the virtuous heroine, who remains decorously, selflessly mute. In this way, the masochistic text authorizes anger in the very act of repudiating it.

This indirect expression of anger toward abusive authorities may well have played an important role in the popularity of the book, enabling readers to feel their own repressed anger toward oppression. And boys, I suspect, could take as much pleasure in that circuitous expression of rage over parental subjection as girls. This is the nasty side of sentimentality, the aspect that rouses the ire of sophisticated readers, who recognize the hypocrisy in its sentimental celebrations of paternal authority and unqualified affirmations of a conservative status quo. But we might also recognize in that hypocrisy a certain, albeit limited, avenue toward agency. Disabled perhaps, by Calvinist prohibitions upon the expression of anger and hostility, the sentimental author found in masochism an indirect avenue toward such expression.[29] And readers anxious to experience release from similar constraints found in masochism the pleasure of venting anger without having to face the causes and the consequences of that anger.

The use of suffering as a circuitous method of expressing anger does not undermine the argument that *Elsie Dinsmore* makes paternal violence look attractive; to the contrary, this circular expression of anger reinforces the construction of masochistic desire in the book. In a study of a book that resembles *Elsie Dinsmore* in this respect, James Machor points out that *The Wide, Wide World* repeatedly produces a rebellion in the reader's heart. "How *dare* Aunt Fortune be so cruel to poor Ellen? How *dare* John find fault in her?" But as he points out, rebellious thoughts such as these reinforce rather than subvert the dominant message, which is that all people harbor rebellious impulses against God's law and are in need of the Christian discipline the book advocates. The reader is positioned to say, "If that nearly perfect girl requires discipline—and I see that she does—do I not require even stricter discipline?" The fact that discipline, punishment, and surveillance are rendered so attractive in the book, and the pleasures associated with them are propped onto internal experiences of painful affect, completes the circle. "Indeed I do," the reader is prompted to think. "In fact, it is my most deeply felt desire."

*Three*_____

"An Ecstasy of Apprehension": The Erotics of Domination in *The Wide, Wide World*

"THOUGH we *must* sorrow, we must not rebel," Ellen Montgomery's mother admonishes in the opening of *The Wide, Wide World* (12). How does one come to terms with the inevitability of suffering and the prohibition of resistance? Mrs. Montgomery has the answer: "Remember, dear Ellen, God sends no trouble upon his children but in love" (12). If Ellen can learn to interpret suffering as a sign of God's love, then her suffering will be not only meaningful but rewarding. As it turns out, these precepts of providential Calvinism actually do determine Ellen's experiences of suffering. When Ellen's mother dies, Ellen's "brother" John takes up where she left off, reminding Ellen that "God loves every sinner . . . never better than when he sends bitter trouble on them" (349).

> Ellen listened, with her face hid on his shoulder.
> "Do you love Christ, Ellen?"
> She nodded, weeping afresh.
> "Do you love him less since he has brought you into this great sorrow?"
> "No," sobbed Ellen;—"*more*." (349)

The predominant discourses of her upbringing make Ellen feel love for the one who afflicts her.

Richard Brodhead implies as much in his influential article "Sparing the Rod." He demonstrates that Ellen is raised under the precepts of a "disciplinary intimacy" that intertwines love and coercion, and she therefore seeks love in the form of discipline and chastisement. "Made into a compulsive love seeker, Ellen shows how the child so determined becomes driven, by her heightened need to win and keep parental favor, not just to accept but really to *seek out* the authority of the parent's moral imperatives" (82, emphasis in original). Brodhead magnificently demonstrates that in *The Wide, Wide World*, modern forms of power "replace the old disciplinary mode with new technologies—less visible but more pervasive, less 'cruel' but more deeply controlling" (69). Yet he fails to address the more perverse implications of this argument: disciplinary intimacy can be erotic as well as affectionate, creating what Foucault calls sensual, "*perpetual spirals of power and pleasure*" between the disciplinarian and the subject (*History* 45, emphasis in original). As Foucault argues, the discourses constructing an individual's subjectivity play a role in shaping this sexualized response to authority.

In this chapter, I propose that Ellen's association of love with chastisement becomes eroticized through the twin discourses of providential Calvinism and true womanhood. True womanhood makes the most basic experiences of the body so problematic for Ellen that pain seems alluring, simply because it affords the basic experience of embodiment. Calvinism, on the other hand, provides a language in which pain is associated with divine love. John Humphreys, consistently associated with God, is in a prime position to benefit from this association of physical pain with divine love. Though, as Brodhead points out, Ellen appreciates John's nurturing, maternal qualities, she is, I propose, excited by his qualities of paternal violence—manifested in his horsewhipping, his authoritative, invasive gaze, and his many associations with a punitive God. Her attraction to his acts of domination is not purely that of a disciplinary subject for its mother; it is erotic.

In arguing that Ellen is masochistic, my argument would at first appear to be at odds with a great deal of recent criticism of books like *The Wide, Wide World*.[1] Nina Baym, for example, explicitly states that *The Wide, Wide World* is not masochistic since Warner never makes drudgery look attractive. Seemingly masochistic behavior such as Ellen's, she claims, should be recognized as "a moderate, or limited, or pragmatic feminism" (*Woman* 18). Numerous subsequent critical analyses have followed through on Baym's notion of a "pragmatic feminism," demonstrating ways that apparently masochistic behaviors in antebellum domestic fiction are comprehensible, functional, or even subversive. But the fact that such behaviors have practical motives and outcomes does not render them less masochistic. Masochists frequently take pleasure in precisely the emotional and practical benefits that these critics spotlight—a functional identity, decreased vulnerability to abuse, self-expression, and social empowerment—but they are people whose environments encourage them to see suffering, submission, and abjection as their best means of filling those needs, and who therefore associate suffering with pleasure.[2] One of the stunning features of *The Wide, Wide World* is that it makes its psychological universe so real that readers can easily recognize the cultural and discursive factors that make suffering a form of pleasure and power. We can *see* how suffering functions as a subversive, strategic, comforting, "limited or pragmatic feminism" for Ellen, licensing expressions of anger, constructing a related and functional identity, and producing a sense of intimacy, fulfillment, and purpose.

Indeed, even sexual masochism can be seen as a perverse but effective form of "moderate feminism" in *The Wide, Wide World*. In a culture in which womanhood is constructed through abjection of the female body, feeling pain is paradoxically a counterhegemonic activity; fantasies (as opposed to real suffering) are particularly ripe for such pleasures, since they express a desire for physical sensation without actually producing pain. Such fantasies, articulated in the voice of Calvinist sentimentalism, can function as expressions of a taboo desire for erotic pleasure.[3] In making available to antebellum authors a volatile and transgressive idiom of desire, sentimental masochism turns one of the greatest weapons of the patriarchy—the eroticization of domination—into a form of pleasure and agency.

Clearly, though, the erotics of domination is double-edged. Such tropes only enjoy expressive force because "true women's" desires and identities are deformed by patriarchal ideology: Ellen actually embraces the chastening rod that oppresses her because her desire has been influenced in such a way that she finds its blows exciting. While it is true that she asserts her will and desire in the closing pages of the book, her "will" is an oppressive longing to be absorbed into others and to be free of will. As Walter Benn Michaels has shown, it is perverse to celebrate all forms of freedom—when such a celebration includes the "freedom" of individuals to relinquish all of their rights or actually to give themselves to another person, such as a sadist or a tyrant. Such a celebration exemplifies the limitations of a "liberal" devotion to pure freedom.[4] If we are inclined to celebrate Ellen's choice to indulge her desire for domination as an expression of her individuality, we must recognize that her individuality itself may be repressive. Moreover, one young fan indicates a potentially disturbing legacy of *The Wide, Wide World* when she writes to Susan Warner, "How I loved little Ellen Montgomery. How I sympathized with her in all her troubles. How I like Mr. Van Brunt for being so kind to her, and wished I had a John as she had."[5] This young reader disturbingly suggests that while she and readers like her liked Mr. Van Brunt for his kindness, they *desired* John. Warner's portrayal of eroticized domination is double-edged; it negotiates oppressive cultural gender norms, but it also risks disseminating them among millions of readers, imparting to men a suspicion that women desire domination, and to women a belief that domination should be their own true desire.

The Making of a Masochist

As *The Wide, Wide World* reveals, one of the principal reasons that suffering and pain can appeal to the antebellum bourgeois woman is that it provides access to the body, an access that ideologies of true womanhood and Calvinism render otherwise problematic for women. The book endorses the bourgeois ideal of bodiless true womanhood, focusing upon the pleasures enjoyed by the woman who achieves that elevated but elusive state. Alice Humphreys is a "true woman." As we have seen, she is like a "transparent glazing . . . unknown it was she gave life and harmony to the whole" (205). In renouncing her status as a potentially self-fulfilling individual, becoming unknown and invisible, such a woman becomes the essential ingredient in everything, privileged to enjoy both self-esteem and widespread admiration. *The Wide, Wide World* demonstrates how abjection of the body is a central process in the construction of sentimental true womanhood. Once Ellen achieves the noncorporeal ideal, her education is complete, but so is her story; only in the last few pages of the book do we feel that she has completely subjugated her corporeal self. The final sentence points toward what Warner represents as an idyllic future, in which Ellen leaves Scotland and goes "back to spend her life with the friends and guardians she best loved, and to be to them . . . 'the light of the eyes.'" Her education complete, Ellen has achieved the paradoxical properties of light: she is visible but insubstantial. She will "be to them," her identity contingent upon others whose vision she can enhance and whose being she can augment. Standing in ironic counterpoint to Emerson's transparent eyeball, the true woman illuminates the vision of others, exists solely through enhancing others' lives.

For the girl who wants to be insubstantial, like "light," the fact of her own embodiment is threatening. In keeping with her Calvinist background, Warner posits the human body as unreliable at best. In the opening pages of the book, Ellen tells her mother, "Why, mamma,—in the first place I trust every word you say—entirely—I know nothing could be truer; if you were to tell me black is white, mamma, I should think my eyes had been mistaken. Then everything you tell or advise me to do, I know it is right, perfectly. And I always feel safe when you are near me, because I know you'll take care of me. And I am glad to think . . . I needn't manage myself, because I know I can't; and if I could, I'd rather you would, mamma" (18). Given Ellen's inability to trust her own senses, it is not surprising that she feels unable to take care of herself—if her most fundamental physical experiences are unreliable, how can she have any basis for making decisions at all?[6] Her suspicion of her own senses and judgment leads even further: even if Ellen *could* take care of herself, she would *rather* be taken care of. Granted, Ellen is only a child here, but her words exemplify a pattern of female dependence that resembles the ideal of the feme-covert, both in its advocacy of female subordination to male subjectivity and in its implication that a woman cannot trust her own body and its sensory input. Even when she has grown up, she fantasizes about John's doing her thinking for her; at the end of the book, we find her deciding how to handle a particular situation not by determining what seems best to her but rather by thinking, "I know what [John] would tell me if he was here, and I'll try to do it" (519). It is indeed true that Warner values female intellectual development; as Lora Romero and Nancy Armstrong point out, domestic ideology arose in reaction against the upper-class commodification of women as purely ornamental objects, and Warner's middle-class domesticity represents women as intelligent creatures with minds hungering for historical, literary, scientific, and theological learning. Nonetheless, Ellen's intellectual training consistently stresses not independent thinking but mimicry of the thoughts of her superiors. Even in adulthood, she requires others to tell her the meaning of her knowledge.

When Ellen insists that she would rather *not* take care of herself, she affirms not only the basic principles of coverture but also the basic principles of Calvinism: "it is just so; it is *just* so: that I wish you to trust in God," Mrs. Montgomery replies (18). Ellen's inability to trust the data afforded by her senses accords with the Puritan notion of the depravity of the senses, which views the information the senses provide as potentially useful if interpreted by reason, but likely to foster a false sense of self-reliance that will lead one away from an appropriate dependence upon God. This basic Puritan (antisentimental) suspicion about the body as a source of knowledge is vividly reinforced in one episode occurring roughly halfway through the novel, when Ellen is wandering around a greenhouse, indulging her passion for flowers. "From the moment the sweet aromatic smell of the plants had greeted her she had been in a high state of delight. . . . She could hardly leave a superb cactus, in the petals of which there was such a singular blending of scarlet and crimson as almost to dazzle her sight; and if the pleasure of smell could intoxicate she would have *reeled* away from a luxuriant daphne odorata in full flower, over which she feasted for a long time" (324, emphasis in original). Left to interpret material phenomena on her own, Ellens tends toward a dangerous sensuality; she is "intoxicated" by a floral "feast." The description of the encounter emphasizes the voluptuous enticement of the carnal world, which Warner characterizes with words like "delight," "dazzled," "pleasure," "reeled away," and "luxuriant." It also indicates the dangers of such carnal experiences: Ellen is a slave to these scarlet and crimson pleasures, so "high" and "reel[ing]" that she can "hardly leave."

This experience in the greenhouse affords an important object lesson in basic Puritan doctrine for Ellen: while God sends physical pleasures, such as flowers, as emblems of the better world to come, it is dangerously easy for the would-be Christian to focus upon these signs rather than on the things they represent. Ellen is so intoxicated by the signifier that she fails to turn her mind to the signified. When John joins her as she admires a white camellia and asks, "What does that flower make you think of, Ellen?" she cannot answer. " 'I don't know,' said Ellen,—'I couldn't think of any thing but itself' " (324). Ellen does not know how to "think" about a flower, which she sees as only "itself." Calvinism suggests that this is precisely the problem with sensory data derived from the material world; they may lead to a damnably carnal fixation upon things themselves—what Harriet Newell called "the glittering toys of the world"—instead of on an appropriate, spiritual attraction to their essential, higher beauty. John, however, models the appropriate response to the flower: " 'It reminds me of what I ought to be— and of what I shall be if I ever see heaven; it seems to me the emblem of a sinless pure spirit,—looking up in fearless spotlessness. Do you remember what was said to the old Church of Sardis?—'Thou hast a few names that have not defiled their garments; and they shall walk with me in white, for they are worthy.' " The tears rushed to Ellen's eyes, she felt she was so very unlike this" (324–25). Ellen had just been reveling in the cactus flower's dazzlingly scarlet and crimson petals, so it is not surprising that she feels her garments are not white; she is dangerously inclined to defile them, for she has not yet learned how to avoid the snares of the material realm through a spiritualized hermeneutic that ignores the materiality of a thing itself and refers everything to a spiritual meaning. "How much you see in every thing, that I do not see at all," she tells John more than once (481). Such experiences teach Ellen to beware of her own body; its sensations must be received cautiously and interpreted carefully—according to principles dictated by someone else.[7]

Of course, suspicion of the senses is fundamental to the Christian tradition, but such a suspicion is particularly important for women invested in the ideology of true womanhood, which places a high value on woman's religiosity, purity, and ethereality. True womanhood frequently seems to suggest that a woman's role is to embody purity, to avoid all situations in which physical experiences might challenge her religious principles. Men must confront the evils of life, while for a woman, as Alice puts it: "when [evil] is forced upon you, see as little of it as you can, and forget as soon as you can what you see" (184). For a woman, a good way to avoid contact with corrosive materiality is to perform tasks that are clean and relatively immobilizing, such as sewing invisible seams, embroidering dainty objects like eyeglass cases and collars, making perfect tea and toast, and drawing copies of others' artwork.

This is not to say that all women's work is simply ornamental in the novel. After all, Aunt Fortune is a productive landowner who churns, spins, preserves food, washes, and runs a farm. And the "bee" scenes foreground the emotionally fulfilling and useful aspects of female labor.

Indeed, from such a perspective, *The Wide, Wide World* could be seen as a celebration of women's productivity. But while Warner does represent the value of working-class women's labor, her primary emphasis is upon the *higher* meaning enjoyed by middle-class women who attain the status of true womanhood. Again, it might be objected that even Alice—the incarnation of true womanhood—performs the important labor of sewing, leading prayer sessions, and cooking. But although Warner celebrates that labor, there's a curiously unlabored air about it as Warner describes it. The Humphreys' two-kitchen system provides an apt metaphor for the clean, pure labor of a true woman. In describing her kitchen, Alice tells Ellen: "I have been in many a parlour that I do not like as well. Beyond this is a lower kitchen where Margery [the servant] does all her rough work; nothing comes up the steps that lead from that to this but the very nicest and daintiest of kitchen matters" (167). Generally parlors are "for show," and in her parlor-kitchen, Alice engages in relatively decorative work, the "daintiest of kitchen matters," while the "rough" work is performed by servants like Margery or working-class women like Aunt Fortune, who "cruelly" dyes Ellen's dainty white stockings an easy-to-wash gray. In her parlor-kitchen, Alice incarnates an industrious purity; though she does roll up her sleeves, asking, "Did you think cakes were made without hands?" hers come in contact only with substances preselected in order to keep her untainted.

Underlying the bourgeois ideals of noncorporeality and laborless labor in the novel is the ideal of passionlessness. At the beginning of the book, Warner writes that Ellen's "passions were by nature very strong, and by education very imperfectly controlled; and time, 'that rider that breaks youth,' had not as yet tried his hand upon her" (11). The novel insists that the passions are *the* problem, both physically and spiritually. Early in the novel, Dr. Green tells Ellen that the one thing she can do to help her mother is make perfect toast, warning that she "must be very careful—if that piece of toast of yours should chance to get burned, one of these fine evenings, I won't answer for the consequences" (19). Such a warning is presumably a friendly effort to afford the little girl a sense of agency in the face of agonizing loss. But just five pages earlier, Ellen had burned a piece of toast in a fit of passion: "she began to think . . . the sickness of heart quite overcame her; she could not go on. Toast and fork and all dropped from her hand into the ashes; and . . . she burst into a fit of sorrow" (14). The effect of the doctor's warning that burnt toast could lead to illness, following so close upon the heels of Ellen's "fit" is to imply that Ellen's passion is partly responsible for her mother's illness. Indeed, the doctor observes, "I'm afraid you haven't taken proper care of her; she looks to me as if she had been too much excited. I've a notion she has been secretly taking half a bottle of wine, or reading some furious kind of a novel . . . she *must not* be excited,—you must take care that she is not,—it isn't good for her. You mustn't let her talk much, or laugh much, or cry at all, on any account" (19). Dr. Green offers the little girl possibilities for meaningful work, but those possibilities only involve perfect self-control, and the stakes for failure are high (he cannot "answer for the consequences"). This is indeed a double-edged sense of agency: Ellen can do next to nothing; the only thing she can actually do is try to help her mother not feel by concentrating upon having no feelings herself.

A sense of power and meaning contingent upon perfectly controlling the body and its feelings is an invitation for masochism, because perfect self-control is impossible, as the always-already-burnt-toast incident suggests. It creates a built-in sense of guilt, for Ellen has few avenues of agency *apart* from self-control open to her, leaving her prone to fear of a mistake. But she has abundant motives for being deeply invested in *trying* to achieve perfect self-control. In fact, that is her major ongoing effort throughout the book. Because Ellen is committed to controlling herself and preventing any spontaneous eruptions of passion, she feels a strong attraction to people who are willing to offer assistance with the task of self-discipline, while people who indulge her are doing her no favor. Dr. Green, for example, is the object of Warner's admiration and affection precisely because he advocates self-restraint and goes so far as to lie to the Montgomery women in his effort to help them discipline themselves. He asks Ellen:

> "[W]hat do you think of this fine scheme of mine . . . of sending this sick lady over the water to get well? . . . "
>
> "*Will* it make her quite well, do you think, sir?" asked Ellen, earnestly.
>
> "'Will it make her well!' to be sure it will; do you think I don't know better than to send people all the way across the ocean for nothing? Who do you think would want Dr. Green, if he sent people on wild-goose chases in that fashion?" . . .
>
> "Poor woman!" said the doctor to himself as he went downstairs (he was a humane man). "I wonder if she'll live till she gets to the other side!" (19)

So why *does* the doctor send Mrs. Montgomery all the way across the ocean for nothing, on a wild-goose chase, which he himself states would be inappropriate? Why not let her stay and die at home? And—an even more interesting question—why does Warner parenthetically comment that "he was a humane man," going out of her way to praise the kindness of someone who deliberately misleads Ellen?

In a sense, Dr. Green is "humane" simply because, unlike Captain Montgomery, he sympathizes with suffering women. But there is also, in the world of *The Wide, Wide World*, something admirable in the doctor's misleading words and actions, which manipulate Ellen's emotions in such a way as to prevent a useless experience of violent passion. Evidently, she is not to feel what is actually happening to her, presumably because passion is bad for her. Like Captain Montgomery, Dr. Green wants the parting of mother and daughter to be as passionless as possible. In this scene, Warner tacitly concedes that women need to be controlled for their own good. The admirable men are those who do it with love.

The authoritarian doctor who provided scripts by which women were to live—of which Dr. Green is an example—was a popular figure of female desire in the nineteenth century. As ideologies of "true womanhood" took greater and greater hold in Victorian America, the popularity of the figure of the doctor increased. Dr. S. Weir Mitchell, whom Charlotte Perkins Gilman rendered notorious for his treatment of hysterical and neurasthenic women, exemplifies the esteemed, domineering, patriarchal doctor. Like Warner's Dr. Green, Dr. Mitchell argued that women needed to control their emotions and passions or they would succumb to internal enemies that would attack them in the form of nerves or even mental illness. When a woman "yield[s] where she should not," he wrote, she "acquire[s] within herself a host of enemies" (131–32). Mitchell reiterates the longstanding notion that a woman is engaged in a lifelong war with her internal demons, and he represents himself as a hero whose willingness to use a strong arm is exactly what women want and need. When a woman is overcome by her passions, he says, "It then becomes the business of her physician to tell her what is real, what is unreal, what must be respected, what must be overcome or fought. . . . The hour for absolute trust has arrived, and she must now believe in her adviser, or, if she cannot, she must acquire one in whom her belief will be entire and unquestioning. . . . You tell her that she must disregard her own feelings. She credits you with knowing, and so wins her fight"(131). This doctrine echoes ideals expressed in *The Wide, Wide World*: a woman is to believe what she is told and must distrust her own feelings. She—and her unreliable feelings—are her own worst enemy. Dr. F. C. Skey, president of the Royal College of Surgeons of England, goes even further, explicitly promoting heroic sadism for doctors treating genteel women: "Ridicule to a woman of sensitive mind, is a powerful weapon . . . but there is not an emotion equal to fear and the threat of personal chastisement. . . . they will listen to the voice of authority."[8] Like Mitchell, Skey attributes hysteria to a woman's indulgence of her feelings and believes that she can regain health only by relinquishing herself to the authority of her doctor. What women really want, he indicates, is a domineering, condescending doctor willing to take control.

Such condescending behaviors won doctors considerable love and gratitude among female patients. Mitchell claimed that after a doctor has cured a woman by helping her with the task of self-control, "nothing seems easier than with . . . a chorus of gratitude in the woman's soul, to show her how she has failed, and to make clear to her how she is to regain and preserve domination over her emotions" (8). And in fact, many women did feel gratitude and love for the authoritative, firm doctor who was armed with knowledge to help them with their war with their bodies.[9] One patient wrote Mitchell, "Whilst laid by the heels in a country-house with an attack of grippe, also an invalid from gastric affliction, the weary eyes of a sick woman fall upon your face in the *Century* of this month—a thrill passes through me—at last I saw the true physician."[10] As this letter makes clear, the relationship of heroic doctor and grateful patient had the potential to inspire love and perhaps even eros: a "thrill passes through" the woman, whose self-representation as a passive and defeated "sick woman" makes "the true physician" appear more vigorously virile by contrast. Because she understands herself as a victim, an object in need of management—going so far as to speak of herself in the third person—she idealizes a doctor renowned for taking control of women's moral flaws and helping them restrain themselves.[11]

The Wide, Wide World, written a half-century earlier, locates the roots of such women's attitudes in religious ideologies. The heroism of a Dr. Green or a Dr. Mitchell derives from his association with the ultimate heroic sadist, God, the heavenly physician who requires his patient's total submission as a precondition for his healing. Mrs. Montgomery tells Ellen, "from the hand that wounds, seek the healing. He wounds that he *may* heal. He does not afflict willingly. Perhaps he sees, Ellen, that you would never seek him while you had me to cling to" (41). Certainly we see that kind Dr. Green does not afflict willingly. Warner glamorizes and idealizes the relationship of domination and submission between doctors and female patients in keeping with her religiously determined belief that salvation requires submission. She appreciates the kindness of a man who lies to women for their own good because she knows how easily women can succumb to addictive carnal pleasures, and consequently lose access to the status of true womanhood and the pleasures and powers accruing to such status—as well as access to heaven.

The pernicious ideal of female bodilessness, as seen in *The Wide, Wide World*, gives rise to an equally pernicious ideal of female contingency. These are the two principal ideologies promoting a masochistic attraction to domination in *The Wide, Wide World*. Exemplified in the grammar of Warner's phrase "be to them," and in Frances Cobbe's theory of woman-as-adjective, contingency strips a woman of subjectivity, representing her as an object who only finds an identity in relation to someone endowed with subjectivity. Contingency is different from intersubjectivity, a term that considers a person's identity as being defined through relations with others. Intersubjectivity denotes an awareness that can lead to a compassionate, progressive, and spiritual sense of the self in relation to the rest of the world. Contingency, by contrast, is a state in which one has no sense of self at all apart from that conferred by others, a conviction that one's personal development and self-realization are irrelevant, that one exists only through and *for* others. Intersubjectivity has appropriately been celebrated in recent feminist scholarship as a feminine trait that offers a positive alternative to what it posits as "male," "Western" individualism, but overemphasizing the limitations of individuation has drawn attention away from the traumatic nature of maturation into conventional female identity in nineteenth and twentieth-century American culture.[12] In a state of contingency, in which relatedness involves subordination, what Jessica Benjamin calls "mutuality" degenerates into a relation of master to slave, of domination and subordination.

The Wide, Wide World emphasizes less the mutuality of intersubjectivity than it does the domination and subordination of contingency. The contingency of Ellen's mature identity is unbalanced and excessive. From childhood, as we have seen, Ellen learns to distrust her own senses, her own interpretations, and her own desires, deferring in all things to her mother. In her last weeks with her mother, Ellen receives a crash course in independence, but the skills she learns emphasize not problem solving, self-reliance, and tenacity, such as a boy might learn, but rather how to be contingent: to submit when the heart rebels; to display appropriately self-effacing manners that will elicit the help of others; to intuit others' thoughts and assume them as her own. When Mrs. Montgomery takes Ellen to buy a Bible, she pretends to allow Ellen to make the decision on her own, but the shopping lesson actually trains Ellen how to figure out what others think through indirect cues and to make her decision by guessing what they would have her do. Responding to her mother's hesitation to approve one of the Bibles that Ellen chooses, Ellen asks, "you don't advise me, then, to take this little beauty?" When her mother answers, "Judge for yourself; I think you are old enough," Ellen says, "I know what you think, though, mamma, and I dare say you are right, too; I won't take it, though it's a pity" (31). In such a scene, even though supposedly Ellen's independent subjectivity and her mature judgment are being affirmed ("Judge for yourself"), in fact, subjectivity is being located outside of herself ("I know what you think"), and she is acquiring a contingent identity. The lesson demonstrates to Ellen that she *cannot* judge for herself, that her best hope lies in intuiting what others think and pretending that she has made the choice herself, either through good judgment or good taste.

Throughout her life, Ellen continues to resort to mind reading in order to figure out what she is *supposed* to think, rather than gradually learning to consider what she *does* think. When Alice Humphreys asks Ellen, "Have you a fancy for curiosities?" Ellen unenthusiastically responds, "Yes, ma'am, I believe so" (163). But Alice's indirect cues indicate that Ellen did not accurately describe her own taste:

> "Believe so!—not more than that?. . ."
>
> "I don't know, ma'am," said Ellen. "I never was where I could get them."
>
> "Weren't you! Poor child! Then you have been shut up to brick walls and paving-stones all your life?"
>
> "Yes, ma'am, all my life."
>
> "But now you have seen a little of the country,—don't you think you shall like it better?"
>
> "Oh, a great deal better!"
>
> "Ah, that's right. I am sure you will." (163)

Alice makes it easy for Ellen to realize what her taste is supposed to be. Although the period in which she was "shut up" with her mother is actually Ellen's private memory of Eden, by the end of the conversation, Ellen realizes that she was a "poor child," that the out-of-doors is now to be preferred; henceforth, she dutifully loves nature. In a subsequent lesson in taste formation, Alice is more direct, and Ellen is not so foolhardy as to consult her own inclinations: "'[W]ait till you see the hemlock branches bending with a weight of snow, and then if you don't say the winter is beautiful I'll give you up as a young lady of bad taste.' 'I dare say I shall,' said Ellen; 'I am sure I shall like what you like'" (185). Such scenes do not simply evince a healthy relatedness, as feminist critics influenced by object-relations models of subjectivity have suggested, for underlying these frantic quests for identity is a traumatic loss of subjectivity. It is no surprise that people think Ellen has such good taste: they consistently see their own reflected back from her.

The scene in which Ellen is torn from her mother's arms foregrounds not only the fact that Ellen inherits from her mother a contingent identity but the fact that this contingency is the basis of a masochistic erotic desire on her part. When Captain Montgomery informs Ellen that she must be separated from her mother the next morning, Ellen displays "a look of blank astonishment at first . . . but very soon indeed that changed into one of blank despair." Because he is a boor, Ellen's father takes comfort from Ellen's passivity, but her mother and the reader recognize in Ellen's blankness not resignation but terror, for she is being deprived not only of her mother's love but of her own interiority. Her training thus far has emphasized the suppression of all inner promptings and the assumption of the ideas and perceptions of others, her mother being the most influential of these. Separation is therefore almost lethal, and not only for Ellen but for Mrs. Montgomery, who also acquires subjectivity vicariously from the relationship:

> [Mrs. Montgomery] said not a word, but opened her arms to receive her little daughter; and with a cry of indescribable expression Ellen sprang upon the bed, and was folded in them. But then neither of them spoke or wept. What could words say? Heart met heart in that agony, for each knew all that was in the other. No,—not quite all. Ellen did not know that the whole of bitterness death had for her mother she was tasting then. But it was true. Death had no more power to give her pain after this parting should be over. His after-work,—the parting between soul and body,—would be welcome rather; yes, very welcome. Mrs. Montgomery knew it all well. She knew this was the last embrace between them. She knew it was the very last time that dear little form would ever lie on her bosom, or be pressed in her arms; and it almost seemed to her that soul and body must part company too when they should be rent asunder. (63)

Living for and through others, the "true woman" finds that separation entails "the whole bitterness of death"—the death of the social self—more powerfully than it would for a man in her culture. Physical death is appropriately seen as "after-work," particularly given the relative insignificance of the body to "true womanhood." There are pleasures in this anguish of separation, however, which will ultimately play into the construction of a masochistic eroticism on Ellen's part. The moment of separation, while painful, offers a rich consolation: the extremity of agony enables those who are being separated to experience a wonderfully complete union ("Heart met heart . . . for each knew all that was in the other"). As we have seen, "Sentimentalism is a manifestation of the belief in or yearning for consonance—or even unity—of principle and purpose" (Barnes, *States* 597). This scene in which Ellen and her mother are torn from each other illustrates the way that sentimentalism itself promotes such unity through pain, which paradoxically enables people to experience unity and separation simultaneously. Released by the supposed universality of that anguish from the loneliness of individuality and from the detachment of conventional social intercourse, selves in pain seem to flow into and out of each other freely through identification with each other's pain. As Adam Smith puts it, in sympathy, "one enters, as it were, into [another's] body." For a moment, Ellen and her mother are one being, and as they lie in bed together, entwined in each other's arms, they are perfectly united. They epitomize the pleasures of sentimental suffering. The paradox of unity-in-separation explains one of the great pleasures that sentimental fiction imagines: pain unites people, transcending individuality and bypassing conventional and imperfect forms of communication, such as language.

This loving union is ruptured through a female version of the classic oedipal paradigm:

> Not many minutes had passed in this sad embrace, and no word had yet been spoken, no sound uttered, except Ellen's first inarticulate cry of mixed affection and despair, when Captain Montgomery's step was again heard slowly ascending the stairs. "He is coming to take me away!" thought Ellen; and in terror lest she should go without a word from her mother, she burst forth with, "Mamma! Speak!"
>
> A moment before, and Mrs.Montgomery could not have spoken. But she could now; and as clearly and calmly the words were uttered as if nothing had been the matter, only her voice fell a little toward the last.
>
> "God bless my darling child! and make her his own,—and bring her to that home where parting cannot be."
>
> Ellen . . . burst into uncontrollable weeping . . . she clung to her mother with a force that made it a difficult task for her father to remove her. (63–64)

A forbidding father, what Lacan calls the "*non*-du-père," interposes itself into the closed, maternal dyad incestuously intertwined in bed. But Ellen does not receive the consolation of the "*nom*-du-père" (a meaningful identity as a subject in a symbolic social system) that the oedipal boy in similar circumstances would acquire. To be sure, like the boy, Ellen seeks in language a consolation for the loss of her mother: "[I]n terror lest she should go without a word from her mother, [Ellen] burst forth with, 'Mamma! speak!'" (63). As she enters a realm of existence independent of her mother, the paternal realm, she pleads for language to compensate for her mother's absence, for a linguistic symbol of the transcendent communion idealized in the wordless mother-child bond. Language is therefore both a symbol of maternal presence and a tragic sign that that bond is irrecoverable. "A moment before, and Mrs. Montgomery could not have spoken," Warner writes, recognizing that language would have destroyed the perfect heart-to-heart union she and her daughter enjoyed. However, after the moment of separation, symbolic communication is no longer superfluous but essential. Words cannot *constitute* the affectional bond (which was perfect during the silent moment when agonized heart met heart), but they can *represent* connection and mutuality and approximate the undivided union of profound heart-to-heart communication in which "neither of them spoke [yet] . . . each knew all that was in the other." Like Lacan, Warner represents language as a means of compensating for the loss of maternal presence. It is both pain (proof of her absence) and pleasure (symbol of her presence).

The language that Mrs. Montgomery offers in response to Ellen's plea for words to compensate for her own lack deprives Ellen of the consolation of subjectivity that the oedipal boy gains at the moment of separation from his mother: "God bless my darling child! and make her his own,—and bring her to that home where parting cannot be." Mrs. Montgomery does not say "you" to Ellen; rather the grammar of her address determines Ellen's new identity as not-subject, as grammatical object contingent upon one who will "make her his own." Whereas a boy's acquisition of language affords him the compensation of meaningful subjectivity within the symbolic social system, Ellen is neither an "I" nor a "you" but rather a "her," or worse yet, "his own." The words that define Ellen's place in the symbolic, and which structure her self-conception, not only strip her of subjectivity but dictate the terms of her desire. While the boy's desire—also born in this moment—would, according to a Freudian paradigm, be for a symbolic substitute for his mother, Mrs. Montgomery determines that Ellen's desire is to be desired, and thereby to acquire vicarious subjectivity. The mother plays an important role in helping her daughter acquire agency, but the agency she teaches is that achieved through vicarious subjectivity and passive obedience to patriarchal law. The relationship Mrs. Montgomery hopes to initiate is between Ellen and God, but the language also lends itself to a more earthly relationship between Ellen and a man who will "make her his own" and "take her to his home"—a husband. Husbands are intimately linked with the divine Master because of their privileged access to the *nom*-du-père, which is off-limits for objects in the symbolic realm. While God may eventually take Ellen to his heavenly home, a man will first take Ellen to his own earthly home. The scene links Ellen's religious desire with her sexual desire; ecstasies of fusion and security await her once she has been possessed by God, and by a Godlike husband. If separation from her mother marks the birth of her sexuality as well as her sociolinguistic identity, the language of this birth propels her toward subordination.[13]

This moment of separation not only imposes upon Ellen a grammar of domination but teaches her an object lesson in the pleasures of pain. Separation creates a heart-to-heart transcendent fusion, but it predicates that ecstasy upon pain, since the ecstatic interpenetration of mother and child arises only by concentrating upon its impending loss. The pain of imminent *dis*union creates the transcendent union. Merging is achieved only through suffering, and thus this moment that witnesses the birth of Ellen's desire also witnesses the birth of her association of pleasure with pain. Ellen intuitively understands the religious dictum that affliction is a sign of love, for she has actually had a basic experience of ecstasy achieved through agonizing suffering, and it occurred at a crucial moment, the birth of her independent, sexual self.

This pivotal experience represents the culmination of Ellen's formation as a sexual masochist, and it puts her in a good position to be erotically attracted to John Humphreys, not *despite* the fact that he is a renowned horsewhipper (while she herself has been compared to a horse in need of breaking), but because of it. She has been educated to seek a strong man in whom to find vicarious subjectivity, one who will help her regulate her unruly passions, and if his discipline is painful, that is all the better, since Ellen empirically knows that pain can produce pleasure. The first introduction of John notes that he is "handsome enough" and bestows upon Alice a "look of love," but also that "one look into his eyes" reveals him as "a person to be feared;—there was no doubt of that" (275). This is, of course, attractive for the little girl seeking not indulgence but severity. Later, Warner explicitly identifies John as Ellen's "master": "Ellen had an excellent lesson, and her master took care it should not be an easy one" (350–51). When Ellen's mother finally dies, Ellen not surprisingly plunges into a deep melancholy, remaining without vitality until John cures her through an exacting course of intellectual and physical training. Warner points out that "Alice had endeavoured to bring this about before, but fruitlessly. What she asked of her Ellen indeed *tried* to do; what John told her *was done*" (350–51). John succeeds where Alice cannot because Alice was only a substitute mother, while Ellen has been trained to seek one "to" whom she can "be"; and lacking the authority of the "*nom*-du-père," Alice lacks the subjectivity that will enable Ellen to come alive. Once John assumes the central position in Ellen's life, she becomes, as it were, a heliotropic plant, drooping when separated from him and coming back to life when he appears. Sophia remarks, "Did you observe [Ellen] last night, Matilda, when John Humphreys came in? . . . I saw the colour come and her eye sparkle . . . her eye went straight as an arrow to where he was standing" (476). Ellen literally "live[s] upon" her conversations with John. Earlier, she had lived upon her conversations with her mother, but now that she has been ejected into the symbolic realm as an adjective in search of a noun, only a man can play this vivifying role for her (564).

Alice's death symbolically completes Ellen's protracted separation from her mother and her development of an identity within a symbolic realm structured according to language and law. A scene immediately following Alice's death reiterates the changes in Ellen's status from one half of a dyad to an object in a patriarchal system, a change that occurred in the momentous maternal separation scene. In this second scene, Ellen rushes away to a hidden mountain retreat to be alone, but John finds her and offers words of religious consolation:

> With an indescribable air of mingled tenderness, weariness, and sorrow, she slowly rose from her seat and put both her arms round the speaker's neck. Neither said a word; but to Ellen the arm that held her was more than all words; it was the dividing line between her and the world,—on this side every thing, on that side nothing.
>
> No word was spoken for many minutes.
>
> "My dear Ellen . . . let sorrow but bring us closer to him. Dear Alice is well—she is well,—and if *we* are made to suffer, we know and we love the hand that has done it,—do we not Ellie?" (443)

In this exchange between Ellen and John, as in that between Ellen and her mother, "no word was spoken," and the two share a moment whose intimate silence bonded by a common suffering invites a comparison and contrast with the perfect union Ellen had shared with her mother. Warner does not say that "heart met heart"; rather, she says that "the arm that held her was more than all words." If the moment transcends language, it is because John's arm brings meaning to it; if they are experiencing an ecstasy of merging, it is not a mutual merge, but a dissolution of her being into his. Their intimate communication is regulated by the symbolic value of John's arm, and John is not a substitute for lost Alice and lost Mrs. Montgomery, but rather a representative of paternal law. He is Ellen's conduit to merging and intimacy, but that merge is symbolic and regulated. As "the dividing line between her and the world," John's arm is an image, not of plenitude, but rather of a division that structures Ellen's social existence through difference and symbolism.

As that which structures division, John's arm has the central organizing power that Lacan ascribes to the phallus in Western culture. It symbolizes the divisions that make all meanings within the symbolic realm, and the law that governs exchange and determines identities. Indeed, like the Lacanian phallus, John's arm seems to be a synecdoche for God's law, for the passage represents God's law as a scourging hand: "if we are made to suffer, we know and we love the hand that has done it." John's arm brings meaning to Ellen's life in the same way that God's law does, and he is linked to God through the arm-hand connection. Ellen does indeed love God, and she also loves his earthly representative, this young clergyman. John tells Ellen to repeat from the very depths of her suffering, "O, how *love I thy Law*"; when she does so, she seems to be addressing both God and John (352, emphasis in original). And she demonstrates her love by embracing the punishments that both inflict.

This scene suggests how John's associations with God make his religiously sanctioned punishments attractive to Ellen. Later, example after example indicates that she thinks of her own erotic desire in terms of punishment because of the connection between John's chastening arm and God's divine law. Consider an experience she has during her Scottish exile, when a glass of wine forced upon her by her relatives inspires a dream of John: "John was a king of England, and standing before her in regal attire. She offered him, she thought, a glass of wine, but raising the sword of state, silver scabbard and all, he with a tremendous swing of it dashed the glass out of her hands; and then as she stood abashed, he went forward with one of his old grave kind looks to kiss her" (520). John's chastening arm is an object of Ellen's romantic interest: the dream links his kisses with the chastisement his arm inflicts. The glass of wine represents the myriad forces conspiring to weaken Ellen's Christian virtue when she is separated from John, and her fantasy that he uses the phallic "sword of state" to abash her, combined with the expectation of his kisses, suggests that his association with discipline and chastisement is eroticized in Ellen's imagination.

The Calvinist environment surrounding Ellen strengthens her inclination to think of her romantic desire in terms of chastisement. As we have seen, the notions of divine constraint and punishment were metonymically linked in Calvinist discourse with the ecstasies associated with submission to him. The many hymns that Warner incorporates in *The Wide, Wide World*, such as the one Mr. Marshman directs Ellen to read, reiterate this familiar association between God's disciplinary punishment and the bliss of religious rapture:

Behold the Saviour at thy door,
He gently knocks,—has knock'd before,—
Has waited long,—is waiting still,—
You treat no other friend so ill.

Oh, lovely attitude!—he stands
With open heart and outstretch'd hands.
Oh, matchless kindness!—and he shows
This matchless kindness to his foes.

Admit him—for the human breast
Ne'er entertain'd so kind a guest.
Admit him—or the hour's at hand
When at *his* door, denied, you'll stand.

Open my heart, Lord, enter in;
Slay every foe, and conquer sin.

Here now to thee I all resign
My body, soul, and all are thine. (75)

This hymn links divine intimacy to the violent assault that is a necessary
prelude to its attainment. But it expresses this linkage in the sentimental
language that increasingly dominated American Protestantism in the
nineteenth century. Sentimentally, the hymn anthropomorphizes God
with such words as "gently" and "kindness," and a "lovely attitude,"
which invite the Christian to experience the maternal intimacy that is
evoked in the domestic trope of heart-as-house. But the tenderness of
God in the first three stanzas is overlaid onto a Calvinist discourse of
wrath in the fourth: God can wear the maternal Bushnellian face of a
friend, but he can also wear the Edwardsian face of an enraged paternal
Jehovah locking his own door. The hymn tacitly concedes that though
people have every reason to love and desire God, it is difficult to "Admit
him." Therefore, while the first three verses urge an implied listener to
seek divine intimacy, the fourth moves to first-person expressions of a
longing for murderous conquest that will *force* the would-be Christian
to submit. In this hymn, as in many of the sentimental novels discussed
in chapter 2, though the desire is ultimately for a maternal nurturer, the
terms of that desire are paternal, and violent.

This intersection of a sentimental discourse of a God apprehended
through the heart with a Calvinist discourse of a God who manifests his
love in mighty acts of violence furthers the eroticization of domination
that characterizes *The Wide, Wide World*. The words "Here now to thee
I all resign" were every bit as much a script for the bride as for the Christian convert, and the language of the hymn prompts Ellen to conceive of
marital as well as religious love in terms of violence. As the scene of separation from her mother indicated, both God and husband are associated with a rapture of maternal fusion, and as we see in this hymn, the
rapture of the fusion requires an act of violence designed to conquer the
independent will of the bride/convert. The intersection of maternal
sentimental ideals with paternal providential notions dictates that the
terms of desire for that merge are masochistic: "open" me, "enter" me,
"slay" and "conquer" those within, possess me "body, soul, and all."

John Humphreys is patterned upon God as portrayed in the hymn: he
has both a "lovely attitude" and a dark streak, indicating that, like God,
he has the power and the character needed to sweep a woman off her
feet and force her to yield to the erotic rapture of fusion with God and
with himself. "Them that sleep in Jesus will God bring with him," John
tells Ellen at the close of the book. "'I am satisfied,' said Ellen softly,
nestling again to his side;—'that is enough. I want no more'" (583).
Sleeping in Jesus is like sleeping with John, and as the word "nestling"

suggests, in sentimental fiction both are like sleeping with one's mother, a utopia of preverbal, maternal presence. But in order to achieve that maternal fusion in a world regulated by symbolic, paternal law, a woman must understand her desire for that fusion in relation to the chastening hand of the father/husband. Nineteenth-century women were not born masochists, but *The Wide, Wide World* suggests that an upbringing under the influence of the volatile intersection of two ideologies—Calvinism and true womanhood—conspired to turn them into masochists.

Horsewhipping and the Exploration of Desire

But while we can read *The Wide, Wide World* as a lurid exposure of the destruction of female subjectivity and the oppressive manipulation of female desire, we can also read it as a text that revels in its own masochism. Working within the culturally overdetermined language of desire of northeastern evangelical culture, it develops what we can recognize as a perverse masochistic discourse of erotic desire. To read the masochism in the text as a voice of sexual desire is neither to essentialize nor endorse masochism. It is rather to recognize that in her representation of a masochistic desire, Warner was not purely a victim; she was also operating as an agent—seizing, crafting and exploiting a discourse that enabled her to explore sexual fantasies.

Fantasies of surveillance are one of the most pervasive modes of erotic dreaming in *The Wide, Wide World*. John's surveillance may seem oppressive to modern readers, but for Ellen, the idea that "there was always somebody by, who whatever he might himself be doing, never lost sight of her" is deeply gratifying (464). John's omniscience bathes Ellen's body in a sensual male desire with which she can identify, vicariously providing access to her own desiring body. Like the warden in a panopticon and like God in heaven, John can say "I saw it all, Ellie" (447); he sees not only everything that Ellen does but everything she thinks: "[H]ow *could* you guess what I was thinking about, Mr. John?" Ellen asks (321); "How did you know—how could you know what I was thinking of?" (481). The transparency implicit in being completely readable is erotically charged not only because it comports with ideologies of coverture, according to which female noncorporeality is erotically desirable to a watching male, but also because it is allied with the religious ecstasies associated with total submission to God. The pleasures of examination and surveillance can be traced to the religious discourses that train Ellen to say, "Open my heart, Lord." Not only is the sentimental image of God as the gentle, lovely guest whose outstretch'd hands offer physical intimacy metonymically evoked by a discourse of conquest and surveillance, but it is also eroticized, when associated with the ecstasies of total fusion with God that are the promised reward for yielding oneself up. The sinner does not willingly open herself up to God, which is why an invasive stare and a severe examination are alluring.

Though John knows everything that Ellen thinks, he compels her to confess it, not for his own enlightenment, which is redundant, but for her own spiritual advancement. When John says, "I want to talk to you a little about this. Will you let me ask you a question or two?" Ellen answers, "Oh, yes—whatever he pleased" [sic] (296). She is so delighted to be examined, subjected to John's scrutiny, that at the end of the novel, when he proposes, "Perhaps I shall try you in two or three things, Ellie," she responds, "Will you! in what? Oh, it would make me so happy—so much happier" (561–63). And when she excitedly adds, "I will tell you everything about myself; and you will tell me how I ought to do in all sorts of things" (564), Ellen demonstrates the extent to which self-exposure and submission to examination express a desire for intimacy in terms that are both effective and acceptable. She also reveals the one-way nature of that exposure.

A scene from the ending of the novel exemplifies not only how surveillance functions as an expression of erotic desire but also how masochism is a way of finding erotic pleasure within the oppressive constraints of true womanhood. In this scene, John has come to visit Ellen during her Scottish exile, but before addressing her, he secretly watches her in order to see how her good character has been faring amidst a crowd of worldly pleasure seekers. He finds Ellen among a group of people singing around a piano, seeing and hearing as little as possible, diligently absorbed in the task of corporeal abjection:

> Ellen's eyes were bent on the floor. The expression on her face touched and pleased him greatly; it was precisely what he wished to see. Without having the least shadow of sorrow upon it, there was in all its lines that singular mixture of gravity and sweetness that is never seen but where religion and discipline have done their work well. . . . Ellen at the moment had escaped from the company and the noisy sounds of the performer at her side; and while her eye was curiously tracing out the pattern of the carpet, her mind was resting itself in one of the verses she had been reading that same evening. (559)

Although Ellen is physically present, all of her bodily signs bespeak her absence. She neutralizes her body with tasks that keep it under restraint: with her "eyes bent on the floor," "curiously tracing out the pattern in the carpet," she prevents her body from yielding to the enticing lures of the nonspiritual and gives off an air of "gravity," an otherworldly orientation that stands in mute, unmistakable separation from the carnal, "noisy sounds of the performer." As if in search for Ellen's "true" presence, the point of view shifts in the course of the passage. The scene begins by looking at Ellen from the perspective of John or an objective narrator, reporting only observable detail. But Ellen's physical presence only bespeaks her absence: she "had escaped." An editorial omniscient narrator therefore takes over and scans Ellen's interior. But she is not there either. Her presence is again deferred. As it turns out, Ellen is "*in* one of the verses," dissolved into a disembodied spiritual state. Ellen had wondered how she would "keep [her]self right," as she put it, without John's ongoing disciplinary presence. This scene suggests that she maintains her "right" self by concentrating upon abjection, continuously consolidating her coherent identity as a "true woman" in the very refusal to be a body present with other bodies. When true womanhood is absence, corporeal abjection is a means of consolidating it.

Grace Ann and Theodore Hovet read this scene as illustrating Ellen's relatively successful accommodation to her culture; where resistance is impossible, wearing a mask of social conformity leaves Ellen free to think what she wants (9–10). But I believe that such a reading of this passage exemplifies the limitations of a "liberal" celebration of freedom. Though Ellen *looks* free, it is her desire itself that is imprisoned. As Foucault observes in *Discipline and Punish*, whereas premodern methods of social control rely upon visible punishments—burning at the stake, flogging, drawing and quartering—modern power works through internalized control based upon religion and bodily discipline. Such modes of internal oppression arise in a world resembling Jeremy Bentham's model panopticon, a model prison built around a central guard tower and designed to enable the warden to see the prisoners while remaining obscured himself. The theory behind this design, Foucault says, is that "[h]e who is subjected to a field of visibility, and who knows it, assumes responsibility for the constraints of power; he makes them play spontaneously upon himself; he inscribes in himself the power relation in which he simultaneously plays both roles; he becomes the principle of his own subjection. By this very fact, the external power may throw off its physical weight" (202–3). Certainly, there are no chains on Ellen, no threats of physical chastisement. Rather, in creating a scene in which Ellen's self-erasure is "precisely what [John] wished to see," Warner represents the way that internal subjection works. She first subjects Ellen to "a field of visibility" and then rewards her for her good behavior with a surprise visit from the warden, a dearly longed-for reward for all of her ongoing, painful renunciations. Because power works through the production of subjectivity rather than through repression, physical abjection is both Ellen's prison and her pleasure. Her "freely chosen" physical abjection and self-dissolution can hardly be celebrated as an illustration of her protofeminist self-determination.

However, there may be a more perverse, and more deeply embedded, kind of "protofeminism" in this passage; for though it can be said to be "about" Ellen's abjection of her body, it is also "about" sexuality. Ellen's ethereal gravity elicits John's desire—it is "precisely what he wished to see"—and he hints at a marriage proposal in the next pages. His desire in turn stimulates Ellen's; "I have wanted you so very much!" she says. Although Warner does not use explicitly romantic language, most readers understand that that is what is implied. A reviewer writing in the 1851 *Godey's Lady's Book* suggests that nineteenth-century readers widely recognized that *The Wide, Wide World*—and particularly the ending of the book—is about romantic desire. In fact, the reviewer chastises Warner for the disingenuousness of the ending:

> One of the best and most carefully drawn characters in the book is the young clergyman, John Humphreys. In his last interview with Ellen, before leaving Scotland, he enjoins upon her—not to read novels! This species of disingenuousness, be it said, is a common thing with novel-writers. Is it not an affectation of humility? Or does each novel-writer, who condemns that sort of work, consider his or her novel an exception to the rule? Such writers forget entirely the homely but wise injunction, to "honor the bridge that carries us in safety." "The Wide, Wide World" is essentially a novel; the author perhaps thinks, because there are no professed love scenes in it, that it may escape this title. Both love and matrimony are insinuated in the concluding pages; and it does not require much knowledge of the mechanism of fiction to detect in John, from the beginning, the embryo husband of Ellen, notwithstanding their dubbing each other brother and sister; this after all, is but an old and hackneyed trick of the sentimental school, which we do not at all approve. The relation of brother and sister is too delicate in its sacredness to be thus made the cover of a more ardent affection.[14]

Not only the cagey modern critic, but the common reader of Warner's day, would recognize that *The Wide, Wide World* is about an "ardent affection" whose sexual implications require the "cover" of pretended innocence.

But Warner's denial of a romantic reading of her novel is no mere hackneyed trick. The schizophrenic attitude toward romance implicit in these last pages is central to the text's ambivalent eroticism. For the air of chastity that Ellen gives off is precisely that which attracts John's romantic desire; it is "precisely what he wished to see." From John's perspective, female purity promotes "ardent affection." And the reader who looks at Ellen from John's perspective gains vicarious access to desire—*his* desire. As we have seen, the point of view encompasses multiple perspectives, enabling the reader both to look *at* Ellen and to be *in* Ellen, to perceive Ellen's desirability and to experience that desirability. The

reader who shifts back and forth from identification with Ellen to identification with John gains access to erotic desire via the fantasy of female
noncorporeality. In other words, imagining the spectacle of chastity
under the admiring male gaze is erotic.

Reader's responses suggest that female chastity was—paradoxically—
romantically alluring. One male reader, for example, wrote Warner a
long fan letter, describing his adoration of "sweet" Alice Humphreys,
signing it "Alice's Admirer." Before addressing this letter, we must keep
in mind that Alice Humphreys is a character who believes that sexual
passionlessness is a sign of moral value, and that sexual desire is a sign of
moral inferiority. Her contempt for sexual desire is implicit in her contrast between her servant Margery and Margery's husband, Thomas.
Margery "came over with us [from England] twelve years ago for the
pure love of my father and mother; and I believe now she looks upon
John and me as her own children . . . [Thomas] isn't equal to his wife.
Perhaps I am partial; Margery came to America for the love of us, and
Thomas came for the love of Margery; there's a difference" (173). Indeed, there is; Thomas is an inferior person because he loves his wife
more than his pious employers. While Margery exemplifies the "pure"
caritas of disinterested devotion to children that she did not produce
but that she looks upon as her own, Thomas is motivated by a more
carnal eros. And since nonerotic love is Alice's implicit yardstick for
moral superiority, she finds Thomas inferior to Margery. The passionlessness that Alice advocates and represents is the mark of the "pure
love" that distinguishes her from lesser people.

It is ironic, then, that Alice should have inspired the following explicitly romantic and implicitly erotic expression of desire in the male
reader's fan letter to Warner:

> Alice—lovely Alice—affectionate, pious, accomplished Alice—thou hast cap-
> tured my heart! O how sorry I felt when she died. Some of my kind friends
> wonder why I dont get married. I have sometimes wondered myself—for I am
> very fond of the social & domestic joys of home. The matter however is now
> explained. Alice is evidently the lady that was intended for me—her early
> death therefore, shut me up to single blessedness—I argue that she was the
> person intended for me, from the fact, that she possesses just the trends of
> character that I would desire in such a relation. It is true, she is *far too good for
> me*. I do not *deserve* any such model of female excellence & female loveli-
> ness—but then she was so sweet in her disposition—that when she knew how
> much I loved her, she would have pitied me & perhaps—she might have done
> more.[15]

The fact that "Alice's Admirer" is unable to find a *real* wife suggests that
a man who bought into the ideal of true womanhood was going to have

to wait a long time for a true woman to come along. Alice is pure, impossibly pure—"far too good" for her admirer. But though he sees himself as inferior to her, he does not repudiate his own carnality; rather, he fantasizes that out of pity his angel would gratify his base desires (too vulgar to be more than alluded to in the final clause: "perhaps—she might [do] more"). Alice's purity provokes his desire—precisely that which women are trained to elicit as the very key to their social existence. The woman who experiences that desire vicariously by fantasizing about the alluring spectacle of her own purity gains circuitous access to her own desire for carnal pleasures in the very act of repudiating that desire.

Ellen also provoked romantic interest in male fans—and it was expressed in a language of domination and subordination. One, who signed his name "Ellen's ardent admirer," expressed to Susan Warner his love for Ellen, and for Susan herself. His long, rambling letter includes the following condescending critique of Warner's writing and self-mockery for his own presumptuousness:

> The first volume is generally the best but then you became a little tired at last, and we cant work well without the heart is in it. (For having written a book or so myself I speak from experience)—You see I am playing Master John, and you must be, for the time, as I strongly suspect in reality you are—Ellen— But I cannot get Ellen out of my mind, I dont try *very* hard. She is a sweet, dear girl—just such as I should like for a wife—at least in most respects—I fear however I stand no chance while that Mr. John is alive, what *could* bewitch the child so for him, he is *far* too old." [16]

Although he claims not to understand Ellen's attraction to John, this fan intuitively understands, since he plays John by criticizing and instructing Susan Warner, with whom he pretends to be in love. He recognizes that *The Wide, Wide World* eroticizes domination, and he is happy to "play" the role of "Master John" by chastizing his beloved Susan. Domination is the language of his romantic fantasy.

Warner revels in fantasies of submission as thoroughly as Ellen's admirer revels in domination. One of the ways she indulges her zest for it is by detailing fantasies of John-as-owner. Mrs. Montgomery had hoped that God would make Ellen "his own" and take her to his heavenly home, and possessive love serves as the mark of love for God's earthly counterpart too. When John says, "I think you belong to me more than to any body," Ellen responds, "That is exactly what I think . . . I am very glad you think so too! I will always do whatever you tell me—just as I used to—no matter what any body else says. . . . I had given myself to you a great while ago" (563). Her desire to give herself to someone who is both willing and worthy to possess her is partly determined by her Puritanism ("Here now to thee I all resign / My body, soul, and all are thine"). Self-surrender serves as a discourse of erotic desire in religious books committed to ideologies of coverture. Hence, in the fairy-tale second ending of *The Wide, Wide World* (excluded from the original publication), Warner writes: "There was in [Ellen's glance] a life-long of feeling and memory; it seemed in its self-renunciation to gather up all the past and lay it and herself with it at [John's] feet" (576). This masochistic rhapsody, when considered in light of Calvinist discourses of the ecstasies of submission to God, functions as a covert expression of desire for the ecstatic erotic merge Ellen imagines as the consequence of giving herself, "body, soul, and all," to a man.

While such renunciations lie at the heart of the romantic and religious motives of *The Wide, Wide World*, they are also exceedingly difficult to perform. When Mr. Marshman asks Ellen in one trying moment, "What is the reason that you do not love the Savior?" she answers, "Mamma says it is because my heart is so hard," to which he replies, "That is true" (70). The metaphor of a "hard heart" to express an unconquerable devotion to the carnal self is fundamental to Calvinist discourses. Harriet Newell, the reader will recall, wrote in her diary, "How awfully depraved is the natural heart! Every day I can see more and more of *my own* apostasy from God. Break, compassionate Immanuel, Oh *break* this stony heart of mine, and *compel* me to live an obedient child" (March 10, 1809). And as we have seen, such longings for God to break the hard heart function in sentimentality as metonyms for erotic desire. A similar metaphor that was widely used to express the difficulty of submission—the breaking of a horse—has the same effect in *The Wide, Wide World*. As the opening of the book states, in order to enjoy the ecstasies of religious and marital rapture, Ellen's will must be broken ("time, 'that rider that breaks youth,' had not as yet tried his hand upon her"). And like Newell, Warner believes that the one who breaks the sinner's will is "compassionate." The will is like a young horse: headstrong, eager to go where it wants rather than where its rider wants, and mostly interested in a good meal and physical pleasure. But in order for a woman to attain the abiding and elevated delights of spiritual enlightenment in Christian marriage, her will must be broken. John Humphreys reiterates the time-honored connection between controlling a woman's will and controlling a horse when he commands, "You must not talk when you are riding, unless you can contrive to manage two things at once; and no more lose command of your horse than you would of yourself" (463).

John's renown as a breaker of horses, therefore, is another means by which Warner explores erotic desire within appropriately chaste terms. Critics who see in John's violent streak only Warner's challenge to the patriarchal system that oppressively dominates women are blind to the attractions of John's domineering ways, perhaps because they downplay the intense religiosity that is Warner's primary motivation. Joanne Dobson, for example, claims that "nuances of characterization" in Warner's representation of John criticize the patriarchy by suggesting that he "will be even more abusive than Ellen's previous 'owners'" (231). As evidence for her claim, Dobson points out that John is called "King John the Second" and "the Grand Turk" by his acquaintances, and that some characters compare him to gunpowder. But Warner explicitly devalues the opinions of those who simply see John as simply "the biggest gobbler in the yard." Shallow people like Sophia, Marianne, and the Scottish relatives confuse permissiveness with love, but Warner insists that lax discipline is merely condescension or indifference. According to Dobson, even God comes under Warner's critique, portrayed as "a sadistic manipulator who 'wounds that he may heal'" (231). But while Warner recognizes very well that God's requirements seem cruel—he takes a mother away in order to draw the daughter to him—many a Puritan has murmured against the hard lessons of providence without subverting them. Indeed, rebellion in one's heart against God has been considered essential for genuine growth. When Harriet Beecher Stowe converted without much struggle, her sister Catharine "was afraid that there might be something wrong in the case of a lamb that had come into the fold without being first chased all over the lot by the shepherd" (Hedrick 35). Rather than fostering an attitude of rebellion, the novel fosters an attitude of exclusivity: those who recognize and appreciate John's spiritual mastery are the rare few who are on the mystical path to a higher religious plane of existence—people Emily Dickinson refers to as "a Dedicated sort—/A Member of the Cloud" (FP#330 JP#273). Like God, John has the characteristics of a "sadistic manipulator," but the text's emotional current does not therefore move away from John any more than it moves away from God. If John's apparent sadism inspires in the reader a rebellious heart, that experience should only reinforce her belief that she, like Ellen, is "very, very weak" and in need of self-control and discipline (296).[17]

With Ellen's soaring spiritual quest in mind, we can read John's notorious history as a brutal horsewhipper as part of a fantasy whose ecstasies are intensified, not undermined, by fear. Consider a scene in which Ellen has been given a new pony, and her friend Sophia advises her to whip it immediately:

> "I don't want to whip him, I am sure; and I should be afraid to besides."
> "Hasn't John taught you that lesson yet?" said the young lady;—"he is perfect in it himself. Do you remember, Alice, the chastening he gave that fine black horse of ours we called the 'Black Prince?'—a beautiful creature he was,—more than a year ago?—My conscience! he frightened me to death."

"I remember," said Alice; "I remember I could not look on."

"What did he do that for?" said Ellen.

"What's the matter, Ellen Montgomery?" said Miss Sophia, laughing,—"where did you get that long face? Are you thinking of John or the horse?" (376–77)

As Sophia recognizes, Ellen identifies with the "Black Prince" and considers with anxiety the necessity of disciplinary violence. Her identification has a religious context; the name "Black Prince" suggests the satanic internal impulses, "the devil within," that lead earthward rather than heavenward. But under the guidance of a masterful hand, Warner insists, the Black Prince of passion can be a "beautiful creature." The disciplinary violence that John inflicts upon the horse is a sign of his love for it, just as his discipline of Ellen is a sign of his love for her. In particular, since Ellen's passions are consistently compared to horses in the novel, the chastening of the Black Prince can be read as a displaced symbolic representation of the discipline and control of women's bodies and carnal desires in the process of bringing them in line with true womanhood.[18] "Is he good?" Ellen asks John of the second horse named Black Prince that he chastens. "'I hope so,' said John, smiling;—'if he is not I shall be at the pains to make him so. We are hardly acquainted yet.' Ellen looked doubtfully at the black horse and his rider, and patting the Brownie's neck, observed with great satisfaction that *he* was very good" (402).[19] Knowing full well that her education at John's hands is intended to make *her* good, it is no surprise that Ellen looks worried. Her insistence that the Brownie is "very good" seems to be a subtle insistence that she herself does not need to be subjected to his chastening whip.

Warner's imagination is powerfully drawn toward the violence latent in "disciplinary intimacy." In fact, John has already whipped one "Black Prince" into submission and is currently in the process of breaking a second horse by that name—a plot detail that enables the past act of chastisement to continue to create tension for Ellen in the present. As Ellen's very first encounter with John suggests, his potential for violence excites her. And although the scene with Sophia may unearth Ellen's latent fear, it also unearths her desire for him; immediately after she worries about John's treatment of her pony, when she and John are back home, Warner writes,

Ellen was left alone on the lawn. Something was the matter; for she stood with swimming eyes and a trembling lip, rubbing her stirrup, which really needed no polishing. . . . What *was* the matter? Only—that Mr. John had forgotten the kiss he always gave her on going or coming. Ellen was jealous of it as a pledge of sistership, and could not want it; and though she tried as hard as she could to get her face in order, so that she might go in and meet them, somehow it seemed to take a great while. She was still busy with her stirrup, when she suddenly felt two hands on her shoulders, and looking up received the very kiss the want of which she had been lamenting. (403)

The references to John's horsewhipping immediately preceding this scene evidently do nothing to lessen the intensity of Ellen's love for John. Rather, they are followed by expressions of desire for him: tears and trembling lips. She also rubs a leather stirrup, part of the very technology by which John disciplines the horse of passion.

Elaine Scarry's theory of the "unmaking" function of pain offers an intriguing hypothesis as to why the very thought of subjection to vicarious whipping stimulates Ellen's desire in this scene. Scarry has argued that pain destroys the constructed universe, restricting a victim's experience of the world to the confines of the body, and she focuses on the misery inherent in such a deconstruction, the agonizing collapse of the mental and imaginative extensions of the self in the world. Scarry's argument also suggests, however, how fantasies of pain might also produce pleasure: when the constructed world is conceived as a prison of social identity, "unmaking" can produce an ecstasy of unshackling.[20] In particular, when social identity precludes physical feelings, identifying with a whipped horse might produce a pleasing vicarious experience of embodiment that undermines that anticorporeal ideological construct. The book consistently associates Ellen with horses, and so the discipline of horses reads as a displaced representation of the violent discipline of herself. In such circumstances, sympathy for whipped horses affords Ellen a socially acceptable form of access to her own body. Such are the transgressive delights of abjection. Pain is paradoxically liberating when the "making" of a woman's identity hinges upon the abjection of her body. It is unequivocally appalling that true womanhood made vicarious pain an attractive (because effective) way for a woman to imagine her own embodiment, but it is also true.

Indeed, the vicarious experience of the abject body conforms to the definition of ecstasy. The word ecstasy derives from the Greek words *ex* (out of) and *histanai* (to cause to stand, set, place), which combine to form the Greek word *existanai*, which means "to put out of place." The intense pleasure we think of as "ecstasy" is caused by an experience of being outside of stasis (ex-stasis), which in Ellen's case is a socially constructed psychic order founded through abjection of the passionate body.[21] Images of horsewhipping, evocative of the abjected female body, express a desire for ecstasy. Hence it should not come as a surprise that in another scene, Ellen's identification with another whipped horse explicitly produces feelings of ecstasy. This time, Ellen is waylaid by Mr.

Saunders, a dastardly sales clerk with a grudge against her. This descendant of Lovelace (as Leslie Fiedler calls Saunders) fashions from a sapling "a very good imitation of an ox-whip in size and length, with a fine lash-like point," and begins to threaten Ellen's pony, "the Brownie," in order that she suffer through sympathetic identification with her horse: "'I'm a going to punish you . . . but it ain't pretty to quarrel with ladies, so Brownie and me'll settle it together'" (399). Warner adds, "His best way of distressing Ellen, he found, was through her horse . . . and he meant to wind up with such a treatment of her pony, real or seeming, as he knew would give great pain to the pony's mistress" (400). Mr. Saunders understands that sympathy works as a mechanism for torture because a sympathizer feels what a victim feels. Ellen introjects a mental representation of her pony and experiences its pain: "a smart stroke of the whip upon his haunches made the Brownie spring in a way that brought Ellen's heart into her mouth" (398). What Mr. Saunders could hardly anticipate, though, is that Ellen would take a covert pleasure from the fantasized experience of pain. But when he begins harrassing her pony, Warner writes that Ellen suffers "in an ecstasy of apprehension." Granted, Warner presumably meant by "ecstasy" something resembling the primary definition of the word in Webster's 1841 dictionary: "a fixed state; a trance; a state in which the mind is arrested and fixed, or as we say, lost; a state in which the functions of the senses are suspended by the contemplation of some extraordinary or supernatural object." But that state, in which one's mind ceases to function, tends to be associated with extreme pleasure, as the second definition suggests: "Excessive joy; rapture; a degree of delight that arrests the whole mind; as, . . . the *ecstasy* of love." Given Ellen's loving feelings toward John, another horsewhipper in the novel, we are invited to associate the suspense Ellen experiences with the latter kind of pleasure.[22]

When Ellen identifies with the punishment of her pony, her painstakingly acquired corporeal tranquillity collapses in a rapid succession of intense bodily sensations. Fear brings "her heart into her mouth"; she feels "her heart beating very fast"; "her heart sprang with a nameless pang"; she "trembl[es] in every nerve from head to foot"(298, 296, 298). With her mind frozen, Ellen is almost purely focused upon her body. This intense physical experience is so far out of the ordinary for Ellen, who normally focuses upon preventing such irruptions of physical sensation, that she is no longer herself. When, at the end of the encounter, Warner writes that Ellen has almost recovered and "looked almost like herself" (402), she implies that in her frenzy of fear, Ellen did not look like "herself." Indeed, the confrontation provokes the following: "'Oh, do not!' cried Ellen, almost beside herself" (397). "Beside herself," Ellen is ex-static—outside of the tranquil, passionless, noncorporeal woman that ideologies of true womanhood say she is. Her self, for a few moments, includes a full range of her body's sensations, so that physical sensations of fear afford her an encounter with her own abjected corporeality. Outside the parameters of her ideologically determined self, intense physical experience really does locate Ellen "beside herself," though, ironically, for a "true woman" that means firmly inside her body.

To the extent that sympathetic identification with the suffering Brownie provokes ecstasy in Ellen, it would appear to be sadistic. Leo Bersani has proposed that there is something sadistic and sexual about the pleasures of sympathy, and that therefore, "the very operation of sympathy partially undermines the moral solidarity that we like to think of as its primary effect" (150).[23] He draws our attention to the synonym "compassion," which means "to feel along with another." In sympathy, an onlooker feels the pain of another, and the resulting disruption of the onlooker's internal equilibrium is erotic, because it is disorderly and transgressive—like sex. Presuming that such transgression is inherently erotic, Bersani suggests that " 'sympathy' always includes a trace of sexual pleasure," and therefore the pleasures of both sympathy and sadism are "inescapably masochistic." We do not need to endorse Bersani's questionable proposition that all internal stimulation is erotic in order to acknowledge that while sympathy may not always be sexual, evangelical sentimentality does provide a language that makes that association likely. The physical affect of sentimental sympathy is particularly liberating for bourgeois Protestant women, for whom the untrammeled experience of their own bodies is unavailable. Genteel characters like Ellen can enjoy a thrill of physical sensation by identifying with tortured pets and with the physical and emotional afflictions of other people. Under the guise of altruism, they can feel others' pain and enjoy the transgressive experience of uncontrollable sensation that puts one "beside [one]self." But this apparently sadistic pleasure is actually an inverted form of masochism, since the pleasure comes from the vicarious experience of pain. In *The Wide, Wide World*, that pain becomes erotic through a chain of associations linking punishment to God's love, and linking God's spiritual love to a man's carnal love.

When viewed as a genre permeated by subtly sadomasochistic pleasures, sentimental fiction is hardly just a collection of what Emily Dickinson called "sweet and true" books that "will do one good," tales about "pure little lives, loving God, and their parents, and obeying the laws of the land" (L#85). Rather, books like *The Wide, Wide World* exploit sympathetic suffering and tropes of violence, discipline, and surveillance to explore female erotic desire. The altruistic humanitarian concern that overtly motivates Ellen's sympathy for her pony on a conscious level is accompanied by an undercurrent of masochistic self-gratification that can actually be seen to exploit the Brownie's pain.

Recognizing these sadomasochistic pleasures radically reconfigures our understanding of this novel, which is neither simply a tool in the victimization of women nor simply a protofeminist affirmation of female nurture and female labor. Rather, it represents a problematic effort to appropriate agency in one of the most contested arenas of women's lives under patriarchy: sexuality. *The Wide, Wide World* is part of an ongoing effort to find a language of female sexual pleasure within the constraints of a culture hostile to that expression. Critics who fail to imagine that a woman like Susan Warner might take pleasure in imagining marriage with a domineering man like John Humphreys miss a crucial opportunity to unravel the problematic complexity of women's sexuality. Insisting that what looks like masochism is really something else not only violates the dominant emotional current of the novel but makes it *less* interesting than it is and strips the feminist inquiry into the novel of the potentially explosive contemporary relevance that it could have. Susan Warner's exploitation of the erotics of domination is not simply a sign of her victimization, a tragic memento to oppression—though it is that. It is also a significant effort on her part to fantasize about female desire, to capture in richly detailed imagery the shape and feel of a woman's pleasure.

Four

The Ecstasies of Sentimental Wounding
in *Uncle Tom's Cabin*

IN THE previous chapter, we saw how desire is both suppressed and expressed through sentimental masochistic discourse, and we considered the implications of this double-edgedness from a feminist perspective. This chapter takes up the political implications of this paradox. The perfect text in which to explore these is Harriet Beecher Stowe's *Uncle Tom's Cabin*, a paradigm of nineteenth-century sentimentality and an indisputably important political novel. Nowhere are the complications of a nineteenth-century woman's exploitation of sentimental masochism for power and pleasure more vividly displayed. Stowe sought to make readers feel the pain that slaves felt in order to force upon them an intuitive, experiential approach to the abolitionist question. Taking advantage of conventional sentimental strategies, she deliberately inflicted emotional wounds and urged readers to identify the pain of these wounds with the suffering of slaves, so that they would *feel* the urgency of the abolitionist cause. Her motive for this political activism was fundamentally religious; she wanted to show that African Americans had souls and a spiritual dimension and to oppose the affront to Christianity represented by slavery. As feminist critics of the past twenty years have observed, Stowe's Christian politics represented a radical feminist intervention into, and critique of, American public life. What they have not recognized, however, is that the contextualization of Stowe's painful sentimental affect within Christian and racial discourses had the effect of eroticizing that affect.

Many readers have confessed that the reading of *Uncle Tom's Cabin* stimulated masochistic erotic desires. In "A Child Is Being Beaten," Sigmund Freud observes that many patients have beating fantasies, and many of them use *Uncle Tom's Cabin* for "onanistic gratification": "In my patients' milieu it was almost always the same books whose contents gave a new stimulus to the beating-phantasies: those accessible to young people, such as the so-called '*Bibliothèque rose*,' *Uncle Tom's Cabin*, etc." (107). In her study of masochistic desire, Marcia Marcus lists the childhood books that provided materials for her own adolescent masochistic fantasies: "There were the books about boarding school, in which small boys slaved for the bigger boys. . . . There were books about the initiation rites of exotic people. There was *Uncle Tom's Cabin*, and other books about black slaves in America. There were books about armies with iron discipline and military justice and punitive expeditions" (16). Likewise, Richard Krafft-Ebing, the sex researcher who coined the term "masochism," includes in his compendium on sexual pathology the following letter from a self-diagnosed masochist (Case 57): "Even in my early childhood I loved to revel in ideas about the absolute mastery of one man over others. The thought of slavery had something exciting in it for me, alike whether from the standpoint of master or servant. That one man could possess, sell or whip another, caused me intense excitement; and in reading 'Uncle Tom's Cabin' (which I read at about the beginning of puberty) I had erections" (137).[1] Case 57 adds that "there are many men who like to play 'slave' . . . this unlimited power of life and death, as exercised over slaves and domestic animals, is the aim and end of all masochistic ideas" (95–99).

In this chapter I illuminate the complex mechanisms by which *Uncle Tom's Cabin* came to function as such a notoriously successful supply of material for masochistic erotic fantasy; readers who read about the transcendent pleasures of mystical martyrdom and interracial bonding and who also felt the gut response typical of sentimental affect frequently associated sentimental pain with pleasures of a private erotic or ecstatic character rather than with disinterested altruistic desires to serve the public good. *Uncle Tom's Cabin* came to function as such a notoriously successful supply of material for masochistic erotic fantasy. I also address the ethical and political implications of the popularity of *Uncle Tom's Cabin* as masochistic fantasy: the pleasures it creates call into question its appropriateness as political discourse, and yet these pleasures played a key role in the popularity of the book that President Lincoln believed started the Civil War, a war that resulted in the emancipation of the slaves.[2] Power and pleasure turn in upon themselves in *Uncle Tom's Cabin*, making a final judgment of the ethics of sentimental masochism as a mode of agency all but impossible. Stowe turned to sentimentalism not to please readers but to promote her own political position: sentimentalism was a tool of political agency. But the book was powerful at least in part because of the illicit pleasures it produced. Readers turned to it—and to the cause it promoted—because of the pleasures associated with its production of sympathy. Though its sadomasochistic tendencies made the book politically effective, they also undermined the spiritual goals that motivated Stowe to write it in the first place. For the sadomasochistic pleasures that made her book so powerful also positioned the slaves as erotic objects rather than fully human subjects. And her spiritual goal—to recognize the humanity and spirituality of slaves—was undermined by that objectification, even as the political goal was energized as never before.

From the perspective of feminism as well as that of abolitionism, the implications of sentimental masochism are doubled-edged. Women, Stowe suggests through her novel, needed to reform the dehumanizing male-dominated political system through a spiritually motivated platform of sympathy and feelings. Yet by effectively promoting suffering as women's most significant form of political agency, *Uncle Tom's Cabin* cut against more affirmative and proactive forms of women's empowerment. Moreover, while eroticized suffering conveniently made passion accessible to middle-class women for whom ideologies of true womanhood and Calvinism rendered passion taboo, it also oppressively suggested that suffering was the central component of a distinctly female variety of sexual pleasure. Because of the high stakes involved in the double-edgedness of its sentimental masochistic erotics, *Uncle Tom's Cabin* offers a uniquely dramatic example of the complexities attending the pursuit of a voice of female pleasure and power.

The Epistemology of Wounds

Stowe had contempt for dishonest forms of sentimentality, claiming that their authors "talk what they cannot have felt" (Rugoff 111). She also recognized, however, that the epithet "sentimental" was all too frequently slapped dismissively onto any discourse that valued feelings. In *Uncle Tom's Cabin*, for example, Senator Bird ridicules "all sentimental weakness of those who would put the welfare of a few miserable fugitives before great state interests" (155). Likewise, St. Clare recalls that his brother had accused him of "a womanish sentimentalism" for sympathizing with slaves (342). Evidently, Stowe distinguishes between two kinds of sentimentality, and she values what Paula Bennett calls "high sentimentality," "an epistemologically based discourse" that grounds judgments of character and ethics in feelings, intuition, and spirituality rather than in logic ("Descent" 593 n2). Female authors turned to high sentimentality in order to redress the cognitive failures of abstract analysis that they believed had led the nation into its great moral crisis. They believed that detached abstraction served as the basis of the corrupt legal system. As Mrs. Bird puts it, "I hate reasoning . . . on such subjects. There's a way you political folks have of coming round and round a plain right thing; and you don't believe in it yourselves when it comes to practice" (145). She advocates a sentimental alternative: "Your heart is better than your head, in this case" (153).[3]

In pursuing her sentimental epistemology, Stowe relied upon a conviction that nonslaves could know what the pain of slavery felt like. When her son Charley died, she identified her emotional anguish with that felt by slave parents whose children were sold to other masters. "It was at his dying bed and at his grave that I learned what a poor slave mother may feel when her child is torn away from her," she wrote.[4] Like many sentimental authors, Stowe saw the anguish of bereavement as a universal emotion that cut through cultural difference, enabling one person to understand perfectly what another was feeling. In *Uncle Tom's Cabin*, for instance, when Tom is torn from his wife and children, Stowe emphasizes the universality of his grief: "Sobs, heavy, hoarse, and loud, shook the chair, and great tears fell through his fingers on the floor; just such tears, sir, as you dropped into the coffin where lay your first born son; such tears, woman, as you shed when you heard the cries of your dying babe. For, sir, he was a man,—and you are but another man. And, woman, though dressed in silk and jewels, you are but a woman, and, in life's great straits and mighty grief, ye feel but one sorrow!" (90–91). The anguish of separation is a unifying force, for all races, classes, and genders experience bereavement as "one sorrow." Here we see the classic paradox of sentimentalism, which is that the pain of separation fosters a unity of feeling among sufferers.

In *Uncle Tom's Cabin* Stowe capitalizes upon the political potential of this paradox of sentimental separation. In order to forge between readers and slaves a union based upon shared feelings, she reinvigorates readers' own anguished memories of bereavement and separation, suggesting that those experiences are qualitatively the same as the miseries of slavery.[5] As Catharine O'Connell has shown, the Senator Bird chapters provide a mise-en-scène illustrating Stowe's own authorial strategy of inducing witnesses to relive old wounds. The senator's approach epitomizes prevailing epistemologies; he supports the Fugitive Slave Law because he thinks in dehumanizing abstractions, such as "fugitives," and never considers the emotions of the human beings represented by these abstractions: "his idea of a fugitive was only an idea of the letters that spell the word,—or at the most, the image of a little newspaper picture of a man with a stick and bundle with "Ran away from the subscriber" under it. The magic of the real presence of distress,—the imploring human eye, the frail, trembling human hand, the despairing appeal of helpless agony,—these he had never tried" (156). He is reformed by a sentimental wound. When Eliza Harris attempts to explain why she ran away from the Shelbys, she interrupts the senator's series of logical questions with a question of her own that shifts the epistemological basis of the discussion. She asks if the Birds have ever lost a child, a question that was "thrust on a new wound." When the Birds answer yes, Eliza explains, "Then you will feel for me. I have lost two" (148). This fictional example illustrates Stowe's own literary method: she thrusts into readers' preexisting wounds, forcing them to "feel for" slaves by reexperiencing their own painful separations and other forms of suffering. This wounding forces a new mode of cognition upon readers, who are to understand slavery through their memories of sorrow rather than through reason, and thereby apprehend the "plain right thing" that logic conceals.[6]

Stowe is not alone in associating her method with wounding; it is also the word readers used to describe the experience of reading her book. William Henry Channing's response to *Uncle Tom's Cabin* not only exemplifies the centrality of wounding as the book's rhetorical strategy but also features the reform of politics that wounding was supposed to effect: "O Heaven! How patient are God and nature with human diabolism! It seems to me that I have never begun to do anything for antislavery yet. And now, with one's whole heart bleeding, what can we do? . . . How this book must cut a true-hearted Southerner to the quick!—cut us all, for we verily are all guilty together" (Gossett 165). With his "whole heart bleeding," Channing seems to feel the pain slaves feel, an experience that causes him to recognize intuitively the urgency of the antislavery cause and to redouble his commitment to it. This kind of political transformation through feelings was precisely the reaction that sentimental abolitionist authors like Stowe sought to provoke. Convinced that Americans had become deadened to the pain suffered by victims of heartless public policies because they, like Senator Bird, thought in impersonal abstractions, authors like Stowe sought to restore feelings as dominant modes of cognition. They "cut . . . to the quick," piercing through anaesthetizing abstractions and making readers think with the subjective responses of intuition, imagination, and sympathetic extension to others.

Unlike authors of what Thomas Laqueur calls "humanitarian sensationalism," Stowe does not wound her readers by displaying literally wounded victims.[7] Even though she suggests that "the imploring eye, the frail trembling hand" might reform the senator, these bodily signs are not necessarily sufficient to transfer meaning from sufferer to observer. After all, when Eliza appears in his kitchen, "with garments torn and frozen, with one shoe gone, and the stocking torn away from the cut and bleeding foot," the senator remains conspicuously detached from her, "tak[ing] up the interrogatory" (148). The physical presence of a real fugitive slave in evident distress does not restore him to his conscience, because physical presence is not "real presence." It is not until Eliza wounds the senator himself by appealing to the universal anguish of separation that his political transformation occurs. Even if a witness is physically present with a victim, if he or she is emotionally disengaged, then he or she is not "truly" present, as Stowe indicates when she chastises her reader: "everything your money can buy, given with a cold, averted face, is not worth one honest tear shed in real sympathy" (167).

The body can never equal "real presence" for Stowe, because she conceives of human identity in terms that resemble what Jessica Benjamin calls "intersubjectivity," an unstable self centered in, but extending beyond, the boundaries of the body. In *Uncle Tom's Cabin*, people are defined by "electric streams" uniting them to others (106). When Eliza loses her first two children, to whom she is "passionately attached," her identity is incomplete. "After the birth of little Harry, however . . . every bleeding tie and throbbing nerve, once more intertwined with that little life, seemed to become sound and healthful" (57). Because Eliza's identity is interfused with that of her children, her bodily presence cannot in and of itself constitute her real presence. Likewise, Chloe sees identity as being defined by cathexes. When wife and husband are torn apart, she claims, they effectively die: "it's jest takin' the very life on 'em" (111). Depriving husband and wife of each other's physical company kills them, because it prevents their emotional connection to each other. Tellingly, the only time Tom comes close to submitting to Legree's efforts to break his spirit is when he is deprived of communion with his fellow slaves, isolated from the human interaction that is essential for true human life, reduced to a merely physical existence.

Though Stowe emphasizes the intersubjective nature of human identity, however, she also emphasizes a bodily dimension to selfhood. Given the Lockean roots of their aesthetic, and in opposition to their own Calvinist heritage, sentimental authors like Stowe tend to see the emotional self as an embodied self. Their use of the sentimental wound is part of their daunting and laudable struggle to appeal to a decentered but embodied notion of personhood within the constraints of a Christian culture that separates self and body. A wound is a site where emotions and senses intersect in pure *feeling*, and in attempting to produce affect in their readers, sentimental authors attempt to communicate through the presence of physical and emotional feelings, rather than through abstract detachment from the body. Stowe idealizes bodily activities—feeding, sitting on laps and touching faces, dancing and rolling on the floor together, tickling one another or pulling one another's toes—as physical means by which individuals construct intersubjective, nonindividuated identities. When, in the opening of the novel, Chloe alternately puts food in the mouth of her baby and then in her own mouth, and when the baby subsequently buries her fat hands in Tom's hair, Stowe offers visual images of the way bodies serve as a means *not* of separating the "me" from the "not-me" but of extending the "me" to the "not-me." The embodied, relational self in sentimentality has "real presence"; by this she means neither a disembodied soul nor a simply emotional being nor simply bodily presence (156). Rather, she means the self defined by its cathexes and its embodied feelings.[8]

Though sentimentalists do not equate "bodily presence" with "real presence," the two are easily confused in sentimental literature, because the body is intimately associated with emotional presence. When Haley carries Tom off, Stowe berates Mr. Shelby for his physical absence, because a face-to-face encounter could have shattered his emotional detachment. In order to provoke emotional connection, sentimental authors emphasize the importance of bodily presence and the bodily signs of emotional presence. They do so with such consistency, in fact, that critics have assumed that they equate the two. According to Karen Sanchez-Eppler, in sentimentality, one "reads internal characteristics from the external signs offered by the body"(37). As a paradigmatic example, Sanchez-Eppler observes that the heroine of Stowe's *Dred*, Nina Gordon, enjoys a capacity for "unproblematic discrimination of good from evil," so that after seeing Mr. Jekyl, she insists "I hate that man! . . . I never saw him before. But I hate him! He is a bad man." When her beau, Clayton, asks with logical detachment, "How can you be so positive about a person you've only seen once?" Nina jokes, "don't you know that girls and dogs, and other inferior creatures, have the gift of seeing what's in people? It doesn't belong to highly cultivated folks like you, but to us poor creatures, who have to trust to our instincts." According to Sanchez-Eppler, this scene illustrates Nina's dubious "[s]kill in reading the body of the stranger," judging books by their covers (36).

But Sanchez-Eppler conflates two separate operations: trust in the advice given by one's own body and trust in the signs provided by the other's body. Nina is describing a gut feeling; however, such a response does not place implicit trust in the other's gut but in one's own gut. Sanchez-Eppler describes a hermeneutic activity, a physiognomy of culturally determined—racially and sexually encoded—bodily meanings. But surely the reference to dogs precludes any hermeneutics: dogs do not "read" symbolic codes; they respond to smell, tone of voice, mannerisms, and other presymbolic modes of communication associated with bodies. Underneath the obsequious self-deprecation that shields Clayton from the full brunt of her criticism of his abstraction, Nina is trying to make a point about different—female—ways of knowing that are superior to abstract thinking. The confusion arises from an absence of a language in Western culture to represent nonabstract, nonverbal modes of communication. Stowe's struggle to represent a mode of cognition relying upon one's own body as an instrument for interpreting data resembles the struggle Jane Gallop describes in *Thinking Through the Body.*[9] For Stowe, thinking through the body is a bodily response to another person's "real presence," not his or her body only—though "real presence" is housed in the body, grounded in the body, and metonymically represented by the body. Proximity to another person's body enables an interpreter to evaluate that person holistically, as a complex nexus of physically grounded cognitive processes and emotional attachments. Intuitive thought is not the same thing as an epistemology presuming "a stable matrix of bodily signs" (Sanchez-Eppler 37).

Recognizing the centrality of bodily cognition in sentimentality encourages us to reinterpret some of the most frequently discussed scenes in the novel. For instance, Sanchez-Eppler reads the following scene as a prime example of how sentimentality can only envisage freedom from racial and sexual oppression in fantasies of transcendence that separate essence from body, thereby unwittingly reinforcing the very oppression they seek to challenge:

> "An't yer mine, now, body and soul?" [Legree] said, giving Tom a violent kick with his heavy boot; "tell me!"
>
> In the very depth of physical suffering, bowed by brutal oppression, this question shot a gleam of joy and triumph though Tom's soul. He suddenly stretched himself up, and looking earnestly to heaven, while the tears and blood that flowed down his face mingled, he exclaimed,
>
> "No! no! no! my soul an't your, Mas'r! You haven't bought it,—ye can't buy it! . . . you can't harm me!" (508)

According to Sanchez-Eppler, Tom's freedom in this passage ("you can't harm me!") is achieved through repudiation of the body: "Tom insists on the irrelevance of his body in identifying himself as a man" (113). However, while it is true that Tom separates himself from the "slave body" that white men have defined as "purchasable," it is equally true that it is the experience of his body that makes Tom conscious of a self not for sale, a self that is literally and physically within his body. The body is precisely *not* irrelevant to Tom's sense of his manhood in this scene. Rather, physical pain draws attention to a zone within which Tom's "real presence" is located. When the pain of Legree's violent kick shoots through Tom's body, that sensation of physical penetration metonymically reveals to Tom the existence of an interior self ("soul") distinct from the outer self (body) that Legree both owns and kicks. Thus, the kick "[shoots] a gleam of joy and triumph through Tom's soul." This passage illustrates how wounding can awaken an empowering self-consciousness that is neither independent of the body nor equal to it. The significance of this self-consciousness is not deferred to the afterlife; rather, it affords a psychic and spiritual transcendence *in the here and now*. It enables Tom to draw strength from his communal, affectional bonds and resist Legree's commands that he whip fellow slaves, betray Cassie, and renounce his religious convictions. His freedom derives from a transcendence not of his body, but of the legal fiction that exploits his body to define him as property.

Sanchez-Eppler is not wrong in her claim that appeals to spiritual freedom such as this one facilitate material exploitation. Another passage makes the repressive implications of idealizing "inner" freedom even more vivid: "the blows fell now only on the outer man, and not, as before, on the heart. Tom stood perfectly submissive; and yet Legree could not hide from himself that his power over his bond thrall was somehow gone" (558). Stowe's advocacy of the paradoxical freedom in perfect submission (a recognizable descendant of Calvin's "Paradox of Christian Liberty") exemplifies the repressive effects of universal humanism. But I want to suggest that there are two voices speaking simultaneously in these passages: the abstract and the presymbolic. I want to listen to that presymbolic voice. Stowe is, I think, trying to do something different from merely deferring freedom to a heaven where all souls are equal. The less familiar voice affirms an embodied, affective personhood empowered to resist repressive legal definitions of personhood and to affirm its own self-definition, grounded in integrity and personal convictions. It should not surprise us that we need to excavate this voice from beneath a counterdiscourse of disembodied transcendence. Literary practice is a symbolic activity, lacking a presymbolic vocabulary. As Stowe struggled to incorporate her female vision of the world and its potential for political transformation into her literary production, she found readily at hand a rich religious tradition describing universal equality in nonempirical terms. If it did not express the emotive ways of knowing grounded in cathexes and bodily experiences that she addressed elsewhere, it did enable her to bring into her work a notion of an interiority for slaves, a conception different from their enslaved bodies—with the deeply problematic ramifications that critics have appropriately noted.

We can recognize the voice of embodied, affective personhood most clearly in the sentimental effort to produce in the reader's body a sensation of sympathetic pain as a grounding for an intuitive understanding of the slave's "real presence" as a living, breathing, feeling human being. Awakening a visceral consciousness, "high sentimental" authors believe, is more likely to provoke action than dispassionate analysis, for it prevents the detachment that the mediation of symbols facilitates. To produce a gut feeling, Stowe draws upon readers' own memories of pain, creating blueprints that guide readers to relive their own experiences of suffering and to associate them with those of slaves. One of Tom's whippings, for instance, is introduced by images designed to stimulate readers' expansive imaginations: "The two gigantic negroes that now laid hold of Tom, with fiendish exultation in their faces, might have formed no unapt personification of the power of darkness. The poor woman screamed with apprehension, and all rose, as by a general impulse, while they dragged him unresisting from the place" (509). However, Stowe leaves the central scene unwritten, for the next chapter opens with a description of the aftermath: "the thick air swarmed with myriads of mosquitos, which increased the restless torture of his wounds; whilst a burning thirst—a torture beyond all others—filled up the uttermost measure of physical anguish" (510). Most readers are intimately familiar with mosquitos and thirst, and Stowe's allusion to these as the incidental details compounding an unspoken central horror grounds their imaginative projections of the scene of horror within their own physical experiences. Here, metonymy provokes the "presence" of the reader's own remembered pain, so that the reader experiences a small taste of "real" physical torture and associates it with slaves' anguish. The chain of metonymic associations enables readers to understand a slave's physical anguish intuitively rather than abstractly.

The device of alluding to the incidental physical details of a vaster horror provides a palpable grounding for Stowe's effort to convey slaves' limitless suffering. A scene in which Cassy attempts to dissuade Emmeline from fleeing by impressing upon her the tortures to which she would be subject were she captured offers a fictional example of this authorial strategy:

> "You'd be tracked by the dogs, and brought back, and then—then—"
> "What would he do?" said the girl, looking, with breathless interest, into her face.
> "What *wouldn't* he do, you'd better ask," said Cassy. . . . "You wouldn't sleep much, if I should tell you the things I've seen . . . There's a place way out down by the grounds, where you can see a black, blasted tree, and the ground all covered with black ashes. Ask anyone what was done there, and see if they will dare to tell you."
> "O! what do you mean?"
> "I won't tell you. I hate to think of it. And I tell you, the Lord only knows what we may see to-morrow. . . ." (534)

Cassy's indication that Legree burns slaves alive grounds Emmeline's comprehension within her body, a grounding that is metonymically reinforced by her repetition of the word "black." But deferring articulation of that torture enables Cassy to invoke an even more powerful sense of all kinds of interior anguish, centering within the victim's body but extending beyond its boundaries. Refusing exact details is not only a gesture toward delicacy, as Karen Halttunen argues, though it is undoubtedly that. It also enables physical torture to function as a *trope* for Legree's *limitless* depravity. We might compare Cassy's speech with that used by Toni Morrison in *Beloved*. As Caroline Rody shows, Morrison also relies upon deferral of articulation in an effort to prevent the containment and oversimplification of the supremely horrifying nature of slavery. The metonymic title of the novel, an adjective detached from a noun, exemplifies the inarticulability of the composite horrors of slavery. The ghost in *Beloved*, Rody argues, represents an embodiment of slave pain, a wish whose fulfillment is impossible in language. Like Stowe, Morrison focuses upon embodiment not as a representation of presence but as a trope for "real presence."

The most famous scene of *Uncle Tom's Cabin* conforms to this pattern of metonymy and deferral. Even though it was supposedly a vision of Tom being whipped to death that inspired Stowe to write the novel, the scene is largely unwritten.[10] Rather, the climax alludes to incidental features associated with it:

> the tick of the old clock could be heard, measuring with silent touch, the last minutes of mercy and probation. . . . Then, Legree, foaming with rage, smote his victim to the ground.
>
> Scenes of blood and cruelty are shocking to our ear and heart. What man has nerve to do, man has not nerve to hear. What brother-man and brother-Christian must suffer, cannot be told us, even in our secret chamber, it so harrows the soul! (583)

Readers construct the images of torture within their minds, drawing upon words like "blood," "nerve," "foaming," and "shocking." Doing so imparts the qualities of horror that they *know* accrue to physical distress, without containing the horror within language. These metonyms for torture stimulate a sensation of pain that feels so real that Stowe's son and biographer claimed that "*Uncle Tom's Cabin* made the crack of the slavedriver's whip, and the cries of the tortured black ring in every household in the land" (C. E. Stowe 155).

A Raging, Burning Storm of Feeling

Of course, it didn't. It is fundamentally impossible to bridge the gap separating one person's experience from another's. Metonymy is not equivalence. And so, while sentimental authors idealized in wounding an epistemological ideal of perfect comprehension in "one sorrow," intuitive knowing could never guarantee that readers would feel exactly what slaves feel.[11] However, that epistemological failure produces an unanticipated result: representations of physical and emotional wounding constitute powerful tropes for the *desire* to achieve a perfect form of knowing, even if they cannot effect it. Physical wounds tantalize a viewer by seeming to make the inner self accessible to scrutiny, while emotional wounds underlie fantasies of emotional equivalence ("I know exactly what you're going through"). Stowe's sentimental wounding so powerfully evokes the fantasy of perfect access to the other's "real presence" that its failure to achieve that presence is partially compensated by its ability to make that *desire itself* present to a reader. A wound is a gap, a metaphor for the absence of the other. While the sentimental wound cannot heal that gap, its representation of the desire for "real presence" partially compensates for the inevitable deferral of "real presence."

In the climax of *Uncle Tom's Cabin*, Stowe repeatedly exploits the rhetorical power of wounding to represent the desire for "real presence." For instance, after Tom is beaten "to the uttermost of physical anguish," Stowe writes: "He did not know but that the day of his death was dawning in the sky; and his heart throbbed with solemn throes of joy and desire, as he thought that the wondrous *all* . . . might all break upon his vision before that sun should set again" (538). As Tom's wounds throb with pain, his heart throbs with joy and desire; as his skin is broken by the whip, he imagines that he is near the presence of "the *all*." "The *all*" is a loose reference to something like "God's presence," and wounding makes available to Tom a fantasy of fusion with God, a merge that is suggested to him by the rupture of his skin, which allows for an ecstatic penetration of his body by alterity. This kind of merge is infinitely desirable for Stowe, who laments the way individuality imposes a lonely separation from God's loving plenitude, as Tom's dying words emphasize: "Who,—who,—who shall separate us from the love of Christ?" (591). Separation from God and other people is inimical to the deepest forms of human fulfillment, as Stowe indicates when isolation leads Tom to the brink of atheism. When human life imposes barriers, that life is a form of death, while death paradoxically offers "life," a state of "continuity" with God, as Bataille puts it. Thus, when little Eva dies, Stowe writes that she "gave one sigh and passed from death unto life!" (428) Eradicating separation from God and from "the *all*" is such an enticing prospect that Tom effuses, "[Legree] an't done me no real harm,—only opened the gate of the kingdom for me; that's all!" (591). Within the Calvinist discourse that governs Stowe's language in the ending of the novel, the wounds that a whipping opens in the skin can be zones of "joy and desire," because they are gates between a person's isolated individuality and God's kingdom. As gates, wounds are metonyms for God's full presence.

In the climactic whipping scene in *Uncle Tom's Cabin*, wounding is so intimately linked with desire that torture seems to express longing and intensity of imagined pleasure more than it does literal physical agony. When a fellow slave taunts Tom that he is about to be whipped to death, Stowe writes, "The savage words none of them reached that ear!—a higher voice there was saying, 'Fear not them that kill the body, and, after that, have no more that they can do.' Nerve and bone of that poor man's body vibrated to those words, as if touched by the finger of God; and he felt the strength of a thousand souls in one. . . . His soul throbbed,—his home was in sight,—and the hour of release seemed at hand" (581–82). As Stowe casts about for powerful imagery to express the desire for "real presence," a desire that is at the heart of these climactic scenes, she turns to a number of words that seem sexual, particularly when they appear together in the same passage: "throbbed,"[12] "release," "vibrated," "touched by the finger," "joy and desire." Sexual desire, like religious desire, is frequently about a longing for the other's "real presence," not simply proximity nor simply emotional or intellectual connection. And this convergence, in the climax of the novel, of sexual language with notions of a desire for real presence, condensed in the trope of the wound, may well explain why *Uncle Tom's Cabin* provided the foundation for the masturbation fantasies quoted at the head of this chapter. Readers experienced the book as a kind of emotional wounding; Stowe identified her strategy as one of thrusting into readers' wounds, and associates wounds with sexualized expressions of ecstatic transcendence. Readers therefore were in a good position to experience the textual affect as a form of sexual transcendence. While literary history abounds with descriptions of innocents suffering cruelty and violent subjugation, few books feature the convergence of ecstatic transcendence, sexual language, and sadistic torture as vividly as does *Uncle Tom's Cabin*.

But the use of this sexual language in association with martyrdom is surely not sufficient to make the book the masochistic chef d'oeuvre so many readers have found it to be, since such language is, for the most part, limited to the ending.

Another, more immediate discourse of the era participates even more directly in the eroticization of wounding in *Uncle Tom's Cabin*. For not all martyrdom is eroticized in the novel. Though Eva experiences the same kind of bissful reintegration with totality at her death as Tom does at his, and though she suffers terribly, the language of her passing is not tinged with the erotic. Rather, fantasies of wounding appear to be most fully eroticized in *Uncle Tom's Cabin* when projected onto suffering *black* bodies, such as those of Tom and Dodo, a beautiful young slave who appears in chapter 28, "Henrique." Stowe embeds her portrait of Dodo within a clearly sexualized discourse by limning a romantic rivalry between him and Eva's white supremacist cousin, Henrique. Henrique's relationship with his "fair cousin" is characterized in romantic clichés: "I could love anything, for your sake, dear Cousin; for I really think you are the loveliest creature that I ever saw" (396). But after Henrique strikes Dodo "across the face with his riding-whip, and, seizing one of his arms, force[s] him on to his knees, and beat[s] him till he was out of breath" (388), Eva pointedly ignores his gestures of "gallantry" toward herself, favoring instead his weeping slave: "But Eva bent to the other side of the horse, where Dodo was standing" (389). When Henrique protests, "Why, Eva, you've really taken such a fancy to Dodo, that I shall be jealous," she does not dispute that there has been a romantic contest and that she has favored his rival, responding instead, "But you beat him," as though there were a causal link between his suffering and her love. "[Y]ou don't *love* your servants," he insists, to which she replies, "I do, indeed" (237, emphasis in original). Henrique's abuse stimulates Eva's love for Dodo and frees her to express it, an expression that would remain taboo if Dodo had not been whipped.

The love for the slave is not entirely chaste. As Hortense Spillers argues, a covert discourse of sexual desire for black men pulses throughout the book, erupting most blatantly when Eva urges her father to buy Tom because, as she puts it, "I want him" (130). The desire of the white woman for the black man is a cliché in America; barred by race from bourgeois respectability, African Americans have traditionally been mythologized as supersexual beings associated with tropical heat, fire, blood, and strength.[13] If eroticism is a desire for the "other," a longing to heal the wounds of an internalized otherness that situates separation from "the *all*" at the core of identity, then in nineteenth-century America, a black man represents the perfect figure of desire for the white woman. Stowe may well express this kind of culturally overdetermined desire for the black man's supermasculinity through explicit expressions of desire, as Spillers suggests, but she also does so by fetishizing the wounds of black men. Feminizing and emasculating these men frees her to desire them, for as tortured objects of pity, they invite the full force of love, tenderness, and longing for intimacy that Stowe could never bestow upon a black man represented as subject. Projecting masochistic desires onto these powerfully sensual (but sentimentalized) figures eroticizes the identification that unites two people in the bonds of one sorrow.[14]

Through the operations of "propping," this unconscious attraction to wounded black slaves intensifies the eroticization of Stowe's rhetorical strategy of sentimental wounding. Stowe strives to make readers experience "the real presence of distress" and to bring them to associate it with the suffering of the wounded slave in a fantasized unity forged through pain. The opening of old emotional wounds produces affect somewhere within the body, that unidentifiable site of an elusive "real presence," and the discourses of sexual desire associated with the suffering slaves are "propped" onto that experience of affect, so that the unity of reader and sufferer can be experienced as a sexual unity. The process by which the sentimental wound is experienced as ecstatic or erotic is metonymic and discursive, culturally specific rather than universal.

Southern reviewers routinely objected to the prurient sexuality that they found overwhelming in *Uncle Tom's Cabin*. An anonymous reviewer in the New Orleans *Picayune*, for instance, charged that Stowe "painted from her own libidinous imagination scenes which no modest woman could conceive of." In his review, or "critical punishment," as he calls it, George Frederick Holmes exhorted: "Are scenes of license and impurity, and ideas of loathsome depravity and habitual prohibition to be made the cherished topics of the female pen, and the familiar staple of domestic consideration or promiscuous conversation? Is the mind of woman to be tainted, seduced, contaminated, and her heart disenchanted of all its native purity of sentiment, by the unblushing perusal . . . of such thinly veiled pictures of corruption? Can a lady of stainless mind read such works without a blush of confusion, or a man think of their being habitually read by ladies without shame and repugnance?" One can only assume that Holmes would feel "shame" if ladies were exposed to "ideas of loathsome depravity" because they would then have firsthand knowledge of the extent to which their husbands, brothers, and fathers are regularly "seduced . . . [by] thinly veiled pictures of corruption" in the books normally reserved for male readers. Surely, the metaphor William Gilmore Simms constructed to express his loathing for Stowe displays an imagination more libidinous than the one he seeks to condemn: "Mrs. Stowe betrays a malignity so remarkable that the petticoat lifts of itself, and we see the hoof of the beast under the table." Because they are immune to the appeal of communal bonding through suffering, these commentators are alert to the pornographic aspects of the book and concerned about the transgressive effects of that eroticism upon their wives and daughters (qtd. in Gossett 190–91).

Northern readers were far less likely to see their experiences of the book as sexual. Nonetheless, many enthusiastic readers experienced what we might call a jouissance, an experience associated with, though not identical to, sexuality. Many of Stowe's contemporary readers describe a physical experience of desire for the real presence of "the *all*" in images of wounding, expressed within racial and religious terms and "propped" on the "real presence" of their own emotional and physical wounds. Consider, for example, the response to sentimental wounding described in a letter written by Stowe's lifelong friend Georgiana May, which Stowe printed in an 1870s edition of *Uncle Tom's Cabin*:

> I sat up last night long after one o'clock, reading and finishing "Uncle Tom's Cabin." I *could not* leave it any more than I could have left a dying child; nor could I restrain an almost hysterical sobbing for an hour after I laid my head upon my pillow. I thought I was a thorough-going Abolitionist before, but your book has awakened so strong a feeling of indignation and compassion, that I seem never to have had *any* feeling on this subject till now. But what can we do? Alas! alas! What *can* we do? This storm of feeling has been raging, burning like a very fire in my bones, all the livelong night, and all through my duties this morning it haunts me,—I *cannot* do away with it. Gladly would I have gone out in the midnight storm last night, and, like the martyr of old, have been stoned to death, if that could have rescued these oppressed and afflicted ones. (Qtd. in Gossett 167)

May's letter encapsulates many of the ways that wounding functions as a trope for desire in sentimentality. The letter opens with a melodramatic identification with heroic motherhood (she "*could* not leave" a dying child).[15] In imagining being unwillingly wrenched from a dying child, she inflicts upon herself precisely the sentimental wound of the separation of mother and child that Stowe so frequently depicts, invigorating within herself an aching desire for intimate union. May follows this indication of a painful sense of absence in herself (implied in the powerless cry "Alas! alas! What *can* we do?") with a second image of literal wounding as a trope expressing her desire to fill that gap: "Gladly would I have gone out in the midnight storm last night, and, like the martyr of old, have been stoned to death." The fantasy of palpable pain counteracts the absence inside the self, and the coherent image of braving a lethal storm gratifies May with a visualizable form of agency that answers her frustrated inarticulateness. It also rewards her with an ecstatic sense of transcendent martyrdom that resembles the martyrdom of Tom. Indeed, her use of heightened language ("like the martyr of old") suggests that Stowe's heightened discourse has provided the terms in which May understands her own experience of inner anguish and her conception of an effective response.

Sentimental wounding also produces a form of jouissance for May. Her use of the image of a storm twice ("storm of feeling," "midnight storm") links her pain to her desire; they seem to be manifestations of each other. The metonymic link of the word "storm" suggests that the idea of religious transcendence "props" itself on the raw feeling of physical affect raging and burning within, so that the burning sensation is associated with the ecstasies that presumably accompany martyrdom. In other words, metonymic exchanges between literal storms and storms of feeling enable May to experience some version of the ecstatic jouissance Stowe associates with Tom's literal wounds. The phrase "these oppressed and afflicted ones" gestures toward solidarity with slaves, but its detached, clichéd character suggests that they serve more as objects facilitating in her a turn inward than as actual subjects leading her outward into public action.

Presumably, Stowe would not object to her friend's experience of elation upon contemplating the spectacle of martyrdom. Indeed, May's response mirrors the ideal Christian response to the Atonement: a deeply felt recognition of Jesus' martyrdom fills the Christian with a blissful recognition of God's love for humanity.[16] Stowe describes this process in the novel when, on the brink of atheism, Tom receives a vision of Christ "crowned with thorns, buffeted and bleeding. Tom gazed, in awe and wonder, at the majestic patience of the face; the deep, pathetic eyes thrilled him to his inmost heart; his soul woke, as, with floods of emotion, he stretched out his hands . . . he saw that same face bending compassionately towards him" (554). Like the reader of *Uncle Tom's Cabin*, Tom *feels* distress by identifying with the pain of another sufferer, and that feeling provokes a "flood[ing]" sense of loving intimacy, a bonding with the other that expands the self. My point is not that May's experience is necessarily objectionable, any more than Tom's is, but rather that it is a physically grounded experience of expansion prompted by sympathy and propped on an ideal of interracial bonding. As such, it has an ecstatic, erotic character.

The ecstasy of sentimental wounding is made available to May because of the involuntary nature of her physical response. The division between two selves—a will that seeks self-control and a body racked by convulsions and hysterical sobbing she "*cannot* do away with"—enables May to experience her jouissance without having to take responsibility for it. Being forced to feel passion might well have been enticing for women in May's social position. The influential British doctor and author William Acton notoriously observed in 1857 that "the majority of women (happily for society) are not very much troubled with sexual feeling of any kind"—particularly "the best mothers, wives, and managers of households."[17] And thirteen years later, George Napheys, an influential Philadelphia doctor, wrote "A vulgar opinion prevails that [women] are creatures of like passions with ourselves; that they experience desires as ardent, and often as ungovernable, as those which lead to so much evil in our sex. . . . Nothing is more utterly untrue. Only in very rare instances do women experience one tithe of the sexual feeling which is familiar to most men" (173–74). As Nancy Cott points out, many women endorsed the dominant narrative of female passionlessness, because they derived from it the privileges their culture accorded its "best" women. Stowe herself had disavowed any passion: "tho I did love you with an almost *insane* love before I married you," she wrote to her husband, "I never knew yet or felt the pulsation which showed me that I could be tempted in that way—there never was a moment when I felt anything by which you could have drawn me astray—for I loved you as I now love God—and I can conceive of no higher love— . . . I have no passion."[18] But racialized masochistic fantasies in *Uncle Tom's Cabin* served as a mechanism enabling her and her female readers to experience such "pulsations" while retaining their self-conceptions as "true women." Scarry's "unmaking" thesis applies here as it does in *The Wide, Wide World*: when one's constructed identity abjects the body and physical passion, fantasies of pain enable one to imagine the ecstasies of unmaking that repressive subjectivity, without experiencing its agonies.

Male readers of *Uncle Tom's Cabin* also indulged the pleasures of unmaking—in their case, of hegemonic norms of manhood. According to George Templeton Strong, a prominent New York lawyer, *Uncle Tom's Cabin* was "a sentimental romance . . . that set all Northern women crying and sobbing over the sorrows of Sambo." The affect of *Uncle Tom's Cabin* was not limited to women, however. Horace Greeley's tears were so uncontrollable that he had to interrupt a trip from Boston to Washington to spend the night in a hotel and, presumably, weep in private.[19] William Lloyd Garrison mentions a feminine "frequent moistening of our eyes, and the making of our heart grow liquid as water, and the trembling of every nerve within us." Rev. Henry Clarke Wright observed, "It has fascinated and repulsed me at the same time, as a reptile that enchants you, while it excites your loathing and abhorrence . . . moving and melting and swaying my heart and sympathies." Longfellow comments that "we read ourselves into despair in that tragic book, *Uncle Tom's Cabin*. It is too melancholy, and makes one's blood boil too hotly." And John Dix, an English immigrant, commented that a friend was "sleeping one night in a strange house," and being "annoyed by hearing somebody in the adjoining chamber alternately groaning and laughing," he "knocked upon the wall and said, 'Hallo, there! What's the matter! Are you sick or reading *Uncle Tom's Cabin?*'" The stranger answered that he was reading *Uncle Tom's Cabin*.[20] These male readers, like female readers, may have found a transgressive pleasure in being forced to shed abjected "female" tears despite themselves, released from oppressive fictions of virile manhood.

The involuntary nature of these responses frees both white men and women to indulge socially unacceptable desires without having to accept responsibility for them. But such compulsion is not merely a veil screening the novel's potential to provoke erotic feelings; rather, the physical compulsion effected by the novel intensified its potential to stimulate sexual feelings. According to D. A. Miller, readers of Victorian sensation fiction experienced an erotic thrill from physical subjection to the adrenaline effects characteristic of sensation fiction: "accelerated heart rate and respiration, increased blood pressure, the pallor resulting from vasoconstriction." These "fight or flight" symptoms are involuntary: "the body is compelled to automatism . . . the rhythm of reading is frankly addictive." And Miller describes this physical subjection to an author's "Pavlovian expertise" as a form of slavery, an "involuntary servitude" that provokes a masochistic titillation (146). Analogously, *Uncle Tom's Cabin* affords the masochistic pleasures of "involuntary servitude" to the visceral power of Stowe's wounding ("I *cannot* do away with it," May says).[21] Slavery is not only the *subject* of the novel but its *effect*. This doubly enslaving textuality reinforces the ability of the reader to fantasize about the kind of ecstatic liberation from hegemonic identity that Tom does when Legree kicks him. Because the author has forced the experience of passion upon her readers, they are not responsible for its transgressiveness. Separated from the body, yet in a heightened relationship to the body, the reader can thrill to a sense of incoherence, a gap in the illusion of unitary identity. Stowe not only represents what Case 57 claimed was "the aim and end of all masochistic ideas"— the "unlimited power of life and death, as exercised over slaves and domestic animals"—but her sentimental wounding subjects her reader to something resembling it.

This freedom through enslavement produces a kind of transcendence for the reader, who can experience a release from the coherence of subjectivity, a transcendence that derives not from rising above the body but rather from experiencing it in a splintered way. This ecstatic experience of incoherence is related to—but crucially different from—the decentered intersubjective identity sentimental authors idealized in the rhetorical technique of wounding. In the sentimental ideal, a sufferer and an observer exceed their own bodily limits through the common bond of pain; the observer knows what the sufferer feels and becomes intertwined with the other. One does unto one's neighbor as unto oneself, because one's neighbor *is*, in a sense, oneself.

But the physical gratification associated with that experience does not necessarily extend the observer outward to a communion with the sufferer; it may turn the observer inward, compensating with a self-satisfying *illusion* of humanitarian altruism that may well not be acted upon at all. After all, as Wendell Phillips says, "There is many a man who weeps over Uncle Tom and swears by the [pro-slavery New York] *Herald*" (qtd. in Gossett 168). The response of a group of Swiss mountaineers, as recorded by Stowe's brother Charles, also indicates a disturbingly exploitative side of sympathy: "It was touching to listen to the talk of these secluded mountaineers. The good hostess, even the servant maids, hung about Harriet, expressing such tender interest for the slave. All had read 'Uncle Tom'; and it had apparently been an era in their life's monotony, for they said, 'Oh, madam, do write another! Remember, our winter nights here are very long!'" (C. E. Stowe 244). While these mountaineers are sympathetic to the slaves' plight, Charles Beecher suggests that their preoccupation with their own dismally long winter nights partially undermines their pretensions to humanitarian altruism. They can do little to help the slave, but they long for another tale about bondage in order to alleviate their boredom. Philip Fisher suggests that, despite its altruistic gesture, self-reflexive pleasures are endemic to the sentimental genre, because it relies upon death as an "analogy for social, remediable suffering." Because sentimentality emphasizes "our general helplessness," "the will to act is weakened if not denied. The feeling of suffering becomes more important than the action against suffering. Tears become more important than escapes or rescues" (110). Thus, in response to her own rhetorical question "What *can* we do?" Georgiana May fantasizes about being stoned to death, if that would help the slaves, an image that gratifies with the *illusion* of heroic agency but identifies no real action. Fisher's sweeping critique of the failure of sentimentality to produce genuine political commitment offers a temptingly appropriate closure. After all, it would be satisfying to observe that not only do sado-masochistic fantasies of torturing members of another race violate all human decency and compassion, degrade the human spirit, and perpetuate racist stereotypes but they fail to produce the presumably desired goal of rescuing "these oppressed and afflicted ones."

But surely history proves that *Uncle Tom's Cabin* did *not* weaken the will of the nation to act.[22] Some readers may have simply indulged the decadent pleasures of enslavement within a private reading situation, but many nonetheless responded to those pleasures by taking arms against enslavement in a public arena. The pleasures of suffering did not invariably prevent outward-oriented action. Rather, they appear to have fostered in many white Americans a fiction of interracial bonding that inspired action on behalf of the community as a whole. Indeed, the pleasures of that fiction, including the pleasures of narcissistic and erotic gratification, encouraged readers around the world to endorse the book's abolitionist message. Though the communal ideal frequently was predicated upon the erasure of the subjectivity of black Americans, it nonetheless awakened abolitionist passions in many citizens who had grown accustomed to rationalizing slavery. Without the fictions of unity that authorized it, emancipation might never have become a national priority. As the complex erotics of the sentimental wound demonstrate, sympathy is a dangerous form of political thought, tending to objectify the other or recreate that other in one's own image. But as history demonstrates, a *lack* of sympathy is even more dangerous.

The political ramifications of the eroticization of sympathy in *Uncle Tom's Cabin* are equally double-edged from a feminist standpoint. Sentimental authors conceived of feeling along with suffering others as an important contribution women could make to the political sphere. Stowe says in the "Concluding Remarks" to *Uncle Tom's Cabin*, "There is one thing that every individual can do,—they can see to it that *they feel right*" (624). But in promoting "feeling right" as a significant form of female political agency, she unwittingly fostered the sadistic exploitation of slaves positioned as erotic objects. She, and sentimental authors like her, also participated in the construction of ideas of an essential female masochism, since the promotion of "feeling right" rewarded women who suffered with both social esteem and sensual gratification, thereby suggesting that women enjoy suffering and should enjoy it. White men could return from their flirtation with the masochistic pleasures of identification with abused slaves to their positions of cultural dominance, while women were led to understand suffering as their particular calling and privilege. However, the masochistic pleasures of *Uncle Tom's Cabin* are not simply a means of brainwashing female readers into accepting their positions within the panopticon. They also represent the fact that bourgeois white women, like everyone else, were already in the panopticon, searching for effective means of experiencing the full range of their feelings and desires within their particular cultural constraints. Fantasies of ecstatic martyrdom did not necessarily describe what women like Stowe and May actually wanted in their lives, but they did make available a language of desire, articulated in codes largely determined by prevailing social discourses, such as Calvinism and racial essentialism. For better or for worse, in antebellum America, tropes of torture and enslavement enabled white middle-class women to articulate their longings for intimacy, ecstasy, reconnection to the body, interracial bonding, and reform of the alienated abstraction that characterized the male-dominated literary and political spheres. Recognizing and understanding the agency and eroticism of sentimental wounding neither naturalizes nor apologizes for it; revealing its historical and cultural contingency takes an important first step toward finding equally exciting and more humane alternatives.[23]

Five

The Revenge of Cato's Daughter:
Emily Dickinson's Uses of
Sentimental Masochism

THE LETTERS and poetry of Emily Dickinson prominently feature sentimental scenarios that bear a striking resemblance to certain passages
in evangelical sentimental works, like *The Wide, Wide World* and *Elsie
Dinsmore*, in which helpless innocent females submit to the abusive
domination of an extremely powerful male. Many of these scenarios are
masochistic, for the victims willingly submit to and even seek to be dominated or hurt.[1] In Dickinson, one important, recurring manifestation of
this scenario is the image of a female flower with her head bowed in
anguished adoration before a domineering, powerful male figure, who
appears as Christ, King, Duke, Master, Caesar, or Sun. (All of these together make up a composite figure St. Armand usefully labels "Phoebus.") Found in many poems, such as "The Daisy follows soft the Sun,"
"Great Caesar," "Ah, Teneriffe,"and implicit in the many flower-bee
poems, the Daisy-Phoebus relationship is an important element in Dickinson's poetic lexicon.[2]

Dickinson turns to these stereotypes of masculinity and femininity for
the possibilities for self-expression they offer her. Historically and culturally specific discursive associations enable the Daisy-Phoebus relationship to express an intense and complex emotion, incorporating such
components as terror, vulnerability, ecstasy, mysticism, eroticism, and
anger. This image manages to encapsulate so much emotional intensity,
not because of a universal meaning associated with it, but rather because
it compresses within a single snapshot the vast allusiveness of two converging discourses—sentimentalism and Calvinism—that provided
many of the terms in which Dickinson understood her life. Like Susan
Warner and Harriet Beecher Stowe, Dickinson takes advantage of this
convergence for aesthetic purposes. However, unlike Warner's and
Stowe's, Dickinson's use of sentimental masochism as an expression of
desire is a self-conscious, ironic, and intentional appropriation of conventional discourse for her own literary aims.

The "man of noon" letter, which Wendy Barker describes as "a letter
so dramatic that nearly every Dickinson critic has observed its significance," exemplifies how sentimental and evangelical discourses con-

verge in the Phoebus-Daisy image.[3] Writing to Susan Gilbert in early
June 1852, twenty-two-year-old Emily Dickinson expresses her ambiva-
lence about marriage:

> Those unions, my dear Susie, by which two lives are one, this sweet and
> strange adoption wherein we can but look, and are not yet admitted, how it
> can fill the heart, and make it gang wildly beating, how it will take *us* one day,
> and make us all it's own, and we shall not run away from it, but lie still and be
> happy!
>
> You and I have been strangely silent upon this subject, Susie, we have often
> touched upon it, and as quickly fled away, as children shut their eyes when the
> sun is too bright for them. I have always hoped to know if you had no dear
> fancy, illumining all your life, no one of whom you murmured in the faithful
> ear of night—and at whose side in fancy, you walked the livelong day; and
> when you come home, Susie, we must speak of these things. How dull our
> lives must seem to the bride, and the plighted maiden, whose days are fed
> with gold, and who gathers pearls every evening; but to the *wife*, Susie, some-
> times the *wife forgotten*, our lives perhaps seem dearer than all others in the
> world; you have seen flowers at morning, *satisfied* with the dew, and those
> same sweet flowers at noon with their heads bowed in anguish before the
> mighty sun; think you these thirsty blossoms will *now* need naught but—*dew?*
> No, they will cry for sunlight, and pine for the burning noon, tho' it scorches
> them, scathes them; they have got through with peace—they know that the
> man of noon, is *mightier* than the morning and their life is henceforth to him.
> Oh, Susie, it is dangerous, and it is all too dear, these simple trusting spirits,
> and the spirits mightier, which we cannot resist! It does so rend me, Susie, the
> thought of it when it comes, that I tremble lest at sometime I, too, am yielded
> up. (L#93)

In this letter, Dickinson represents marriage as an institution that transforms the bride into a masochist. Relinquishing autonomy and locating
all of her being, happiness, and identity in another, a bride is precari-
ously vulnerable to the threat of abandonment. While the idea of marriage may initially seem to be all gold and pearls, a husband may well
lose interest in his wife and either physically or emotionally abandon her.
But because her life has now become "henceforth to him," she will require her husband's presence for her very identity as completely as a
flower requires the sun's beams. Even if he causes her anguish, she will
crave it, since it comes from him. Dickinson seems amazed that though
the act of giving oneself to a man is so potentially lethal, women—
"these simple trusting spirits"—go through with it all the time, becoming so dependent upon the presence of their mighty man that they
masochistically cry and pine for the one who hurts them.

The central image of this letter—a husband who is as powerful and
resplendent as the sun—is drawn from an intersection of sentimental ro-

mances and evangelical Christianity. I suspect that Dickinson's usage of it here is at least partially influenced by the 1851 domestic novel *Head of the Family*, by Dinah Maria Mulock Craik, a Scottish author well known in her day for her novels *John Halifax, Gentleman* and *Olive* and her children's story *The Little Lame Prince*. In a letter to her close friend Abiah Root written in April 1852, Dickinson mentioned that she would soon be receiving and reading *Head of the Family*. She apparently read it soon thereafter, for two months later, she loosely quotes from it in the "man of noon" letter. The novel tells the story of Rachel Armstrong, an abandoned wife who—like the flowers in Dickinson's letter—perversely loves her faithless husband and masochistically pines for his (abusive) presence. Rachel had been an innocent country virgin until she fell in love with a seductive rake who "married" her in a ceremony attended only by the two of them and then abandoned her in order to pursue richer, fresher women. Devastated by the loss of both virginity and husband, Rachel becomes a famous but miserable tragedian, towering in her grief. Before she finally plunges into an amnesiac dementia, she goes through a masochistic phase, telling a mild-mannered friend, Ninian:

> I am not afraid of you, as I always was of—him that is my husband. But then he was like a god compared with me; in knowledge, in power, in beauty. I felt that from the first moment I ever saw him. It was just the story of Clytie and the Sun. Ah! he taught me that story—all things I ever knew he taught me, or I learned them for his sake. . . . I loved him! Nay, not loved, that is too low a word. It was adoration, as wild, as daring, as hopeless as Clytie's for the Sun. Until at last the Sun, looking down from his sphere, saw the flower which his beams had wakened into life—saw it, loved it, lifted it up into his heart. And the poor flower would have been content, even if his brightness had scorched it to death—knowing it had lived one hour there. (23)

Though Ninian is attracted to Rachel, she is indifferent to him; his kindly ways lack the magnificence, glory, and arrogance that provokes her "wild," "daring" "adoration." Her attraction, rather, is for a man like a god, who offers an infinitely rich and rewarding life to his bride, who opens to a girl ecstasies of fulfillment, meaning, and purpose—even if they come at the cost of pain and anguish. As we have seen, such fantasies were fostered in part by discourses of spousal unity idealizing the absorption of a woman into a man, who alone has subjectivity and significance for both.

Marriage transforms Rachel into a masochist; the male power she loves is, in her imagination, most palpable in violence directed against herself. Even the idea of death at the hands of her Sun-like husband provokes desire and pleasure, if such a death were to buy an hour with him. The reason for this masochistic attraction to a crushing power appears to be the contingency of her being as wife. Rachel's husband "wakened [her] into life," gave her a new, rich existence in which she not only partook of his grandeur but required it to survive. His scorching beams are essential to her. The pattern for this masochism originates in what she represents as a familiar story, that of Clytie and the sun-god Apollo, which is found in Ovid's *Metamorphoses*.[4] In this myth, Apollo grows indifferent to his former lover Clytie, who remains desperately in love with him and is doomed to a despairing existence watching him as he traces his fiery path across the sky. So rooted is she in her position of mute desire that she turns into a heliotrope, a flower that turns its face toward the sun throughout the day. Rachel wishfully revises Ovid by imagining that the Sun looks down, pities Clytie, and lifts her back to his heart. She also elaborates on the masochism implicit in Ovid: even if the sun scorched the flower to death, she "would have been content" just to be near him.

The mystical allure of the Sun-Husband lies at least partially in his association with God. Later in *Head of the Family*, Craik indicates that marital and religious union are virtually interchangeable when she describes heaven as "that Kingdom where all earthly marriage will be done away, and that marriage only remain, which being an union spiritual and complete, is as indissoluble as the union of the soul with God" (30). Such links between God and husband inform the "man of noon" letter. Its images of "gold," "pearls," brilliant sunlight, and resplendent power are drawn from the discourses of the Second Great Awakening. Charles Wadsworth, Dickinson's "shepherd from little girlhood," for example, enticed his followers with a vision of future bliss, when the gospel itself "meets the soul, as it casts off the burden of flesh, and clothes it in heavenly robes, and indues it with heavenly faculties, and bears it to heavenly places—through the gates of pearl, along the streets of the golden city, through the opening ranks of cherubim and seraphim to sit down in the midst of the Throne of God" (51). That vision, a staple of revival rhetoric, is in turn drawn from *Revelation*: "And I John saw the holy city, new Jerusalem, coming down from God out of heaven, prepared as a bride adorned for her husband. . . . And the twelve gates were twelve pearls; every several gate was of one pearl: and the street of the city was pure gold, . . . And the city had no need of the sun, neither of the moon, to shine in it: for the glory of God did lighten it, and the Lamb is the light thereof" (Revelation 21:2, 21, 23). At the time that she wrote the "man of noon" letter, Dickinson was intellectually and emotionally absorbed in the fervor of the Second Great Awakening, the massive revival movement that dominated life in Amherst during her formative years as well as her year at Mount Holyoke. And as Cynthia Griffin Wolff documents, Dickinson was intimately familiar with marriage as a metaphor for God's relationship to human beings (272–73).[5] Because the pearls and gold and sunlight of marriage were widely associated with heavenly rapture, the complex emotion evoked by the image of flowers kneeling before the Sun-God-Husband includes notions of religious transcendence.

The terror that also obviously characterizes the relationship of Phoebus and Daisy is another important component of this image, intensifying its capacity to express ecstatic desire. Dickinson associates both marriage and sex with a mixture of agony and ecstasy; the same mixture characterizes her feelings about a mystical union with God. In her way of seeing it, yielding autonomy in order to "be to" God puts a convert in a position as precarious as that of a bride: vulnerable to an agonizing dependence upon the presence of the other upon whom his or her being has become contingent. She captures this precipitous vulnerability she associates with conversion in a letter she wrote to Abiah Root on March 28, 1846: "I feel that I am sailing upon the brink of an awful precipice, from which I cannot escape & over which I fear my tiny boat will soon glide if I do not receive help from above. There is now a revival in College & many hearts have given way to the claims of God" (L#11). Though "giv[ing] way to" God struck her as a perilous plunge with an unpredictable outcome, all around her she saw "simple trusting spirits" yielding to the persuasions of the revivalists, seduced, perhaps, by ecstatic visions of the gold and pearls adorning God's own bride. In her mind, the ecstasies of uniting oneself with another are inseparable from terror.

The "man of noon" letter represents both evangelical and sentimental ideologies as protomasochistic: the contingency of being they entail will induce the convert/bride to long for affliction from the hands of her God-like husband. The potential for agony in both forms of relinquishment would seem here to be the cause of Dickinson's famous rejection of both conversion and marriage. However, the letter also suggests that in the masochistic sensibility generated by the convergence of those discourses lies possibilities for powerful forms of aesthetic representation and private pleasure. The liminality that Dickinson associates with proximity to a Godlike other—while too risky to indulge *actually*—is exciting as an imaginative *fantasy*. The notion of being "yielded up" suggests possibilities of sublime rapture, and even an erotic merging. After all, in referring to the "sweet and strange" union "by which two lives are one" Dickinson refers not only to marriage but to sexual intercourse. She imagines that it will "fill the heart," "take *us*," and "make us all it's own," and adds that "we shall not run away" but rather "lie still and be happy." And though that kind of being "yielded up" seems hostile or dangerous, it is a "sweet and strange adoption." In part, the sweet erotics of a violent sexual union derives from the association in this letter with the religious union of God and human. In part, it also seems to derive from the liminal state that is invoked, the thrill of feeling life so intensely precisely because it is on the brink of annihilation.

In fact, as she writes the letter, Dickinson may even feel some version of the erotic thrill of fear that she describes. She not only describes the terror of being "yielded up"; she actually experiences something resembling it. Her description of her own bodily sensations as she thinks about sex and marriage mirrors the sensations she imagines the bride experiencing. The idea of wives "yielded up" "rend[s]" her. The flowers are scorched by the sun's powerful rays, and in response her own body "tremble[s]." The idea "fill[s]" her heart and makes it "gang wildly beating." This similarity between her experience and that of her imaginary victims suggests that to a certain extent, Dickinson identifies with the perilous plight of the abandoned flowers, experiencing in response the classic "fight or flight" symptoms of pounding heart, stimulated nerves, and increased respiration. And while these fight-or-flight symptoms are presumably provoked by fear of spousal or divine abandonment or violence, the sensations produced by fantasized identification with such a situation can evoke the rapture that sentimentalism and Calvinism associate with the anguish of being "yielded up." As we have seen, in Calvinist discourse, the idea of pain can trigger feelings of pleasure associated with salvation.[6] Given such a context, the physical sensations associated with fear might well be experienced as some form of religious or erotic pleasure. The physical reaction to identifying with the flower-sun scenario is a crucial component of its power as an expression of desire. It re-presences the body abjected by dominant ideologies, achieving the kind of semiotic expressiveness that Julia Kristeva prizes in poetic language.[7] As Robert McClure Smith notes, "What is so intriguing about Dickinson's . . . poetic fusion of body and text, is that with minimal fuss it anticipates in practice one of the major theoretical goals of an *écriture féminine*," writing into presence a female body written out of Western literature (*Seductions* 128–29).[8]

As the wealth of recent feminist criticism demonstrates, Dickinson is far from unequivocally supportive of this violent scenario, however. Wendy Barker, for example, demonstrates that many of Dickinson's poems evince considerably more anger at the violent aftermath than attraction to the seductions of the powerful Sun.[9] She singles out for particular attention "Of this is Day composed":

Of this is Day composed
A morning and a noon
A Revelry unspeakable
And then a gay unknown
Whose Pomps allure and spurn

And dower and deprive
And penury for Glory
Remedilessly leave
  (FP#1692 JP#1675)[10]

This poem does indeed criticize mythologies of marriage. But the line
"A Revelry unspeakable" also hints at another use for scenarios of abusive husbands joined with adoring brides; they enabled Dickinson to
speak things that were otherwise unspeakable, both ideologically and
linguistically. Likewise, the "man of noon" letter foregrounds with relative straightforwardness Dickinson's rejection of culturally produced
representations of female desire but also exploits their economical expressiveness in order to capture a notion of a "Revelry unspeakable."

The expressive potential of this sentimental-masochistic Daisy-Phoebus relationship fascinated Dickinson, and throughout her career she
mined it for the nuances of emotional expression that it made available
to her. Nowhere is the full array of such expressive potential more vividly
displayed than in the notorious "Master" letters, particularly the third,
beginning "Oh, did I offend it," in which a vulnerable Daisy cringes
adoringly at the knee of a ruthless, judgmental Master.[11] Whatever else
they may be, the "Master" Letters—three abject love letters to an
unidentified recipient——are literary experiments with the aesthetics of
sentimental masochism. "Oh, did I offend it" in particular can be read
as a style exercise exploring the uses of the sentimental masochistic scenario introduced in the "man of noon" letter (substituting the abstract
figure of Master for the Sun).[12] In it, two clichéd figures—Daisy and
Master—perform many of the stock scenes of sentimental dramatics,
variations on the theme of feminine submission and male domination.
The poet develops her repertoire of sentimental masochistic fantasy in
this letter, exploring the expressive potential of masochistic images of
wounding, domination, submission, guilty terror, and abjection. This
expressive potential can be seen as falling into three overlapping but still
distinct categories: it provides a lexicon of a desire for power, a desire for
erotic pleasure, and a desire for presence. All three rhetorical functions
come into play in this virtuoso performance in the Victorian theatre of
sentimental masochism:

Oh, did I offend it . . . Daisy—Daisy—offend it—who bends her smaller life
to his (it's) meeker (lower) every day—who only asks—a task—[who] something to do for love of it—some little way she cannot guess to make that master glad—

A love so big it scares her, rushing among her small heart—pushing aside
the blood and leaving her faint (all) and white in the gust's arm—

Daisy—who never flinched thro' that awful parting, but held her life so tight he should not see the wound—who would have sheltered him in her childish bosom (Heart)—only it was'nt big eno' for a Guest so large— . . .

Low at the knee that bore her once unto [royal] wordless rest [now] Daisy [stoops a] kneels a culprit—tell her her [offence] fault—Master—if it is [not so] small eno' to cancel with her life, [Daisy] she is satisfied—but punish [do not] dont banish her—shut her in prison, Sir—only pledge that you will forgive—sometime—before the grave, and Daisy will not mind—She will awake in [his] your likeness.

Wonder stings me more than the Bee—who did never sting me—but made gay music with his might wherever I [may] [should] did go—Wonder wastes my pound, you said I had no size to spare—

You send the water over the Dam in my brown eyes—

I've got a cough as big as a thimble—but I dont care for that—I've got a Tomahawk in my side but that dont hurt me much. [If you] Her master stabs her more—. . .

Oh how the sailor strains, when his boat is filling—Oh how the dying tug, till the angel comes. Master—open your life wide, and take me in forever, I will never be tired—I will never be noisy when you want to be still. I will be [glad] [as the] your best little girl—nobody else will see me, but you—but that is enough—I shall not want any more—and all that Heaven only will disappoint me—will be because it's not so dear (L#248)[13]

This is pure sentimental melodrama, reiterating over and over the pain of separation from Master, the desperation of her yearning for fusion with him, and the ecstasy that would accompany such fusion. The sentimental voice of the little girl predominates; not only does Daisy self-consciously refer to her "childish bosom" and "your best little girl," but like a child she naively claims "a love so big it scares her, rushing among her small heart." Sounding like Ellen Montgomery, she longs for Master to open his life and take her in, just as Ellen repeatedly longs for the adults in her life to take her into their laps and lives. Though Daisy promises not to be noisy, ironically, the child voice frees Daisy to *be* noisy, to take advantage of the liberty children normally have to speak out on subjects adults politely avoid. She pours out expressions of desire that would be difficult for the adult woman to express without restraint, a series of variations upon a single unremitting theme: "I desire you so much that separation from you is killing me."

This use of the innocent voice of a child importuning a powerful other as a means of expressing desire is far from unprecedented in Dickinson's culture. As Judith Farr has demonstrated, this letter is informed by similar rhetorical gestures in *Jane Eyre*, and Gilbert and Gubar and Betsy Erkkila demonstrate that it uncannily mimics Brontë's private expressions of love for her own "Master," Constantin Heger. Susan Howe has proposed that the letter is informed by Little Em'ly's abject expressions of desire for Steerforth in *David Copperfield* (whose protagonist is nicknamed "Daisy"). We can further compare it, though more loosely, to books like *Head of the Family*, which concludes with an image of Ninian's wife, whom he calls "my child," kneeling beside him, after which "Ninian Graeme lifted her up, little creature as she was, and folded,— nay, almost buried her in his breast" (169). As similar images in books like *The Wide, Wide World, The Planter's Northern Bride, Elsie Dinsmore, St. Elmo*, and many other popular fictions suggest, the image of an innocent girl-woman submitting in adoration to a powerful master and longing to be his "best little girl" is a staple of nineteenth-century representations of heterosexual love. The dense intertextuality of letters like this one suggests that Dickinson is drawing broadly upon this sentimental discursive convention, mining it for associations that will enable her own prose to resonate widely with an intense desire.

The speaker does not just long for parental nurture from her master, though; she also longs for affliction from him: "Punish don't banish her—shut her in prison, Sir." To judge from this letter, the reason Daisy turns to masochistic expressions of desire is the same one that inspired many sentimental heroines to long for punishment from their beloved or from God: punishment is not banishment, and above all else, the sentimental heroine fears abandonment from the one who defines her. Daisy's longing to be enslaved, punished, absorbed, or imprisoned by Master is a longing for a sign of his presence. As the flower in the "man of noon" letter must have the sun in order to live, so for Daisy, Master is an ontological necessity. It is more important that she exist in relation to Master than that she end her suffering or have pleasure. Indeed, he is so essential that—confronted with the appalling fact of his absence— Daisy ingeniously invents methods to perpetuate her ontological state of relatedness to him. His absence is a punishment he is inflicting upon her, she imagines, a punishment that refigures her lonely suffering as something intentional. She is not abandoned; she is doing penance. "I've got a Tomahawk in my side but that dont hurt me much. Her master stabs her more—." Master is the one afflicting her, Daisy imagines, and the presence of the stabbing pain he is causing partially alleviates the horror caused by his absence. As the tomahawk example indicates, the pain of absence paradoxically becomes the very sign of presence—for if he is stabbing her, and she actually feels a tomahawk in her side, then he must be present. Because it hurts, absence is presence. Like Ellen Montgomery, Daisy intuitively understands that if she can experience pain as punishment, then she will never have to feel abandoned; and if that punishment is inflicted in love, then she need never feel unloved. Suffering

offers almost magical consolations in this letter. It is a trope for the expression of desire (your separation from me feels like a tomahawk in my
side—come back and relieve me) and it is a form of presence in itself
(you are stabbing me; you are present). Need and satisfaction collapse in
this sentimental masochistic fantasy.

Whoever the real Master was, it is likely that receiving this letter made
him feel uncomfortable, since it casts him in the unflattering role of
"Daisy's abuser." Though Daisy's overt message is one of abject guilt,
the covert one is the opposite: she does not really believe that she is
guilty, and neither do we. For the histrionic Daisy, the pose of self-ab-
jection not only perpetuates relatedness but accuses the Master, puts him
in his place, and makes him look like a heel for being so abusive to such
an undeserving innocent. As this letter shows, sentimental masochism is
a mode of power similar to that of the stereotypical Jewish or Italian
mother who manipulates through suffering ("Don't worry about me; I'll
just sit here . . . alone . . . in the dark"). But the controlling aspects of
suffering, it must be recognized, threaten to undermine the ontological
security Daisy derives from pain. If she is in control, then Master may not
be imprisoning her but simply ignoring her—a possibility that haunts
this letter with the spectre of meaninglessness and psychic collapse and
propels her more desperately toward the presence found in pain.

As this discussion indicates, sentimental masochism serves three inter-
related modes of expression for Dickinson: representing a vulnerable
Daisy submissive before a ruthless Master is a mode of fantasizing about
power and expressing anger; alluding to sentimental and religious links
between pleasure and pain is a mode of expressing erotic desire; and col-
lapsing desire for presence with the presence of pain is a mode of addressing ontological anxieties relating to abandonment. The impetus for
such modes of expression is psychological, but the most significant
benefits are aesthetic: sentimental masochism infuses Dickinson's poetry
with a passion and tension that resonates widely with many readers. As
readings of key poems exemplifying these three principal uses of sentimental masochism in the rest of this chapter will reveal, the poet was not
confined by the original or intended meanings of sentimental and evangelical discourses. Rather, she appropriated and exploited them, forging
an extraordinarily powerful, exciting, and assertive form of expression
within prevalent discourses of her culture, discourses that were frequently hostile to a female poetics ranging beyond appropriately sentimental, religious verse. As Joanne Dobson observes, while women were
publishing extensively in Dickinson's era, "absent from, or apologized
for, or negated in the writing of most women of the white middle class
in that period are what were seen as "deviant" qualities for women—
sexual passion, personal (as opposed to altruistic) anger, and aspiration

for achievement or recognition outside the private sphere of the family. Although some women wrote in open violation of these expressive tenets, mainstream women writers, many of whom were excellent stylists and perceptive commentators on the cultural scene and women's place in it, had to find avenues of expression either within the boundaries of the acceptable, or at least not in obvious violation of expressive norms" (*Reticence* 3). Dickinson was not a mainstream writer, and her writing features many open violations of convention. Nonetheless, she also sought avenues for the expression of inappropriate subjects within— rather than in flagrant violation of—the discourses of her day. Sentimental masochism was one such avenue.

The Power of Sentimental Masochism

> Power is only Pain—
> Stranded—thro' Discipline

Many twentieth-century discussions of masochism point out that masochism can be a form of control. In *Masochism and Modern Man*, Theodor Reik notes that the masochist "forces another person to force him. . . . It is strange and worthy of meditation that the masochist whose character is one of complete submission to his object, of utter obedience, insists in his approach that his will alone be carried out— disregarding his object's wishes" (84, 87). Likewise, in a 1969 article, V. N. Smirnoff writes: "Masochism is a defiance. It is expressed through the masochist's apparently passive behaviour, by his compliance with the inflicted pain and humiliation, by his claims of being enslaved and used. In fact, the masochist knows that his position is simply the result of his own power: the power of endowing the executioner with the obligation of playing the role of a master, when indeed he is only a slave, a creation of the masochist's desire" (668). And as practitioners of sadomasochistic sex invariably insist, the masochist is in control of the script.[14] The self-avowed, practicing sadist Pat Califia, for example, sarcastically derides the "fluffy-sweater types" who presume "I'm the one who is ostensibly responsible for manipulating or coercing the M into degradation— all 130 pounds 5'2" of me" ("Secret" 130).

Emily Dickinson certainly understood how masochism can function as a fantasy of power.[15] Consider, for example, the brief poem "Bind me—I still can sing":

Bind me—I still can sing—
Banish—my mandolin
Strikes true, within—

Slay—and my Soul shall rise
Chanting to Paradise—
Still thine—
        (FP#1005 JP#1005)

Masochistic self-representation as a tortured possession ("thine") paradoxically empowers the speaker: in a peremptory tone, she insists upon
her right to praise her tormenter. No matter how he attempts to thwart
her, she asserts her will to be will-less, using three imperatives in six
lines. Although the general meaning of the poem is "If you bind me, I
will still sing," the speaker does not, in fact, say "if." She demands to be
bound, banished, and slain, asserting not only her prerogative to sing
but her superiority over the other, who, in the eyes of an imagined onlooker, is a brute, while *she* is an innocent, virtuous, passionate, and
faithful martyr to a cruel and domineering love. In fact, within the logic
of this poem, the more the other abuses her, the more that other empowers her. Indeed, the poem collapses the distinction between abuse
and empowerment, since "my mandolin / Strikes true, within" refers
both to the pain she suffers and her artistry. In this poem, suffering is
self-assertion.

Nick Mansfield, in *Masochism: The Art of Power*, agrees that manipulation of a seemingly powerful other through suffering lies at the heart
of all masochistic expression. Like Stoller, Smirnoff, Reik, Kamel, and
Weinberg, he observes that "the masochistic subject wants the dominating other's desire to be represented in the scene, but the representation
has to conform completely to his [the masochist's] own desire of her
desire. He wants her [the sadist's] subjectivity to be present, and to appear to be present in and of itself. But an autonomous desire arising
outside of the guidelines he has set down, and rejecting the parameters
of the masochistic scene, is to be ignored, run down by the momentum
his own desire is producing. The subjectivity of the other has to be a
nothingness that can present itself as a totality" (6–7).[16] In "Bind me,"
Dickinson's sadistic other has no desire apart from the presumed desire
to slay the speaker. His desire is completely produced by the speaker's
masochistic imagination. But the question naturally arises, Why would
one seek power by fantasizing about being controlled by another? Why
seek the power that inheres in dictating that the other desire only to slay
oneself? If this is agency, it is certainly a peculiar and limited form of it.

Stollers, Smirnoff, and Reik all interpret the turn toward masochism
as an expression of an otherwise inexpressible anger. But while "Bind
me" does express anger, its imagery of rising to paradise gestures toward
transcendent pleasures in this masochistic fantasy that are more important than merely the expression of anger. Mansfield offers an intriguing

analysis of the masochist's fantasy of power that helps make sense of this transcendent dimension in Dickinson's sentimental-masochistic poetics. He proposes that masochists seek a state of "total subjectivity," in which they are both a strongly centered ego and everything else. The sadistic "other," a product of the masochist's own fantasy, represents everything "that the subject is supposed to define as its exterior and alternative" (29). In the fantasy, the self is being annihilated, but the fantasizer scripts the sadist's desire to annihilate the masochist. Masochistic fantasy imagines an impossible state: the fantasizer is simultaneously a strongly centered ego *and* an annihilated self, thoroughly merged in the subjectivity of another who represents limitlessness. Annihilation allows for the possibility of totality, or limitlessness, while the careful scripting protects the ego of the fantasizer. The state of "total subjectivity" resembles the decentered state celebrated by poststructuralist psychoanalysis, but unlike the self in that fragmented state, the masochist remains intact by controlling the entire aesthetic process.

"Bind me—I still can sing" exemplifies the way that masochism strives for a state of total subjectivity: though it describes docile submission to annihilation, it is also a poem about the speaker, her body, and her desires. In six lines, the words "me," "my," or "I" occur four times, and the focus is upon both the speaker's artistic and religious aspirations and her own body. Though it is a fantasy of annihilation, it ensures that the fantasizer is, as Mansfield puts it, "never not anything." And what is particularly alluring for the genteel Victorian female about masochistic fantasy is that the masochist "can operate power while remaining technically removed from it, even highly critical of it," since she is "capable of (being) anything" (42).[17] Embracing every possible abasement removes the speaker of "Bind me" from subjection to power in the very gesture of refusing power, since to be annihilated—slain—is to "rise / Chanting to Paradise." This observation renders irrelevant much of the sparring that characterized early discussions of sentimentalism. Ann Douglas, for example, claimed that sentimental novels were masochistic in their idealization of "true womanhood," while Jane Tompkins countered that their representations of women's roles were efforts to redefine power. However, as the present discussion demonstrates, masochism is itself a form of redefining and seizing power, a form that was available for women to exploit.

Gary Lee Stonum has noticed a similar quest for mastery through refusal of mastery in Dickinson's poetry. The "deferential sublime," a quality he finds in an important cluster of Dickinson's poems, resembles what I am calling sentimental masochism, with its drive for total subjectivity. Dickinson recognizes that the poet of the sublime assaults the reader with "bolts of melody"; as she told Thomas Wentworth Higginson, "If I read a book [and] it makes my whole body so cold no fire ever can warm me I know *that* is poetry. If I feel physically as if the top of my head were taken off, I know *that* is poetry."[18] Stonum argues that Dickinson uses the pose of abjection to assert the violent "mastery" that poets of the sublime must exert over their readers without asserting mastery, remaining (as Mansfield puts it) "technically removed from" power. In her "deferential sublime" poems, he argues, Dickinson avoids the brutal assault of the sublime poet by emphasizing the victim's experience of the sublime and enabling the reader to identify with experiences of submission to a potentially lethal power. But, like Mansfield, Stonum understands that this position is no less masterful; it is simply a form of mastery achieved through hyperbolic refusal of mastery. As he writes, "Within the differential and comparative hierarchy of the sublime the emperor's is not the only role" (155).

The correspondence between masochism and the sublime is striking. Both combine pleasure and displeasure, offering what Kant describes as "a negative pleasure," a sense of elation associated with being overwhelmed by a threatening, dominating force. In both cases, one experiences the impossible and ecstatic state of being simultaneously overwhelmed by the infinite and superior to it. In masochistic fantasy, this impossibility is imagined through simultaneous identification with a subject on the brink of annihilation and with the infinitely powerful other bent upon that annihilation. In experiences of the Kantian sublime, one is dwarfed by something infinitely large yet simultaneously supersedes that sublime object through the act of attempting to imagine it.[19] Noting that the label "masochism" is indebted to a novelist, Mansfield argues that these sexual and aesthetic experiences are essentially the same thing, only separated (erroneously) in the taxonomy-obsessed nineteenth century.[20]

Dickinson frequently achieves this masochistic or deferential sublime in scenarios in which a small female figure is dominated or annihilated by a Godlike husband who represents totality. As David Morris demonstrates in *The Religious Sublime*, Christian poetry in eighteenth-century England (including that of Dickinson's beloved Milton) found in Protestant theology a discursive foundation for a religious—as opposed to a "natural" or "rhetorical"—sublime. God represents the infinitely huge "other," contemplation of which elevates the soul of the contemplative. In Dickinson's sentimental-masochistic poems, the scenario of a bride's abjection to a Godlike husband who represents totality to her appropriates a Calvinist sublime—with a twist. For unlike the convert[21] (though like the Kantian subject), she takes advantage of the consolidation of self that is available in her role as fantasizer, an arrogant control *through* the fantasy of total relinquishment. In "Bind me," she can be read as scripting even God's desire, ordering him to slay her in order to evoke the fantasy of fusion with his hugeness, experience the physical affect of vicarious terror, *and* remain in control of the aesthetic process.[22]

Dickinson's description of the effects of pain in "A nearness to Tremendousness" illuminates the kinds of empowerment inherent in the sublime or masochistic encounter. This poem is crucial in a study of Dickinson's uses of sentimental masochism because its basic situation—proximity of a vulnerable entity to an infinitely powerful one—is fundamental to sentimental aesthetics.

> A nearness to Tremendousness—
> An Agony procures—
> Affliction ranges Boundlessness—
> Vicinity to Laws
>
> Contentment's quiet Suburb—
> Affliction cannot stay
> In Acres—It's Location
> Is Illocality—
>
> (FP#824 JP#963)

The experience of affliction, this poem suggests, is intrinsically transgressive. While contentment quietly remains within the confines of the law, pain will not stay in its place. It defies laws and the boundaries that regulate them and (as Scarry demonstrates) the language that articulates them. Pain destroys the peaceful illusion of coherence that is indulged by the bourgeois residents of "Contentment's quiet Suburb." Pain splits the illusion of identity apart, exposing the gaps that lie at its core. Located only in "Illocality," pain represents the prospect of a lawless, boundless heterogeneity of personal identity and poetic meaning, an unmaking of constraining systems of thought. And when such proximity to tremendousness appears in an imaginative framework, the result is a fantasy of the splintering of self *and* the consolidation of self through the act of fantasizing. For example, in "the man of noon" letter, the fantasy of a Daisy "near" to a tremendous Master or Sun evokes the inevitability of pain that he will inflict; that pain allures with its boundlessness. As author of a masochistic scenario, Emily Dickinson can be both the afflicted Daisy and the sublime, infinite Master. The pleasure of identifying with the self splintered by pain is that it enables an otherwise impossible simultaneous experience of "Illocality" and "Location."

It also grounds that experience in the body of its reader. As we have seen, sentimentalism is an intensely bodily genre, producing tears, trembling, and a variety of physical responses to its core scenario. Cathy Davidson describes this scenario as a fundamentally Gothic drama that an onlooker is helpless to prevent: the combination of terror and passivity produces the characteristic physicality of the reading experience. A poem like "A nearness to Tremendousness," to be sure, does not produce such physical feelings; it describes them. But the intense affect of such nearness is fundamental to sentimentalism. And for the "true woman," whose identity is defined by abjection of the body, reading a sentimental work that produces such an experience *is* a form of "Illocality" "Locat[ed]" in the body.

The brief poem "Great Caesar! Condescend" exemplifies how poetic representations of "A nearness to Tremendousness" achieve the absolute totality of the sublime through absolute repudiation of power and at the same time ground the experience of that sublime in the affective body:[23]

> Great Caesar! Condescend
> The Daisy, to receive,
> Gathered by Cato's Daughter,
> With your majestic leave!
> (FP#149 JP#102)

According to Johnson, Dickinson sent the poem to her brother in 1859. When read as a message to him, it conveys a message of anger from a sister who abjects herself in histrionic terms, perhaps in order to make her brother feel ashamed of his own professional education and the respect accorded by his parents, since both are denied to his equally deserving sister. As Robert Stoller writes, the masochist's credo is "Suffering is my revenge" (*Sexual* 125).

But Dickinson copied it into a fascicle, and the multiple allusions in this fifteen-word poem harness that private expression of aggression for a more sublime end. For as classically educated Dickinson and her brother would have known, Caesar was the arch-enemy of Cato, who committed suicide rather than submit to Caesar when defeated by him. In offering a "Daisy" to Caesar, Dickinson is offering a girl as tribute to someone the girl hates and fears, someone who caused her father's death and could well cause hers. In other words, the poem is essentially about "A nearness to Tremendousness." Daisy is in a vulnerable situation, subject to whatever abuse her conqueror might choose to inflict. And this vulnerability to the possibility of annihilation draws into the poem not only a sublime fear of an infinite other but the idea, if not the experience, of a trembling, breathless, stimulated body. The poem exploits the physical and emotional tension in this hierarchical dilemma, the current of implied violence and anger surging beneath its obviously fake pose of abject submissiveness. The potential for pain implicit in this fragment invokes the infinite illocality that is always the sought-after sensation in this kind of sentimental masochistic fantasy. The excitement of this precarious situation is also tinged with the erotic: what, after all, is Caesar likely to do with his virginal female war booty?

The poem not only *is* a masochistic fantasy of power; it also comments obliquely upon its own methodology, since its speaker, Cato's Daughter, is one of history's most renowned masochists. As Plutarch reports, Portia, daughter of Cato and wife of Brutus, was a strong-minded woman, "addicted to philosophy, a great lover of her husband, and full of an understanding courage," but she had no outlets for her talents because of her gender. Although her husband believed that "she has a mind as valiant and as active for the good of her country as the best of us," he refused to share secrets with her, because she was a woman and therefore naturally prone to gossip. In order to prove that she merited her husband's confidence, Portia turned to masochistic self-mutilation. "She made this trial of herself. She . . . gave herself a deep gash in the thigh; upon which followed a great flow of blood, and soon after, violent pains and a shivering fever" (807). "In the height of all her pain," Portia explains to Brutus that she has inflicted this wound on herself because she wanted to test—and prove—her worthiness through extraordinary trials of pain: "what evidence of my love, what satisfaction can you receive, if I may not share with you in bearing your hidden griefs, nor to be admitted to any of your counsels that require secrecy and trust? I know very well that women seem to be of too weak a nature to be trusted with secrets; but certainly, Brutus, a virtuous birth and education, and the company of the good and honourable, are of some force to the forming of our manners; and I can boast that I am the daughter of Cato, and the wife of Brutus, in which two titles though before I put less confidence, yet now I have tried myself and find that I can bid defiance to pain" (807). Education, breeding, and character did not win her her husband's confidence; nor could they alone assure her that she merited it. So Portia turned to self-wounding in order to prove herself worthy of Brutus's love and trust. And to judge from Brutus's response—he "lifted up his hands to heaven and begged . . . that he might show himself a husband worthy of such a wife as Portia"—her masochistic gambit worked (Plutarch 807). Stoicism was highly prized in Portia's culture (as in Dickinson's), but there is a difference between facing adversity and creating it for yourself, and presumptions of female physical inferiority in both cultures often made it difficult for women to be recognized for their strength. In identifying with "Cato's Daughter," Dickinson associates herself with someone who empowers herself through submission, with a vengeance.[24] In abjecting herself before Caesar, Daisy asserts her right to intellectual respect through a mocking variation on Portia's histrionic masochism. As the "man of noon" letter suggests, Dickinson had no intention of actually hurting herself. But that letter also suggests, as does this poem, that she understood that masochistic discourse offered a rhetorical device to express anger (indirectly) and to assume (deferentially) the mastery of the sublime poet, who creates for readers aesthetic experiences of total subjectivity.

The Erotics of Sentimental Masochism

> Herein a Blossom lies—
> A Sepulchre, between—
> Cross it, and overcome the Bee—
> Remain—'tis but a Rind.

As we have seen, in *Erotism*, Georges Bataille proposes that sexual desire is essentially a desire to close a gap at the core of identity. Like his contemporary Jacques Lacan, he believes that identity is formed through separation from everything other than the self, a separation that agonizingly situates otherness at the center of one's own identity. Like Lacan, who posits what Wilden describes as an "eternal and irreducible human desire . . . for the nonrelationship of zero, where identity is meaningless,"[25] Bataille believes we are divided between an obsession with achieving a state of "continuity" and an obsession with protecting our "evanescent individuality." Eroticism, he proposes, addresses these conflicting obsessions. Through physically and emotionally transgressing the boundaries of the self, lovers are led to the liminal edge between life and death, a state in which they experience primal continuity even as they remain themselves. There is always a possibility of violence in eroticism, since it drives toward a dissolution of individuality, a violation "bordering on murder" (17). He offers an analogy to explain not only his understanding of the simultaneous continuity and discontinuity sought in sex but also why violence is implicit in it. Imagine, he proposes, the reproduction of a single-celled organism: it splits itself into two. At the moment of splitting, that organism is both itself and no longer itself; it is simultaneously two and one. This metaphor encapsulates his understanding of the impossible simultaneity of oneness (continuity) and twoness (discontinuity) sought by lovers. It also exemplifies why he sees eroticism as essentially violent, since the union that is born implies the annihilation of the individual.

The impossible state of simultaneous identity and nonidentity in this image is precisely the state produced by Dickinson's sentimental masochism: as fantasizer, she can imagine being simultaneously herself and her own infinite object. As the anxiety of the "man of noon" letter suggests, Dickinson understands heterosexual union as potentially violent or lethal to the individuality of its practitioners. But as the subtle eroticism of a poem like "Great Caesar!" suggests, she also recognizes aesthetic benefits to be derived from representing the liminal threshold between continuity and discontinuity. Masochistic fantasy can function as a rhetorical device for describing an ecstatic, sublime act of erotic fusion that does not lead to the obliteration of a person's individuality.[26]

Consider, for example, the sentimental poem "The Daisy follows soft the Sun":

> The Daisy follows soft the Sun—
> And when his golden walk is done—
> Sits shily at his feet—
> He—waking—finds the flower there—
> Wherefore—Marauder—art thou here?
> Because, Sir, love is sweet!
>
> We are the Flower—Thou the Sun!
> Forgive us, if as days decline—
> We nearer steal to Thee!
> Enamored of the parting West—
> The peace—the flight—the amethyst—
> Night's possibility!
>   (FP#161 JP#106)[27]

This core scenario of a flower in proximity to a powerful and hostile Sun is highly charged in Dickinson's private lexicon. Read in the context of the "man of noon" letter and "A nearness to Tremendousness," this poem about a Daisy's irresistible attraction to danger can be seen to exploit fear in its expression of erotic desire. The poem takes advantage of the tension associated with the liminal zone separating fear from desire; the Daisy, vulnerable before a potentially violent Sun, evokes the possibility of a painful assault and consequent sublime continuity with his infinite magnitude. The erotics implicit in such language as "love is sweet" and "Night's possibility" is therefore tinged with the sublime.

While the poem plays with the erotics of power, it subverts any conventional meanings that might be associated with its sentimentality. In deliberately seeking out the Sun's cold and unwelcoming rebuke and the possibility of an even greater punishment, Daisy appropriates for herself the lawless, transgressive possibilities made available by suffering. Daisy's willing submission to (potential) pain is a pose that puts her in control of this poem. She follows the Sun for her own reasons and in defiance of his wishes, while he, in all his resplendence, remains oblivious to her presence, and the pleasure she takes in that presence. Furthermore, Daisy's attraction to the *parting* West not only diminishes his power relative to his most powerful position at noon but also effectively pushes him offstage altogether. "I love you; leave me," she masochistically says, intensifying her own suffering. Her desire for the "Night's possibility" also displaces the Sun, since the eroticism implied in that possibility is precisely contingent upon his absence—it is *night*, after all. It appears that Daisy is most in love with the Sun when he is asleep or absent, and she manipulates him throughout this poem in order to procure for herself his desired absence. That absence is welcome both because it allows her to desire him and because it is painful, enabling her to indulge a frisson of pain and desire, the tension between longing to merge and needing to remain autonomous.

This nearness to tremendousness procures for Daisy the lawless pleasures associated with affliction. Despite Daisy's pose of absolute innocence, the Sun appropriately calls her a "Marauder," a word with implications both of lawless plundering and roving vagrancy. Daisy refuses to keep in her place, to respect the limits that are implied by the poem's hierarchy. She herself uses the word "steal" to describe her naughty actions. But that which Daisy actually steals from the Sun is the autonomy and desire that are supposed to be his prerogative. Referring to herself with the royal "we" while calling him "thou," she reduces him to the role of a player in her own private drama. She also appears to have had an illicit love affair with him, unbeknownst to him. In the first stanza, Daisy sits at the Sun's feet at sunset; and in the second stanza, when he wakes, it should therefore logically be morning (his "waking" is the sunrise). This would imply that they have already spent the night together, though he does not even know why she is there. Through sentimental masochism, Daisy controls this love affair, taking it on her own terms, pushing him offstage in order to thrive on the ecstatic pain of his abandonment, and stealing his powers and prerogatives in the act of refusing them. The pose of willing submission is a powerful device for taking exactly what she wants, and what she wants most in this poem is erotic union—"Night's possibility"—a union for which her submission to his hostility paves the way.

In "The Daisy follows soft the Sun," Dickinson seems to see the merging in heterosexual eroticism as gendered, as does Bataille: Daisy is the partner willing to be dissolved, while the Sun is the absorbing male partner into whom she can dissolve and expand. But as we have just seen, masochistic fantasy also subverts that conventional hierarchy by allowing the masochist to control the sadistic other, to force the sadist's desires and actions to conform to the will of the masochist. Dickinson is not confined by conventional gender categories; she exploits them.

A similar strategy of covert manipulation can be found in another one of Dickinson's erotic paeans to self-dissolution, "My River runs to thee":

> My River runs to thee—
> Blue Sea! Wilt welcome me?
> My River waits reply—
> Oh Sea—look graciously.
> I'll fetch thee Brooks
> From spotted nooks—
> *Say*—Sea—
> Take *Me*!
> (FP#219c JP#162)

The tone of this poem echoes that of many sentimental works, in which a winsome little female wishes to merge her small life-stream with that of a powerful sea-husband but wonders what she can offer such a mighty being that he would not already have. In keeping with the conventions associated with such works, the river in this poem attempts to win the sea's regard with the allure of "Brooks / From spotted nooks," fresh, uncorrupted waters. The poem draws in general upon the sentimental convention that privileges fresh, pure simplicity and, more particularly, upon the elaboration of it in *Jane Eyre*. Like Dickinson's winsome river, Brontë's Jane has nothing tangible to offer Rochester, but he is captivated nonetheless by her enthusiastic and refreshing candor. The night before their wedding, Jane tells Rochester, "I thought of the life that lay before me—*your* life, sir—an existence more expansive and stirring than my own: as much more so as the depths of the sea to which the brook runs, are than the shallows of its own strait channel" (294). Dickinson echoes Brontë's use of the brook-sea image as a metaphor for the total subjectivity promised to the bride: dissolving herself in the sea of an encompassing man affords access to a stirring, deep existence. "Least Rivers—docile to some sea. / My Caspian—thee," another poem says (FP#206 JP#212), reiterating the way that docility can function as a metonym for the depth of existence in deep, stirring love (the "Caspian"). However, like Brontë, Dickinson also recognizes the possibilities of self-assertion within self-erasure: just as "My River runs to thee" ends with a string of imperatives (say, sea/see, take), so too Brontë's novel ends with a blinded, maimed Master in a relationship of equality or even submission to Jane. Moreover, Dickinson's self-representation as a "river," an entity that can be quite large on its own, marshaling "brooks" on behalf of the sea, claims a fair amount of independent strength for the speaker.

To interpret such poems as merely ironic jabs at male pretensions to grandeur, however, would be to strip them of the erotic desire that their imagery of dissolution and merging expresses. These poems of female dissolution and male absorption are grounded in the prevailing ideology of spousal unity, according to which a woman becomes invisible in marriage, her identity covered by that of her husband. While they may assume an ironic stance toward that ideology, they also exploit the eroticism that is associated with it. Though the poem "Forever at His side to walk," for example, can be read as an ironic commentary on conventional gender roles in Victorian marriage, it operates at multiple levels, including an earnest consideration of the potentially sublime erotic pleasures inherent in the female's disappearance into spousal unity.

> Forever at His side to walk—
> The smaller of the two!
> Brain of His Brain—
> Blood of His Blood—
> Two lives—One Being—now—
>
> Forever of His fate to taste—
> If grief—the largest part—
> If joy—to put my piece away
> For that beloved Heart—
>
> All life—to know each other
> Whom we can never learn—
> And bye and bye—a Change—
> Called Heaven—
> Rapt Neighborhoods of men—
> Just finding out—what puzzled us—
> Without the lexicon!
>
> (FP#264 JP#246)

This poem explores Victorian ideologies of marriage, according to which subservience and self-renunciation are the keys to eternal joy. Although Dickinson saw most of the actual marriages around her as debased and debasing, in this poem she finds that conventional mythologies of marriage facilitate her expression of her own expansive desires for erotic and religious union.

The basic premise of this poem is the notion, introduced in the "man of noon" letter, that female self-renunciation is the key to a marital union that can perhaps be best compared to the mystical rapture of fusion with God. In marriage a couple can experience the religious delights of eternity ("forever") in an earthly temporal existence ("now").

Marriage is a mystical state of eternal divine presence. This idealized view of marriage, as we have seen, is rooted in both the law of coverture and the Christian view of marriage as a microcosm of God's universal hierarchical order. According to these legal and religious traditions, just as God is the supreme lord of the cosmos and it is the privilege and duty of his chosen people to serve him, so the husband is the head of the family and it is the woman's privilege and duty to serve him.

The first stanza alludes to the scriptural foundation for such ideologies: in Genesis, it is written that God first made Adam and then made Eve from Adam's rib, to be his helpmeet. "And Adam said, This is now bone of my bones, and flesh of my flesh: she shall be called Woman, because she was taken out of Man" (2:23). The unity of body yet separateness of being that the Genesis story implies—"Two lives—One Being"—was deeply attractive to Dickinson, since, as Albert Gelpi writes, the "problem of the One and the Two" was "the dilemma that determined her response to experience on all levels."[28] Longing simultaneously for autonomy and fusion, Dickinson was deeply attracted to the merge idealized in spousal unity. While we normally distinguish people related "by blood" from people related "by marriage," Dickinson insists upon a miraculous physical unity in marriage: a wife is "blood of his blood." Likewise, the reference to the concrete, anatomical "Brain," rather than the more ethereal "soul," "psyche," or "spirit," reiterates the (impossible) bodily dimension of marital conjoining.

The second stanza indicates that female submission is the price required for the mystery of marital unity. If a woman renounces all personal, individual experiences, she will be able to participate completely in the totality of her husband's experiences. The stanza elaborates its discussion of marriage by analogy to eating a dish of food. If the food is bad, a woman should eat most of it, since her own, individual experiences are insignificant. If it is good, she should let her husband eat all of it, because, if she identifies with him, she can enjoy it vicariously through him. If she can give herself up entirely, and if he is willing to accept the offering, to allow her to live, in a sense, inside him, then the two will be able to enjoy on earth the kinds of joys otherwise reserved for heaven.

The third stanza suggests that this kind of representation of marriage can function as a metaphor for understanding spiritual union, which is merely a "change" that—occurring "bye and bye"—is hardly an interruption. Christians, like brides, can only experience the empowerment and pleasure of union by renouncing all particular concerns. Just as women find their joy in putting aside their partial pleasures in order to participate in the greater pleasures of powerful male identity, so in heaven, men and women will take joy in dissolving their individuality in order to be absorbed into a state of continuity with God.

The last three lines are enigmatic. They can be read as suggesting that women understand the potential for rapturous fusion in marriage but are "puzzled" because they lack a "lexicon" that enables them to think about simultaneously being one and two. The most prominent lexical element featured in this poem is the body: devotion is best conceived through the image of "walk[ing]" at his side; identity is known through the "Brain"; kinship is known as "Blood"; fate is experienced as a "taste[ing]"; love is experienced as sharing body parts; a lover is represented as a "Heart"; and eroticism is expressed as a relationship of a small body to a larger one. Because the body is the "lexicon" for earthly human understanding, earthly marriage—according to which two lives are made one—is puzzling. Bodies, after all, are the basis of individuation. They visibly separate one person from another: people have separate brains and separate blood—ideologies of spousal unity notwithstanding. Our body-centered sense of self makes it difficult for us to comprehend how we can fuse with another being without dying. In heaven, however, whole "Neighborhoods" of people are able to experience and understand perfect love, because they no longer are confined by a bodily lexicon separating one from another; they have access to a heavenly lexicon in which thought is not limited by binary oppositions. If we take Dickinson's use of the word "men" in the third stanza to refer to "males," then the scenario in heaven may be one in which males are just beginning to learn what women have puzzled over for a long time: in dissolution lies the possibility of ecstatic expansion of being.

However, the last stanza also invites an opposite reading, one in which bodies are considered as the basis, not of individuation, but of sexual conjoining. Rather than implying that comprehension is more perfect in heaven, where people do not think in terms of the body but rather of the soul, this stanza can be read as saying that the heavenly "Neighborhoods of men"—just learning about the joys of submission to a corporate identity—are hampered by *lacking* the lexicon, the body. The body may be a *better* lexicon of love than some heavenly lexicon of disembodiment. It is no accident that to "know" someone is a euphemism for sexual intercourse—suggesting that it is through the body that we gain a total, nonintellectual, intuitive comprehension of another being. Two people can "know" each other again and again and again with their bodies, enjoying a holistic experience of the other that does *not* consume and encompass the other, "Whom we can never learn."[29]

Such a reading reverses the seemingly doctrinal representations of both religion and marriage invoked in the first two stanzas. Here, as Porter observes of Dickinson's poetry in general, "the tone is established and then upset so that the reader is plundered of his first invested consent in the poem" (91). If heaven is impoverished because it lacks a bodily lexicon, then it is merely a symbolic existence, the reality of which can be more fully and directly experienced on earth. The final stanza suggests that marriage may not be simply a microcosm of divine love; it may also be the original, and divine love the copy. In other words, spiritual union of the human and the divine might simply be a metaphor for sexual union. In such a reading, the ecstasies of sexual knowing can be understood by analogy to conventional religious associations, but they are not subordinate to religion. Rather, religious ideologies of submission to a larger being can be seen as providing a discourse of love that the deft poet can appropriate and invert for the expression of carnal, erotic desire. Gary Lee Stonum reads this poem as a variation on the Dickinsonian sublime, and though he recognizes that it and other poems of sublime abjection are love poems, in which the speaker "clearly cherishes her bondage" (as in 273), he does not thoroughly trace the relationship between the sublime and the masochistic eroticism that an attraction to bondage implies (157). But "Forever at His side" indicates that Dickinson's "deferential sublime" enables her to fantasize about a supreme and distinctly embodied experience of erotic ecstasy. The experience of being dissolved and absorbed in something infinitely large, which we associate with the romantic sublime, is linked in "Forever at His side" to the expression of an embodied female sexuality.

Dickinson's most masterful use of sentimental masochism for erotic expression is found in the lyric "I started Early—Took my Dog," a poem that exemplifies how total subjectivity and erotic desire are twinned in her masochistic aesthetic. Longing for the absorption depicted in "Forever at His side to walk" and "My River runs to thee," but also emphasizing her own role as "the one who longs," the speaker in this poem is both her own autonomous self and erotically merged with everything else. Like the "man of noon" letter, "I started Early—Took My Dog" vacillates between a longing to be overpowered and outrage over violation. It plays with the idea that, if it is female destiny to be consumed, then there may be pleasures in fantasizing about it.

Read on the most literal level, the poem is about a vulnerable speaker who goes to the beach, where a wave washes over her. She flees, but the wave pursues her, fills her shoes with pearl-like foam, and then recedes. The presence of the protecting dog and the image of the mouse identify the speaker as a variation on the Daisy figure, an identification that locates this poem within Dickinson's sentimental mode.[30]

I started Early—Took my Dog—
And visited the Sea—

The Mermaids in the Basement
Came out to look at me—

And Frigates—in the Upper Floor
Extended Hempen Hands—
Presuming Me to be a Mouse—
Aground—opon the Sands—

But no Man moved Me—till the Tide
Went past my simple Shoe—
And past my Apron—and my Belt
And past my +Boddice—too—   +Bosom/Buckle

And made as He would eat me up—
As wholly as a Dew
Opon a Dandelion's Sleeve—
And then—I started—too—

And He—He followed—close behind—
I felt His Silver Heel
Opon my Ankle—Then My Shoes
Would overflow with Pearl—
Until We met the Solid Town—
No +One He seemed to know—   +man—
And bowing—with a Mighty look—
At me—The Sea withdrew—

                    (FP#656 JP#520)

The symbolic meaning of the Sea in this poem has been extensively discussed; it has been read as the unconscious, immortality, sexual desire,
God, infinity, the universe. All of these, however, can be subsumed
under a rubric reading the Sea as an expansive metaphor for totality of
being: Kant's "absolute totality," Bataille's "continuity," Kristeva's
"*chora*," Lacan's "Real," Stowe's "the *all*." The speaker's visit to the Sea
of totality of being begins safely, because she does not abandon the ego
barriers that protect her from dissolution. She has her dog, perhaps for
protection, and is merely visiting the Sea, not submerging herself in it.
She indulges a number of fantasies of connection with the others—mermaids look at her and frigates extend their hands to her—but she is
merely observing, "unmoved." She hesitates, understandably, to yield
to the obliteration that she associates with liberation from lonely isolation.[31] Like many a Puritan, Dickinson represents intimacy as a threat to
the self.

The collapse of the me/not-me distinction—the complete dissolution of herself in the gigantic Sea—is enticing even as it is threatening,

and the poet turns to a masochistic fantasy of erotic domination to represent her simultaneous fear of and desire for merging. She simultaneously indulges and disavows her desire by projecting it onto a mighty Tide/Man who moves the speaker without her volition or participation. As a passive recipient of the actions he performs, she does not have to own up to her desire, and she can remain physically intact and morally pure in her own eyes as the observer of her own encroaching dissolution. The Tide/Man who appears to desire the speaker begins to overwhelm her. His creeping up and over her body is both seductive and insidious. The repetition of "past . . . and past . . . and past . . . too" gives the impression both of his threatening, unwavering encroachment upon her and of a kind of "ecstasy of apprehension" in her, as she experiences her nearness to his tremendousness. She neither flees nor participates as he "ma[kes] as He would eat" her up as he would the "Dew" on a (vaginal?) "Sleeve." Her state of paralysis compresses the longing for union with the agony of dissolution ("eat me up"). The poem exploits this tension as it creeps closer to the line between life and death. As Bataille might put it, eroticism in this poem is "assenting to life up to the point of death" (11).

At a certain moment, the intensity reaches a climax. The space between the fourth and fifth stanzas conceals the crucial reversal in the speaker's emotional state, but as the fifth stanza begins, she is running, and he is following. Perhaps terror has outweighed the pleasure of the near-seduction. She fears getting in over her head. He almost overtakes her; she feels his silver heel right at her ankle, an image with overtones of imminent violence. Shifting to the conditional (a marker, Miller notes, of the fantasized or repetitive nature of the poem), she worries that if he caught her, her "Shoes / Would overflow with pearl."[32] But the question is, Which of the two would produce the pearly fluid overflowing the shoes? He or she? Does she fear his desire to eat her up, or her own desire to be eaten? Is this a rape, or a masochistic revelry in her own near-obliteration?

If he really is a projection of her own desire, then the distinction is insignificant. It is the dissolution of her being that she both desires and fears, and it is the fantasized situation of eroticized domination that produces the secretions. Fleeing the flood of pearly foam, she arrives back in the solid town of conventional behavior, curtailed desire, and stable identity. The solidity of the town suggests that the speaker has not suffered the irrevocable psychic collapse she feared because the masochistic *fantasy* enables her to indulge the desire to be "yielded up" without losing her strong, controlling self, to be simultaneously dissolved in the sea of continuity and to be safely observing her own ecstatic dissolution. Fantasized identification with both members of a scenario of eroticized domination enables her to achieve the long-desired, elusive "Art to stun [her]self / With Bolts—of Melody!"

The Presence of Sentimental Masochism

> If *He dissolve*—then—there is *nothing*—*more*—
> *Eclipse*—at *Midnight*—
> It was *dark*—*before*—
>
> *Sunset*—at *Easter*—
> *Blindness*—on the *Dawn*—
> *Faint* Star of Bethlehem—
> *Gone down!*

Dickinson frequently suggests that an inexplicable loss is fundamental to her being. One poem begins:

> A loss of something ever felt I—
> The first that I could recollect
> Bereft I was—of what I knew not
> Too young that any should suspect
>
> A Mourner walked among the children
>   (FP#1072 JP#959)

The poem goes on to say that this inexplicable sensation of loss, felt as long as she can remember, inspires a search for her lost "Dominium," her "Delinquent Palaces." And the end of the poem suggests that this lost "something" is "the Kingdom of Heaven," essentially religious and unattainable on earth.

One of the fascinating uses of her sentimental masochism is that it partially appeases this intrinsic sense of loss, for in emphasizing the pain of absence, the poet experiences a sense of presence—albeit only the presence of pain rather than the presence of that which was lost. We have thus far considered Dickinson's sentimental masochism to be a series of variations upon the theme of a vulnerable female bowed in anguish before an exceptionally powerful other. But that image of submission to domination is fundamentally appealing because it responds to the terror of separation and abandonment. An equally important facet of Dickinson's sentimental masochism is an emphasis upon feeling the emotional pain of separation itself. As readers of *The Wide, Wide World*, *Uncle Tom's Cabin*, or virtually any other nineteenth-century sentimental novel invariably observe, such an emphasis is central to the sentimental imagination. Feeling the presence of the pain of absence is only a consolation for absence rather than a cure, of course. But Dickinson nevertheless repeatedly foregrounds the way that intensifying her feelings of loss provides partial but real consolation for the absence of her loved ones.

In her letters, Dickinson emphasizes the anguish of separation with astonishing regularity. This emphasis, however, is hardly iconoclastic; rather, it reflects Dickinson's immersion in sentimental culture.

> Oh my darling one, how long you wander from me, how weary I grow of waiting and looking, and calling for you . . . you'll never go away, Oh you never will—say, Susie, promise me again, and I will smile faintly—and take up my little cross again of sad—*sad* separation. (L#73; to Susan Gilbert, February 6, 1852)

> I cannot believe, dear Susie, that I have stayed without you almost a whole year long. . . . And now how soon I shall have you, shall hold you in my arms; you will forgive the tears . . . there's something in your name, now you are taken from me, which fills my heart so full, and my eye, too. (L#93; to Susan Gilbert, early June 1852)

> And now five days have gone, Emily, and long and silent, and I begin to know that you will not come back again. There's a verse in the Bible . . . a little like this—"I can go to her, but she cannot come back to me." I guess that isn't right, but my eyes are full of tears. (L#146; to Emily Fowler Ford, December 21, 1853)

> I would tell you about the spring if I thought it might persuade you even now to return, but every bud and bird would only afflict you and make you sad where you are, so not one word of the robins, and not one word of the bloom. . . . . nothing forgets you, Emily, not a blossom, not a bee . . . in their little faces is sadness, and in their mild eyes, tears. (L#161; to Emily Fowler Ford, spring 1854)

> Dear Susie, you are gone—One would hardly think I had lost you to hear this revelry, but your absence insanes me so—I do not feel so peaceful, when you are gone from me— (L#107; to Susan Gilbert, March 12, 1853)

> Susie . . . to wear the loneness next your heart for weeks, when you sleep, and when you wake, ever missing something, *this*, all cannot say, and it baffles me. I would paint a portrait which would bring the tears, had I canvass for it, and the scene should be—*solitude*, and the figures—solitude—and the lights and shades, each a solitude. I could fill a chamber with landscapes so lone, men should pause and weep there . . . "They say that absence conquers." It has

vanquished me. (L#176; to Susan Gilbert, November 27–December 3, 1854)

Each of these quotations from her letters (except the penultimate) uses a distinctly sentimental voice. Most also mention a present sign of pain that partially compensates for the absence of the beloved. The tears Dickinson sheds as she sentimentally probes the pain of her own wound partially alleviate the sensation of "ever missing something, *this*"; as she puts it, there is "something in [Sue's] name" that "fills my heart so full, and my eye, too." While something is missing, something is nonetheless filling her full. If the beloved is absent, at least the signs of Dickinson's feelings about that absence are not. Hence, she would like to paint landscapes of solitude; representing absence is itself a consoling form of presence.[33] We find here the seeds of that impulse that Sandra Gilbert describes as Dickinson's tendency to transform "the pain associated with the puzzle at the center of her life," "a kind of absence or blank, the enigmatic wound," into "the miracle of her art" ("Nun" 25).

Though Dickinson's sentimentalism is an effort to achieve such presence, it is not a drive toward the "real presence" that Stowe strives to capture in her uses of sentimental wounding, for the fundamental alienation described in poems like "A loss of something ever felt I" and the overall deliberate self-fragmentation that Dickinson consistently portrays suggest a doubt on her part as to the possibility of there existing anything such as "real presence" in human existence. As Karl Keller writes, "Emily Dickinson cannot find a center in (male-made) society . . . [only] in herself—and even that isn't reliable" (70).[34] But as a poem like "Rehearsal to Ourselves" suggests, the presence of pain does afford perverse, intrinsic pleasures, despite the inaccessibility of some essential self. The central question of the poem—"Why is it pleasurable to experience again and again a painful memory of separation?"—bears directly upon any exploration of the pleasures of sentimental pathos, and while the poem suggests answers less transcendent than those that Stowe proposes, it shares with a text like *Uncle Tom's Cabin* an idealization of the paradoxical pleasures of the presence of pain, that "ecstasy of parting" (71).

Rehearsal to Ourselves
Of a Withdrawn Delight—
Affords a Bliss like Murder—
Omnipotent—Acute—

We will not drop the Dirk—
Because We love the Wound

The Dirk Commemorate—Itself
Remind Us that We died
    (FP#664 JP#379)

The first stanza of this poem establishes the masochistic paradox that the
second stanza proposes to explain: rehearsing the memory of a painful
separation can produce bliss. It relates the cause of this perverse pleasure
to the fact that the memory is "Omnipotent" and "Acute"; the painful
experience is a sentimental variation on the experience of the sublime, in
which the encounter with the infinite power of a painful memory penetrates and vanquishes one, producing a sensation of elation. The murderous memory resembles the "Heavenly Hurt" of that "certain Slant of
light" that penetrates to the interior where "the Meanings, are—"
(FP#320 JP#258).

However, "Rehearsal to Ourselves" questions the ability of anything,
be it dirk or slants of light, to penetrate through layers of seeming to
where meanings are. The second stanza makes a series of symbolic references: it proposes that the speaker loves the dirk that stabbed her, because it "Commemorate[s]" the wound that it made, and loves the
wound, because "Itself" reminds her that she died. The chain of symbols spilling from line to line, where repeated enjambments make one
line an essential though distinct component of another, seems a little
indirect. If she loves the dirk for causing her to remember the wound,
then why not love the wound directly? And if she loves the wound because it reminds her that she died, then why not (like Whitman) love
death itself? If she loves death because of the promise of resurrection,
then why not focus on resurrection rather than leave it out of the poem
altogether? Why this interest in traces and symbols?

Apparently, the problem is that when the poet traces each symbol
back to its referent, that referent only refers her further back to another
referent. Tracing all the way back to the origin, she finds only an absence
of meaning and speech—death. In this poem, there appears to be no
core of meaning but only a shifting system of unattached signifiers, with
absence at its core. And in such a case, the poem suggests, one might
just as well "love" a symbol—a dirk or a wound, for instance—since the
only thing they commemorate, in any case, is an absence: death. The
dirk and the wound, after all, offer the gratifying compensations of
tangibility and presence. Even if the dirk caused pain, it is a present object; or as Dickinson puts it, while "The Dirk Commemorate[s]" the
"Wound," it also "Commemorate[s]—Itself." Likewise, even if the
wound is a reminder of a painful separation, it is also palpable proof that
the other was at one time present. Moreover, a wound can be seen as a

visual metaphor not only for separation from the other but for the gaps in language that are the necessary negative spaces between signifiers, spaces that are the precondition for all signification. Even if dirks and wounds signify absence, they are comfortingly concrete signs of absence. This presence of symbols is fundamentally what deconstructive lovers of philology—from Dickinson to Derrida—appreciate about words, or "the consent of language" (JP#1651).

But even if symbols only refer to each other, what is the particular pleasure of representing absence? This question is even more forcefully framed in the poem "Struck, was I," in which the first three stanzas actually do "rehearse" the pain of a "withdrawn delight":

Struck, was I, nor yet by Lightning—
Lightning—lets away
Power to perceive His Process
With Vitality—

Maimed—was I—yet not by Venture—
Stone of Stolid Boy—
Nor a Sportsman's +Peradventure—   +ruthless pleasure—
Who mine Enemy?   /wanton leisure—

Robbed—was I—+intact to Bandit—   +yet met no Bandit—
All my Mansion torn—
Sun—withdrawn to Recognition—
Furthest shining—done—

Yet was not the foe—of any—
Not the smallest Bird
In the nearest Orchard +dwelling   +waiting
Be of Me—afraid—

Most—I love the Cause that slew Me—
Often as I die
+It's beloved Recognition   +That
Holds a Sun on Me—

Best—at Setting—as is Nature's—
Neither +witnessed Rise   +Noticed
Till the infinite Aurora
In the Other's Eyes—

(FP#841 JP#925)

As Judith Farr points out, this poem's subject, "the *coup de foudre* of love," is familiar in romantic poetry. However, she fails to observe that the violent aspects of love's assault in this poem stem from the possibility of *separation* from the beloved. The idea that the sun has "withdrawn to Recognition," that the "Furthest shining" is "done," and that "Neither [is] witnessed" of the other suggests that the anguish suffered by this speaker is not merely the thunderbolt of love but the anguish of separation from that love. Indeed, love and the threat of separation were inseparable for Dickinson. Her comment to Samuel and Mary Bowles after a visit, "I am sorry you came because you went away," epitomizes the way that she has difficulty indulging in the pleasure of love because of the pain of possible separation, a possibility of pain that generates the violent striking and maiming she associates with love.[35]

What pleasure might there be in rehearsing so insistently the torturous aspects of love—as opposed to its raptures? The answer to this question may be partially implicit in the underlying tone of these first three stanzas, which read like a conversational fragment embedded in a much larger context (in the first line, the words "nor yet" seem to refer back to a previous remark by someone else). The tone is one of insistence: "I tell you I was *struck*, and it wasn't simply by lightning," the speaker seems to say, implying that her interlocutor requires convincing. Despite what the other thinks, the pain the speaker experienced did not feel random or without purpose for her (not a "venture," nor a stone thrown by some unintelligent boy, nor a random "Peradventure" or "ruthless pleasure" or "wanton Leisure"). She insists that the encounter with the other was *real* and that the suffering she experienced was intentional, not random. The pleasure, then, of reliving this wounding relates to its realness—with an implied intentionality on the part of a specific other.

The fourth stanza approaches this self-inflicted wounding in a sentimental style that dramatically differs from that of the rest of the poem. It interrupts the poem's anatomy of the anguish of love, departing from the "[verb]-was-I" pattern of the first three stanzas and the "one word dash" pattern that appears in the first-line of all other stanzas besides this and the first. The fourth stanza features none of the dense or complex imagery of the other five. It instead considers love's sublime from a deferential viewpoint, pathetically seeming to say, "but *I* wouldn't hurt anyone." The speaker's wistful insistence that she does not deserve to be hurt has a number of effects. Structurally, it plays an important role in the poem's representation of the sublime nature of love by drawing attention to the smallness of the speaker, in order to amplify by contrast the hugeness in the fifth stanza. The sentimentalism, then, produces an effect of "nearness to Tremendousness," a situation of precarious vulnerability that is suspensefully sustained before the climactic, fatal assault of the fifth stanza. The expression of love in those fifth and sixth stanzas is intensified not only by the erotic liminality invoked in the fourth but also by the physical affect that is latent in the "nearness to Tremendousness" in that stanza. For a poet who wrote "I am afraid to own a Body" (FP#1050 JP#1090), the production of physical affect through terrified representations of the vulnerable female body in peril of love's thunderbolt was a paradoxical, but by now familiar, way of re-presencing that body.

But eroticism is not the only motive prompting the invention of the exaggeratedly weak, sentimental figure of the fourth stanza; rather, that invention seems designed to stabilize the speaker's identity for herself. In the face of a situation of abandonment like that implicit in the first three stanzas, sentimental masochism can serve, as James Sacksteder writes, as "the precarious center of a functioning and stable identity": "A masochistic identity is a type of negative identity, which, however costly and pathological, nonetheless represents for some individuals their best possible effort at creating and maintaining a separate and au-tonomous sense of self, one that salvages for them a modicum of satis-faction, security, and self-esteem and thereby staves off tugs toward identity diffusion, psychotic regression, and/or suicide" (106). The speaker derives "beloved Recognition" from the pain she associates with love. And that recognition enables her to maintain a stable sense of self, a self understood as "innocent victim." But in order to be this innocent victim, she requires someone who is intentionally afflicting her who will enable her to experience a coherent sense of self as "not the foe—of any." The gaze of the other is an "infinite Aurora" because she finds in it the "beloved Recognition" that she is who she thinks she is: an inno-cent victim.

But the poem is haunted by the possibility that she might no longer have access to the other's recognition, since the other is "withdrawn to Recognition— / Furthest shining—done." The problem with this with-drawal is that it would mean not only that the transcendent intimacy they shared is at an end but also that she is no longer herself. Without the presence of an afflicting other, she is simply an unidentified victim with no coherent relationship to define her and to justify her suffering. And existence under such circumstances is impossible. The masochistic affirmation "Most—I love the Cause that slew Me" in the fifth stanza, stating "I" love something that killed "me," suggests that independent selfhood ("me") was annihilated in order to bring into being the "I" who lives in relationship to "the other" whose recognition holds a sun on her. Like the flowers in the "man of noon" letter, the speaker in "Struck, was I" not only enjoys the "beloved Recognition" that the sun holds on her but *requires* that "infinite Aurora / In the Other's Eyes."[36]

The very wording of that masochistic affirmation indicates anxiety: rather than saying "Most I love the reason for which the other slew me" or "Most I love the one who had a reason for slaying me," the speaker suggests that there might have been no agent behind the slaying. She was simply slain by that which slew her, a wording that belies any intentionality to the cause. But Dickinson is playing with semantics in the phrase "Cause that slew Me." Obviously, all acts of slaying have a cause, if not intention, and by embracing that cause, she implies intention; for "cause" means not only "the reason why something happened" but also "that goal for which things are done." In embracing the former, the speaker implies the existence of the latter. And while her embrace of the cause cannot fully alleviate the anxious suspicion that her suffering in fact has no intended goal but simply happened, it does seem sufficient for the recognition she requires. What it does, specifically, is keep alive the idea of "cause" as "goal for which I am suffering." And the perpetuation of that purpose makes her suffering meaningful and stabilizes the identity that is constructed around that goal and that suffering. Indeed, the double meaning of "Cause" enables the speaker to consolidate her identity through renunciation, since each act of renunciation amplifies the "Cause."[37]

As this reading of "Most—I love the Cause that slew Me" reveals, masochistic fantasy is a way of feeling oneself to be a stable entity in an equally stable world. To the extent that "causes" are intentional, one's suffering is made meaningful. This kind of turn to violence for ontological security is not unprecedented in Dickinson. She repeatedly seems to ask in her poetry, "How do I know I am real?" and even more frequently, "How do I know others around me are real?" and, as Benfey has shown in his study of this philosophical skepticism in Dickinson, a turn to violence for answers to these questions also has ample precedent. As he points out, Dickinson is attracted to pain and death because one "knows" they are true: "I like a look of Agony, / Because I know it's true," she sadistically writes. People do not fake death, and so the act of dying convinces an onlooker that the other was real, not a product of her own mind. As Benfey argues, "I like a look of Agony" and "Split the Lark" demonstrate "the tendency of skepticism to erupt in sadism" (95). But we might add that poems like "Struck, was I" demonstrate that philosophical skepticism can equally erupt in masochism. Feeling the fatal assault of the other can console the anguish of skepticism in ways that resemble the consolations of sadism. Pain feels indisputably present to us, and it connects us to the world by reassuring us of the presence, outside ourselves, of that which has caused our pain.

This function of sadism and masochism as a response to skepticism lies at the heart of Hegel's "master-slave" dialectic.[38] All people require recognition from another that they are alive, he says, and they will fight each other to the death to wrest that recognition from the other. One will enslave or hurt another, forcing that other to recognize him, and both will temporarily find in that master-slave relationship the ontological assurance they require, until the slave realizes that the master is dependent upon him, and the master realizes that his slave controls him. While Hegel imagines an upward spiraling phenomenology emerging from this shift, Dickinson tends to focus upon the ontological instability she associates with any diminishment in her master. "If *He dissolve*—then—there is *nothing—more*" (FP#251 JP#236). But "Struck, was I" precludes the possibility of that diminishment, since it feels the master's presence in the pain of his absence, and the speaker can therefore remain in a *permanently* hierarchical relation to an infinitely powerful master without risking the profound psychological turmoil she would suffer from his diminishment. As long as he is absent, he is stable and infinite, which is why his beloved recognition holds a sun on her "Best—at Setting." The pain of his absence can be experienced as one more manifestation of his infinite power. Feeling pain and imagining herself intentionally hurt is (almost) sufficient recognition of her existence.[39]

The attraction in the final stanza to the *setting* sun—rather than the sunrise it promises—is particularly masochistic, privileging the pain of the present over the anticipated pleasure of the future. In *Beyond the Pleasure Principle* Freud describes a similar phenomenon in his analysis of the masochistic "fort-da" game, in which his grandson symbolically enacts his mother's departure by throwing a wooden spool on a string out of his crib and saying "fort" ("gone") and then joyfully reeling it back in saying "da" ("here"). Freud writes, "The child cannot possibly have felt his mother's departure as something agreeable . . . It may perhaps be said in reply that her departure had to be enacted as a necessary preliminary to her joyful return, and that it was in the latter that lay the true purpose of the game" (15). Similarly, the speaker in "Struck, was I" presumably rehearses the sun's departure as a way of anticipating its return in the morning's "infinite Aurora." But Freud observes that the child (like the speaker of "Struck, was I") stages the "departure . . . as a game in itself and far more frequently than the episode in its entirety, with its pleasurable ending." The reunion is implicit in the "fort" half of the game, but the child prefers representing the painful absence of the beloved. Freud suggests that this repetition compulsion represents the child's effort to control through self-infliction a suffering that is inevitable.

Lacan elaborates Freud's analysis of the "fort-da" game, emphasizing the pleasures of symbolization itself. He reads the "fort-da" game as the birth of the child's desire, a birth that is tied to the birth of his language. Language substitutes for the absent mother, and the pleasures of signification substitute for the pleasures of her presence. In "Function and Field of Speech and Language," he writes, "These are the games of occultation which Freud, in a flash of genius, revealed to us so that we might recognize in them that the moment in which desire becomes human is also that in which the child is born into language. . . . [We see that] the subject is not simply mastering his privation by assuming it, but that here he is raising his desire to a second power. . . . Thus the symbol manifests itself first of all as the murder of the thing, and this death constitutes in the subject the eternalization of his desire" (*Écrits* 103–4). The departure of the mother inaugurates for the child the birth of desire, and it simultaneously gives birth to his language. Having risen from a desire for maternal presence to a desire to reconnect with her symbolically, he effectively murders the mother (the thing) in order to privilege the desire that is "eternalized" in linguistic representations of desire for her presence. Language represents an effort to control through representation the traumatic separation that one must inevitably undergo; it is therefore always restless with desire for a presence it can only symbolize but never achieve. Because language is predicated upon the pain of absence, pain is inseparable from the pleasures of signification.

But emphasizing that pain underlying signification—representing the gaps in language rather than representing that which is desired—offers the distinct pleasure of foregrounding the presence of language itself. One might prefer the representation of maternal absence to presence, sunset to sunrise, pain to pleasure because it makes one conscious of the fact that one actually *has* language at hand (or a spool *in* hand). One may well achieve some abstract, "infinite Aurora" in heaven, and that aurora may ultimately compensate for the pain we feel now, but *now* we can derive sustenance from the presence of that pain. In "I shall know why—when Time is over" (FP#215 JP#193), Dickinson presumes that in heaven she will learn the cause of her earthly suffering, but she concludes: "I shall forget the drop of anguish / That scalds me now—that scalds me now!" The repetition of the final phrase (a rare occurrence in Dickinson's poetry) emphasizes the incontrovertible fact of present suffering. The intolerable anguish of "scalding" not only challenges the platitudes in the beginning of the poem but also foregrounds the material presence of that pain; whatever airy promises the speaker may hear, her pain is indisputably present. And in that presence lies consolation. This is the lesson Freud's grandchild learned in throwing away the spool representing his mother; to experience the trauma of her absence on his own terms was to substitute a presence of his own choosing for an absence he could not control. If pain is not the desired maternal presence, pain is still a form of presence on his own terms. Likewise, if language cannot provide access to maternal nurture, it can approximate and symbolize the desire for that presence, and that symbol is materially present.

Once we recognize that the pleasures of representing absence in both "Rehearsal to Ourselves" and "Struck, was I" derive at least in part from the consoling presence of symbols, we are in a good position to understand the pleasures of symbolizing gaps rather than presences. Once one relinquishes hope for a one-to-one correspondence between signifier and signified, one can revel in the delightful slippage between signifiers, the way one word or phrase can be part of more than one phrase at the same time, the way lines spill into each other. For example, resisting unitary meaning, the third line of "Rehearsal to Ourselves" means both "a bliss that resembles murder" and "a murder that feels like bliss." It delights in its own "Bliss[ful]" defiance of the coherence of meaning—the murder of the sentence. Such a murder delightfully opens up the possibility of multiple meanings unconfined by logic or bondage to an original signified.[40] As Lacan writes, "the symbol manifests itself first of all as the murder of the thing" (*Écrits* 103–4). Dickinson revels in that very murder in "Rehearsal to Ourselves."

Fetishizing one's own wounds, as Dickinson does in this poem and in "Struck, was I," is a way of thinking about these gaps between people and gaps between words, the gaps that are the negative space necessary for both signification and for identity. The indisputable here-and-nowness of the pain one experiences in dwelling upon the painful gap between oneself and one's beloved seems to close that very gap, because there *is* no gap if that which separates the two people is fully present. If all the space between them is present—palpably—then how separate can the two be? As an example of how the pain of absence achieves pure presence, recall the scene in *The Wide, Wide World* in which Ellen and her mother are about to be separated: "Heart met heart in that agony, for each knew all that was in the other" (63). Feeling the *presence* of the pain of impending absence eradicates all conventional boundaries, enabling the two to experience a peak moment of oneness of being. And at that moment, they also enjoy a form of communication that is perfect: "What could words say?" Words are superfluous because there is no gap between the two of them; they have a oneness of thought. As their example demonstrates, ironically, dwelling upon separation creates an experience of pure presence, an experience in which two selves are indistinguishable from each other. In the absence of the other, or in jointly anticipating separation, one can fantasize about the total fusion that would occur if the other *were* present, and one can almost *feel* that total fusion, because one has a strongly *present* experience of that other's absence.

Dickinson appears to have appreciated this pleasurable capacity of wounds to represent and produce presence. In early 1864, for example, to "Sweet Sue," she writes: "There is no first, or last, in Forever—It is

Centre, there, all the time. . . . for the Woman whom I prefer, Here is Festival—Where my Hands are cut, Her fingers will be found inside . . . Take the Key to the Lily, now, and I will lock the Rose—" (L#288). The image of Sue's fingers in Emily's wounds, like the idea of her key in Emily's lock, is a graphic metaphor for the total fusion and absolute presence ("Centre, there, all the time") that Dickinson associates with love, a fusion that is inseparable from anguish, given both the inevitability of separation and the loss of identity that are inseparable from love as she understands it. The wound with Sue's fingers in it is a physical image of the merging of their corporeal (and psychic) boundaries, a display of the thoroughly intersubjective nature of their identities. It conveys the sense of rupture that Dickinson would feel were they separated, and in doing so, it keeps alive the tantalizing ideal of pure presence ("Centre"). Of course, Dickinson proposes that Sue's fingers are *already* inside of her—when Emily's skin is cut, Sue's fingers will be found already inside. Wounding would only reveal the fact of their prior fusion. This image may well allude to a lesbian desire for Sue to dip her fingers in a slit in Emily's flesh—appropriating gendered images of keys, locks, and wounds to express homoerotic desire[41]—but it also has a less specific meaning as an expression of the intensity and corporeality of Dickinson's love. In a letter to Sue, Dickinson writes, "in thinking of those I love, my reason is all gone from me, and I do fear sometimes that I must make a hospital for the hopelessly insane, and chain me up there such times, so I wont injure you" (L#77). Because love entails the complete merging of identities, if it were expressed, it would injure the other. Therefore, given the impossibility of achieving her desire, Dickinson turns to a language of wounding to describe it.

The intensity of her conception of love made Dickinson chary of conventional social intercourse: she could not actually murder her friends and become one with them. Real human contact threatened to degrade the ideal of love Dickinson associated with the few friends her soul selected. Relationships were therefore more intense and more satisfying at imaginary and epistolary levels, which allowed her to keep alive the ideal of total fusion, complete presence. Thus, in a letter to the Hollands, she recalls that during a recent visit, she felt the pain of separation more keenly than she would have if she had stayed at home: "when at your house, the nights seemed much more long than they're wont to do, because separated from you" (L#175). Ironically, physical proximity feels like separation, while in letters, she can enjoy a perfect intimacy untrammeled by barriers such as skin and decorum. In the same letter, she writes, "When father rapped on my door to wake me this morning, I was walking with you in the most wonderful garden, and helping you pick— roses. . . . I count impatiently the hours 'tween me and the darkness, and the dream of you and the roses" (L#175). While physical presence foregrounds the inevitable separation of the human condition, in the solitary privacy of her bedroom she enjoys perfect union with her friends:

> I see thee better—in the Dark—
> I do not need a Light—
> The Love of Thee—a Prism be—
> Excelling Violet—
>   (FP#442c JP#611)

By not actually seeing the beloved, Dickinson can protect her love that "Excel[s] Violet."

Dickinson notoriously resisted being physically present with her friends while paradoxically attaching a greater-than-average value to friendships. To have permitted casual encounters with her friends would have debased her inflated sense of them.[42] One of Dickinson's most sustained poetic treatments of the consequent agonizing necessity of separation is "I cannot live with You— / It would be Life." The body of this poem directly focuses upon all of the reasons why she cannot, indeed must not, see the one she so desperately craves to see. This poignant recitation of all of the forces conspiring against their love is framed by the first and last stanzas, which establish how she has come to terms with her present state of affairs. These two framing stanzas maintain that a symbolic lover is preferable to the physically present lover:

> I cannot live with You—
> It would be Life—
> And Life is over there—
> Behind the Shelf
>
> . . . .
>
> So we must meet apart—
> You there—I—here—
> With just the Door ajar
> That Oceans are—and Prayer—
> And that White +Sustenance—   +exercise—/privilege—
> Despair—
>
>   (FP#706 JP#640)

The poem opens with a paradox: "I cannot live with You— / It would be Life." I read the capitalized word "Life" as a vehicle for expressing the ideal of the pure presence of the other. Conventional individuality is not "Life" but living. The tragedy of existence is that overcoming lonely individuality in the interest of "Life" necessarily destroys "life." The poem clarifies a number of reasons why "Life" is not possible. First, it would make a heaven out of earth, and this reversal is contrary to Christian law: "They'd judge Us" for the blasphemous inevitability that "Your Face / Would put out Jesus'," and she would look for signs of her lover in Jesus, rather than looking for signs of Jesus in her lover. Second, "Life" cannot be sustained because it would render the two inextricable from each other, and this fusion of being is unthinkably perilous in a world in which one must remain behind "To shut the Other's Gaze down" and suffer the intolerable agonies of abandonment. Third, simply by definition, one really "cannot live with" another, because being is defined by separation from others. "Living near" is not "living with." The only way she could "live with" her lover would be to permit "I" to die. "I" exists only in relation to the "not I," and, unfortunately, that second category must include the Lover.

The only source of consolation can be found in a *conceptual* "liv[ing] with," "meet[ing] apart." If they meet conceptually, their real separation is relatively inconsequential; such meeting protects the possibility of seeing each other in the future, consolidating the stable identity that is firmly grounded in the other's absence. The present term of separation is painful, but the two can "meet apart— / You there—I—here— / With just the Door ajar / That Oceans are." The oceans may be barriers, but they are also barriers encountered mutually, providing a means for communication and can therefore be thought of as a "Door ajar."

Restimulating the "cause" of her "Despair"—rehearsing to herself the withdrawn delight—affords her "Sustenance," a reminder that is sufficient to alleviate the threat of complete psychic collapse underlying her separation. Undoubtedly, hurting herself is an unpleasant necessity, but at least it works. When the lightning singes us, "then—Ourselves are conscious He exist" (FP#595 JP#630). Like fantasizing about oceans, experiencing pain is a way of bridging the distance. The "White Sustenance" may also be, as Cynthia Griffin Wolff suggests, a reference to language. Letters and poetry enable her to unite with the lover without diminishing his infinite magnitude, and without inflicting upon him the violence that is the logical endpoint of her quest for total presence. Dickinson values the almost limitless possibilities of words to enact the intimacy of symbolic relationships. "Your precious letter, Susie, it sits here now, and smiles so kindly at me" (L#85). Like masochism, writing provides physical presence, a presence whose pleasure is contingent upon the other's (painful) absence. The compensation of that pleasure was so considerable that Dickinson could write: "A Letter is a joy of Earth— / It is denied the Gods—" (FP#672 JP#1639).

The enormously consoling presence of writing, with its possibilities for a fusion unattainable with fleshly people, is vividly exemplified in the poem "Unto my Books—so good to turn":

Unto my Books so good to turn—
Far ends of +tired Days—   +Homely—
It half endears the Abstinence—
And Pain—+is missed—in Praise.   +Forgets—for—

As Flavors—cheer Retarded Guests
With Banquettings to be—
So Spices—stimulate the time
Till my small Library—

It may be Wilderness—without—
Far feet of failing Men—
But Holiday—excludes the night—
And it is Bells—within—

I thank these Kinsmen of the Shelf—
Their Countenances Kid
Enamor—in Prospective—
And satisfy—obtained—

(FP#512 JP#604)

After a long day of labor, it is good to turn to books, the "Far ends" of hours spent abstaining from true pleasure. Turning away from abstinence is so pleasurable that it makes the abstinence itself half enjoyable simply by building up desire. Indeed, it can endear the pain itself. There is a double meaning of "missed" in the observation that "Pain—is missed." Certainly, she means that there is no more pain when one is reading a book. However, the more masochistic reading also applies. Just as a prison becomes a friend, so the pain of abstinence can become a pleasure in its own right, its pain "missed," because absence-of-pain holds out no more bright *promises* of absence-of-pain. As Lacan says, "desire" has been raised to "a second power."

Libraries offer holidays not only from the real world of obligations, failing men, and the wilderness but from other people. Noticeably absent from Dickinson's edenic library are flesh-and-blood "Kinsmen." Rather, in solitude she can perpetuate the ideal relationships that are impossible when others are physically present.[43] The image of books excluding the night, setting bells to ringing within, echoes a letter written in autumn 1853 to the Hollands: "Dear Dr. and Mrs. Holland—dear Minnie—it is cold tonight, but the thought of you so warm, that I sit by it as a fireside, and am never cold any more. I love to write to you—it

We must an anguish pay
In keen and quivering ratio
To the extasy—
      (FP#109 JP#125)

Ecstasy is so inseparable from anguish that the keenness and the quiver-ingness of making the payment is itself a pleasure. The ecstasy of writing poetry, for instance, arises from a "keen and quivering" dwelling upon the painful ontological consciousness of partiality and ephemerality, and the subsequent transformation of that suffering into an enduring art that is itself present.[1]

While we, as readers, cannot help but grieve over the tragic facts of mortality and lack-of-presence that produced Dickinson's poetry, we can nonetheless be grateful for the immensely rich "gift of screws" that arose from Dickinson's masochism. Confronting the misery of the human condition—erotically reveling in the presence of that misery—Dickinson produced a poetry that has afforded readers intellectual and sensual pleasures for over a century, with no foreseeable decline in her relevance for contemporary readers. Dickinson's successful grasp of aes-thetic power through the deliberate cultivation of suffering suggests that we should rethink our attitudes toward masochism.

This empowerment through masochism, it should be noted, is rela-tively conservative with regard to direct transformation of social injus-tice. The power of masochism is attained not through subversion or transgression of dominant discourses but rather by intentionally deploy-ing them. In saying that "a prison gets to be a friend," Dickinson does not rail against the limitations of life in the panopticon but points out that she finds pleasure in prison life. While, in a strict sense, locating a female voice is a priori subversive of the patriarchy, in the sense of direct political action it is not necessarily so. After all, when Phyllis Schlafly or Clarence Thomas expresses conventionally conservative views, the sim-ple fact that they are, respectively, female and black is not enough to make their speech acts subversive. But Dickinson is not a public figure publicly advocating female submission to dominant social norms. Her masochism is not a social program; it is a private form of self-expression, indulged in for the purpose of exploring her own desires and of creating art from her fantasies. In her masochistic poetic fantasies, Dickinson does not obviously challenge sentimental and Calvinist discourses, not-withstanding their repressive positioning of women like herself. Rather, she exploits them for her own erotic and aesthetic pleasure, creating a space for herself to achieve stellar heights of aesthetic production.

To conclude, however, that Dickinson's masochism is "conservative" would be to do it and her an injustice, for Dickinson's masochism differs dramatically from that of Susan Warner, Caroline Lee Hentz, and

Martha Finley. In her use of masochism, Dickinson, I suggest, is closer to contemporary novelist and advocate for sadomasochism Dorothy Allison (author of *Bastard Out of Carolina* and *Cavedweller*) than to these sentimental novelists, for Dickinson's uses of a masochistic voice are self-conscious and intentional. Consistently, in poems such as "Rehearsal to Ourselves / Of a Withdrawn Delight," "Struck, was I," and "I cannot live with You," she not only uses masochism but also investigates when and why pain is associated with pleasure. None of the other authors studied in this book turns such an analytical, self-referential eye on her own masochism or muses, as Dickinson does, upon the apparently interesting fact of the erotics of pain and domination. She does not simply submit to her desire; she explores it. The erotic fantasies of Warner, Hentz, and Finley are more unconscious; their artistry centers on creating a compelling, visualizable representation of desire rather than on interrogating that desire. To that extent, they achieve considerable power, in the form of dramatic intensity, great readability, and commercial success, but this power of "voice" is at least partially offset by the disempowering long-term effects of these popular sentimental-masochistic novels. In indulging in the pleasures of eroticized domination, these texts, and even Dickinson's poetry, reinforce negative cultural patterns, presenting coherent and attractive visions of female destiny that readers young and old might be tempted to reproduce in their own lives (young girls associating sexiness in men with abusiveness and therefore seeking abusive men and young men seeking to attract women by being abusive). Even *Uncle Tom's Cabin* falls into this generally negative pattern of the sentimental construction of female masochistic desire. Though it can hardly be viewed as unequivocally disempowering, given its explosive impact on national political life, it does idealize suffering as a particularly appropriate, effective, and ecstatic form of political action for women.

But while, as a feminist, I obviously endorse the long-term goal of breaking down the deeply entrenched patterns of eroticized male domination that I discuss here, I think that simply to reject masochism out of hand for these reasons is neither practical nor desirable. Masochism is not a single nor simple phenomenon: it comes in a variety of forms, on a continuum that ranges from dysfunctional, literal self-inflicted pain to an aesthetic of the sexualized sublime. Dickinson frequently explores the latter kind of masochism by intentionally exploiting the discourses of the former. Unlike male masochists, who transgress conventional gender roles in their quest for a jouissance, women can revel in aesthetic performances of such roles. But the pleasures for both sexes can partake of a sublime transcendence and are not necessarily repressive reactions to social determination.

Whereas masochism is not a priori bad for women (or men), women's attraction to dominating men *is* always at least dangerous. An aesthetic of masochistic ecstasy is different from an attraction to abuse. But even when self-deprecating, male-identifying attractions to submission, and not self-conscious, aesthetic varieties of masochism, are present, I still think it is important to allow for the play of female masochistic desire. Genuine self-exploration must precede any transformation. If masochistic desire is so beyond the pale that no one can own it in private, then few people feeling it will examine their own desire sufficiently either to grow beyond it through heightened awareness *or* to recognize that it is not a purely negative force in their lives.

Honest self-recognition is the first step, and the key step, toward transformation, and the feminist movement needs to welcome it if it is to remain a relevant and vital force in American political life. Women who self-identify as feminists but who also have fantasies that involve domination or pain are as likely to stay out of the movement altogether as they are to challenge criteria for membership. And they are even more likely to choose nonparticipation if membership threatens to deprive them of a significant avenue toward agency that they have identified within the patriarchy.

Dorothy Allison argues similarly:

> for me S/M was a road out of being unable to connect with my body on any level. . . . Some social theories say that the reason incest survivors are attracted to S/M is because they're incapable of feeling anything and therefore they go for extremes in pain as a way to feel anything at all—and this becomes a criticism, a reason why you should not do this. If you are a person who can not feel and they tell you that this one place you can feel you are not supposed to do, then all you are left with is still being that person who can not feel. The theory has no compassion. (Interview 29)[2]

Characters like Ellen Montgomery and Elsie Dinsmore likewise have little access to feeling—in their cases because of ideological constraints upon female corporeality and sexuality—and masochistic fantasies work for them as they do for Allison: making available a form of feeling. For those in such a position, saying "you should not feel this" is more likely to alienate than to change them. The same line of thinking applies to masochism as an expression of anger. For the person to whom the expression of anger is off-limits, masochism represents a sad but effective means of self-expression. Making it off-limits without recognizing the need it serves and proposing an alternative is likely to be counterproductive. Many psychotherapists recognize this truth, asserting that it is important not to attack clients on their defenses. Therapists strive to help clients see how certain behaviors have been undermining their lives *and* serving them, so that the clients may voluntarily change these behaviors when they identify viable, less self-destructive alternatives.

The worst aspect, however, of a blanket rejection of masochism and masochistic fantasy is that it does not enable women who are drawn toward one or the other to grow as human beings through an honest encounter with what turns them on. Therefore, while books like *The Wide, Wide World* and *Elsie Dinsmore* present deplorable visions of life, I nonetheless see them as positive signs of female empowerment in that they present images of their authors' fantasies. If we do not like what turns these authors on, we should nonetheless appreciate their vivid imagining of their desire, if for nothing else than the understanding it affords us of the forms of desire that a society constructs and the repressive effects that might have stemmed from such artworks. Moreover, can we know that the fantasies are simply bad? So what if Ellen is turned on by an image of John swinging a scepter at her? Is that always and only to be read as a sign and agent of patriarchal manipulation? Perhaps, as Laplanche and Pontalis might argue, she identifies with both John *and* herself in her fantasy, thereby breaking down, rather than reifying, repressive forms of coherent identity.[3] Sex is weird; sexual fantasies, notoriously bizarre. Petrarch is fixated on the hand of a woman he doesn't know; Hamlet is attracted to his mother; Angelo in *Measure for Measure* is sexually aroused by the chastity of a young nun; Leopold Bloom in *Ulysses* grovels before a hermaphroditic creature whom he calls "Mistress"; the self-educated man in Sartre's *Nausea* is turned on by little children in the public library; Quentin Compson can't stop thinking about his sister's dirty underwear. For a woman to own her desire is to own herself in all her human complexity and human weirdness. Her desire is not immutable, nor is her identity, but knowing who she *is* is as significant as knowing who she *wants* to be. To repudiate a fantasy because it differs from an ideal desire is to refuse full aliveness.

In an essay entitled "Public Silence, Private Terror," Dorothy Allison recalls a phone call she received from a fellow-lesbian speaking in a tone "choked with shame and desperation" about her own masochistic fantasies. "She had tried to stop herself, stop the fantasies, masturbation, stray thoughts. But it didn't go away, either her fear or her desire," and Allison sorrowfully recalls the woman's "terror, her disgust with herself" (102). Allison advises the caller to accept her desire and read a book on how to practice it safely, but the caller does not want to accept her desire; she wants to get rid of it, to not-desire that which she desires. Her shame over the exposure to which the call subjects her causes her to hang up abruptly. Allison muses:

> Throughout my life somebody has always tried to set the boundaries of who and what I will be allowed to be . . . What is common to these boundary lines

is that their most destructive power lies in what I can be persuaded to do to myself—the walls of fear, shame and guilt I can be encouraged to build in my mind. Like that woman who called me, I am to hide myself, and hate myself and never risk exposing what might be true about my life. I have learned through great sorrow that all systems of oppression feed on public silence and private terrorization. But few do so more forcefully than the systems of sexual oppression, and each of us is under enormous pressure to give in to their demands. (116)

Self-hatred. Shame. These go along with the rigid imposition of standards of sexual political correctness. If one needs to hate anything in masochism, one might appropriately hate any negative behaviors that might spring from culturally determined desires, but not one's own desiring self. Allison's caller is only fantasizing, yet she is overwhelmed with terror over what her desire says about her. It is normal, not "sick," to have sexual fantasies that are not "nice." I do not share the conviction that public talk about our kinkiest desires is necessary in order to free us from "systems of oppression," but I do think that frank speech about the nature of sexual fantasy and its tangential relationship to identity and behavior would go a long way toward liberating people like Allison's caller from terror and shame. The unconscious—that perverse hotbed of masochistic, sadistic, incestuous, narcissistic, fetishistic, voyeuristic, necrophilic fantasies—is not the same as the conscious self. And the fantasies it revels in scripting, rehearsing, and staging—while they may provide some insight into one's deeper motives—are not "the true self." People should feel free to confront these dark artworks emanating from their own unconscious, to celebrate their artistry with humor and pride. According to Allison, the masochistic protagonist in *Bastard Out of Carolina* "is deeply ashamed of her S/M fantasies, but at the same time, they're a source of energy for her. *She is not only a victim*—she finds some heroism which isn't possible in her everyday life" (Interview 28, emphasis added). If people uncomfortable with their desires cannot celebrate the heroism of their fantasies, at the very least they can recognize that many "good," "normal" people also have surprising erotic fantasies, and this recognition would ease the shame and self-loathing that surely do little to promote healthy sexuality and self-esteem. As the situation of Allison's caller indicates, willing desires to go away because one is ashamed of them simply does not work.

Allison's caller resembles Zenobia in Nathaniel Hawthorne's *Blithedale Romance*: she is a feminist and a masochist, tortured by her desire and rendered desperate by its incompatibility with her conscious sense of herself. I would like to close with a brief consideration of Hawthorne's representation of masochism in *Blithedale* because it contains in miniature the entire argument made in this book, including the difficulties in both acknowledging and *not* acknowledging women's maso-chistic desires. Among other things, *The Blithedale Romance* explores the hypothesis that women—whether by nature or by nurture—are at-tracted to abusive men, and that this attraction will undermine the women's movement, which Hawthorne vaguely idealized as our last best hope for the spiritual redemption of the world. Miles Coverdale is amazed and dismayed to observe both his beloved Priscilla and her sis-ter, the woman's-rights activist Zenobia, irresistibly attracted to Hol-lingsworth, a man with a spirit of holy righteousness, an iron will, and a cruel and egotistical attitude toward women. Hollingsworth reveals the violent underside of the discourses of true womanhood and coverture:

> [Woman] is the most admirable handiwork of God, in her true place and character. Her place is at man's side. Her office that of Sympathizer, the unre-served, unquestioning Believer. . . . All the separate action of woman is, and ever has been, and always shall be, false, foolish, vain, destructive of her own best and holiest qualities . . . woman is a monster—and thank Heaven, an almost impossible and hitherto imaginary monster—without man, as her ac-knowledged principal! . . . were there any possible prospect of woman's tak-ing the social stand which some of them—poor, miserable, abortive creatures, who only dream of such things because they have missed woman's peculiar happiness, or because Nature made them really neither man nor woman!—if there were a chance of their attaining the end which these petticoated mon-strosities have in view, I would call upon my own sex to use physical force, that unmistakable evidence of sovereignty, to scourge them back within their proper bounds! But it will not be needful. The heart of true womanhood knows where its own sphere is, and never seeks to stray beyond it! (128)

The insipid girl Priscilla responds to this violent speech with "entire ac-quiescence." Ethereal and atmospheric rather than fully present, Pris-cilla, "the very woman whom he pictured—the gentle parasite, the soft reflection of a more powerful existence—sat there at his feet" (128). She revels in the thought of a contingent existence relative to a man who alone has subjectivity, because she is "the type of womanhood, such as man has spent centuries in making it," formed by the same ideologies that Hollingsworth cites (127). We might speculate that Hol-lingsworth's violence pleases her as a sign of what he says it is, "evidence of [man's] sovereignty." According to Zenobia, she is the kind of woman who needs her consciousness raised, who needs to learn that her parasitism is not "natural" but rather the product of patriarchal condi-tioning.

But the book explores the likelihood that consciousness raising will not necessarily change her desire. For Zenobia is equally attracted to Hollingsworth, notwithstanding (or perhaps because of) his attitude of violence and derision toward feminists like herself. With tears in her eyes, she says, "Well; be it so," adding: "Let man be but manly and god-like, and woman is only too ready to become to him what you say!" (129). What Coverdale calls "some necromancy of his horrible injus-tice" brings women to Hollingsworth's feet, and the novel probes the deeper social and biological roots of this necromancy, by which cruelty is transformed into male desirability. Hawthorne questions, but seems to agree with, the idea that marriage is women's natural state and high-est calling. Perhaps women seek a "godlike" husband because they can thereby partake of the highest state possible to them, the book suggests. If women wish to be absorbed by godlike men, and if violence is a neces-sary component of godlikeness, then women will be attracted by vio-lence and submit to it. Whether or not that explains Zenobia's attraction to Hollingsworth, the novel is at least clear on one point: raising female consciousness does not necessarily redeem female desire. The presence of masochistic desire in a strong feminist leads Miles to voice what con-temporary women will recognize as a familiar male complaint: " 'Women almost invariably behave thus!' thought I. 'What does the fact mean? Is it their nature? Or is it, at last, the result of ages of compelled degrada-tion? And, in either case, will it be possible ever to redeem them?' " (129). As the word "redeem" implies, Hawthorne sees masochistic de-sire as a problem, and the book implies that the problem lies in what female masochism will do to the cause of women's rights. Indeed, the plot of *Blithedale* turns upon this, for in the competition for the abusive Hollingsworth, Zenobia the feminist betrays her sister. Women, Haw-thorne worries, will not fulfill their highest destiny—that of purifying and spiritualizing the world—until they stop competing with each other for "godlike" men in whom to find a parasitic existence, particularly when "horrible injustice" is their distorted benchmark of male godli-ness.

Hawthorne shows that the stakes in confronting masochism in partic-ular and issues of female sexuality in general are high: in despair over the incompatibility between the very fact of her unruly, uncontrollable sex-ual nature and society's hostility toward "the woman who swerves one hair's breadth out of the beaten track," Zenobia first wildly announces she will become a nun but then gives up the fight and commits suicide (201). It is not exactly her masochism that causes her suicide, but rather her guilt over the corruption to which she is led by her sexual desire. Zenobia cannot meaningfully integrate her sexuality with her feminist idealism, and she responds with self-hatred ("It was my fault all along"; "He did well to cast me off" [202]) and self-destruction.

A truly supportive women's rights movement would be compassion-ate toward and receptive to such a woman's sexual desire, encourage her to know and perhaps embrace the darker, inconsistent aspects of her personality, and live. Embrace the weird curves of her own sexuality. Even as it sought a critical understanding of the repressive aspects of such desires—studying, for example, their origins in nineteenth-century sentimental novels—a truly supportive women's rights movement would foster a broad spirit of tolerance toward impulses and fantasies that, in people's actual lives, do not necessarily change at will. The combination of self-knowledge and self-affirmation in such an attitude would enable women to be that which Hawthorne is incapable of imagining: embodied, fleshy, passionate, sexually arousing and aroused feminists who are aware of and striving to change the constraints of life in the patriarchy, *and* comfortable with the mystery of their own humanity.

Notes

Introduction
"Weird Curves": Masochism and Feminism

1. My interpretation of the poem is indebted to that of Cheryl Walker in *The Nightingale's Burden*. I do not find Shirley Marchalonis's challenge to Walker persuasive. She argues that the poem is religious and *not* about men and women, without acknowledging that many of Larcom's poems are quite clearly about both, simultaneously. Ironically, Marchalonis herself offers a succinct cultural background that perfectly glosses the line, "O man with your beautiful power of presence and speech." In the introduction to her biography of Larcom, she characterizes Larcom's predicament as a poet in these words: "A talented woman was in a difficult position, caught between her drive to use her gifts and the male-generated standards of womanly behavior that, at their extremes, would have made her *invisible and inaudible* (4, emphasis added).

2. Walker, *The Nightingale's Burden*, 50. Though relatively unknown today, Brooks was widely admired by important male authors of her day, including Rufus Griswold and Robert Southey, for her long poem *Zophiel*, a passionate tale of death and erotic obsession. See Bennett's headnote in *Nineteenth-Century American Women's Poetry*.

3. Masse argues that the masochism in women's Gothic literature represents what Freud calls a repetition compulsion: women, psychically afflicted by their traumatic loss of autonomy and subjectivity, continually repeat that very loss in Gothic literature, not for pleasure but in an effort to control it through representation, to bring to light and discharge the repressed affect that is haunting the edges of their consciousness. Her reading of masochism as a drive toward stability and pleasure usefully demonstrates the functional role masochism often plays. Rosemary Jackson and Terry Heller posit more ecstatic, perverse pleasures in masochism, delineating the implications of Lacanian theory for criticism of the Gothic. In *In the Circles of Fear and Desire*, William Patrick Day acknowledges that feminine masochism in the Gothic can be positive for women, not simply a capitulation or repetition compulsion. He argues that in the Gothic, "the self is defined through conflict, as a giver or receiver of pain in a sadomasochistic dynamic," and he claims that Gothic subversion plays this game of domination and subordination; the self acquires agency by turning the tools of power against itself rather than overtly challenging it: "The passivity and acceptance we see in the heroines is not a surrender to their situation, but a style of resistance and self-assertion" (85, 20).

4. For discussions relating the Gothic and the sentimental, see Mary Patterson Thornburg, *The Monster in the Mirror*; Cathy Davidson, *Revolution and the Word*; Richard O. Allen, "If You Have Tears: Sentimentalism as Soft Romanticism"; Leslie Fiedler, *Love and Death in the American Novel*; Noble, "An Ec-

stasy of Apprehension." Allen specifically classifies *The Wide, Wide World* as a Gothic melodrama in a tradition that includes *Rosemary's Baby* (135).

5. Luce Irigaray and Hélène Cixous are the two most prominent theorists seeking a woman's own language, and their experimental prose styles model the form such a voice might take, resisting singularity of meaning or meanings predicated upon binary oppositions. Jessica Benjamin theorizes the possibility of a female desire not patriarchally determined but predicated, rather, upon a "holding" ethic, a form of desire suggested both by the containing aspects of the vagina and by maternal impulses. Julia Kristeva develops a "semiotic" theory of language that emphasizes sensual presymbolic modes of communication, such as rhythm and rhyme, which disrupt the central structures of linguistics. The subject influenced by this disruptive language is no longer a coherent subject but a "subject-in-process," capable of apprehending nondictated desires. All of these fascinating and speculative inquiries into women's language invariably run across the essentialism question: do women considered en masse actually have innate desires that are mutated by culture? Do men? Is there a gender-based "true" desire prior to its cultural and linguistic determination? Diana Fuss responds that it is appropriate to essentialize about race and gender when it is socially and politically expedient to do so.

6. Every essay in Linden's *Against Sadomasochism* falls into the "voluntarist" category. See also the essays by Sheila Jeffreys, Liz Kelly, Deborah Cameron, and Elizabeth Frazer in *Feminism and Sexuality*; the section "Sexual Practice" in Alison M. Jagger's collection, *Living with Contradictions*; and Sheila Jeffrey's "Sadomasochism: The Erotic Cult of Fascism" in *The Lesbian Heresy*. Sandra Lee Bartky, Ruby Rich, Stevi Jackson and Sue Scott, and Linda Singer all offer useful surveys of the conflict between "libertarianism" and "voluntarism." Voluntarist studies frequently equate the practice of heterosexuality with eroticized dominance. Theorists who oppose the "libertarian" position but who are not intrinsically opposed to heterosexuality frequently take the position that what looks like masochism is really something else. At the end of chapter 3 of *In the Name of Love*, for example, Michelle Masse quotes from Margaret Atwood's *Lady Oracle* as a way of summing up her attitude toward uses of masochism in female Gothic fiction: "If you find yourself trapped in a situation you can't get out of gracefully, you might as well pretend you chose it. Otherwise you will look ridiculous" (Masse 106). What appears to be feminine masochism, she suggests, is actually a pose struck to maintain self-esteem. But this enticing approach to the problem of feminine masochism, also featured in Caplan and Radway, exemplifies the central limitation of the voluntarist position, which is that in fact desire frequently is not "pretending," nor is it "other" than one's identity.

7. In "Sexual Skirmishes and Feminist Factions," Stevi Jackson and Sue Scott delineate the same impasse, arguing that "the pursuit of [sexual] pleasure is a positive goal for feminists" but that such pleasure is difficult to imagine within patriarchal society, since "pleasure has long been defined from a masculine perspective." They write: "we need to retain a critical stance on the ways in which our desires have been constructed within a heterosexually ordered patriarchal society, and remain aware of the material constraints which limit the pleasure we can currently attain. The polarisation of the debate between libertarian and anti-

libertarian feminists has made it difficult to theorise a space between these two positions in which we can explore both power and pleasure and their interconnections" (20). Part 3 in Jackson and Scott's collection features a range of feminist responses to the highly fraught question of feminism and the erotics of domination.

8. Works that fall into this "liberal," or "libertarian," category include those by Pat Califia, Amber Hollibaugh, and Dorothy Allison; most of the contributions to *Pleasure and Danger: Exploring Female Sexuality* (Carole S. Vance, ed.), d'Aury's discussions of *The Story of O* in John de St. Jorre; many of the essays in *SandM: Studies in Sadomasochism* (Weinberg and Kamel, eds.); Lynda Hunt's "Doing it Anyway"; and the entire collection entitled *Coming to Power*, and other productions of the sadomasochistic organization SAMOIS.

9. See Jean Wyatt for a theory of how reading can aid in the transformation of both desire and identity. She claims that when a reader is attuned to the preoedipal, nonsymbolic aspects of communication embedded in a text, his or her consciously maintained sense of identity is destabilized, making it possible to fantasize about and desire something new.

10. Many such studies have focused upon Dickinson, and consideration of these gives a good sense of the variety of subversions or resistances critics have identified. One of the most prominent examples of this kind of work is Margaret Homans's "Syllables of Velvet," which considers metonymy in Dickinson's poetry as a literary device for expressing norms of female desire that are not patriarchally dictated. "All men say what to me," Dickinson observes, and in refusing linguistic clarity, she resists the objectification and commodification that was the fate of many of her poetic sisters. Joanne Feit Diehl also analyzes Dickinson's subversions of the male tradition exemplified by Wordworth, Keats, Shelley, and Emerson: by conceiving of herself apart from this male line of poets, Dickinson creates a space that provides her the freedom to experiment. Mary Loeffelholz explores such feminist deconstructive approaches in light of Lacan's language-based theory of the formation of female subjectivity in patriarchal culture: Dickinson resists the gendering gaze, preferring nonobjectifying modes of apprehension, such as the aural. Christanne Miller's *A Poet's Grammar* classifies Dickinson's use of squinting modifiers; unexpected juxtapositions; irregular syntax, verb forms, and punctuation; and many other devices that resist coherent meaning as antipatriarchal linguistic strategies.

11. Poststructuralism often denigrates the author's struggle to express an idea replacing "authors" with "the author function." It is often assumed that there are no ideas in search of articulation, only discourse seeking an agent to express it. Women, from such a point of view, have not been wrestling with a patriarchal language to articulate their eroticism; patriarchal language has been creating their desire and inciting them to discourse, prodding and creating—not impeding—their articulation of eroticism. However, while it is true that forms of expression bear the imprint of the culture in which their authors lived or are even allegories of a political unconscious, as Jameson proposes, authors are not simply vessels for the dissemination of ideology. Thought is stamped, not determined, by language. How else can we explain diametrically oppositional thinking within any given culture?

12. Granted, supposedly gender-neutral ontological theories of subjectivity have frequently been shown to have a male bias. Bersani intelligently addresses such objections to his ontological theory of masochistic pleasure in "Is the Rectum a Grave?" But even if women had to identify with men in order to experience ontological pleasures in masochism, the fact remains that they actually could find pleasures through such identification. See also Carol Siegel's discussion of Deleuze and Guattari's anti-psychoanalytic, culturally specific interpretation of literary manifestations of male masochism. Rejecting Freudian theories of essential gender traits and oedipal conflict, she addresses the multiple powers and pleasures of masochism, including mystical rapture and the thrill of being dominated. On the other hand, some theories of the pleasures of male masochism would make those pleasures by definition unavailable to women. Both Kaja Silverman and D. A. Miller relate the pleasures of male masochism to the transgression of conventional gender categories, a transgression that opens up an ecstatic sense of release from men's ideologically determined positions as the world's dominators and empire builders, and makes available instead revelry in the ecstasies of "feminine" yielding.

13. There are, of course, exceptions to this rule. Both Kaja Silverman and Michelle Masse discuss ways that masochism functions to challenge gender norms.

14. Mary Chapman denies the subversive potential of masochism, arguing that the daughter is usually "disciplined by her own masquerade of compliance" (9). She astutely points out that Deleuze fails to address how gender complicates his model; he overlooks, for example, that women had no right to engage in the contract that is central to his understanding of the empowerment of women. But her argument for the ultimate recontainment of a subversive "masquerade" focuses upon masochistic agency as something that would arise solely in opposition to power rather than in complicity with it.

15. Nancy Armstrong makes a similarly polemical argument, deliberately overstating her case about the extent to which women have been powerful. She says she does so "as a means of countering those who would emphasize woman's powerlessness—and we are certainly rendered powerless in specifically female ways—and therefore as a means of identifying for critical consideration that middle-class power which does not appear to be power because it behaves in specifically female ways. . . . I want to consider the ways in which gender collaborates with class to contain forms of political resistance within liberal discourse. I want to use my power as a woman of the dominant class and as a middle-class intellectual to name what power I use as a form of power rather than to disguise it as the powerlessness of others" (26).

16. Studies of women's victimization through the eroticization of violence are legion, including the foundational studies of Catharine MacKinnon and Andrea Dworkin. More recently and specifically, Liz Kelly has identified a continuum of men's sexual violence that locates coercive heterosexual practice at one end and rape and murder at the other. Deborah Cameron and Elizbeth Frazer claim that the eroticization of male violence leads some men to commit sex murders, and therefore, like Kelly, they challenge the "libertarian" approach to danger and feminine desire. Addressing the woman who might say, "I have discov-

ered these desires in myself—you cannot ask me to repress them," they reply, "not repress, but question" (Cameron and Frazer 214). They urge feminists to "look at the social consequences of acting out [sadomasochistic] desires in order to reconstruct desire such that sado-masochism is no longer erotically charged" (214).

17. Rich offers an insightful survey of the history of scholarship on feminism and sadomasochism in the 1980s, discussing SAMOIS's *Coming to Power* (1982), *Against Sadomasochism* (Robin Ruth Linden et al., eds., 1982), *Powers of Desire* (Ann Snitow, ed., 1983), *Pleasure and Danger* (Carol Vance, ed., 1984), Pat Califia's *Sapphistry* (1983), *Pleasures* (Lonnie Barbach, ed., 1984), and Beatrice Faust's *Women, Sex and Pornography* (1980). There are, of course, some studies of the double-edgedness of women's masochism. In chapter 5 of *Passions of the Voice*, Clare Kahane considers the benefits Olive Schreiner derived from writing about masochism in *The Story of an African Farm*. Kahane argues that Schreiner represents masochism as a reaction to the problematics of female identity: forced to separate from a nurturing maternal presence and individuate, the masochistic subject expresses her desire for unity through a masochistic melancholy and death drive. Masochism, then, is a useful rhetorical device for Schreiner's efforts to find a voice in which to articulate her anxiety of gender. See also Smith, Barnes, Chapman, Masse.

18. Nancy Armstrong's *Desire and Domestic Fiction* represents probably the best, most detailed working out of the ways that domestic fiction empowers women, not through resisting or subverting power, but through wielding it. She demonstrates that late-eighteenth- and nineteenth-century British domestic fiction (and I would add, similar works in America) were agents by which women gained social power. Domestic novels, frequently written by women and in which women played starring roles, preceded and fostered the way of life they represented, shaping the new view of middle-class women as pivotal figures in the culture, not mere ornaments. And this shift was central to the rise of middle-class cultural hegemony. As an example of how this ultimately led to a reconfiguration of power, Armstrong suggests that by the mid-nineteenth century, the gendering of identity in women's domestic fiction led to widespread representations of the working classes in terms of personal deficiencies (deficient women were deemed masculine and deficient men were deemed effeminate), and middle-class intellectuals were thereby able to represent the problems caused by rapid industrialization as sexual scandals brought about by workers' lack of personal development and self-restraint. Reformers were then in a good position to step forward and offer themselves and their institutions as the remedy for growing political resistance. Domestic fiction—with its insistent interiorization and gendering of identity and its idealization of sexual restraint, and its focus upon the essential interiority of identity—played a critical role in stabilizing bourgeois hegemony by determining the ideologies of identity and morality central to that social formation. Domestic fiction, therefore, is both a document in and an agent of cultural history.

19. In *The Wicked Sisters*, Betsy Erkkila similarly challenges the tendency among feminist critics to find in female authors voices of powerless, innocent victimization rather than powerful, complicitous women. Erkkila draws our at-

tention to the following argument in Teresa de Lauretis's "Eccentric Subjects," which I quote at greater length than does Erkkila: "The subject of this [new feminist historical] consciousness is unlike the one that was initially defined by the opposition of woman to man on the axis of gender and purely constituted by the oppression, repression, or negation of its sexual difference. For one thing, it is much less pure. Indeed, it is most likely ideologically complicit with the "oppressor" whose position it may occupy in certain sociosexual relations (if not in others). Second, it is neither unified nor singly divided between positions of masculinity and femininity but multiply organized across positions on several axes of difference. . . . Finally, and most significantly, it has agency (rather than 'choice'), the capacity for movement or self-determined (dis)location, and hence social accountability" ("Eccentric Subjects" 137). Nancy Armstrong, Laura Wexler, and Karen Sanchez-Eppler, among others, also make this point.

20. Before the 1970s, this large body of work received virtually no recognition, except of the contemptuous, dismissive sort. Sentimental fiction was the oppressive background that enabled men's literature to shine forth in dramatic and heroic relief. The best example of how it did this is found in *Huckleberry Finn*, in which Emmeline Grangerford's maudlin sentimental poetry serves as a foil for Twain's own tell-it-how-it-is writing. In the '70s, the American feminist movement took an "androgynous" stance: women and men are essentially the same, but culture reifies gender through rigorous socialization. Read through this lens, sentimental fiction was seen as collaborationist; its authors were victims of patriarchal ideological manipulation, constrained to celebrate antifemale values dictated by women's abusive rulers. The most notorious proponent of this position was Ann Douglas, who represented Little Eva as the perfect emblem of what is wrong with this fiction: Eva is a purely decorative creature whose passivity, Stowe oppressively insists, is the key to women's cultural empowerment. Nineteenth-century women, Douglas maintains, struck a Faustian bargain, selling their autonomy and intellectual aspirations for the narcissistic pleasures of being represented as Christlike icons of passive martyrdom and hence the most important figures in their cultures. Sentimental fiction, from this perspective, is a flattering mirror celebrating dominant ideologies and gratifying women with portraits of happy and fulfilled wives and mothers. Other works that largely conform to this early feminist perspective on sentimentalism include Barbara Welter's *Dimity Convictions* and Martha Vicinus's *Suffer and Be Still*.

21. The androgyny mode of feminist thought was challenged in the '80s by a school of feminist thought that celebrated female difference. This movement was perhaps most popularly theorized by Carol Gilligan's *In a Different Voice* and Nancy Chodorow's *The Reproduction of Mothering*. Gilligan insisted that men and women are fundamentally different, and that the feminist effort to emphasize androgyny was actually a form of collaboration with the oppressor, since the universal norm remained implicitly male. Women think differently from men, Gilligan proposed, and the goal of feminism should be to revalue women's ways of thinking and approaching things. From this perspective, traditional womanly interests like domestic preoccupations, childrearing, relationship building, and fashion became not signs of women's ideological manipulation but the very essence of womanly being, expressions of legitimate female inter-

ests. Nancy Chodorow contributed to this effort by revising the oedipal paradigm to foreground a girl's healthy sense of relatedness and attachment, in contrast to a boy's loneliness, brought on by the excessive individuation mandated by Western culture. Like Gilligan, Chodorow underwrote efforts to revalue women's emphases upon relationships and community building as healthy and of greater moral value than men's emphases upon empire building and individual excellence. Literary criticism influenced by this perspective no longer denigrated sentimentalism but instead celebrated its richly portrayed social worlds and its realistic representation of female emotion. Jane Tompkins's *Sensational Designs* epitomizes the approach to nineteenth-century sentimental fiction that this development in feminist theory inspired. Insisting that sentimental works were antipatriarchal in their very domesticity, she argued that they posited an alternative form of power—domestic power—that positioned women as the most important members of society. These fictions, she maintained, promulgated women's ways of thinking and approaching things, not in a spirit of collaboration with patriarchal values but in a spirit of opposition to them. They positioned feelings and religion higher than materialism and aggressive individualism, and they thereby constituted important challenges to the major patriarchal myths of their day.

22. The following crucial observation in the Masters and Johnson report on sex and human loving bears consideration: "Fantasies about rape are possibly the most misunderstood of all sex fantasies. Some people think that women who fantasize about rape are really yearning for such an event to occur and suggest that the fantasy represents an unrealized wish. This distorted interpretation has no basis in fact. It is more useful to look at rape fantasies as providing reassurance to some women that they are being sexually passive rather than aggressive, since this conforms to our cultural stereotypes about sexual behavior" (Masters & Johnson 278–79). Just because women's romances have included fantasies of rape and domination is no reason to presume that these are the secret wishes of authors and readers. But to deny the abiding power of such fantasies is to reify rather than dissipate their power. If a woman really does not *want* to have masochistic fantasies, is repression really the best way of achieving a personally transformative liberation? Particularly if she is secretly deriving power and pleasure from fantasies of submission?

23. One readily understands the impetus of authors like Radway and Paula Caplan to dispute the notion that women have masochistic desires. Caplan wrote *The Myth of Female Masochism* in order to rebut the psychoanalytic assumption that women are masochistic, a belief deriving from Freud's theory of an essential female masochism. In a late essay called "The Economic Problem of Masochism," Freud identifies three types of masochism: erotogenic masochism, feminine masochism, and moral masochism. Only the first and third of these require analysis, he writes, since feminine masochism is "the most accessible to our observation and least problematical" (276). Unlike female masochism, Freud believes male masochism is not biologically determined and therefore is interesting. Throughout his career, Freud alludes to an essential female masochism, as for instance when he writes in a 1918 essay on virginity: "We regard it as the normal reaction to coitus for a woman to . . . press [a man] to her at the

climax of gratification, and this seems to us an expression of her gratitude and an assurance of lasting thraldom to him" (78). While I do not specifically engage Freudian theory, as do Silverman, Bersani, Deleuze, and Laplanche, his basic insights are crucial to this book. In particular, Freud laid the foundation for theorizing the relationship between desire and culture. In the case study of Dora, for example, he explores how a particular bodily experience—say, a hysterical symptom, such as a twitch—can become associated with a particular idea—say, anxiety—through the coincidence of their occurring at the same time. Though the connection is purely accidental, the body takes advantage of that connection, so that the next time the person feels anxiety, his or her body will express it with a twitch. In "Instincts and their Vicissitudes," he suggests that a similar process of association can govern sexuality. In infancy, libidinal impulses can become associated with nonsexual physiological activities like sucking, so that the act of sucking can remain eroticized. In other words, as Laplanche proposes in *Life and Death in Psychoanalysis*, Freud theorizes the notion that bodily experience is not necessarily a pure experience, but rather can be influenced by ideas, and language.

24. Feminist responses to the question of whether women actually are masochistic are bifurcated. Self-identifying radical feminists, frequently lesbians, argue that masochistic female desire is pervasive, that the patriarchy fosters masochism in women, and that heterosexual sex is an intrinsically masochistic activity. In this vein, Andrea Dworkin writes: "I believe that freedom for women must begin in the repudiation of our own masochism. . . . I believe that ridding ourselves of our own deeply entrenched masochism, which takes so many tortured forms, is the first priority: it is the first deadly blow that we can strike against systematized male dominance" (111). On the other hand, many feminists insist that women are *not* masochistic, that they are not turned on by fantasies of domination, and that it is men committed to the benefits they themselves derive from this Freudian perspective on femininity who make this false claim. Caplan's book aims largely at challenging a tendency in the psychoanalytic community to label specific female behaviors "masochistic," i.e., sick, rather than seeing them as coping strategies. Relying heavily upon Caplan, Roy Baumeister's survey of the research on gender and masochism concludes that "Masochistic sexuality is apparently more common among men than among women" (146); on the other hand, he adds that "men engage in nearly all forms of deviant sexual activity more than women" (146). But his book only addresses the actual practice of sadomasochistic sex, leaving aside the entire issue of fantasy and the vagaries of erotic attraction; his argument, therefore, differs fundamentally from studies in the humanities. The editors of *The Essential Papers on Masochism* observe, "Few would now assert that women are 'more' masochistic than men, except as child-rearing, socialization, maternal ego-ideals and male power lead them toward the 'seduction of the aggressor.' Nonetheless, women's fiction, from Charlotte Brontë to Alice Munro, shows a strong fascination with the female psyche in its particular sexual submissions and humiliations. . . . The possibility of a feminine masochism . . . has not quite been laid to rest" (Hanly 406). Though masochistic eroticism may in fact be no more prevalent among women than men, it is indeed characteristic of some women's literary expressions of de-

sire. Statistics are not easy to come by. A 1970s Playboy Foundation report (hardly an impartial source) stated that a quarter of all American women under thirty-five had had rape fantasies while masturbating (Marcus 46). Johns Hopkins sex researcher John Money suggested in 1980 that "women have only two predominant 'core' fantasies—masochistic fantasies and fantasies of soft objects and touch" (Masters and Johnson 280).

25. Ethel Person argues that, particularly in modern Western culture, where many former mainstays of identity, such as class and geography, are now less fixed, sexuality is experienced as a central component of identity. This is particularly true for men in our culture, she argues. She locates the genesis of the sex print in a conflation of biological ("drive") factors and cultural ("object-relations") factors predominating during the first three years of age, and she details the shortcomings of studies that use only one model.

26. Other theorists who implicitly or explicitly privilege male subjectivity in their understanding of masochism include Silverman, Deleuze, Bersani, and Frost.

27. Benjamin does takes the critical second step of observing how the operations of the all-important family dynamic are themselves governed by culture, and so *The Bonds of Love* does not feature the reductive character of many psychoanalytic writings. Consider, as an example of the latter, what Esther Menaker theorizes about one masochistic patient: "In her estimation her body was immature, unwomanly. Unconsciously she perceived the truth about her emotional infantility which she projected onto her body" (225). Surely the woman's body image derives as much from cultural messages as from some universally theorizable "emotional infantility."

28. Cited in Sharon Lieberman's review of Pam Carter's *Feminism, Breasts and Breast Feeding* and of Naomi Baumslag and Dia L. Michel's *Milk, Money, and Madness: The Culture and Politics of Breastfeeding*, in the *Women's Review of Books* 14.1 (October 1996).

29. Robert McClure Smith emphasizes the subversive potential of masochistic fantasies: "Thus, a literary text apparently invested in masochism may conceivably subvert the masochistic positioning of the female subject by refusing hermeneutic possession and exploiting masochistic pleasure; that is, pleasure in the loss of a stable identity" (1).

30. The notion that there is no universal, transhistorical experience of sexuality is vividly dislayed simply in the title of Michel Foucault's *The History of Sexuality*. "Sexuality must not be thought of as a kind of natural given which power tries to hold in check, or as an obscure domain which knowledge tries gradually to uncover. It is the name that can be given to a historical construct" (105). That thesis is thoroughly elaborated in Thomas Laqueur's *Making Sex*. Caroll Smith-Rosenberg, writing in *Disorderly Conduct*, concurs that physical experiences such as desire are socially constructed: "there is no natural way to experience the human body. Our mind, shaped by its social experiences . . . interprets the physical body's impulses, requirements, and sensations, shaping them into culturally anticipated categories" (48). And Judith Butler specifies that language is the agent of that social construction. In the introduction to *Bodies That Matter*, she proposes that while there is, after all, a dimension of bodily experience

prior to language, we have no access to such experience, nor can we speak meaningfully about it.

31. The essays collected in *Rethinking Linguistic Relativity* demonstrate the
variety of ways that linguistic determinism as originally articulated in the Sapir-
Whorf hypothesis remains a meaningful concept. Wilhelm von Humboldt an-
nounced in 1836 that "Language is the formative organ of thought. Intellectual
activity, entirely mental, entirely internal, and to some extent passing without
trace, becomes through sound, externalized in speech and perceptible to the
senses. Thought and language are therefore one and inseparable from each
other" (qtd. in Gumperz and Levinson 21). Developing this notion, Edward
Sapir and Benjamin Lee Whorf inaugurated the twentieth-century trend of
thought that concepts have no existence apart from the language in which they
are conceived. The following two oft-quoted passages from Whorf exemplify
this hypothesis: (1) "Users of markedly different grammars are pointed by their
grammars towards different types of observations and different evaluations of
externally similar acts of observation, and hence are not equivalent as observers
but must arrive at somewhat different views of the world" (1940); and (2) "We
dissect nature along lines laid down by our native languages. The categories and
types that we isolate from the world of phenomena we do not find there because
they stare every observer in the face; on the contrary, the world is presented in
a kaleidoscopic flux of impressions which has to be organized by our minds—
and this means largely by the linguistic systems of our minds" (1956) (qtd. in
Gumperz and Levinson 5 and 70). It is poststructuralist psychoanalytic theory—
the work of Lacan and Kristeva, as well as French feminists Luce Irigaray and
Hélène Cixous—that has done the most to apply these doctrines of linguistic
relativity to the study of the influence of language on desire. See, as an obvious
example, Kristeva's *Desire in Language*.

32. Montaigne 68. Alan Levine argues that such experiences lie at the heart
of Montaigne's advocacy for toleration, since sympathetic pain leads the essayist
who is "at home" within himself to believe that his own self-interest will be
promoted by the existence of a compassionate environment for his fellow human
beings. His argument demonstrates the origins in the Renaissance of a position
more typically associated with the Enlightenment.

33. Many recent object-relations and relational psychoanalytic theorists dispute Lacan's notion that language silences women. They point out that children
normally learn language from their mothers; that meaningful relational dialogues between mother and infant precede the child's use of symbolic speech;
that while the acquisition of symbolic speech is significant, the child has *already*
been constituted as an interpreted social subject during the symbiotic phase;
that symbolic communication is not necessarily individualized and purely cognitive but rather is an interpersonal agent of connection (rather than separation),
drawing upon somatic forms and subject to contextual contingencies. Adrienne
Harris describes a transitional period between semiotic and symbolic levels of
communication, during which a child's sense of self is constructed not purely in
oppressive symbolic terms but rather through a dialogic interplay of symbolic
speech with the use of transitional objects. Selfhood, then, is not purely an alienated structure imposed by symbolic language but rather is an interpersonal en-

tity in which symbols can be playful as well as humbling. Her article suggests by implication that entry into a fully linguistic state of existence does not exercise a unilaterally oppressive grip upon female subjectivity but rather evolves fluidly from a transitional period in which language is plastic. No theory of women's masochistic desire, therefore, can presume the truth of a Lacanian framework according to which women are silenced by their entry into the Symbolic. However, such a framework, I believe, plays a crucial role in how nineteenth-century women conceived of the relationship between femininity and language, even if that conception is not in fact true. In "Adventures in the World of the Symbolic," Suzanne Juhasz offers a lucid and persuasive challenge, grounded in object-relations theory, to Lacanian psycholinguistics. See also many of the articles in Skolnick and Warshaw, including that of Harris, and Juhasz's introduction to the section on object relations in *The Women and Language Debate*.

Chapter One
Masochistic Discourses of Womanhood

1. The author of the first, "Gracious Jesus, Lord most dear," is unidentified (*Plymouth* 147); "And can my heart aspire so high" is by Mrs. Steele (225); the author of the third, "Wait, O my Soul, thy Maker's will," is Beddome (237). It is important to note that celebrations of the chastening paternal rod are far more characteristic of hymnology in the eighteenth and early nineteenth centuries, abounding in Watts but appearing less frequently in New Light Theology, which focuses more upon maternal affection than paternal discipline. This point is fully developed in chapter 2.

2. Mary Poovey discusses the naturalization of female dependence in *Uneven Developments*.

3. Quoted in Caine 131.

4. Quoted in Poovey, *Uneven Developments* 1. William Rathbone Greg, "Why Are Women Redundant?" *National Review* 14 (1862): 436.

5. Masse cites Jill Montgomery (45) for this story (Masse 34).

6. Karen Halttunen analyzes the intersection of these two opposed attitudes toward female nature in the nineteenth-century murder trial of Lucretia Chapman; the trial rhetoric foregrounds the clash between residual ideologies of women as carnal inheritors of Eve's curse and dominant ideologies of women as ethereal angels. See also Cott's "Passionlessness."

7. In "Passionlessness," Nancy Cott explores the many reasons why women endorsed the belief in passionlessness, preeminent among which were freedom from unwanted sex and the social rewards associated with such beliefs. Barbara Caine extensively documents these and other reasons why British feminists endorsed notions of female passionlessness and the allied purity movements. See also Herndl. Frances Cogan, on the other hand, while not denying the forceful presence of an ideology of "true womanhood," argues that it has received excessive attention in recent scholarship, perniciously fostering a view of nineteenth-century women as weak, passive, powerless creatures, whereas in reality they were frequently powerful, energetic, and physically active. She documents an alternative ideal of "real womanhood"—strong, healthy women devoted to their

families—that was equally important in the era. Paula Bennett also argues against the notion of passionlessness in nineteenth-century women in "Critical Clitoridectomy" and " 'Pomegranate Flowers' "; although women did not write explicitly about their sexuality, their imagery reveals an awareness of (and often delight in) their own erotic feelings. And in "The Descent of the Angel" and "Not Just Fillers and Not Just Sentimental," she argues that by the late 1850s, many female poets publicly expressed the dangers of the "l in the House" ideal for women, and by the 1890s many women probably found that ideal as alien as we do today. Nonetheless, as Sojourner Truth's (apocryphal) "Ain't I a Woman?" speech indicates, the conviction that true women were physically weak and small was so widespread that a strong woman had to insist that she was, in fact, a woman.

8. Quoted in Salmon 42. Tapping Reeve, *The Law of Baron and Feme, of Parent and Child, of Guardian and Ward, of Master and Servant, and of the Powers of Courts of Chancery* (New Haven, Conn., 1816): 98.

9. A number of recent studies of the relationship between class and representations of the female body argue that another reason why women endorsed the ideal of ethereal "true womanhood" was that it positioned them in the middle, rather than lower, class. Herndl observes that according to the "cult of female frailty," middle-class women were seen as sick but pure, while lower-class women were seen as able-bodied but contaminated. In "Tender Violence," Laura Wexler demonstrates that many nonwhite women were indoctrinated with the ideology of "true womanhood"; the result, however, was often alienation, confusion, and ultimately repudiation of bourgeois white values. She documents the impact domestic ideology had upon women's relationships to their bodies in a series of photographs of Native American girls before and after time spent at boarding schools devoted to inculcating middle-class values. See also Lynda Nead's *Myths of Sexuality* for an art-history perspective on this class-based schism in representations of women's bodies.

10. In *Bodies That Matter*, Judith Butler expands the psychological theory of abjection to a culture-wide paradigm, focusing specifically on the construction of hegemonic genders. She proposes that cultures negate desires that run counter to dominant norms, but that those negated desires remain as "the abject," aspects of being that are always absent from discourse but present as "the constitutive outside to the domain of the subject. The abject designates here precisely those 'unlivable' and 'uninhabitable' zones of social life which are nevertheless densely populated by those who do not enjoy the status of the subject, but whose living under the sign of the 'unlivable' is required to circumscribe the domain of the subject" (3).

11. Hannah More was a celebrated English conversationalist, poet, dramatist, abolitionist, and educator, whose only novel, *Coelebs in Search of a Wife*, was such a huge success that the first edition sold out in three days, and twelve editions appeared that year (1803). *Coelebs* sold at least thirty thousand copies in America. A copy of the fifth American edition was found in Emily Dickinson's library. And in 1826 and 1827, Dickinson's father published five articles on female education under the pseudonym of "Coelebs."

12. See, for example, Welter 76.

13. See Mary Kelly for an in-depth exploration of how the taboo against female physical display forced constraints upon mid-nineteenth-century women who played a role in public life.

14. Sprague believes careful female education is crucial, because "the character of a young female, at the close of her education, is formed for life—of course, formed for eternity." His rationale indicates a view of girls as static beings: "what you [girls] are at the age of 18 or 20 you will probably be . . . in every future period of life. In other words, your character will, by that time, in all probability have acquired a fixed direction" (14). A boy's character, by contrast, is dynamic, and his education should prepare him to meet the exigencies of the world with flexibility and resolution. In the counterpart conduct book for boys, *Letters to a Young Man*, Sprague advises young men to model themselves on Joseph in Genesis, whom he sees as embodying the principle of dynamism and flexibility, traits that enable him to make his way in the world despite severe setbacks.

15. *New York Ledger*, July 30, 1859. The ideal of invisible women had striking longevity in the nineteenth century. An 1879 American conduct book proposed that a true woman who wanted to appear in public should be "wrapped in a mantle of proper reserve . . . seeing and hearing nothing that she ought not to see and hear . . . [She is] always unobtrusive, never talks loudly, or laughs boisterously, or does anything . . . to attract the attention of the passers-by" (Young 143–44). Manners and behaviors that minimized the impression of female presence served as markers of class distinction and were widely adopted by middle-class women.

16. *Women and the Alphabet* 66. Originally published as "Ought Women to Learn the Alphabet?"in *Atlantic Monthly*, February 1859.

17. Quoted in Haller and Haller 147. Theodora Wilkins, "Pelvic Congestion from Moderate Compression of the Waist," *Southern California Practitioner* 5 (1890): 134.

18. Included in Rufus Griswold's *The Female Poets of America* 322. Howe can hardly be seen as an unabashed advocate for "true womanhood," though. "True womanhood" represents more the ideal that permeated her society, and the role her husband wanted her to play, than it does her own life ambition. During Julia's first pregnancy, her husband was delighted to observe her making infant clothing rather than writing poetry, and he wrote to his friend Charles Sumner that Julia had changed for the better since becoming pregnant: "No true woman ever considered it a burden to bear her infant within her, to nourish it with her own blood, & to furnish every fiber of its frame from her own flesh; hardly has she become conscious of the existence of her infant, when an intense and absorbing love for it fills her bosom. . . . I doubt not that most of her day and night dreams, are about it" (October 16, 1843; qtd. in Williams 66–67). Three months earlier, however, a month or so pregnant, Julia had written to her sister Louisa: "I am not good with children—for their sakes, I should almost be willing not have any" (July 2, 1843; qtd. in Williams 66). And four years later, she wrote to Louisa, "It is a blessed thing to be a mother, but there are bounds to all things, and no woman is under any obligation to sacrifice the whole of her existence to the mere act of bringing children into the world" (68). She did,

however, feel guilty for her inability to be what a wife and mother was supposed to be: "I am trying to press all the bitterness out of my heart, and to live in a more gentle and loving spirit" (December 1845; qtd. in Williams 75).

19. I am indebted to Barnes's discussion of this scene in "Whipping Boy."

20. Sprague wrote to the Warners: "I venture to thank you for your late admirable work entitled *The Law and the Testimony*. As for your other works, the whole world would have thanked you for them already. . . . you might help to keep some of us [ministers] in the old ways, who might otherwise be in danger of wandering after novelties. I congratulate you sincerely that you have set out on a mission of such extensive usefulness" (Baker 63).

21. Elizabeth Oakes-Smith, for example, wrote that women who want to discuss politics receive the epithet "'*female* politicians.' Pardon the phrase, it is a quotation—I recognize only the appropriate term of woman" (*Woman* 91).

22. Since she wrote these words in a letter of 1850 and received *Letters on Practical Subjects* on her thirtieth birthday, in 1860, there is no direct link between Sprague's *Letters* and her own letter. Rather, the attitude of hostility toward the body that she expresses was widely promulgated by Protestant clergymen and popularized by the discourses of the Second Great Awakening. All citations from Dickinson's letters are from the three-volume Johnson edition and are noted in the text, identified by an *L* preceding the number he ascribed.

23. Bercovitch, in *Puritan Origins of the American Self*, and Taves, in *Religion and Domestic Violence in Early New England*, describe the Puritan self-obsessed effort to deny the self.

24. Rather than considering the role of ideology and discourse in the production of such fantasies, an earlier, Freudian, generation of theorists posited an innate, repressed sexuality expressed under the cover of martyrdom fantasies; their explanations are less useful than the patterns they identify. Peter T. Cominos identifies a characteristic type, "The Sublimated Evangelical," typified by Annie Besant, born in England in 1847. In her autobiography she specifically claims that as a child and young woman, she had no sexual inclinations. According to Cominos, she sublimated "the budding tendrils of passion" into love for Christ and her mother and expressed her erotic passion through blatantly masochistic fantasies: "Tales of the early Christian martyrs inspired fantasies wherein she vicariously experienced martyrdom, being 'flung to lions, tortured on the rack, burned at the stake.' She passionately lamented that these heroic religious deeds could not be realized again in her own lifetime" (163). Sublimated evangelicals, he argues, turned to masochistic narratives through which they could punish the guilt that religious doctrines fostered. But these narratives at the same time stimulated their passions—which had the effect of reinforcing their sense of guilt—which led them to read more masochistic narratives. Thus was formed a hermetic circle of pleasure and fantasized violence. In *Dimity Convictions*, Barbara Welter represents the eroticism in Victorian women's descriptions of religious ecstasy as being predominantly masochistic, as, for example, when she compares the hymns women sang and their conversion narratives to "fantasies of rape" by God (93). She notes that the "physical sensations which a woman expected to receive and did receive in the course of conversion" were erotic: "A trembling of the limbs," "a thrill from my toes to my head," "wave

after wave of feeling," "the great blessing of fullness . . . [feeling] perfectly emptied of self and filled with the Spirit of God" (93).

25. Woods's words may well exemplify Cogan's argument that reiterated discourses of true womanhood can frequently be read as signs of opposing ideas in the culture at large. His counsel that the grieving parents find "particular satisfaction" in the usefulness of their daughter's life (terminated at age nineteen) might actually indicate opposition in those same parents.

26. For example, in 1848 Horace Bushnell wrote, "Being the body of Christ, she [the church] is, in some sense . . . a perpetual Christ in the earth. . . . By this she becomes the light of the world, as her Savior was—a perpetual manifestation of the Spirit, or what is the same, of the Divine Nature. . . . she lives a life above nature" (*Selected* 101).

27. In a summary account of her religious exercises found among her papers, dated August 27, 1809, Newell uses these words to characterize the effects of a sermon preached on June 28, 1809 (30, Armstrong ed.).

28. This quotation appears in both the 1830 edition published for Abel Brown and the 1814 edition published by Samuel T. Armstrong. It is taken from a letter written by Mr. Newell to Harriet's mother. The text of this letter (supposedly transcribed) is substantially different in the revised edition published by the Sunday School Union in 1831. All quotations are from the American Sunday School Union edition (1831) unless otherwise noted.

29. I am indebted to Michael Manson's essay "Poetry and Masculinity on the Anglo/Chicano Border" for drawing my attention to the violence of Calvinist discourses of transcendence. Manson cites Bercovitch and demonstrates the usefulness of Gloria Anzaldua's distinction between fluid borders and rigid boundaries for a discussion of Calvinist and Catholic representations of sexuality.

30. First quotation, January 5, 1807. The second is from a letter, "To her sister M. at Charlestown," undated but positioned between a letter dated April 1811 and another dated May 1811.

31. September 20, 1806.

32. First two quotations from Armstrong edition, 33–34 (December 31, 1806; January 3, 1807). Third quotation from American Sunday School edition, 36 (August 10, 1809).

33. Caroline Dean historicizes "the decentered self" in Lacan and Bataille, analyzing the social discourses prevalent in mid-twentieth-century Paris that gave rise to ontological theories grounded upon the assumption of a split self. Baumeister also suggests a need to historicize particular notions of selfhood. He notes that literary instances of erotic masochism are rare prior to the Enlightenment—the era when the self became a more individuated and constraining entity. Sadomasochism is conspicuously absent from many very explicit premodern catalogues of sexuality.

34. In a discussion of the true meaning of freedom, Winthrop criticizes the anarchic idea that freedom is the absence of social regulation, and then continues: "The other kind of liberty I call civil or federal. It may also be termed moral, in reference to the covenant between God and man, in the moral law, and the politic covenants and constitutions amongst men themselves. This liberty is the proper end and object of authority. . . . This liberty is maintained and exercised

in a way of subjection to authority. It is the same kind of liberty wherewith Christ hath made us free. The woman's own choice makes such a man her husband, yet being so chosen he is her lord and she is to be subject to him, yet in a way of liberty, not of bondage, and a true wife accounts her subjection her honor and freedom, and would not think her condition safe and free but in her subjection to her husband's authority. Such is the liberty of the church under the authority of Christ her King and husband" (233). In explicitly referring to the relationship of husband and wife as a covenant, Winthrop indicates a different notion of marriage from the one that Blackstone developed into the law of spousal unity in the next century, according to which no contract was conceivable between husband and wife because they were one and the same person.

35. All Bailey citations are from Taves's edition of the *Memoirs*.

36. A number of historians have attempted to explain the resurgence of religiosity in the Second Great Awakening in sociohistorical terms. Donald Mathews argues that "the Awakening in its social aspects was an organizing process that helped to give meaning and direction to people suffering in various degrees from the social strains of a nation on the move into new political, economic and geographical areas" (27). A number of more recent feminist histories have shown how this thesis applies to women. Nancy Cott's "Young Women in the Second Great Awakening" observes that the role of women changed dramatically with the industrialization of fabric production, leaving young unmarried women unrooted and destabilized. Christianity appealed because, "As opposed to the vagaries encountered in social and economic pursuits, the Christian's struggle was comprehensible, its consequences were well-defined, and a supportive community echoed the individual's experience" (22). Caroll Smith-Rosenberg's "The Pedestal and the Cross," in *Disorderly Conduct*, demonstrates how the assertion of disorder in the Awakening's antiritualism provided a language for expressing the emotional qualities associated with the experiences of social transition. Mary Ryan, in *Cradle of the Middle Class*, emphasizes the changes in women's roles in accordance with changes in religious practices and beliefs during the Awakening; she particularly illuminates the complex relationships among class, gender, family, and religion.

Chapter Two
Sentimental Masochism

1. Z. Isham, *A Sermon* (1700). Quoted in Crane 225.

2. Though Shaftesbury studied under Locke, his notion of an innate moral sense, it should be observed, diverges significantly from Locke's tabula rasa theory. His optimistic belief in an essential benevolence in human nature and his emphasis upon the morality of human feeling are the direct precursors to the ideal of "the good-natured man," which underlies much English and American sentimentality. On the intellectual roots of this ideal, see Camfield, Crane, Greene, Halttunen, Kaplan, Sheriff, Todd, and Turnbull.

3. Cited in Camfield 23. While the influence of Common Sense philosophy on the Founding Fathers is a subject of vigorous debate among political historians, its influence on American sentimental authors is clear.

4. Terhune's father, Samuel Pierce Hawes, quoted in Kelley 93. The passages on the influence of Common Sense are from Herbert W. Schneider, *A History of American Philosophy* (New York: Columbia UP, 1946), 246; and Leon Howard, "The Late Eighteenth Century: An Age of Contradiction," *Transitions in American Literature and History*, ed. Harry H. Clark (Durham: Duke UP, 1954), 68. (Both qtd. in Simpson 60).

5. This is David Denby's central argument. Claudia Johnson also addresses the relationship between Enlightenment ideals and sentimentalism, focusing on politics and gender. She specifically points to the reactionary conservatism of male sentimentality, which idealized the "man of feeling" while marginalizing and even criminalizing women's feelings, thereby positioning feeling women as "equivocal beings." Edmund Burke, Johnson argues, epitomizes the conservative nature of male sentimentalism, and she explores the ways that female authors combat the legacy of male sentimentality. On the intersections between sentimentalism and the Enlightenment, see also Burgett.

6. Such a body-centered epistemology conflicts with the noncorporeality idealized in sentimental notions of true womanhood. This contradiction is addressed directly in chapters 3 and 4, which explore the implications of the fact that sentimental suffering was a way to experience one's body without violating the principal values of true womanhood.

7. "Letter to the Delegation of the State of Connecticut," written by Sigourney on behalf of an "Association of Ladies," March 12, 1831. Quoted in Bennett, *Nineteenth-Century* 7.

8. Barnes addresses the influence of this sentimental ideal of unification on the rhetoric of the Founding Fathers, arguing that affective, familial bonding is the central metaphor for the founding of the national union.

9. As Winfried Fluck writes, the popularity of sentimental novels (her example is *Charlotte Temple*) "can be attributed to a skillful . . . exploitation of a basic, elementary fear underlying and generating, in my opinion, all sentimental fiction: that of a painful separation from an object of affection and thus from an experience of union and wholeness" (18).

10. The unity achieved through sympathy, however, is both limited and problematic. Since we can never really know another's experiences with certainty, the best we can do is imagine what we would feel in that other's place, or what we have felt in analogous circumstances. And so the union occurs through the erasure of the difference between sufferer and observer. As Barnes observes, "while an individual may be taught to see others as her- or himself, what she learns is that difference is to be negated rather than understood" (22). Denby points out that at a certain level, sympathy is therefore self-pity. Quoting and analyzing Lessing's sentimentalism, he observes: "Pity and fear are not felt for the person to whom they occur; they arise from 'our similarity to the suffering person,' and are 'for ourselves.'" And since therefore "'the misfortune of those whose circumstances are closest to our own must naturally touch us more deeply,'" sympathy can be exclusive, its unity predicated upon erasure of diversity of experience and opinion (80). I discuss this problem extensively in chapter 4.

11. She claims, in her discussion of 1940s films for women, that in some of

them, "an enforced or threatened separation between mother and child tends to produce an alignment of the mother with the figures of masochism" (36). Doane claims that the pleasures of anguished spectatorship are de-eroticized, because the spectator of a sentimental woman's film is "a bodyless woman." She cannot identify with a male because such identification is discouraged in the genre, and since female characters are represented in ways that suggest bodilessness, viewers have little access to an embodied identification. The viewing experience, Doane therefore concludes, is not erotic. While nineteenth-century sentimental melodramas also idealize bodiless women, their readers are not left bodiless, for the physical affect produced by the text recuperates the experience of the physical body for its female reader, enabling her to enjoy her fantasy as a sexualized participant rather than as a nonsexual, detached observer. See also Ann Cvetkovich's discussion of "maternal melodrama" in her analysis of the affective power of maternal separations.

12. Leslie Fiedler discusses the rise of a maternalized, sentimental "love religion" in *Love and Death in the American Novel*, as do Ann Douglas in *The Feminization of American Culture*, Barbara Welter in "The Feminization of American Religion," Lawrence Buell in "Calvinism Romanticized," and Paula Bennett in *Emily Dickinson: Woman Poet*.

13. See Armstrong's *Desire and Domestic Fiction* for a fully theorized account of how domestic fictions were less like mirrors imitating life than they were coherent images, starring women, that were imitated *by* their readers.

14. Kristeva borrows the word "chora" from Plato, who uses it to designate unformed matter.

15. In positing a desire that is both regressive *and* captive to symbolic, postoedipal structures of desire, my argument differs from that of Deleuze, who sees masochism as a purely regressive urge toward maternal fusion that eschews forms of sexual desire shaped by oedipal crises. I suspect that the difference between Deleuze's theory and mine lies in the fact that he discusses male masochism, and I female; male masochism actively rejects conventional symbolic sexual norms, while female masochism exploits them. See also note 18.

16. I mean, in terms of the text: we cannot, for example, help Uncle Tom, though it is true that nineteenth-century readers could join the antislavery cause. Robyn Warhol challenges the passivity Fisher posits in sentimentalism, demonstrating that readers may well respond to pitiful sentimental scenes with both tears *and* activism. Certainly, books like *Uncle Tom's Cabin* and *Life in the Iron Mills* sparked significant humanitarian activism *along with* tears. Nonetheless, I agree with Fisher that the tears themselves represent a thwarted sense of agency arising from the reader's detached perspective on the suffering. Sentimental activism may arise simultaneously, but from a different, engaged perspective.

17. Davidson writes, "The reader vicariously accompanies the [Gothic] heroine throughout her various trials. This relationship between reader and text marks another departure from the sentimental form. As Fielding early observed and as numerous subsequent critics have pointed out, the sentimental novel, especially in its seduction format, necessarily flirts with prurience and readily beds down with pornography. The reader is sidelined by the conventionally sen-

timental, is cast as a voyeuristic observer of the protagonist's private affairs. . . . By contrast, the Gothic reader and the Gothic protagonist all along occupy much the same position. Both are mostly in the dark, and the reader, as much as the protagonist, can fear those things that go bump in the night. No overview perspective is provided" (223). See also Introduction, note 3.

18. Deleuze challenges Freudian and Lacanian theories of masochism, disputing the idea of a link between sadism and masochism and also the centrality of the father in the beating fantasies described in "A Child Is Being Beaten." For Deleuze, masochism is a male attraction to a cold and punitive mother, a sexuality that rejects Freudian notions of conventional, postoedipal male sexuality. But his description of a resexualized Thanatos figured as maternal symbiosis is not incompatible with the basic outline of Lacanian thought, according to which desire is born out of separation from the mother and all sexual objects compensate only partially for the true desire, which is to remerge with the mother in a state of symbiotic plenitude that would entail the death of the self. Certainly, Deleuze's argument is not dramatically different from that of Lacan's friend Bataille, except that Bataille does not use the word "mother" to signify "continuity."

19. See, for example, Nancy Cott, *Bonds of Womanhood*; Linda Kerber, "The Republican Mother"; John D'Emilio and Estelle Freedman, *Intimate Matters*. Many literary critics, including Ann Cvetkovich and Joel Pfister, have addressed the social construction of a "natural" moral motherhood. As Elizabeth Ammons, for example, writes in "Stowe's Dream of the Mother Savior," "It is essential to remember that motherhood—as idea, myth, institution, experience— is always a cultural variable. . . . the maternal ideology that Stowe (and we) take for granted is a relatively new invention—the result of a shift in white Western thinking from parenting to mothering as the dominant ideal around the end of the eighteenth and the beginning of the nineteenth centuries. . . . as men left this shared environment to work in mills and offices, a theory of feminized parenthood, of "motherhood," developed" (158–59). The rise of mothering is symptomatic of such changes in the economy as industrialization and increasing urbanization, which raised "the possibility of economic self-sufficiency for large numbers of women" for the first time. As Ammons wryly notes, "the promotion of motherhood as a full-time occupation for women conveniently emerged at just the time that a fundamental change in the traditional pattern of female dependence might have occurred" (158).

20. Barthes's description of sentimental wounding is largely secular, though as Jane Gallop points out, it is tinged with mystical overtones, such as are found in nineteenth-century sentimental fiction. See "The Prick of the Object," *Thinking Through the Body*, 152ff.

21. A certain looseness characterizes recent discussions of the utopian preoedipal period. Many feminist critics celebrate the preoedipal mother-child dyad with its intense and mutually affirming language of bodily caress, glance, and sympathy. This period, which Lacan calls "the Imaginary," is blissful, according to these critics, in that the infant is diffused with the mother. Madelon Sprengnether, for example, writes that "During [Lacan's] Imaginary period there is neither language nor differentiation for the infant, who has no self-

hood," a construct that appears only later, when the oedipal alignment in accordance with the father's phallus separates children from the realm of maternal plenitude along strictly gendered lines. However, Sprengnether collapses the two phases that Lacan calls "the Real" and "the Imaginary." It is during "the Real" that the infant has no differentiation. During the Imaginary, Lacan proposes, the infant is a "moi"; it already knows itself through differentiation from its mother, though it has not yet recognized that the self and its desire can be represented in symbolic form ("I" and "sexuality"/"language," respectively). The gap, then, between mother and self has *already* occurred and has *already* given birth to a desire that is neither gendered nor primarily genital. As I read Lacan, desire is ontological, born at the mirror moment of self-recognition and gendered and eroticized at the oedipal moment.

22. Quoted in Bennett, *Nineteenth-Century* 5–6.

23. Halttunen demonstrates that the pleasures associated with the experience of vicarious pain in sentimentalism were routinely accused of having an unethical and vaguely sexual character. As she writes, "William Godwin called sensibility a 'moon-struck madness, hunting after torture,' and an essay in *The Watchman* (1796) agreed, saying of the sentimental reader, 'She sips a beverage sweetened with human blood, even while she is weeping over the refined sorrows of Werther and Clementina'" (308). Halttunen traces the origin of such spectacles to Common Sense philosophy, and while she emphasizes a sadistic aspect to the pleasures of sentimental suffering, her own genealogy suggests a primary masochism beneath a secondary sadism. See also Leo Bersani's persuasive and thorough argument in "Representation and Its Discontents" for seeing masochistic pleasure as the primary mechanism in a great deal of sadistic pleasure. See also Laura Hinton's *The Perverse Gaze of Sympathy*, which argues for the centrality of sadomasochistic patterns in sentimentalism, beginning with *Clarissa*, whose peeping-through-the-keyhole erotics, she claims, characterizes the entire genre.

24. For discussions of this poem and of Sigourney more broadly, see Baym, Okker, Petrino, Woods, and Zagarell.

25. The passage illustrates David Denby's astute observation that sentimental narratives frequently interrupt the advance of time in order to offer a static tableau, in which the narrator or another character contemplates an exemplary spectacle of suffering, feels sympathy, and responds with tears and/or material aid.

26. The term "resisting reader" is Judith Fetterley's, coined to dispute the simplistic assumption that the values a text preaches are passively absorbed by readers; they might well have taken pleasure in resisting the overt message and in discovering such resistance within the text itself. On the complexities of reader responses to nineteenth-century sentimentalism, see also Susan K. Harris, "Responding to the Text(s)" and "But is it any *good*?" and Barbara Sicherman, "Reading *Little Women*."

27. Deleuze, Mansfield, Frost, and Siegel all make this point.

28. See chapter 7 of Stoller, *Sexual Excitement*.

29. See Taves's introduction to *The Memoirs of Abigail Bailey*, Greven's *Spare the Child*, and Capps's *The Child's Song* for discussions of the Christian tendency to repress anger and the negative results of such repression.

Chapter Three
"An Ecstasy of Apprehension": The Erotics of Domination
in *The Wide, Wide World*

1. Joanne Dobson, Nancy Schnog, and Grace Ann Hovet and Theodore Hovet imply that what earlier critics like Ann Douglas wrongly saw as masochistic tendencies in sentimental fiction are actually wily survival strategies necessitated by patriarchal constraints upon women's lives. According to Dobson, *The Wide, Wide World* is subversive, for Ellen's identification with a whipped horse has the effect of exposing and criticizing the terror tactics of the patriarchy: "Although the surface narrative concentrates on Ellen's genuine movement from anger to acceptance, there exists, nonetheless, a strong emotional undertow that pulls the reader in the opposite direction. The subversion of Warner's lesson in obedience comes in a manipulation of characterization that subtly undercuts the message" (230). Schnog suggests that the "psychological realism" in *The Wide, Wide World* empowered women by enabling them to express concerns about separation that were particularly painful for nineteenth-century women, adding that the apparently repressive ideologies promoted in such fiction actually help women, because "they attempt to reduce women's vulnerability to dependency and isolation" (17). Hovet and Hovet suggest that Ellen's saga negotiates between the need to meet others' expectations and the need to address one's own concerns. Ellen, they argue, moves from a purely "related self" to a "performing self," which masks self-expression in order to retain others' approval, to a mature "constructing self," which balances social and personal needs. The fact that Ellen is almost never represented in the third phase and completely collapses into infantilization at the novel's conclusion, they argue, is a sign that she resists the narrative logic of her own novel. Warner *meant* for her to achieve autonomy, and her failure to represent stable autonomy in Ellen is Warner's "perceptive analysis of the way masculine vision silences feminine voice" (4). Veronica Stewart also argues for the subversive resistance of *The Wide, Wide World* in her analysis of the character Nancy Vawse. "If Ellen's acceptance of the cultural terms prescribed by domestic ideology implies a reticence on the author's part, then Nancy Vawse's defiant rebellion against those constructs must enact a more subversive and creative dimension of Warner's personality and work" (1). In distinct contrast to all of these readings, Erica R. Bauermeister more accurately observes, "Unfortunately for any feminist reading of the text, Ellen's submission to John is usually just that, submission" (21).

2. See Hanly's collection, *Essential Papers on Masochism*, for thorough discussions of the agency of masochism.

3. Jane Tompkins appropriately compares *The Wide, Wide World* to the masochistic classic *Story of O*, in which the heroine derives erotic pleasure from increasingly lethal gestures of self-annihilation. Both books revel in the erotics of domination, Tompkins observes, though she believes only a modern readership would see Warner's that way. Tompkins's chapter on *The Wide, Wide World* extensively documents its teleological religiosity and persuasively analyzes both the book's realism and the reasons why it appealed to its readers.

4. See "The Phenomenology of Contract," *The Gold Standard and the Logic of Naturalism*, especially 131–33.

5. Mary Salter to Susan Warner, Constitution Island Association Warner Collection, Special Collections, U.S. Military Academy, West Point, N.Y. Hereafter letters from this collection will be cited as "Warner Collection."

6. This expression of extreme doubt about sensory experience clashes with the basic tenets of sentimental aesthetics, which as we have seen follows Locke in privileging bodily experience as a site of epistemological certainty. Sentimental Calvinism is an oxymoron, a point that is exemplified in John's final appeal to Ellen to "Read no novels!" Through the voice of a Calvinist clergyman, Warner expresses her opposition to the capacity for emotional stimulation in novels, but she does this within the context of a novel that was one of the most popular tear-jerkers of the nineteenth century.

7. Susan S. Williams, in a reading of manuscript variants for *The Wide, Wide World*, argues that the evangelical thrust of the novel was added later, evidently to accommodate the requirements of Warner's readers. Warner did not turn naturally to sentimental evangelical fiction, Williams claims, but did so deliberately, for economic reasons. This is an intriguing hypothesis, but there is no proof that Warner's edits were motivated by economics; the entire thrust of the book is evangelical.

8. Quoted in Ehrenreich and English 139. Frederic Carpenter Skey was an influential surgeon, a professor of anatomy, and a fellow of the Royal Society. He held many important positions, including president, at the Royal College of Surgeons of England, and he was the personal doctor and friend of many influential citizens, including Disraeli.

9. Certainly not all women doted upon such oppressive doctors. Charlotte Perkins Gilman wrote "The Yellow Wallpaper" specifically to chronicle the devastating effects of Mitchell's infantilizing attitude toward women, though the story implies a marginality in its opposition to the revered figure of Mitchell. Ann Dally notes that Mary Livermore, a women's suffrage worker, spoke against "the monstrous assumption that woman is a natural invalid" and that she denounced "the unclean army of 'gyneacologists' who seem desirous to convince women that they possess but one set of organs—and these are always diseased" (95). Dally also notes that P. Jalland's study of the lives of women in more than fifty privileged families concludes that "women's negative comments about their doctors outweighed the positive and their dominant tone was sceptical" (Dally 115). For example, she notes that Alice James, sister of Henry and William, resented the position of inferiority she had to assume before her pompous society doctor, Sir Andrew Clark. James wrote in her diary, "I suppose one has a greater sense of intellectual degradation after an interview with a doctor than from any human experience" (Dally 114).

10. Quoted in Dally 113.

11. Among the many feminist approaches to the relationship between doctors and their female patients, see Ann Dally, Elaine Showalter, Judith Walzer Leavitt, Ann Douglas Woods, Diane Price Herndl, and various essays in Jacobus, Keller, and Shuttleworth's collection and in Catherine Golden's casebook on "The Yellow Wallpaper."

12. Jessica Benjamin defines and discusses intersubjectivity in *The Bonds of*

Love. Discussions of the benefits of an intersubjective awareness are legion. See, for example, Roberta Rubenstein's analysis of representations of intersubjectivity in the contemporary fiction of nonwhite American women.

13. See Ethel Specter Person's claim that patterns of sexual desire are acquired along with an identity, and that therefore representations of key stages of identity formation can afford useful information for understanding a person's sexuality.

14. Review, *Godey's Lady's Book*, 1851.

15. "Alice's Admirer" to Susan Warner, Warner Collection.

16. "Ellen's Admirer" to Susan Warner, New York, September 27, 1851, Warner Collection.

17. Machor 75–79. I suspect that what Dobson reads as a "strong unconscious conflict" was not so unconscious on Warner's part. When Ellen exclaims, "Oh, it's not right!—it's not right!" (553), Warner foregrounds the traumatic aspects of submission. Machor is closer to the mark when he suggests that Warner and other evangelical sentimental authors intentionally stimulate readers' indignation at tyranny so that they can *participate* in, rather than merely observe, the flaring up of individual will and can feel the difficulty *and* the necessity of submission. Readers feel the abuse of power and are made to resent its wielder—which then luridly exposes to them their own hard hearts. The autocratic actions of Aunt Fortune and Uncle Lindsay particularly produce this effect. Warner, Finley, Cummins, and many other evangelical sentimental writers never say submission is easy; it exacts an excruciating toll in virtually every action of life. That is why the heroines are attracted to the one who assists them in that task: not because they find the actual process of submission a pleasure, but because they find it difficult and the outcome a pleasure.

18. Elizabeth Barnes and Caroline Levander both address the displacement of violence and erotics in sentimental works. Barnes argues that in Louisa May Alcott's sentimentalism, aggression is displaced onto "the whipping boy of love." The cultural paradigm of atonement represents suffering on behalf of others as the mark of one's lovability, so that frequently aggression turned against oneself is an expression of love or lovability. Levander suggests that both Melville's *Pierre* and E.D.E.N. Southworth's *The Fatal Marriage* articulate women's erotic desire through strategies of displacement, the former through projection onto a guitar that sings a sensual love song, the latter, through projection of a chaste heroine's desire onto a "fallen woman."

19. This moment in the text exposes the violence and fear that are the repressed underside of the ideal of a pure, passionless, noncorporeal woman. It exemplifies what Michelle Masse labels "marital Gothic" fiction, in which a variety of representations of violence can be read as displaced or coded representations of patriarchal violence.

20. Baumeister makes a similar use of Scarry's thesis in his analysis of masochism.

21. See also Jane Gallop's discussion of the etymology of "ecstasy" in "Prick of the Object," in *Thinking Through the Body*.

22. Goshgarian offers a similar reading of the Saunders scene and delineates multiple connections between Saunders and John.

23. Bersani's theory of the masochistic roots of sadistic pleasure would ac-

count for why sadistic Mr. Saunders enjoys tormenting Ellen thus: Saunders introjects a representation of Ellen and experiences a sexual gratification in feeling through identification the pain he is causing her. The text invites such a reading. "Ever since [their first encounter] Ellen . . . had lived in his memory as [an] object of the deepest spite" (400). To the extent that Ellen lives within his memory, in punishing her, Saunders is stimulating his own internalized representation of her. The origin of his sadism, therefore, would be masochism.

Chapter Four
The Ecstasies of Sentimental Wounding in *Uncle Tom's Cabin*

1. His seminal definition of masochism is quoted in chapter 2.
2. In *Harriet Beecher Stowe: A Life*, Joan Hedrick writes that when Stowe "met Abraham Lincoln at the White House in 1862, the lanky, angular president is said to have greeted Stowe, who stood less than five feet high, with the words, 'So you're the little woman who wrote the book that started this great war!'" (vii).
3. Even an ambitious, feminist author such as Margaret Fuller can be called sentimental. In *Woman in the Nineteenth Century*, Fuller promotes a recognizably "high sentimental" epistemology, calling for a greater fluidity between genders that would restore to men their repressed, female "intuitive" and "electrical" qualities. High sentimentality is an epistemology devoted to emotive and kinetic cognition. It can produce rigorous writing or "rancid writing," as Ann Douglas puts it, depending upon the talent of its user. Douglas, however, is quite right to observe that sentimentality frequently fails to meet the high literary goals of its theorizers. Camfield offers a useful hypothesis that high sentimentality degenerated as its practitioners lost sight of the genre's roots in Common Sense philosophy. See Sandra Gustafson for a discussion of Fuller's sentimentality.
4. C. E. Stowe, 203–4.
5. See Nudelman's analysis of the sentimental authors' ideal of a community of free and enslaved women bonded through suffering.
6. This presumption that sympathy will reveal the "plain right thing" characterizes Martha Nussbaum's recent appeal on behalf of the literary imagination in public discourse, *Poetic Justice*. Grounding her argument in Smith's *Theory of Moral Sentiments* which she unequivocally endorses, Nussbaum argues that contemporary judges and economists would benefit from the "put-yourself-in-his-shoes" kind of reasoning that Smith and Stowe idealize; they would then be more likely to perceive the right course of action, which purely rational arguments are less liable to reveal. I address the political limitations of sympathy more fully at the end of this chapter.
7. Thomas Laqueur, "Bodies," 179. Laqueur excludes *Uncle Tom's Cabin* from the category of humanitarian narrative that relies upon "details about the suffering bodies of others [to] engender compassion," implicitly disputing recent critical emphases upon bodies as the predominant expressive tropes in sentimentality (176). I agree that while the inspiration for *Uncle Tom's Cabin* was in fact a sensational scene of physical torture, the physical mutilations in the

novel serve largely as graphic images for and metonymic representations of the psychological trauma of separation that is the central "imaginative vehicle"for all sentimental literature. Karen Halttunen, by contrast, includes *Uncle Tom's Cabin* in her study of humanitarian reform literature. In "Sparing the Rod," Richard Brodhead also discusses the whipped body as the central imaginative vehicle in the book, arguing that whipping epitomizes the evils of slavery, while Stowe endorses discipline through loving intimacy.

8. In failing to appreciate the sentimental effort to articulate an embodied intersubjective "real presence," recent criticism has obcured an important feminist dimension of this genre. *Uncle Tom's Cabin* can, in this respect, be usefully read in the context of Homans's *Bearing the Word* and Helena Michie's *Flesh Made Word*, which explore the nineteenth-century female author's effort to articulate the sense of female presence that they argue is central to women's experiences in Western culture but that is all but erased from the dominant language.

9. Gallop describes a variety of efforts, within the limitations of an individualistic, androcentric culture, to affirm and understand a cognition that relies upon one's own body—a site of nonintellectual thought processes—as an instrument for interpreting data. She calls for an epistemology that will heal "the mind-body split." In her introduction, she quotes Adrienne Rich's *Of Woman Born* to explain her own project: "I am really asking whether women cannot begin, at last, to *think through the body*, to connect what has been so cruelly disorganized" in Western culture (1). Gallop documents the embodied—and erotic—responses to literature she experiences in her quest for alternatives to a hermeneutics of intellect.

10. The anecdote is widely recorded. See, for example, C.E. Stowe 148.

11. As Glenn Hendler observes, sentimentality tends to "confuse the *equivalence* it posits between subjects with a dangerous *identity* between them" (689). The danger lies in the presumption that one's own subject position is the universal norm, which can lead to the abuses so ably delineated by Baldwin, Sanchez-Eppler, Nudelman, Wexler, and Hendler. However, the dangers of sympathy pale before the dangers of a *lack* of sympathy, as exemplified in a Southern review written in 1893. The author, Francis Shoup, takes Stowe to task for the same "dangerous" reliance on sympathy as does Hendler. "She did what most women are wont to do . . . She translated herself in fancy to the cotton-fields of the South as a slave, and then interrogated herself as to how she felt. She did not reflect that in the put-yourself-in-his-place method of testing a state of case, it is clearly implied that it shall be—not *you*, any longer, in the new place, but—*he* as he is, who is to feel. In her transmigration she carried with her all her intellectual vigor . . . the suppositious personality of the cotton-field was no longer poor Sambo, but the high-strung, highly cultured Mrs. Stowe. It is not wonderful that she did not like her hypothetical situation." (Quoted in Ammons, *Critical Essays*, 50–52.) Anticipating antihumanist arguments, Shoup rightly observes that the sentimental "put-yourself-in-his-place" method presumes an impossible identification between sufferer and witness. However, Shoup's remarks vividly demonstrate how the assumption that sympathy cannot afford any comprehension at all can also protect and rationalize racism and misogyny.

12. The word "throb" in particular was a recognized euphemism for sex in general and orgasm in particular. In *The House of the Seven Gables*, Hawthorne writes: "The bed-chamber, no doubt, was a chamber of very great and varied experience, as a scene of human life; the joy of bridal nights had throbbed itself away here" (72). In *Moby Dick* Melville also uses the word as a euphemism for intercourse: "the sun seemed giving this gentle air to this bold and rolling sea; even as bride to groom. And at the girdling line of the horizon, a soft and tremulous motion—most seen here at the equator—denoted the fond, throbbing trust, the loving alarms, with which the poor bride gave her bosom away" (589).

13. In *Soul on Ice*, Eldridge Cleaver consolidates this mythology in his contrast between the black male "Supermasculine Menial" and the white male "Omnipotent Administrator"—associated with frailty, cowardice, impotence, and abstraction (174). And, he argues, the "Ultrafeminine" white female, whose "basic fear is frigidity," desires the black man because she feels a "psychic lust for the flame, for the heat of the fire: the Body" in proportion to her fear of her own frigidity (170). Among the many literary representations of the myth of black supersexuality and white women's corresponding desire for black men, see Richard Wright's *Native Son*, James Baldwin's "Going to Meet the Man," and William Faulkner's *Light in August*. See also Gerda Lerner, "The Myth of the 'Bad' Black Woman," a section in *Black Women in White America*.

14. In "Heroines in *Uncle Tom's Cabin*," Ammons demonstrates that Tom is characterized as a stereotypical Victorian heroine. And Baldwin too points out that Tom is emasculated. As for Dodo: Stowe writes, he "had been only a few months away from his mother. His master had bought him . . . for his handsome face." When Eva is kind to him, "the blood rushed to his cheeks, and the tears to his eyes" (232).

15. May's self-inflicted wound of separation from a dying child resembles what Mary Ann Doane calls a "maternal melodrama," but as May's remarks indicate, the pleasures of nineteenth-century sentimentalism are not deeroticized through disembodiment, as Doane claims is the case in films of the 1940s. We see in May how the physical affect produced by identification with someone else's suffering recuperates the experience of the physical body for the female reader. As Ammons observes, women can easily identify with Tom's experiences, pleasures, and desires—and, I would add, partake vicariously of the embodied nature of his experiences.

16. There is no single "correct" meaning of the Atonement, of course. I refer to the meaning it had for many Christians in Victorian America, which was given classic expression in Horace Bushnell's *The Vicarious Sacrifice* (1866).

17. William Acton, *The Functions and Disorders of the Reproductive Organs*, 3d American ed. (Philadelphia, 1871). Quoted in Haller 163–64.

18. Letter of July 1845. Quoted in E. Wilson 22.

19. Cited in Ammons's introduction to the Norton edition of *Uncle Tom's Cabin*.

20. Strong, Garrison, Wright, Longfellow, and Dix quoted in Gossett 165–71.

21. Hawthorne similarly indicts popular fiction on the grounds of a questionable sexuality in its enslaving qualities. For example, in "Alice Pyncheon," in

The House of the Seven Gables, he writes that Alice becomes a "slave" to Matthew Maule, who violates her "virgin" spirit by reading her a story that is likely to be sent to *Godey's* or *Grahams*. Among discussions of the connection between sentimental or sensational fiction and sex, see Halttunen, Miller, and Cvetkovich.

22. See Robyn Warhol's opposing discussion of the activist—rather than regressive—impact of sentimental tears within nineteenth-century American culture. She explicitly disagrees with Fisher.

23. My closing remarks are indebted to Sandra Lee Bartky's analysis of the limitations of both (a) the "liberal" notion that any expression of sexual freedom, including sadomasochism, is liberating and (b) what she calls "sexual voluntarism"—the notion that one can repudiate repressive desires at will. As I indicated in the introduction, while the "liberal" position fails to recognize the manipulation of desire through the ideologically determined production of subjectivity, the "voluntarist" position fails to recognize the deeply systemic nature of patriarchal oppression. I agree that in order to challenge the eroticization of male dominance, it is important to understand the cultural production of desire. On the production of repressive norms of subjectivity in *Uncle Tom's Cabin*, see also Lora Romero, "Bio-Political Resistance."

Chapter Five
The Revenge of Cato's Daughter: Emily Dickinson's Uses of Sentimental Masochism

1. Relatively little explicit critical attention has been paid to masochism in Emily Dickinson. John Cody and other early, psychological critics tended to see her masochism as a pathological manifestation of "an unconscious commitment to the expiation of guilt feelings" (Cody 267). Recent feminist works have tended to address this issue tangentially, reading apparent manifestations of masochism in Dickinson's letters and poetry not as indicators of the poet's own psychology but as explorations of the social *causes* of masochism. According to Helen McNeil, in her masochistic poetry Dickinson explores the social factors that make a woman think, "if I am unloved, it is because I am unlovable. Whatever is done to me, I deserve it" (45). Indicating aesthetic benefits in addition to these sociological ones, Paula Bennett argues that Dickinson finds in hierarchically arranged relationships aesthetic possibilities for poetic "fervor and angst," "both the drama of the speaker's 'elevation' (her 'Queenship') and the pathos and anguish of her 'fall,' qualities lacking in her woman-centered poetry based on sameness rather than difference (*Woman Poet* 162). Both McNeil and Bennett implicitly address the critical silence on this vexed aspect of Dickinson's poetry by emphasizing how risky such discussions are. As McNeil writes, "No matter how carefully or specifically a woman depicts it, no matter how much she emphasizes the general case, she does so at the risk of being thought typically feminine" (46).

The risks of addressing Dickinson's uses of masochism are showcased in Camille Paglia's discussion of sadomasochism in Dickinson. Paglia finds in Dickinson's masochism a parody of an essential female masochism. She and Dickinson, she believes, are sterile freaks in revolt against nature, women who rage against an essential femininity that they loathe. Dickinson is Amherst's "Madame de Sade," a woman whose sadism expresses her detestation of the prison of her own gender. Images that McNeil reads as an exploration of the *social causes* of masochism, Paglia reads as an attack on *nature*. Paglia's absolute belief in biological determinism leads her to pronouncements about female nature that are not only detestable but dangerous, because they routinely receive serious widespread attention in the contemporary culture at large—such as her notorious claim that rape (rooted in male nature) is always the responsibility of the woman, who must protect herself against (intrinsic) male aggression rather than expect an (impossible) self-restraint on the part of men. And yet, though Paglia derives appalling social conclusions from her take on the nature/nurture question, she nonetheless offers three useful insights into Dickinson's masochism. First, there is no reason to assume that Dickinson herself was immune to essentialism: her obsession with the sadistic spectacle of flowers ravished by lover-bees suggests that she was worried about a barbarism against women rooted in nature, not merely culture. Margaret Fuller, it is worth pointing out, worried about precisely the same thing. Secondly, Paglia usefully spells out how Dickinson's sentimental masochism can function as camp, a pose donned for the pleasures of indulging the sensations associated with hierarchy. And third, Dickinson does exhibit the decidedly sadistic streak that is so lovingly and humorously detailed in *Sexual Personae*. Overall, Paglia foregrounds the important point that Dickinson finds pleasure—not simply an informed feminist consciousness—in the sensations associated with fantasies of hierarchy. I do not want to be misconstrued as an essentialist with a misogynist social agenda; I do, however, want to suggest that Dickinson's masochism is not simply a sociological critique of the patriarchy (though it is partly that) but is instead a much more risky, and interesting, appropriation of the dominant discourse of patriarchal desire. Dickinson's use of the language of sentimental masochism is neither simply pathological nor simply antipatriarchal: it is a strategy that afforded the poet significant powers and pleasures, though these did not necessarily come through opposition to men.

2. Adrienne Rich, Albert Gelpi, and Joanne Dobson all read Dickinson's fascination with scenes of the Phoebus-Daisy type as a fascination with the universal, ahistorical meanings of these stereotypes. Rich reads such scenes as representations of the poet's relationship to her own power, as do both Gelpi and Dobson, who add that these are dialogues between the poet and her creative imagination, dialogues grounded in Jungian archetypes. In *The Seductions of Emily Dickinson*, Robert McClure Smith appropriately challenges the ahistoricity of such readings, but he fails to acknowledge the importance of these critics' demonstrations that Dickinson arrogates to herself the qualities associated with the Master.

3. It is typically read as an explanation of Dickinson's anxious rejection of marriage. Gilbert and Gubar appropriately link the letter to related poems that feature "an almost masochistic sexual fascination" combined with a fear of death. The letter, they claim, "reveals, more frankly than most of the poems, the poet's keen consciousness of her own warring feelings about that solar Nobodaddy who was both censorious 'Burglar! Banker—Father,' and idealized

Master/Lover" (596). Similarly, Mossberg sees in the letter an explanation of why Dickinson refused marriage and conversion, both of which would "eclipse" or "scorch" her, and adopted instead a child persona, which "is in large measure a reflection of Emily Dickinson's systematic refusal to become a conventional woman" (63). Pollak points out that the letter represents marriage as "an encounter with a primal source of natural energy for which [Dickinson] herself, like her sexually insatiable 'flowers,' yearns. She describes marriage as a risk-fraught venture . . . [yet] describes a compulsion to risk this experiment. Within this style, 'peace' is not a sufficient goal; exceptionally powerful experience is" (64). Erkkila comments that the women featured in the "man of noon" letter resemble Dickinson's own quiet, passive, dependent mother, who "represented the very model of true womanhood against which Dickinson had to rebel in order to escape dutiful daughterhood" (*Wicked* 45).

4. Dobson connects this letter's imagery to the story of Zeus and Semele. Semele desired to "see [Zeus] in his full splendor as King of Heaven and Lord of the Thunderbolt"; he obliged, "and before that awful glory of burning light she died" (83). The imagery of Dickinson's letter may be linked to this myth, but it alludes more directly, I think, to the story of Clytie and Apollo, which details the origin of the heliotrope, the flower that fascinates Dickinson in this letter.

5. See also Ronald Lanyi's discussion of the relationship between Calvinist theology and Dickinson's marriage poetry.

6. Salvation was consistently represented as being inseparable from pain. Heman Humphrey, for example, president of Amherst College from 1823 to 1845 and renowned author of *Revival Sketches and Manual*, claimed that the unregenerate "must come to the point of unconditional submission" (381). Such submission, he recognizes, is exceptionally painful. "You must seek salvation, but it must be with an earnestness which you have not yet felt. You must '*strive*' to enter in at the strait gate. The original here is a great deal stronger than the translation. The word is *agonize* to enter in. Summon all the energies of your awakened soul; let them be concentrated in the anguish of the sharpest pangs of an awakened conscience. Strive with all the agony of a broken and contrite heart. Cast yourself at once upon the mere mercy of God, through Jesus Christ, and he will save you" (388).

7. See Cynthia Hogue's *Scheming Women* for an extended discussion of the presence of a Kristevan semiotic motility in Dickinson, as well as in other female poets.

8. See Robert McClure Smith's discussion of how Dickinson uses sentimentalism as a means of re-presencing an abjected female body and writing about embodied personhood. With its characteristic blend of physical affect and physical signs of emotional affect, he writes, sentimentalism made available to nineteenth-century female authors a means of representing and stimulating the female body (130–33).

9. Poems supporting her claim include "The *Sun—just touched* the Morning" (JP#232), "God permits industrious Angels" (JP#231), "A full fed Rose on meals of Tint" (JP#1154), and "Angels, in the early morning" (JP#94).

10. All quotations from Dickinson's poems are taken from the Franklin variorum edition, and the numbers he ascribes are noted parenthetically in the text,

preceded by "FP#." Numbers from the Johnson edition are also provided, preceded by "JP#." Letters are indicated parenthetically with "L#."

11. There has been some disagreement about the dating of the second and third "Master" letters, both of which are written in the stylized "Daisy" voice. Based upon an analysis of changes in Dickinson's handwriting, Franklin suggests that the letter most desperate in tone (L#248: "Oh, did I offend it—"), which Johnson places third in the sequence and dates in early 1862, is actually the second, written in early 1861. Because I quote from the Johnson edition of letters, I retain his ordering and numbering for the sake of convenience.

12. The internal evidence of the "Master" letters indicates the existence of a real recipient of these letters. The "Master" is therefore not purely an epistolary fiction. But they can nonetheless be understood as a style exercise, in which Dickinson takes advantage of an actual occasion to generate prose. Erkkila convincingly reads these letters (and Charlotte Brontë's series of "Master" letters) as abstract and autoerotic. She interprets them in the context of Simone de Beauvoir's argument that when women are positioned as "other," a self-effacing love can be read as an effort to acquire the subjectivity enjoyed by men, while the absence of the lover protects the self from him. She usefully quotes de Beauvoir, who writes: "It is one thing to kneel before one's personally constructed god who remains afar off, and quite another to yield oneself to a male of flesh and blood" (*Second Sex* 326, qtd. in *Wicked Sisters* 66).

13. Johnson explains the transcription symbols: "The letter is a penciled rough draft. The alternative suggested changes are placed in parentheses; words crossed out, in brackets."

14. Weinberg and Kamel note: "S&M scenarios are *willingly and cooperatively* produced; more often than not it is the *masochist*'s fantasies that are acted out. Many S&Mers claim, therefore, that the masochist, rather than the sadist, is really in control during a sadomasochistic episode. The partners jointly limit their mutual activities and these restrictions are rarely exceeded. Sadists who are known to disregard previously agreed upon limits are avoided and quickly find themselves without partners" (20).

15. As Barbara Mossberg writes in a discussion of "'Twas Love—not me—," "Beneath the depiction of a masochistic sensibility ('Oh punish—pray—') a tremendous ego is revealed as the daughter describes her ultimate fantasy . . . she is Christ's equal—if not better. Proving how she surpasses her rival brother (Austin, Jesus) has been all that the poet has ever really wanted" (132—33). Diehl and Loeffelholz make similar suggestions about what Dickinson's strategy was in readings of "Sang from the Heart, Sire."

16. In her discussion of James Joyce's masochistic letters to his wife, Nora, Laura Frost makes a similar observation. Although Joyce's letters are explicitly sadomasochistic and pornographic, they nonetheless mention an "unspeakable word," a word so dirty it cannot be spoken. Frost interprets this allusion as representing Joyce's desire that he not be scripting his wife's abusive behavior, that he not be dictating every aspect of the script. It is an effort to retain the illusion that she abuses him of her own free will, that she, not he, is in control of their relationship of domination and subordination.

17. As we have seen, Laura Wexler and Nancy Armstrong provide clear illustrations of how domestic fiction—with its apparently repressive ideologies of femininity—actually was itself a form of female agency in that it consolidated the power of the middle class, a social order that offered significant roles for middle-class white women. Middle-class white female characters and readers were therefore hardly purely passive victims of male oppression.

18. This remark is included in a letter dated August 16, 1870 that Higginson wrote to his wife after meeting Emily Dickinson. Collected in Johnson as L#342a.

19. Monk discusses the development toward increasing subjectivity in English theories of the sublime, a development culminating in Kant.

20. In fact, most discussions of masochistic practice consistently emphasize its aesthetic qualities. Paul Gebhard, for example, writes, "pain *per se* is not attractive to the masochist . . . Accidental pain is not perceived as pleasurable or sexual. The average sadomasochistic session is usually scripted: the masochist must allegedly have done something meriting punishment, there must be threats and suspense before the punishment is meted out, etc. *Often the phenomenon reminds one of a planned ritual or theatrical production*" (37, emphasis added).

21. The Calvinist who undergoes a conversion experience would certainly consciously seek to avoid any sense of consolidation of self. However, historians frequently point to the contradiction between the introspective self-examination typical of Calvinist piety and the ideal of selflessness. While the Christian is supposed to shed the self, he or she also focuses extensively upon the self in that process. It might be said, then, that the Calvinist introvert accomplishes precisely what Dickinson does with her sentimental masochism: he or she consolidates the self through fantasies of dismantling or annihilating it.

22. The Phoebus-Daisy scenario is informed, then, not only by sentimental and Calvinist discourses, but also by those of the romantic sublime. The image both encapsulates and subverts the three discourses that, according to Adrienne Rich, were most oppressive for the nineteenth-century woman. She writes, in "Vesuvius at Home," that Dickinson's "was a life deliberately organized on her terms. The terms she had been handed by society—Calvinist Protestantism, Romanticism, the nineteenth century corsetting of women's bodies, choices, and sexuality—could spell insanity to a woman of genius" (102). But I am arguing that one of the ways she lived life "on her terms" was through the cagey manipulation of the terms she was "handed by society."

23. See Smith chap. 3 for a clear and compelling overview of the way this and similar, obviously gendered, poems achieve "a power inversion" (89).

24. Dickinson probably knew Plutarch's account of Portia. "[B]eing desirous to die, but being hindered by her friends, who continually watched her, she snatched some burning charcoal out of the fire, and, shutting it close in her mouth, stifled herself, and died" (824). But the scene in which she stabs herself in the thigh and the tortured, masochistic death scene also appear in Shakespeare's *Julius Caesar*, which Dickinson knew well.

25. See Wilden's commentary in his edition and translation of Lacan's *The Language of the Self* (191).

26. As many recent feminist critics have argued, no claim can be made to represent a single eroticism on Dickinson's part and critics should more appropriately speak of eroticisms (Henneberg). Judith Farr has presented clear, convincing cases for simultaneous lesbian and heterosexual desire in the poet, which she labels "The Narrative of Master" and "The Narrative of Sue." My exploration of the erotics of her sentimental masochism makes no claim to being an exclusive or exhaustive study of Dickinson's erotic sensibility. Sentimental masochism is one device among many for the articulation of a female erotics. Paula Bennett convincingly indicates in Dickinson's poetry a nonhierarchical, lesbian sensibility; she points to a cluster of erotically charged clitoral images that express lesbian desire without participating in the angst-ridden discourse of Dickinson's heterosexual love lyrics. Martha Nell Smith's analyses of the original manuscripts indicate a startling, systematic pattern of erasures and substitutions of "he's" for "she's," bespeaking a "desperate" effort on the part of Austin Dickinson or one of the other early editors to prevent public awareness of a lesbian sensibility permeating the manuscripts, including the Master Letters. On the other hand, Pollak convincingly describes a heterosexual sensibility thwarted by the limited possibilities for women's romantic fulfillment in the mid-nineteenth century. The gender of the lover is irrelevant for the purposes of my argument, which is that Dickinson exploits dominant rhetorical patterns for the aesthetic and erotic goal of creating a poetry that captures a largely symbolic, fantasized female erotics. The Master is an obviously masculine figure in the letters and poetry because Dickinson is exploiting the eroticism of conventional discourses, not because she is succumbing to it. The argument that runs most notably counter to the one I advance here is that of Margaret Homans, who argues in "Syllables of Velvet" that Dickinson refuses to participate in a conventional, hierarchical discourse of desire but instead turns to metonymic (not representational, metaphoric) language to describe a nonhierarchical erotic desire. My argument is not intended to challenge Homans's, but simply to complement it: I offer evidence in Dickinson's work of another strategy for the expression of a female erotics, one that appropriates and exploits the discourse that, according to Homans, Dickinson does not use (except perhaps in order to criticize its ideological foundations).

27. In *Feminist Critics* alone, the poem is discussed by Gilbert (26), Keller (73), Mossberg (94), Morris (104–5), Homans (118–19), and Miller (143). I contribute to this conversation the observations that in the poem Dickinson exploits masochism for a re-presencing of the body, by concentrating upon the pain of abandonment and by making it clear that Daisy has already spent the night with the sun. I am endebted to Jim Berg for the latter point.

28. In *Emily Dickinson: The Mind of the Poet* (1). Gelpi attributes this fundamental conflict in Dickinson to her devotion to Emerson. In *The Tenth Muse*, he writes, "Emerson was an inspiration and model—perhaps the inspiration and model—for Dickinson when she was choosing to be a poet" (223). Unity and variety, he indicates, are the essential poles for Emerson, who writes in *Representative Men*: "Two cardinal facts lie forever at the base; the one, and the two. —1. Unity, or Identity; and 2. Variety. . . . Oneness and Otherness. It is impossible to speak or think without embracing both" (27–28). See, however, Mary Loef-

felholz's challenge to Gelpi's claim for a direct line of descent from Emerson to Dickinson.

29. The final stanza, with its simultaneous idealization and denigration of a bodiless knowing in heaven exemplifies both sides of the body-soul dialectic that Karen Sanchez-Eppler describes. On the one hand, she writes, Dickinson longs for freedom from the body, but on the other hand, she seems to "sense that what has no body cannot be known or named" (*Touching* 122). Sanchez-Eppler claims that Dickinson cannot imagine a bodiless self, "not only because corporeality makes complex claims on identity, but also because Dickinson understands language itself to be bound up with physicality" (122). If the very mechanism by which we "know" requires a body, it is impossible to imagine bodiless knowing: "Dickinson's fantasy of a fleshless liberty constantly collides with the sensual desire for a fully palpable freedom" (123).

30. Eberwein includes "I started Early" in a cluster of sentimental poems that speak in the child voice, "a mask that apparently struck the poet as a safe refuge from responsibility and as representing a status that allowed free articulation of fears" (56). Other poems she includes in the cluster are " 'Arcturus' is his other name" (JP#70); "What is 'Paradise' " (JP#215); "We dont cry—Tim and I" (JP#196); "I tried to think a lonelier Thing" (JP#532); "What shall I do—it whimpers so" (JP#186); "You love me you—you are sure" (JP#156); "Good Morning—Midnight" (JP#425).

31. Cody argues that such a yielding represents "the loss of one's psychic integrity in psychosis." He adds: "To be submerged, drowned in a vast sea, lost, alone, hopeless—this is the subject of many Dickinson poems. . . . The common denominator in all these 'sea poems,' however . . . is the poet's experience of a diffusion of herself—of the blurring of her own boundaries until she becomes lost in the infinite or expands into infinity herself . . . Emily Dickinson both courted and feared this experience of ego expansion and weakening of psychological boundaries" (304–5). Cody's exclusive focus upon psychological pathology seems to prevent his recognizing in this poem a pattern that is conventional in the romantic sublime.

32. Miller 74.

33. See Peter Sacks's full-scale elaboration of this point in the introduction to *The English Elegy*. In a discussion of Freud's *fort-da* scene, he observes that Freud's grandson "learns to represent absence, and to make the absent present, by means of a substitutive figure" (11).

34. As Sanchez-Eppler writes, "The divisions within identity that her poems chart are not, for her, reconcilable. Indeed, what interests her about identity is precisely its unresolvable doubleness" (*Touching* 107).

35. L#189, circa June 1858. Cody cites multiple examples of the same cluster of ideas: "Good night, dear Mrs. Haven! I am glad I did not know you better, since it would then have grieved me more that you went away." To Kate Anthon: "Why did you enter, sister, since you must depart?" To Edward Dwight: "I think it sad to have a friend, its sure to break the Heart so." To Reverend Dwight: "[I wonder] why a love was given—but just to tear away." To Abiah Root: "I always try to think in any disappointment that had I been gratified, it had been sadder still, and I weave from such supposition, *at times*,

considerable consolation; consolation upside down as I am pleased to call it" (Cody 266–67).

36. The focus on the aurora to be found in the other's eyes and the beams of recognition that the sun sheds upon the speaker invites us to interpret this poem in light of Cynthia Griffin Wolff's object-relations paradigm for Dickinson's psychology. Wolff attributes this kind of "clamoring" for visual relationships in Dickinson to a flawed visual relationship between Dickinson as an infant and her mother. According to Wolff, their unsatisfactory eye-to-eye relationship left the preverbal child with an insufficiently grounded sense of personal identity and a consequent overvaluation of the gaze of the other as a means of affirming her existence. It also led Dickinson to overvalue language, an imperfect compensation for the connection and affirmation of her identity that she sought but did not get from her mother. But as Mary Loeffelholz points out, by using words such as "inadequate," "distorted," "tragic," and "perverse," Wolff implies that Dickinson deviated from a hypothetical "proper" norm of identity formation in which language is a supplemental skill tacked onto an already coherent self, rather than something that *produces* the self. Loeffelholz also points out that Wolff's hypothesis does not take into account the fact that while Dickinson may have craved the presence of her friends, she also assiduously avoided physical contact with them. Loeffelholz suggests that Dickinson eschews visibility in order to evade the powerlessness Lacan says is inevitable for women in the visual realm, which is structured around the (visible) phallus, and she understands Dickinson's quest for recognition as something largely symbolic rather than maternally focused. Therefore she proposes it makes more sense to discuss Dickinson's quest for recognition in terms of Lacanian theory, since the latter understands identity to be a symbolic construct governed by law and exchange.

37. Diehl argues that "the Cause" in this poem represents a "desire to reveal, through her poems, a responsive, wholly alive consciousness" (*Romantic* 156). Diehl relates Dickinson's use of the word to Emerson's in "Self-Reliance": "Let us sit at home with the cause." Reading "Most—I love the Cause that slew Me" through this lens produces another compelling interpretation: the conventional woman was killed by the poet's decision to commit herself to the cause of her own self-expression. This reading effectively equates the goal and the cause; where the "Cause" is "self-expression," aim is indistinguishable from impetus.

38. See "Independence and Dependence of Self-consciousness: Lordship and Bondage," a subsection of the section entitled "The True Nature of Self-Certainty" in *Phenomenology of Mind*. There, Hegel speculates that since the slave, in struggling with nature, learns its secrets, he supersedes the master, a shift that will ultimately lead to an upward-spiraling phenomenology. See chapter 1 of *The Bonds of Love* for Jessica Benjamin's object-relations elaboration of this Hegelian explanation of the origins of masochism. She attempts to imagine ways out of that gendered master-slave dynamic, hoping that social changes in child rearing influenced by feminism will produce a more desirable mutuality of recognition. See also "The Master-Slave Relation in the Psychoanalytic Impasse" for a clear and useful Lacanian elaboration of the Hegelian master-slave dialectic. The authors, Gorney and Muller, link Hegel to Lacan's analysis of transference and countertransference, arguing that a masochistic patient will

present a series of distorted (masochistic) self-representations in order to secure from the (sadistic) psychoanalyst a reaction that reinforces those false self-conceptions. The "cure" lies in the therapist's refusal to reinforce these false ego images, which will lead to what Lacan calls "the disintegration of the imaginary unity constituted by the ego" (*Ecrits* 137).

39. As Karl Keller recognizes, Dickinson probably "knew she had the potency to drive [even God] out, to displace him, to be sufficient. This cannot have been a satisfying position for her, however, unsure as she sometimes was that there was really anybody there to oppose her" (70).

40. Just as such acts of the murder of meaning excite with an exhilarating freedom from logic and coherence, so too the murder of self envisaged in this poem invites an exhilarating possibility of total subjectivity. As we have seen, Julia Kristeva posits precisely such an association between ecstasy and murder in her theory of abjection, advanced in *Powers of Horror*. Abjected entities like wounds, pus, feces, urine, corpses, and the like are charged with ontological meaning, for they "show me what I permanently thrust aside in order to live"; they are "the border of my condition as a living being" (3)—and "How can I be without a border?" (4). A "vortex of summons and repulsion," the abject is both a terrifying site that "murderously" threatens to unravel all meaning and an alluring one where one might slip out of the bondage of unitary identity. The abject opens up to representation all that is unsaid and unsayable in coherent language: it is that which has been withdrawn in order to create the gaps that are essential for symbolic meaning.

41. Morris characterizes this quotation as "elaborate imagery of identity": it implies, she says, that Emily and Sue are identical. But the key-and-lock imagery associated with it belie this tranquil identity. Rather, I think that the imagery exploits the tension implicit in nonbalanced heterosexual relationships in order to capture the intensity of Dickinson's desire for Sue.

42. Another reason is that the object of desire, once attained, can, by definition, no longer be divine or "other," and the identity defined in relation to a "divine other" collapses. On this point, see Eberwein, chapter 3.

43. She first drafted the image of the interior bells and a private religion in a letter written around February 1852 to Sue: "and thank you, too, dear Susie, that you never weary of me, or never *tell* me so, and that when the world is cold, and the storm sighs e'er so piteously, I am sure of one sweet shelter, *one* covert from the storm! The bells are ringing, Susie, north, and east and south, and *your own* village bell, and the people who love God, are expecting to go to meeting; dont *you* go Susie, not to *their* meeting, but come with me this morning to the church within our hearts, where the bells are always ringing, and the preacher whose name is Love—shall intercede there for us!" (L#77).

Conclusion
The Possibility of Masochism

1. Hélène Cixous similarly represents the act of writing as fundamentally masochistic in her playfully titled *Coming to Writing*. The book begins with a joyful description of maternal fusion, quickly followed by the anguished sense of

the loss of that fusion with postbabyhood individuation. As she grows up, Cixous takes up writing as a response to that miserable gap between self and the primary love object who literally means everything to the infant. She describes turning to the wall in despair, feeling her own pain, and writing from that pain. In Cixous's imagination, like Dickinson's, writing is sensual, masochistically elegiac, yet a miraculous transformation of tragedy into art.

2. I am grateful to Helen Elaine Lee for sending me a copy of this interview.

3. I am indebted for this point to Smith's "Dickinson and the Masochistic Aesthetic," which discusses Laplanche and Pontalis's argument that fantasy is a performance in which the fantasizer identifies with all roles simultaneously.

Works Cited

Alcott, Louisa May. *Little Women*. 1868. New York: Signet, 1983.

Allen, Richard O. "If You Have Tears: Sentimentalism as Soft Romanticism." *Genre* 8.2 (1975): 119–45.

Allison, Dorothy. Interview by Melissa Murphy. *On Our Backs*, July/August 1993.

———. "Public Silence, Private Terror." *Skin: Talking about Sex, Class and Literature*. Ithaca, New York: Firebrand, 1994.

Ammons, Elizabeth. "Heroines in *Uncle Tom's Cabin*." *Critical Essays on Harriet Beecher Stowe*. Ed. Elizabeth Ammons. Boston: G. K. Hall, 1980.

———. "Stowe's Dream of the Mother-Savior: *Uncle Tom's Cabin* and American Women Writers before the 1920s." *New Essays on "Uncle Tom's Cabin."* Ed. Eric Sundquist. New York: Cambridge UP, 1986.

Anzaldua, Gloria. *Borderlands: The New Mestiza = La Frontera*. San Francisco: Aunt Lute, 1987.

Armstrong, Nancy. *Desire and Domestic Fiction: A Political History of The Novel*. New York: Oxford UP, 1987.

Bailey, Abigail. *Religion and Domestic Violence in Early New England: The Memoirs of Abigail Abbot Bailey*. Ed. Ann Taves. Bloomington: Indiana UP, 1989.

Baker, Mabel. *Light in the Morning: Memories of Susan and Anna Warner*. West Point, New York: Constitution Island Association, 1978.

Baldwin, James. "Everybody's Protest Novel." *Uncle Tom's Cabin*. Ed. Elizabeth Ammons. New York: Norton, 1994.

Barker, Wendy. *Lunacy of Light: Emily Dickinson and the Experience of Metaphor*. Carbondale: Southern Illinois UP, 1987.

Barnes, Elizabeth. *States of Sympathy: Seduction and Democracy in the American Novel*. New York: Columbia UP, 1997.

———. "The Whipping Boy of Love: Atonement and Aggression in Alcott's Fiction." *Journal X: A Journal of Culture and Criticism* 2.1 (1997): 1–17.

Barthes, Roland. *Camera Lucida: Reflections on Photography*. New York: Hill & Wang, 1981.

Bartky, Sandra Lee. *Femininity and Domination: Studies in the Phenomenology of Oppression*. New York: Routledge, 1990.

Bataille, Georges. *Erotism: Death and Sensuality*. 1957. Trans. Mary Dalwood. San Francisco: City Lights, 1986.

Bauermeister, Erica R. "*The Lamplighter, The Wide, Wide World* and *Hope Leslie*: Reconsidering the Recipes for Nineteenth-Century American Women's Novels." *Legacy* 8 (1991): 17–28.

Baumeister, Roy. *Masochism and the Self*. Hillsdale, N.J.: L. Erlbaum Associates, 1989.

Baym, Nina. "Reinventing Lydia Sigourney." *American Literature* 62.3 (1990): 385–404.

Baym, Nina. *Woman's Fiction: A Guide to Novels by and about Women in America, 1820–1870*. New York: Cornell UP, 1978.

Beecher, Henry Ward, ed. *The Baptist Hymn and Tune Book: Being "The Plymouth Collection."* New York: Sheldon, Blakeman & Co., 1858.

Benfey, Christopher E. G. *Emily Dickinson and the Problem of Others*. Amherst: U of Massachusetts P, 1984.

Benjamin, Jessica. *Bonds of Love: Psychoanalysis, Feminism, and the Problem of Domination*. New York: Pantheon, 1988.

———. "Master and Slave." *The Powers of Desire*. Ed. Ann Snitow, Christine Stansell, and Sharon Thompson. New York: Monthly Review, 1983.

Bennett, Paula. "Critical Clitoridectomy: Female Sexual Imagery and Feminist Psychoanalytic Theory." *Signs* 1.2 (1995): 235–59.

———. "'The Descent of the Angel': Interrogating Domestic Ideology in American Women's Poetry, 1858–1890." *American Literary History* 7.4 (1995): 591–610.

———. *Emily Dickinson: Woman Poet*. Iowa City: U of Iowa P, 1990.

———. *Nineteenth-Century American Women Poets*. Malden, Mass.: Blackwell, 1998.

———. "Not Just Filler and Not Just Sentimental: Women's Poetry in American Victorian Periodicals, 1860–1900." *Periodical Literature in Nineteenth-Century America*. Ed. Kenneth M. Price and Susan Belasco Smith. Charlottesville: U of Virginia P, 1995, 202–19.

———. "The Pea That Duty Locks: Lesbian and Feminist-Heterosexual Readings of Emily Dickinson's Poetry." *Lesbian Texts and Contexts: Radical Revisions*. Ed. Karla Jay and Joanne Glasgow. New York: New York UP, 1990, 104–25.

Bercovitch, Sacvan. *The Puritan Origins of the American Self*. New Haven.: Yale UP, 1975.

Berliner, Bernhard. "Libido and Reality in Masochism." *Psychoanalytic Quarterly* 9.3 (1940): 322–33.

Bersani, Leo. *The Freudian Body: Psychoanalysis and Art*. New York: Columbia UP, 1986.

———. "Is the Rectum a Grave?" *AIDS: Cultural Analysis/Cultural Activism*. Ed. Douglas Crimp. Boston: MIT Press, 1988.

———. "Representation and Its Discontents." *Allegory and Representation*. Ed. Stephen Greenblatt. Baltimore: Johns Hopkins UP, 1981.

Blackstone, William. *Commentaries on the Laws of England*. 4 vols. Vol. 1, *Of the Rights of Persons*. 1765. Chicago: U of Chicago P, 1979.

Bloch, Ruth. "American Feminine Ideals in Transition: The Rise of the Moral Mother, 1785–1815." *Feminist Studies* 4.2 (1978): 101–26.

Brodhead, Richard. "Sparing the Rod: Discipline and Fiction in Antebellum America." *Representations* 21 (Winter 1988): 67–95.

Brontë, Charlotte. *Jane Eyre*. Oxford: Oxford UP, 1998.

Buell, Lawrence. "Calvinism Romanticized: Harriet Beecher Stowe, Samuel Hopkins, and *The Minister's Wooing*." *Critical Essays on Harriet Beecher Stowe*. Ed. Elizabeth Ammons. Boston: G. K. Hall, 1980.

Burgett, Bruce. *Sentimental Bodies: Sex, Gender, and Citizenship in the Early Republic*. Princeton: Princeton UP, 1998.

Bushnell, Horace. *Christ in Theology*. 1851. Ed. Bruce Kuklick. New York: Garland, 1987.

———. *Christian Nurture*. 1861. Cleveland: Pilgrim, 1994.

———. *Moral Uses of Dark Things*. New York: Scribner, 1868.

———. *Selected Writings on Language, Religion and American Culture*. Ed. David L. Smith. Chico, Calif.: Scholars, 1984.

———. *The Vicarious Sacrifice. Grounded in Principles of Universal Obligation*. New York, Scribner's, 1866.

Butler, Judith. *Bodies That Matter*. New York: Routledge, 1993.

Caine, Barbara. *Victorian Feminists*. New York: Oxford UP, 1992.

Califia, Pat. "Feminism and Sadomasochism." *Feminism and Sexuality*. Ed. Stevi Jackson and Sue Scott. New York: Columbia UP, 1996.

———. "A Secret Side of Lesbian Sexuality." *S and M: Studies in Sadomasochism*. Ed. Thomas Weinberg and G. W. Kamel. Buffalo, New York: Prometheus, 1983.

Cameron, Deborah, and Elizabeth Frazer. "The Murderer as Misogynist?" *Feminism and Sexuality*. Ed. Stevi Jackson and Sue Scott. New York: Columbia UP, 1996.

Camfield, Gregg. *Sentimental Twain: Samuel Clemens in the Maze of Moral Philosophy*. Philadelphia: U of Pennsylvania P, 1994.

Caplan, Paula. *The Myth of Women's Masochism*. 1985. Toronto: U of Toronto P, 1993.

Capps, Donald. *The Child's Song: The Religious Abuse of Children*. Louisville, Ky: Westminster, John Knox, 1995.

Chapman, Mary. "The Masochistic Pleasures of the Gothic: Paternal Incest in Alcott's 'A Marble Woman.'" *American Gothic: New Interventions in a National Narrative*. Ed. Robert K. Martin and Eric Savoy. Ames: U of Iowa P, 1998.

Chasseguet-Smirgel, Janine, C. J. Luquet-Parat, et al. *Female Sexuality: New Psychoanalytic Views*. Ann Arbor, Mich.: U of Michigan P, 1970.

Chodorow, Nancy. *Reproduction of Mothering: Psychoanalysis and the Sociology of Gender*. Berkeley: U of California P, 1978.

Cixous, Hélène. *"Coming to Writing" and Other Essays*. Ed. Deborah Jenson. Cambridge, Mass.: Harvard UP, 1991.

Cleaver, Eldridge. *Soul on Ice*. New York: Dell, 1970.

Cody, John. *After Great Pain: The Inner Life of Emily Dickinson*. Cambridge, Mass.: Harvard UP, 1971.

Cogan, Frances. *All-American Girl: The Ideal of Real Womanhood in Mid-Nineteenth-Century America*. Athens: U of Georgia P, 1989.

Cominos, Peter T. "Innocent Femina Sensualis in Unconscious Conflict." *Suffer and Be Still: Women in the Victorian Age*. Ed. Martha Vicinus. Bloomington: Indiana UP, 1972.

Cott, Nancy. *Bonds of Womanhood: "Woman's Sphere" in New England, 1780–1835*. New Haven: Yale UP, 1977.

———. "Passionlessness: An Interpretation of Victorian Sexual Ideology, 1790–1850." *Signs* 4.2 (1978): 219–36.

———. "Young Women in the Second Great Awakening." *Feminist Studies* 3.1/2 (1975): 15–29.

Craik, Dinah Maria Mulock. *Head of the Family*. 1851. New York: Harper, 1859.

Crane, R. S. "Suggestions Toward a Genealogy of the 'Man of Feeling.'" *English Literary History* 1.3 (1934): 205–30.

Cummins, Maria. *The Lamplighter*. 1854. New Brunswick, N.J.: Rutgers UP, 1988.

Cvetkovich, Ann. *Mixed Feelings: Feminism, Mass Culture, and Victorian Sensationalism*. New Brunswick, N.J.: Rutgers UP, 1992.

Dally, Ann. *Women under the Knife: A History of Surgery*. New York: Routledge, 1992.

Davidson, Cathy N. *Revolution and the Word: The Rise of the Novel in America*. New York: Oxford UP, 1986.

Day, William Patrick. *In the Circles of Fear and Desire: A Study of Gothic Fantasy*. Chicago: U of Chicago P, 1985.

Dean, Carolyn. *The Self and Its Pleasures: Bataille, Lacan, and the History of the Decentered Subject*. Ithaca, N.Y.: Cornell UP, 1992.

de Beauvoir, Simone. *The Second Sex*. Trans. H. M. Parshley. New York: Vintage, 1989.

de Lauretis, Teresa. "Eccentric Subjects: Feminist Theory and Historical Consciousness." *Feminist Studies* 16.1 (1990): 115–50.

Deleuze, Gilles. *Masochism: Coldness and Cruelty*. New York: Zone Books, 1989.

d'Emilio, John, and Estelle B. Freedman. *Intimate Matters: A History of Sexuality in America*. New York: Harper & Row, 1988.

Denby, David. *Sentimental Narrative and the Social Order in France, 1760–1820*. New York: Cambridge UP, 1994.

de St. Jorre, John. "The Unmasking of O." *New Yorker* 50.23 (1994).

Dewey, Orville. *Autobiography and Letters of Orville Dewey, D.D.* Boston: Roberts Brothers, 1883.

Dickinson, Emily. *Letters of Emily Dickinson*. Ed. Thomas H. Johnson. Vols. 1–3. Cambridge, Mass.: Belknap P of Harvard UP, 1958.

———. *The Poems of Emily Dickinson*. Variorum ed. Ed. R. W. Franklin. Vols. 1–3. Cambridge, Mass.: Belknap P of Harvard UP, 1998.

Diehl, Joanne Feit. *Dickinson and the Romantic Imagination*. Princeton: Princeton UP, 1981.

———. "'Ransom in a Voice': Language as Defense in Dickinson's Poetry." *Feminist Critics Read Emily Dickinson*. Ed. Suzanne Juhasz. Bloomington: Indiana UP, 1983.

Doane, Mary Ann. *The Desire to Desire*. Bloomington: Indiana UP, 1987.

Dobson, Joanne. *Dickinson and Strategies of Reticence: The Woman Writer in Nineteenth-Century America*. Bloomington: Indiana UP, 1989.

———. "The Hidden Hand: Subversion of Cultural Ideology in Three Mid-Nineteenth-Century Women's Novels." *American Quarterly* 38.2 (1986): 223–42.

Doriani, Beth Maclay. *Emily Dickinson: Daughter of Prophecy*. Amherst: U of Massachusetts P, 1996.

Douglas, Ann. *The Feminization of American Culture*. New York: Knopf, 1977.

Dworkin, Andrea. *Our Blood: Prophecies and Discourses on Sexual Politics*. New York: Penguin, 1976.

Eberwein, Jane. *Dickinson: Strategies of Limitation*. Amherst: U of Massachusetts P, 1985.

Edwards, Jonathan. "Personal Narrative." *Norton Anthology of American Literature*. 5th ed. Vol. 1. New York: Norton, 1998.

Ehrenreich, Barbara, and Deirdre English. *For Her Own Good: 150 Years of the Experts' Advice to Women*. New York: Doubleday, 1978.

Emerson, Ralph Waldo. *Representative Men*. Cambridge, Mass.: Belknap P of Harvard UP, 1996.

———. *Selections from Ralph Waldo Emerson*. Ed. Stephen E. Whicher. Boston: Houghton Mifflin, 1957.

Erkkila , Betsy. *The Wicked Sisters: Women Poets, Literary History and Discord*. New York: Oxford UP, 1992.

Evans, Augusta J. *A Speckled Bird*. New York: G. W. Dillingham, 1902.

———.*St. Elmo*. 1866. New York: Grosset & Dunlap, 1896.

Farr, Judith. *The Passion of Emily Dickinson*. Cambridge, Mass.: Harvard UP, 1992.

Ferguson, Robert A. *The American Enlightenment 1750–1820*. Cambridge, Mass.: Harvard UP, 1997.

Fern, Fanny [Sara Parton]. *Ruth Hall & Other Writings*. Ed. Joyce W. Warren. New Brunswick, N.J.: Rutgers UP, 1988.

Fetterley, Judith. *The Resisting Reader: A Feminist Approach to American Fiction*. Bloomington: Indiana UP, 1978.

Fiedler, Leslie. *Love and Death in the American Novel*. 1960. New York: Stein and Day, 1982.

Finley, Martha. *Elsie Dinsmore*. 1867. New York: Garland, 1977.

———.*Elsie's Womanhood*. New York: A. L. Burt, 1930.

Fisher, Philip. *Hard Facts: Form and Setting in American Fiction*. New York: Oxford UP, 1985.

Fluck, Winfried. "Sentimentality and the Changing Functions of Fiction." *Sentimentality in Modern Literature and Popular Culture*. Ed. Winfried Herget. Tübingen: Gunter Narr Verlag, 1991.

Foster, Edward Halsey. *Susan and Anna Warner*. Boston: Twayne, 1978.

Foucault, Michel. *Discipline and Punish: The Birth of the Prison*. Trans. Alan Sheridan. New York: Vintage, 1995.

———. *The History of Sexuality*. Part 1. Trans. Robert Hurley. New York: Vintage, 1988.

———. "A Preface to Transgression." *Language, Counter-Memory, Practice: Selected Essays and Interviews*. Ed. Donald F. Bouchard. Trans. Donald F. Bouchard and Sherry Simon. Ithaca, N.Y.: Cornell UP, 1977.

Franklin, R. W. *The Master Letters of Emily Dickinson*. Amherst, Mass.: Amherst College Press, 1986.

Frederic, Harold. *The Damnation of Theron Ware*. New York: Prometheus, 1997.

Freud, Sigmund. *Beyond the Pleasure Principle.* Trans. James Strachey. New York: Norton, 1989.

———. "A Child Is Being Beaten." *Sexuality and the Psychology of Love.* Ed. Philip Rieff. New York: Collier, 1963.

———. *Civilization and Its Discontents.* Trans. James Strachey. New York: Norton, 1961.

———. "The Economic Problem of Masochism." *Essential Papers on Masochism.* Ed. Margaret Ann Fitzpatrick Hanly. New York: New York UP, 1995.

———. "The Taboo of Virginity." *Sexuality and the Psychology of Love.* Ed. Philip Rieff. New York: Collier, 1963.

Friday, Nancy. *My Secret Garden: Women's Sexual Fantasies.* New York: Trident, 1973.

Frost, Laura. "'With This Ring I Thee Own': Masochism and Social Reform in *Ulysses.*" *Sex Positives? The Cultural Politics of Dissident Sexualities.* Ed. Thomas Foster, Carol Siegel, Ellen E. Berry. New York: New York UP, 1997.

Fuller, Margaret. "The Great Lawsuit." Boston *Dial,* July 1843. *Norton Anthology of American Literature.* 5th ed. Vol. 1. New York: Norton, 1998.

Fuss, Diana. *Essentially Speaking: Feminism, Nature & Difference.* New York: Routledge, 1989.

Gallop, Jane. *Thinking Through the Body.* New York: Columbia UP, 1988.

Gebhard, Paul H. "Sadomasochism." *SandM: Studies in Sadomasochism.* Eds. Thomas Weinberg and G. W. Kamel. Buffalo, New York: Prometheus, 1983.

Gelpi, Albert. *The Mind of the Poet.* New York: Norton, 1965.

———. *The Tenth Muse: The Psyche of the American Poet.* Cambridge: Cambridge UP, 1991.

Gilbert, Sandra M. "The Wayward Nun beneath the Hill: Emily Dickinson and the Mysteries of Womanhood." *Feminist Critics Read Emily Dickinson.* Ed. Suzanne Juhasz. Bloomington: Indiana UP, 1983.

Gilbert, Sandra, and Susan Gubar. *The Madwoman in the Attic.* New Haven: Yale UP, 1979.

Gilligan, Carol. "In a Different Voice: Women's Conception of Self and Morality." *The Psychology of Women: Ongoing Debates.* Ed. Mary Roth Walsh. New Haven: Yale UP, 1987.

Golden, Catherine, ed. *The Captive Imagination: A Casebook on "The Yellow Wallpaper."* New York: Feminist, 1992.

Gorney, James E., and John P. Muller. "The Master-Slave Relation in Psychoanalytic Impasse." *Masochism: The Treatment of Self-Inflicted Suffering.* Ed. Jill D. Montgomery and Ann C. Greif. Madison, Conn.: International Universities Press, 1989.

Goshgarian, G. M. *To Kiss the Chastening Rod: Domestic Fiction and Sexual Ideology in the American Renaissance.* Ithaca, New York: Cornell UP, 1992.

Gossett, Thomas F. *Uncle Tom's Cabin and American Culture.* Dallas: Southern Methodist UP, 1985.

Greene, Donald. "Latitudinarianism and Sensibility: The Genealogy of the 'Man of Feeling' Reconsidered." *Modern Philology,* November 1977, 159–83.

Greven, Philip. *Spare the Child: The Religious Roots of Punishment and the Psychological Impact of Physical Abuse.* New York: Knopf, 1991.

Griswold, Rufus Wilmot. *The Female Poets of America*. Philadelphia: Carey & Hart, 1849.

Grosz, Elizabeth. "Feminism, Women's Studies and the Politics of Theory." Paper delivered at American University, November 6, 1997.

———. *Jacques Lacan: A Feminist Introduction*. London: Routledge, 1990.

Gumpers, John, and Stephen Levinson, eds. *Rethinking Linguistic Relativity*. New York: Cambridge UP, 1996.

Gurko, Miriam. *The Ladies of Seneca Falls: The Birth of the Woman's Rights Movement*. New York: Macmillan, 1974.

Gustafson, Sandra. "Choosing a Medium: Margaret Fuller and the Forms of Sentiment." *American Quarterly* 47.1 (1995): 34–65.

Haller, John S., and Robin M. Haller. *The Physician and Sexuality in Victorian America*. Urbana: U of Illinois P, 1974.

Halttunen, Karen. "'Domestic Differences': Competing Narratives of Womanhood in the Murder Trial of Lucretia Chapman." *Culture of Sentiment*. Ed. Shirley Samuels. New York: Oxford UP, 1992.

———. "Humanitarianism and the Pornography of Pain in Anglo-American Culture." *American Historical Review*, April 1995, 303–35.

Hanly, Margaret Ann Fitzpatrick, ed. *Essential Papers on Masochism*. New York: New York UP, 1995.

Harris, Adrienne. "Dialogues as Transitional Space: A Rapprochement of Psychoanalysis and Developmental Psycholinguistics." *Relational Perspectives in Psychoanalysis*. Ed. Neil J. Skolnick and Susan C. Warshaw. Hillsdale: Analytic Press, 1992.

Harris, Susan K. "'But is it any *good*?': Evaluating Nineteenth-Century American Women's Fiction." *American Literature* 63.1 (1991): 43–61.

———. "Responding to the Text(s): Women Readers and the Quest for Higher Education." *Readers in History: Nineteenth-Century American Literature and the Contexts of Response*. Baltimore: Johns Hopkins UP, 1993.

Hawthorne, Nathaniel. *The Blithedale Romance*. Boston: Bedford, 1996.

———. *The House of the Seven Gables*. New York: Norton, 1967.

Hedrick, Joan. *Harriet Beecher Stowe: A Life*. New York: Oxford UP, 1994.

Heller, Terry. *The Delights of Terror: An Aesthetics of the Tale of Terror*. Urbana: U of Illinois P, 1987.

Hendler, Glenn. "Louisa May Alcott and the Limits of Sympathy." *American Literary History* 3.4 (1991): 685–706.

Henneberg, Sylvia. "Neither Lesbian nor Straight: Multiple Eroticisms in Emily Dickinson's Love Poetry." *Emily Dickinson Journal* 4.2 (1995): 1–19.

Hentz, Caroline Lee. *The Planter's Northern Bride*. 1854. Chapel Hill: U of North Carolina P, 1970.

Herget, Winfried. "Towards a Rhetoric of Sentimentality." *Sentimentality in Modern Literature and Popular Culture*. Tübingen: Gunter Narr Verlag, 1991.

Herndl, Diane Price. *Invalid Women: Figuring Feminine Illness in American Fiction and Culture, 1840–1940*. Chapel Hill: U of North Carolina P, 1993.

Higginson, Thomas Wentworth. *Women and Men*. New York: Harper, 1887.

Higginson, Thomas Wentworth. *Women and the Alphabet: A Series of Essays.* Boston: Houghton Mifflin, 1881.

Hinton, Laura. *The Perverse Gaze of Sympathy: Sadomasochistic Sentiments from Clarissa to Rescue 911.* Albany: State U of New York P, 1999.

Hogue, Cynthia. "'I Did'nt Be—Myself': Emily Dickinson's Semiotics of Presence." *Emily Dickinson Journal* 1.2 (1992): 30–53.

———. *Scheming Women: Poetry, Privilege, and the Politics of Subjectivity.* Albany: State U of New York P, 1995.

Hollibaugh, Amber. "Desire for the Future: Radical Hope in Passion and Pleasure." *Pleasure and Danger: Exploring Female Sexuality.* New York: Pandora, 1984.

Homans, Margaret. *Bearing the Word: Language and Female Experience in Nineteenth-Century Women's Writing.* Chicago: U of Chicago P, 1986.

———. "Syllables of Velvet: Dickinson, Rossetti and the Rhetorics of Sexuality." *Feminist Studies* 11.3 (1985): 569–93.

———. *Women Writers and Poetic Identity: Dorothy Wordsworth, Emily Brontë, and Emily Dickinson.* Princeton: Princeton UP, 1980.

Hovet, Grace Ann, and Theodore Hovet. "Identity Development in Susan Warner's *The Wide, Wide World*: Relationship, Performance and Construction." *Legacy* 8.1 (1991): 3–16.

Howe, Julia, W. *Passion-Flowers.* Boston: Ticknor, Reed, & Fields, 1854.

Howe, Susan. *My Emily Dickinson.* Berkeley, Calif.: North Atlantic Books, 1985.

Humphrey, Heman. *Revival: Sketches and Manual.* Pittsfield, Mass.: American Tract Society, 1859.

Hunt, Lynda, "Doing It Anyway: Lesbian Sado-Masochism and Performance." *Performance and Cultural Politics.* Ed. Elin Diamond. New York: Routledge, 1996.

Hutcheson, Francis. *A System of Moral Philosophy.* 1755. New York: Kelley, 1968.

Irigaray, Luce. *This Sex Which Is Not One.* Trans. Catherine Porter. Ithaca, N.Y.: Cornell UP, 1985.

Jackson, Rosemary. *Fantasy: The Literature of Subversion.* London: Methuen, 1981.

Jackson, Stevi, and Sue Scott. "Sexual Skirmishes and Feminist Factions." *Feminism and Sexuality: A Reader.* New York: Columbia UP, 1996.

Jacobus, Mary, Evelyn Fox Keller, and Sally Shuttleworth. *Body/Politics: Women and the Discourses of Science.* New York: Routledge, 1990.

Jagger, Alison M., ed. *Living with Contradictions: Controversies in Feminist Social Ethics.* Boulder, Colo.: Westview, 1994.

Jameson, Frederic. *The Political Unconscious: Narrative as a Socially Symbolic Act.* Ithaca, N.Y.: Cornell UP, 1981.

Jeffreys, Sheila. *The Lesbian Heresy.* North Melbourne, Australia: Spinifex, 1993.

Johnson, Claudia L. *Equivocal Beings: Politics, Gender and Sentimentality in the 1790s: Wollstonecraft, Radcliffe, Burney, Austen.* Chicago: U of Chicago P, 1995.

Judson, Ann H. *A Particular Relation of the American Baptist Mission to the Burman Republic*. Washington: John S. Mehan, 1823.

Judson, Emily. *An Olio of Domestic Verses*. New York: Colby, 1852.

Juhasz, Suzanne. "Adventures in the World of the Symbolic: Emily Dickinson and Metaphor." *Feminist Measures: Soundings in Poetry and Theory*. Ed. Lynn Keller and Cristanne Miller. Ann Arbor: U of Michigan P, 1994.

———."Object Relations and Women's Use of Language." *The Women and Language Debate: A Sourcebook*. Ed. Camille Roman et al. New Brunswick, N.J.: Rutgers UP, 1994.

———, ed. *Feminist Critics Read Emily Dickinson*. Bloomington: Indiana UP, 1983.

Kahane, Clare. *Passions of the Voice: Hysteria, Narrative, and the Figure of the Speaking Woman, 1850–1915*. Baltimore: Johns Hopkins UP, 1995.

Kaplan, Fred. *Sacred Tears: Sentimentality in Victorian Literature*. Princeton: Princeton UP, 1987.

Keller, Karl. "Notes on Sleeping with Emily Dickinson." *Feminist Critics Read Emily Dickinson*. Ed. Suzanne Juhasz. Bloomington: Indiana UP, 1983.

Kelley, Mary. *Private Woman, Public Stage: Literary Domesticity in Nineteenth-Century America*. New York: Oxford UP, 1984.

Kelly, Liz. " 'It's Everywhere': Sexual Violence as a Continuum." *Feminism and Sexuality: A Reader*. Ed. Stevi Jackson and Sue Scott. New York: Columbia UP, 1996.

Kerber, Linda. "The Republican Mother: Women and the Enlightenment: An American Perspective." *Toward an Intellectual History of Women: Essays by Linda K. Kerber*. Chapel Hill: U of North Carolina P, 1997.

Krafft-Ebing, Dr. Richard von. *Psychopathia Sexualis*. 1886. Trans. Franklin S. Klaf. New York: Stein & Day, 1978.

Kristeva, Julia. *Powers of Horror: An Essay on Abjection*. New York: Columbia UP, 1982.

———. "Revolution in Poetic Language." *The Kristeva Reader*. Ed. Toril Moi. New York: Columbia UP, 1986.

Lacan, Jacques. *Ecrits: A Selection*. Trans. Alan Sheridan. New York: Norton, 1977.

———. *The Four Fundamental Concepts of Psycho-Analysis*. Ed. Jacques-Alain Miller. Trans. Alan Sheridan. New York: Norton, 1981.

———. *The Language of the Self: The Function of Language in Psychoanalysis*. Ed. and trans. Anthony Wilden. Baltimore: Johns Hopkins UP, 1968.

Lane, Haddie. "Woman's Rights." *Godey's Lady's Book*, January 1850.

Lang, Amy Schrager. "Class and the Strategies of Sympathy." *Culture of Sentiment*. Ed. Shirley Samuels. New York: Oxford UP, 1992.

Langstroth, F. C. *Harriet Atwood Newell: A Sketch*. Philadelphia: American Baptist Publication Society, 1915.

Lanyi, Ronald. " 'My Faith that Dark Adores—': Calvinist Theology in the Poetry of Emily Dickinson." *Arizona Quarterly* 32.3 (1976): 264–78.

Laplanche, Jean. *Life and Death in Psychoanalysis*. Trans. Jeffrey Mehlman. Baltimore: Johns Hopkins UP, 1976.

Laqueur, Thomas. "Bodies, Details and the Humanitarian Narrative." *The New Cultural History*. Berkeley: U of California P, 1989.

———. *Making Sex: Body and Gender from the Greeks to Freud*. Cambridge, Mass.: Harvard UP, 1990.

La Roche, Anna Mercer [Francis]. "Journal—Note book: 1856–1879." Columbia University Special Collection.

Leavitt, Judith Walzer, ed. *Women and Health in America: Historical Readings*. Madison: U of Wisconsin P, 1984.

Lerner, Gerda. "The Myth of the 'Bad' Black Woman." *Black Women in White America: A Documentary History*. New York: Pantheon, 1972.

Levander, Caroline. *Voices of the Nation: Women and Public Speech in Nineteenth-Century American Literature and Culture*. New York: Cambridge UP, 1997.

Levine, Alan. "Skepticism, Self, and Toleration in Montaigne's Political Thought." *Early Modern Skepticism and the Origins of Toleration*. Ed. Alan Levine. Lanham, Md.: Lexington Books, 1999.

Linden, Robin Ruth. *Against Sadomasochism: A Radical Feminist Analysis*. San Francisco: Frog in the Well, 1982.

Loeffelholz, Mary. *Dickinson and the Boundaries of Feminist Theory*. Urbana: U of Illinois P, 1991.

Loewenstein, Rudolph M. "A Contribution to the Psychoanalytic Theory of Masochism." *Journal of the American Psychoanalytic Association* 5.2 (1957): 197–234.

Machor, James L. "Historical Hermeneutics and Antebellum Fiction: Gender, Response Theory, and Interpretive Contexts." *Readers in History: Nineteenth-Century American Literature and the Contexts of Response*. Baltimore: Johns Hopkins UP, 1993.

Mansfield, Nick. *Masochism: The Art of Power*. Westport, Conn.: Praeger, 1997.

Manson, Michael. "Poetry and Masculinity on the Anglo/Chicano Border: Gary Soto, Robert Frost, and Robert Hass." *The Calvinist Roots of The Modern Era*. Ed. Aliki Barnstone, Michael Tomasek Manson, Carol J. Singley. Hanover, N.H.: UP of New England, 1997.

Marchalonis, Shirley. *The Worlds of Lucy Larcom, 1824–1893*, Athens: U of Georgia P, 1989.

Marcus, Macia. *A Taste for Pain: On Masochism and Female Sexuality*. Trans. Joan Tate. New York: St. Martin's, 1981.

Masse, Michelle. *Women, Masochism and the Gothic*. Ithaca, N.Y.: Cornell UP, 1992.

Masters, William H., Viginia E. Johnson, and Robert C. Kolodny. *Masters and Johnson on Sex and Human Loving*. Boston: Little, Brown & Co., 1985.

Mathews, Donald G. "The Second Great Awakening as an Organizing Process." *American Quarterly* 21 (1969): 23–43.

McIntosh, Maria Jane. *Two Pictures; or, What We Think of Ourselves, and What the World Thinks of Us*. 1863. Freeport, New York: Books for Libraries Press, 1972.

———. *Woman in America: Her Work and Her Reward*. New York: Appleton, 1850.

McLoughlin, William G. *The Meaning of Henry Ward Beecher*. New York: Knopf, 1970.

McNeil, Helen. *Emily Dickinson*. London: Virago, 1986.

Melville, Herman. *Moby Dick; or, The Whale*. New York: Penguin, 1988.

Menaker, Esther. "Masochism—A Defense Reaction of the Ego." 1953. *Essential Papers on the Psychology of Women*. Ed. Caludia Zanardi. New York: New York UP, 1990.

Michaels, Walter Benn. *The Gold Standard and the Logic of Naturalism: American Literature at the Turn of the Century*. Berkeley: U of California P, 1987.

Michie, Helena. *Flesh Made Word: Female Figures and Women's Bodies*. New York: Oxford UP, 1987.

Miller, Cristanne. *Emily Dickinson: A Poet's Grammar*. Cambridge, Mass.: Harvard UP, 1987.

Miller, D. A. *The Novel and the Police*. Berkeley: U of California P, 1987.

Mitchell, Juliet, and Jacqueline Rose. *Feminine Sexuality: Jacques Lacan and the Ecole Freudienne*. New York: Norton, 1982.

Mitchell, S. Weir. *Doctor and Patient*. Philadelphia: Lippincott, 1887.

Moi, Toril, ed. *The Kristeva Reader: Julia Kristeva*. New York: Columbia UP, 1986.

Monk, Samuel H. *The Sublime: A Study of Critical Theories in XVIII-Century England*. New York: Modern Language Association of America, 1935.

Montaigne, Michel de. *Essays*. Book 1, Essay 21. Trans. Donald Frame. Stanford UP, 1957.

Montgomery, Jill D. "The Return of Masochistic Behavior in the Absence of the Analyst." *Masochism: The Treatment of Self-Inflicted Suffering*. Ed. Jill D. Montgomery and Ann C. Greif. Madison, Conn.: International Universities Press, 1989.

More, Hannah. *Coelebs in Search of a Wife*. 1809. New York: Derby, 1861.

Morris, Adelaide. "'The Love of Thee—a Prism Be': Men and Women in the Love Poetry of Emily Dickinson." *Feminist Critics Read Emily Dickinson*. Ed. Suzanne Juhasz. Bloomington: Indiana UP, 1983.

Morris, David B. *The Religious Sublime: Christian Poetry and Critical Tradition in 18th-Century England*. Lexington: UP of Kentucky, 1972.

Mossberg, Barbara Antonina Clarke. *Emily Dickinson: When a Writer Is a Daughter*. Bloomington: Indiana UP, 1982.

Napheys, George Henry. *The Transmission of Life: Counsels on the Nature and Hygiene of the Masculine Function*. Philadelphia, 1870.

Nead, Lynda. *Myths of Sexuality: Representations of Women in Victorian Britain*. Cambridge, Mass.: Blackwell, 1988.

Newell, Harriet. *The Life and Writings of Mrs. Harriet Newell*. Rev. ed. Philadelphia: American Sunday School Union, 1831.

———. Selections from Letters and Diaries. Published as Leonard Woods, *A Sermon, Preached at Haverhill, Mass. In Rememberence of Mrs. Harriet Newell, wife of the Rev. Samuel Newell*. Boston: Samuel T. Armstrong, 1814.

———. Selections from Letters and Diaries. Published as Leonard Woods, *A Sermon, Preached at Haverhill, Mass. In Rememberence of Mrs. Harriet Newell, wife of the Rev. Samuel Newell*. 9th ed. N.P.: Abel Brown, 1830.

Noble, Marianne. "'An Ecstasy of Apprehension': The Gothic Pleasures of Sentimental Fiction." *American Gothic: New Interventions in a National Narrative*. Ed. Robert K. Martin. Ames: U of Iowa P, 1998.

Noyes, John K. *The Mastery of Submission: Inventions of Masochism*. Ithaca: Cornell UP, 1997.

Nudelman, Franny. "Harriet Jacobs and the Sentimental Politics of Female Suffering." *ELH* 59 (1992): 939–64.

Nussbaum, Martha. *Poetic Justice: The Literary Imagination and Public Life*. Boston: Beacon, 1995.

Oakes-Smith, Elizabeth. *Selections from the Autobiography of Elizabeth Oakes [Prince] Smith*. 1924. Ed. Mary Alice Wyman. New York: Arno, 1980.
———. *Woman and Her Needs*. New York: Fowlers & Wells, 1851.

O'Connell, Catharine. "'The Magic of the Real Presence of Distress': Sentimentality and the Competing Rhetorics of Authority." *The Stowe Debate: Rhetorical Strategies in Uncle Tom's Cabin*. Ed. Mason I. Lowance, Jr., et al. Amherst: U of Massachusetts P, 1994.

Okker, Patricia. "Sarah Josepha Hale, Lydia Sigourney, and the Poetic Tradition in Two Nineteenth-Century Women's Magazines." *American Periodicals* 3 (1993): 32–42.

Ovid. *Metamorphoses*. Trans. David R. Slavitt. Baltimore: Johns Hopkins UP, 1994.

Paglia, Camille. *Sexual Personae: Art and Decadence from Nefertiti to Emily Dickinson*. London: Yale UP, 1990.

Person, Ethel Spector. "Sexuality as the Mainstay of Identity: Psychoanalytic Perspectives." *Women: Sex and Sexuality*. Ed. Catherine Stimpson and Ethel Spector Person. Chicago: U of Chicago P, 1980.

Petrino, Elizabeth A. "'Feet so precious charged': Dickinson, Sigourney, and the Child Elegy." *Tulsa Studies in Women's Literature* 13.2 (1994): 317–38.

Pfister, Joel. *The Production of Personal Life: Class, Gender, and the Psychological in Hawthorne's Fiction*. Stanford, Calif.: Stanford UP, 1991.

Plutarch. *The Lives of the Noble Grecians and Romans*. Dryden trans. University of Chicago, The Great Books ser. Chicago: Encyclopedia Britannica, 1952.

Pollak, Vivian R. *Dickinson: The Anxiety of Gender*. Ithaca, N.Y.: Cornell UP, 1984.

Poovey, Mary. *The Proper Lady and the Woman Writer: Ideology as Style in the Works of Mary Wollstonecraft, Mary Shelley, and Jane Austen*. Chicago: U of Chicago P, 1984.
———. *Uneven Developments: The Ideological Work of Gender in Mid-Victorian England*. Chicago: U of Chicago P, 1988.

Porter, Carolyn. *Seeing and Being: The Plight of the Participant Observer in Emerson, James, Adams and Faulkner*. Middletown, Conn.: Wesleyan UP, 1981.
———. "Emily Dickinson: The Poetics of Doubt." *Emerson Society Quarterly* 60 (1970): 86–93.

Radway, Janice A. *Reading the Romance: Women, Patriarchy, and Popular Literature*. Chapel Hill: U of North Carolina P, 1984.

Ragland, N. M. *Leaves from Mission Fields; or, Memoirs of Mrs. Harriet Newell, Mrs. Ann Judson, Miss Hattie L. Judson, Mrs. Josephine Smith, Charles E. Garst.* St. Louis, Mo.: Christian Publishing, 1900.

Reik, Theodor. *Masochism in Modern Man.* Trans. Margaret H. Beigel and Gertrud M. Kurth. New York: Farrar & Rinehart, 1941.

Reinisch, June M. *The Kinsey Institute New Report On Sex: What You Must Know to be Sexually Literate.* New York: St. Martin's, 1990.

Reynolds, David S. *Beneath the American Renaissance: The Subversive Imagination in the Age of Emerson and Melville.* New York: Knopf, 1988.

Rich, Adrienne. "Vesuvius at Home." *Shakespeare's Sisters: Feminist Essays on Women Poets.* Ed. Sandra Gilbert and Susan Gubar. Bloomington: Indiana UP, 1979.

Rich, B. Ruby. "Review Essay: Feminism and Sexuality in the 1980s." *Feminist Studies* 12.3 (1986): 525–61.

Rody, Caroline. "Toni Morrison's *Beloved*: History, 'Rememory,' and a 'Clamor for a Kiss.'" *American Literary History* 7.1 (1995): 92–120.

Romero, Lora. "Bio-Political Resistance in Domestic Ideology and *Uncle Tom's Cabin.*" *American Literary History* 1.4 (1989): 715–34.

———. "Domesticity and Fiction." *The Columbia History of the American Novel.* New York: Columbia UP, 1991.

Rowlandson, Mary. "A Narrative of the Captivity and Restoration." *Norton Anthology of American Literature.* 5th ed. Vol. 1. New York: Norton, 1998.

Rubenstein, Roberta. *Boundaries of the Self: Gender, Culture, Fiction.* Urbana: U of Illinois P, 1987.

Rugoff, Milton. *The Beechers: An American Family in the Nineteenth Century.* New York: Harper & Row, 1981.

Ryan, Mary P. *Cradle of the Middle Class: The Family in Oneida County, New York, 1790–1865.* Cambridge: Cambridge UP, 1981.

Sacks, Peter. *The English Elegy: Studies in the Genre from Spenser to Yeats.* Baltimore: Johns Hopkins UP, 1985.

Sacksteder, James L. "Thoughts on the Positive Value of a Negative Identity." *Masochism: The Treatment of Self-Inflicted Suffering.* Ed. Jill D. Montgomery and Ann C. Greif. Madison, Conn.: International Universities Press, 1989.

Salmon, Marylynn. *Women and the Law of Property in Early America.* Chapel Hill: U of North Carolina P, 1986.

SAMOIS. *Coming to Power: Writings and Graphics on Lesbian S/M.* Boston: Alyson, 1987.

Sanchez-Eppler, Karen. "Bodily Bonds: The Intersecting Rhetorics of Feminism and Abolitionism." *Representations*, Fall 1988, 28–59.

———. *Touching Liberty: Abolition, Feminism, and the Politics of the Body.* Berkeley: U of California P, 1993.

Scarry, Elaine. *The Body in Pain: The Making and Unmaking of the World.* New York: Oxford UP, 1985.

Schnog, Nancy. "Inside the Sentimental: The Psychological Work of *The Wide, Wide World. Genders* 4 (1989): 11–25.

Sheriff, John K. *The Good-Natured Man: The Evolution of a Moral Idea, 1660–1800.* University: U of Alabama P, 1982.

Showalter, Elaine and English Showalter. "Victorian Women and Menstruation." *Suffer and Be Still.* Ed. Martha Vicinus. Bloomington: Indiana UP, 1973.

Shuttleworth, Sally. "Female Circulation: Medical Discourse and Popular Advertising in the Mid-Victorian Era." *Body/Politics: Women and the Discourses of Science.* Ed. Mary Jacobus, Evelyn Fox Keller, and Sally Shuttleworth. New York: Routledge, 1990.

Sicherman, Barbara. "Reading Little Women." *United States History as Women's History.* Ed. Linda K. Kerber, Alice Kessler-Harris, and Kathryn Kish Sklar. Chapel Hill: U of North Carolina P, 1995.

Siegel, Carol. *Male Masochism: Modern Revisions of the Story of Love.* Bloomington: U of Indiana P, 1995.

Sigourney, Lydia. *Poems.* Boston: Goodrich, 1827.

Silverman, Kaja. "Masochism and Male Subjectivity." *Camera Obscura* 17 (1988): 31–67.

Simpson, Lewis David. *The Relationship of Common Sense Philosophy to Nathaniel Hawthorne, Poe and Melville.* Doctoral dissertation, Ohio State University, 1987.

Singer, Linda. "Bodies—Pleasures—Powers." *Feminism and Sexuality.* Ed. Stevi Jackson and Sue Scott. New York: Columbia UP, 1996.

Smirnoff, V. N. "The Masochistic Contract." *International Journal of Psychoanalysis* 50 (1969): 665–71.

Smith, Adam. *The Theory of Moral Sentiments.* 1759. 6th ed., 1817. Washington, D.C.: Regnery, 1997.

Smith, Martha Nell. *Rowing in Eden: Rereading Emily Dickinson.* Austin: U of Texas P, 1992.

Smith, Robert McClure. "Dickinson and the Masochistic Aesthetic." *Emily Dickinson Journal* 7.2 (1998): 1–21.

———. *The Seductions of Emily Dickinson.* Tuscaloosa: U of Alabama P, 1996.

Smith-Rosenberg, Carroll. *Disorderly Conduct: Visions of Gender in Victorian America.* New York: Knopf, 1985.

Soelle, Dorothee. *Suffering.* Trans. Everett R. Kalin. Philadelphia: Fortress, 1975.

Southern Women's Writing Collective. "Sex Resistance in Heterosexual Arrangements." *Living with Contradictions: Controversies in Feminist Social Ethics.* Ed. Alison M. Jaggar. Boulder, Col.: Westview, 1994.

Spillers, Hortense. "Changing the Letter: The Yokes, The Jokes of Discourse, Or, Mrs. Stowe, Mr. Reed." *Slavery and the Literary Imagination.* Ed. Deborah McDowell and Arnold Rampersad. Baltimore: Johns Hopkins UP, 1989.

Sprague, William B. *Letters on Practical Subjects to a Daughter.* 1822. New York: Haven, 1831.

———. *Letters to Young Men on the History of Joseph.* Albany, N.Y.: E. H. Pease, 1845.

Sprengnether, Madelon. *The Spectral Mother: Freud, Feminism, and Psychoanalysis.* Ithaca, N.Y.: Cornell UP, 1990.

St. Armand, Barton Levi. *Emily Dickinson and Her Culture: The Soul's Society.* New York: Cambridge UP, 1984.

Stewart, Veronica. "The Wild Side of *The Wide, Wide World*." *Legacy* 11.1 (1994): 1–16.

Stoller, Robert J. *Pain & Passion: A Psychoanalyst Explores the World of S & M.* New York: Plenum, 1991.

———. *Sexual Excitement: Dynamics of Erotic Life*. New York: Pantheon, 1979.

Stoller, Robert J., and Gilbert Herdt. *Intimate Communications: Erotics and the Study of Culture*. New York: Columbia UP, 1990.

Stonum, Gary Lee. *The Dickinson Sublime*. Madison: U of Wisconsin P, 1990.

Stowe, Harriet Beecher. *Key to Uncle Tom's Cabin*. London: Clarke, Beeson, 1853.

———. *The Minister's Wooing*. Library of America ser. New York: Viking, 1982.

———. *Uncle Tom's Cabin, or Life among the Lowly*. 1851. Ed. Ann Douglas. New York: Viking Penguin, 1981.

Stowe, Charles Edward. *Life of Harriet Beecher Stowe compiled from Her Letters and Journals*. 1889. Detroit: Gale Research Company, 1967.

Studlar, Gaylyn. *In the Realm of Pleasure: Von Sternberg, Dietrich, and the Masochistic Aesthetic*. Chicago: U of Illinois P, 1988.

Thornburg, Mary Patterson. *The Monster in the Mirror: Gender and the Sentimental/Gothic Myth in Frankenstein*. Ann Arbor, Mich.: UMI Research Press, 1987.

Todd, Janet. *Sensibility: An Introduction*. London: Methuen, 1986.

Tompkins, Jane. *Sensational Designs: The Cultural Work of American Fiction 1790–1860*. New York: Oxford UP, 1985.

Turnbull, Archie. "Scotland and America, 1730–90." *Hotbed of Genius: The Scottish Enlightenment 1730–1790*. Ed. David Daiches, et al. Edinburgh: Edinburgh UP, 1986.

Vance, Carole S., ed. *Pleasure and Danger: Exploring Female Sexuality*. London: Pandora, 1992.

Wadsworth, Charles. *Sermons*. New York: A. Roman & Co., 1869.

Wald, Priscilla. *Constituting Americans: Cultural Anxiety and Narrative Form*. Durham, N.C.: Duke UP, 1995.

Walker, Cheryl. *American Women Poets in the Nineteenth Century: An Anthology*. New Brunswick, N.J.: Rutgers UP, 1992.

———. *The Nightingale's Burden: Women Poets and American Culture before 1900*. Bloomington: Indiana UP, 1982.

Warhol, Robyn R. "As You Stand, So You Feel and Are: The Crying Body and the Nineteenth-Century Text." *Tattoo, Torture, Mutilation, and Adornment: The Denaturalization of the Body in Culture and Text*. Ed. Frances E. Mascia-Lees and Patricia Sharpe. Albany: State U of New York P, 1992.

Warner, Marina. *Alone of All Her Sex: The Myth and the Cult of the Virgin Mary*. New York: Vintage, 1983.

Warner, Susan. *The Wide, Wide World*. 1851. New York: Feminist, 1987.

Weinberg, Thomas, and G. W. Kamel, eds. *SandM: Studies in Sadomasochism*. Buffalo, N.Y.: Prometheus, 1983.

Weisbuch, Robert. *Emily Dickinson's Poetry*. Chicago: U of Chicago P, 1975.

Welter, Barbara. *Dimity Convictions: The American Woman in the Nineteenth Century*. Athens: Ohio UP, 1976.

Welter, Barbara. "The Feminization of American Religion." *Clio's Consciousness Raised: New Perspectives on the History of Women*. Ed. Mary Hartman and Lois W. Banner. New York: Harper, 1974.

Wexler, Laura. "Tender Violence: Literary Eavesdropping, Domestic Fiction, and Educational Reform." *The Culture of Sentiment: Race, Gender and Sentimentality in Nineteenth-Century America*. Ed. Shirley Samuels. New York: Oxford UP, 1992.

Williams, Gary. *Hungry Heart*. Amherst: U of Massachusetts P, 1999.

Williams, Susan S. "Widening the World: Susan Warner, Her Readers, and the Assumption of Authorship." *American Quarterly* 42.4 (1990): 565–86.

Wilson, Edmund. *Patriotic Gore*. New York: Oxford UP, 1962.

Winthrop, John. *The Journal of John Winthrop, 1630–1649*. Norton Anthology of American Literature. 5th ed. Vol.1. New York: Norton, 1998.

Wolff, Cynthia Griffin. *Emily Dickinson*. Reading, Mass.: Addison-Wesley, 1988.

Wood, Ann Douglas. "Ms. Sigourney and the Sensibility of the Inner Sapce." *New England Quarterly* 45.2 (1972): 163–81.

Wyatt, Jean. *Reconstructing Desire: The Role of the Unconscious in Women's Reading and Writing*. Chapel Hill: U of North Carolina P, 1990.

Young, John H. *Our Deportment; or, The Manners, Conduct and Dress of the Most Refined Society*. Detroit: F. B. Dickerson & Co., 1879.

Zagarell, Sandra A. "Expanding 'America': Lydia Sigourney's *Sketch of Connecticut*, Catharine Sedgwick's *Hope Leslie*." *Tulsa Studies in Women's Literature* 6.2 (1987): 225–47.

Index